MARILYN MONSTERS

TOMMY REDOLFI

Life Drawn

Fabrice Giger
Publisher

Rights & Licensing - licensing@humanoids.com
Press and Social Media - pr@humanoids.com

MARILYN'S MONSTERS
This title is a publication of Humanoids, Inc. 8033 Sunset Blvd. #628, Los Angeles, CA 90046.

Life Drawn is an imprint of Humanoids, Inc.

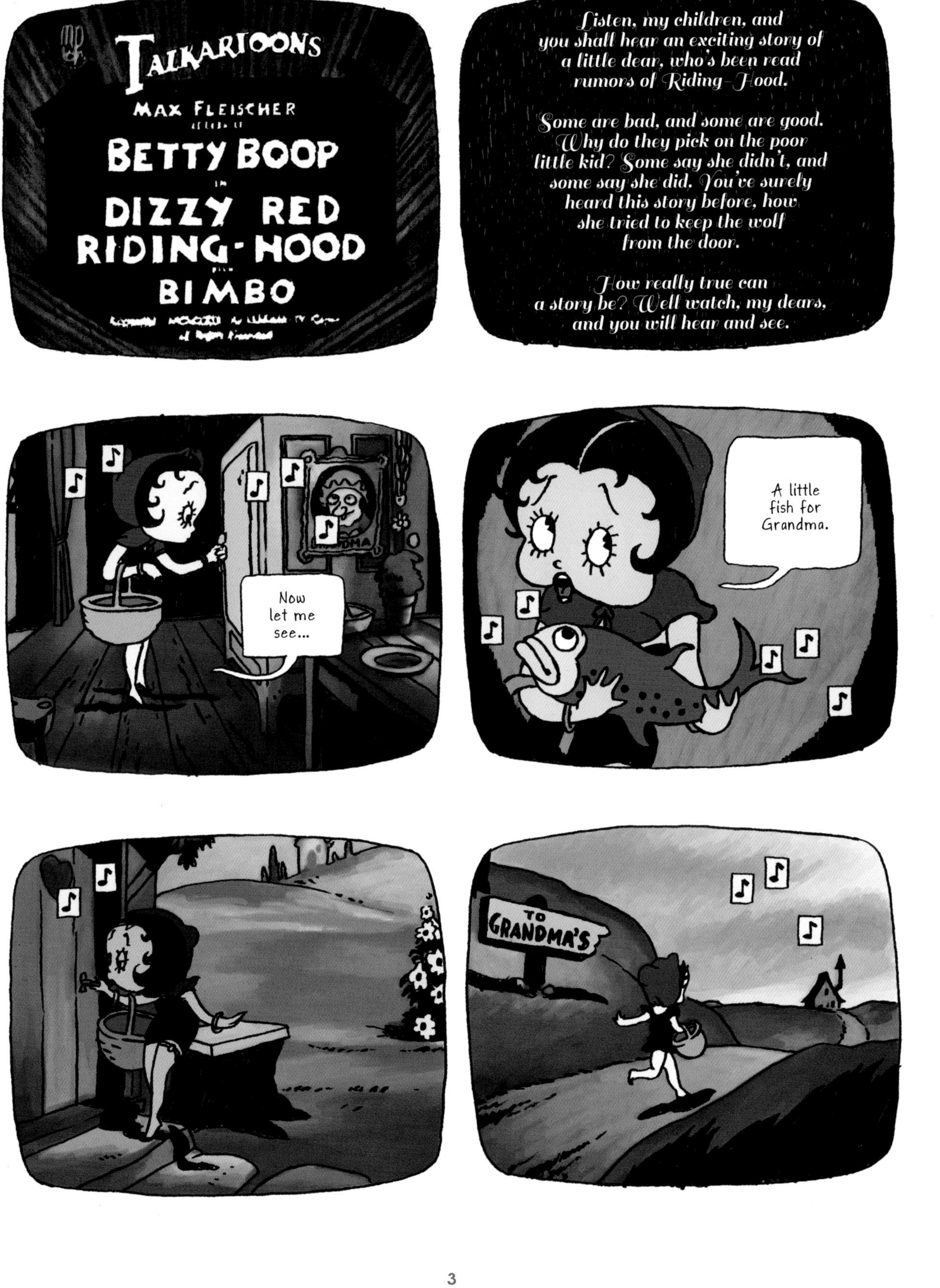
TALKARTOONS
MAX FLEISCHER
BETTY BOOP
DIZZY RED RIDING-HOOD
BIMBO
Listen, my children, and you shall hear an exciting story of a little dear, who's been read rumors of Riding-Hood.
Some are bad, and some are good. Why do they pick on the poor little kid? Some say she didn't, and some say she did. You've surely heard this story before, how she tried to keep the wolf from the door.
How really true can a story be? Well watch, my dears, and you will hear and see.
Now let me see...
A little fish for Grandma.
TO GRANDMA'S

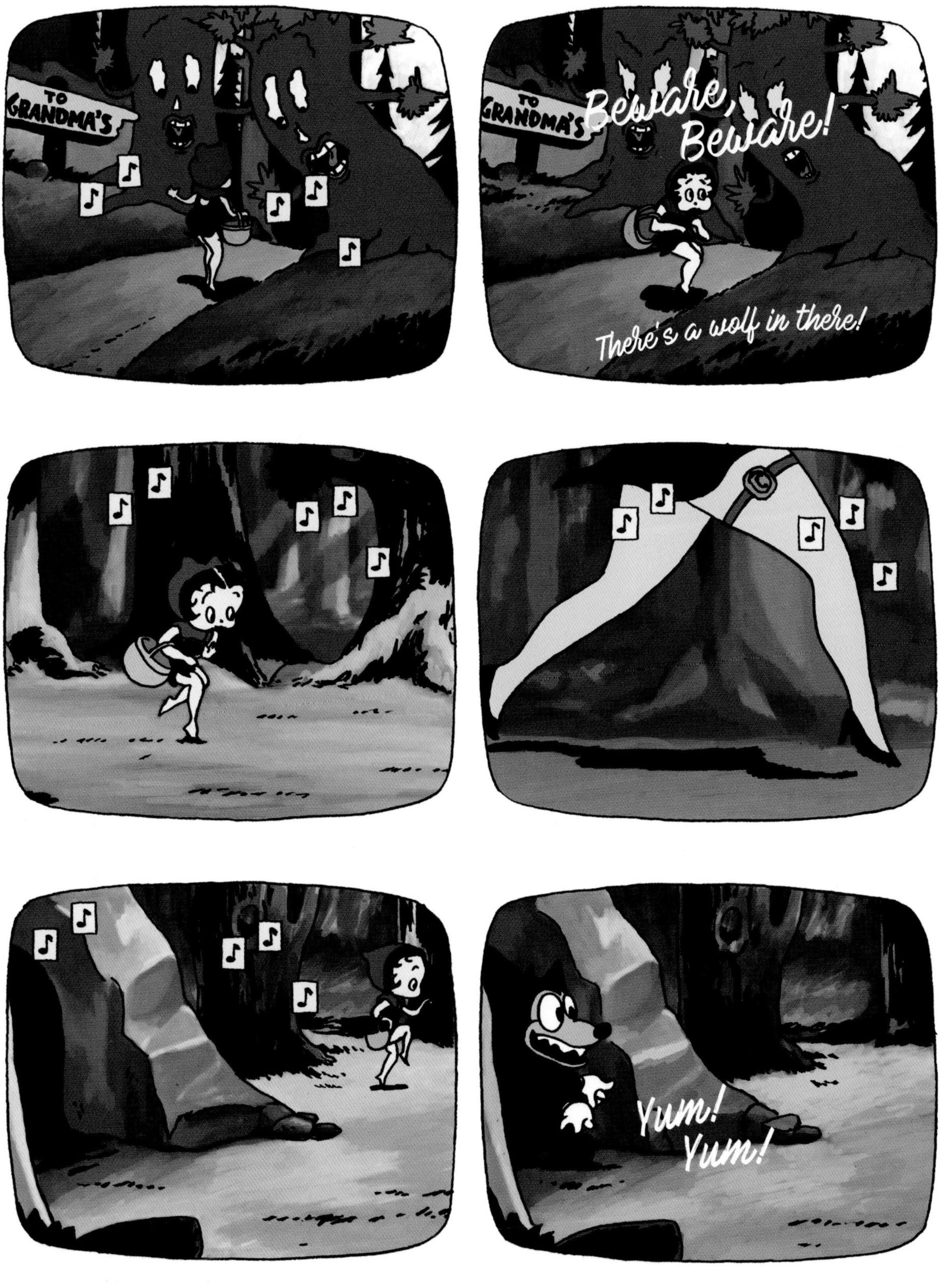
TO GRANDMA'S
TO GRANDMA'S
Beware, Beware!
There's a wolf in there!
Yum! Yum!

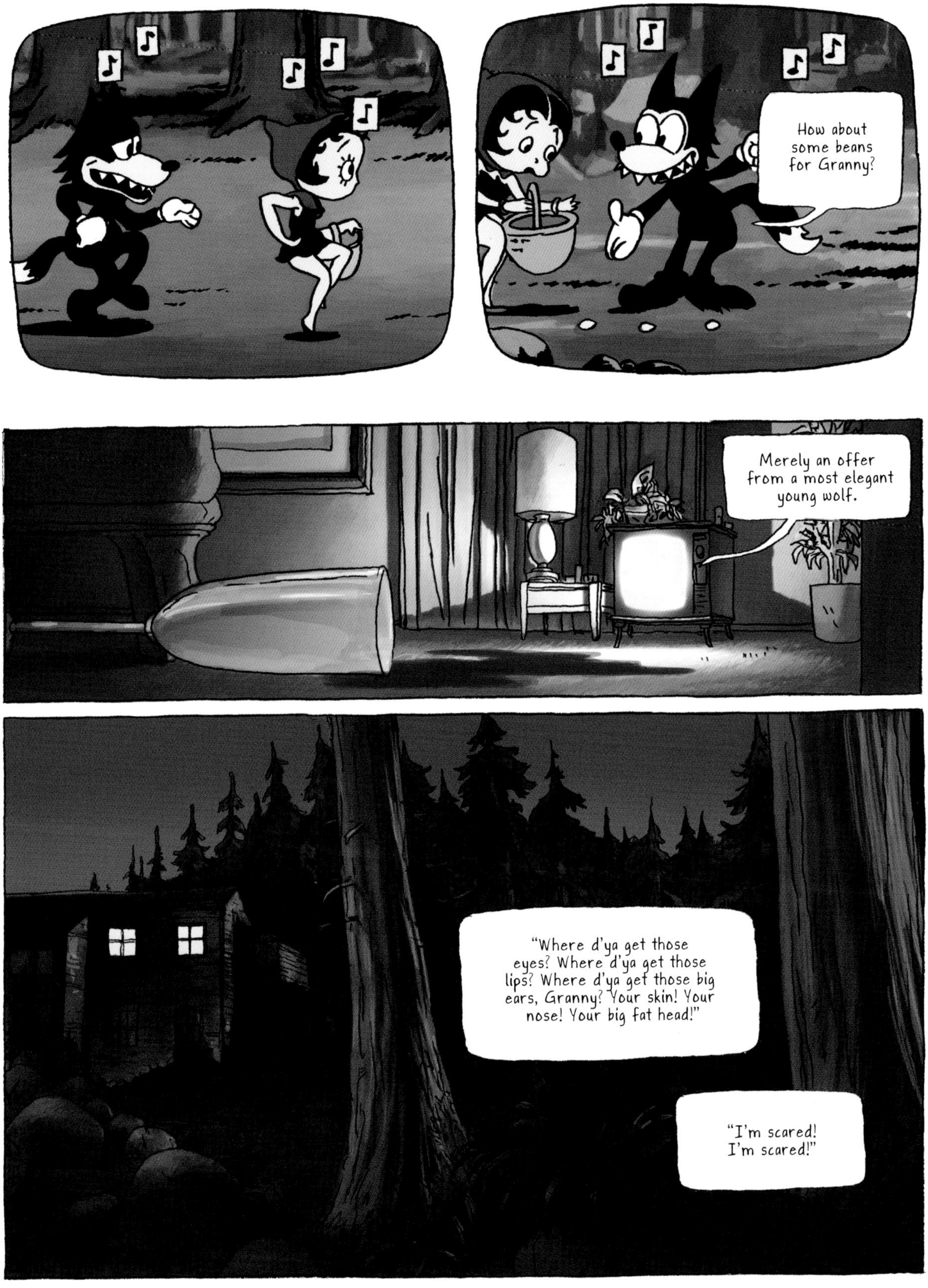
How about some beans for Granny?
Merely an offer from a most elegant young wolf.
"Where d'ya get those eyes? Where d'ya get those lips? Where d'ya get those big ears, Granny? Your skin! Your nose! Your big fat head!"
"I'm scared! I'm scared!"

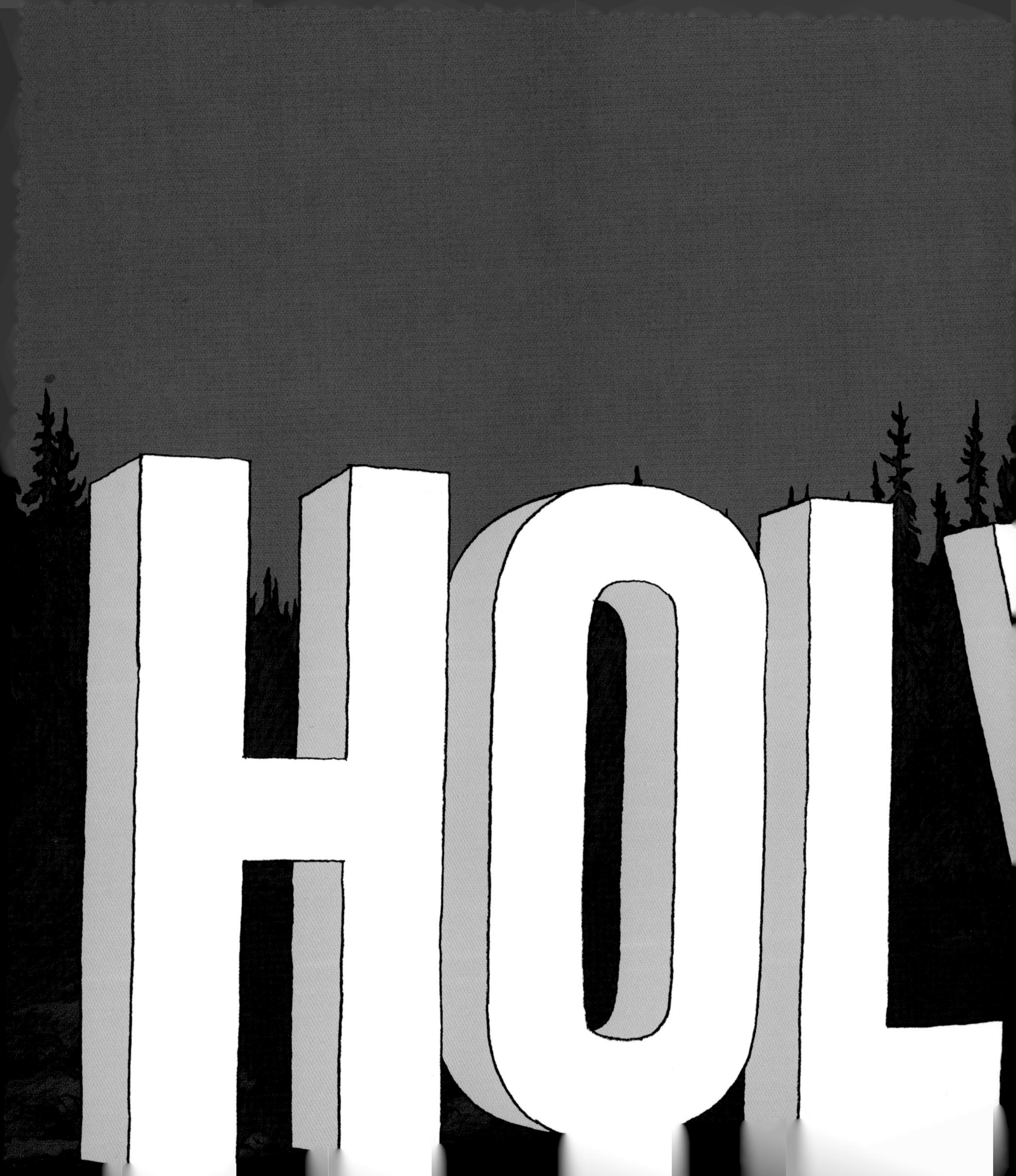
HOL

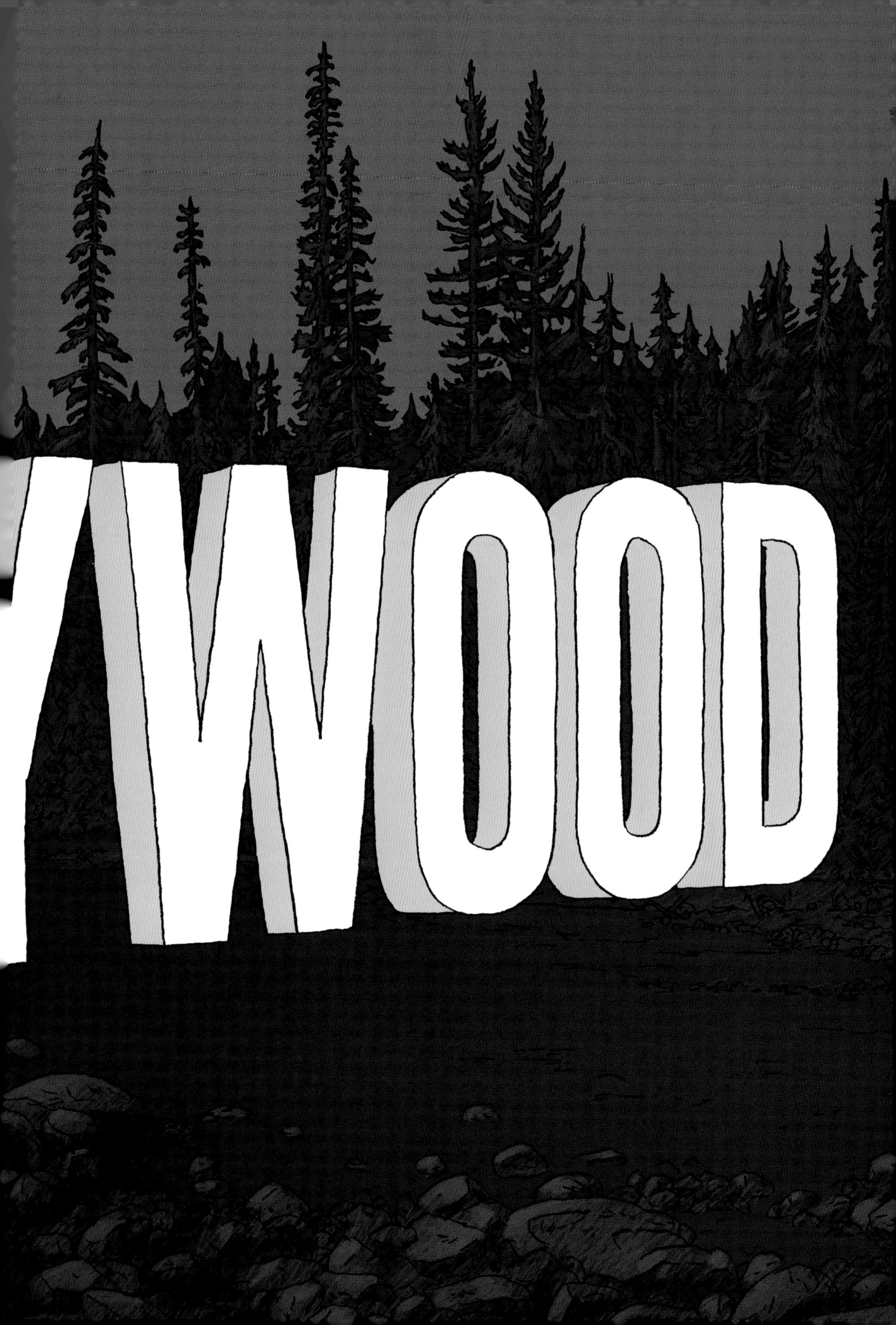

WOOD

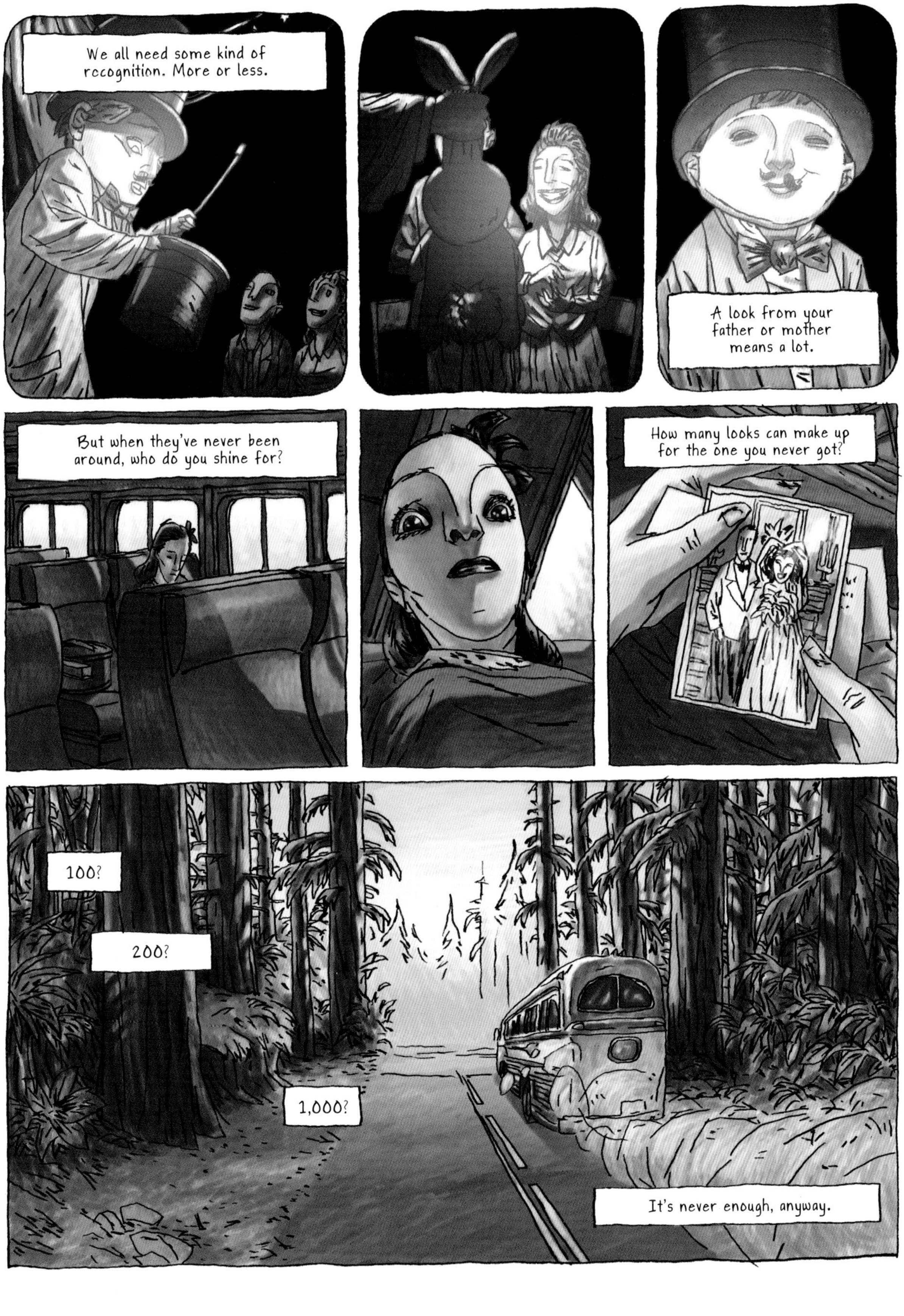

We all need some kind of recognition. More or less.
A look from your father or mother means a lot.
But when they've never been around, who do you shine for?
How many looks can make up for the one you never got?
100?
200?
1,000?
It's never enough, anyway.

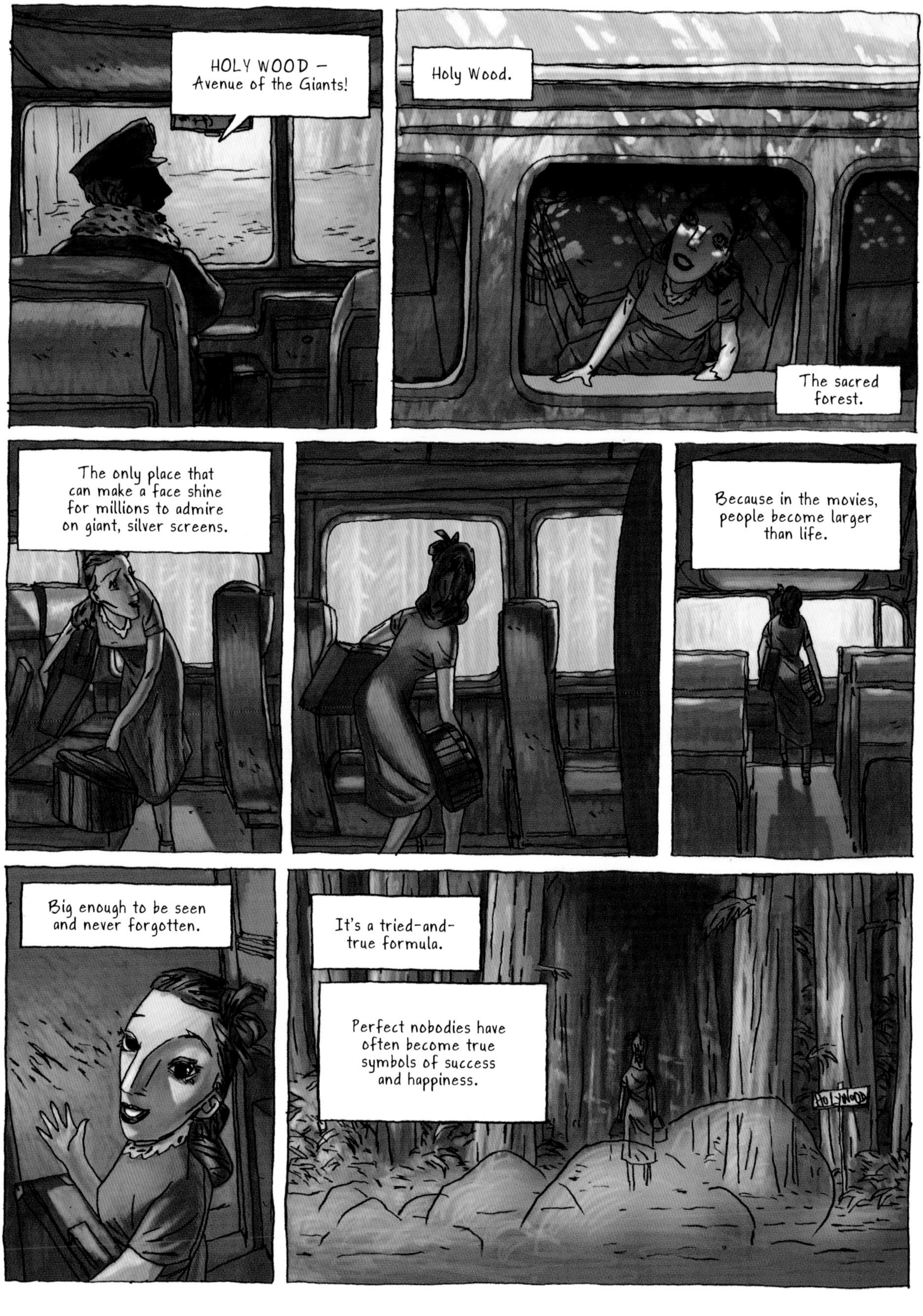
HOLY WOOD – Avenue of the Giants!
Holy Wood.
The sacred forest.
The only place that can make a face shine for millions to admire on giant, silver screens.
Because in the movies, people become larger than life.
Big enough to be seen and never forgotten.
It's a tried-and-true formula.
Perfect nobodies have often become true symbols of success and happiness.
HOLYWOOD

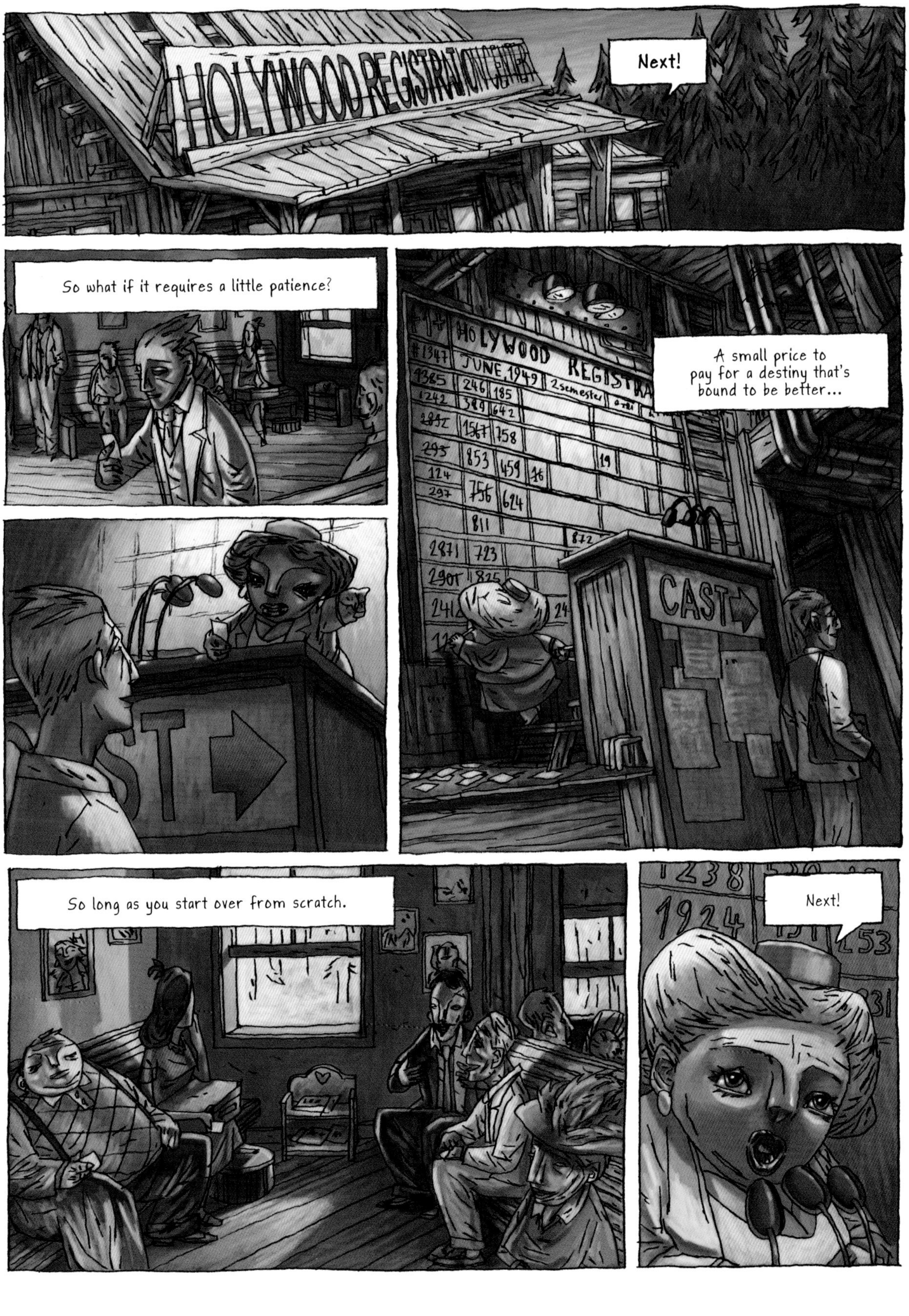
HOLYWOOD REGISTRATION
Next!
So what if it requires a little patience?
A small price to pay for a destiny that's bound to be better...
JUNE 1949
CAST
So long as you start over from scratch.
Next!

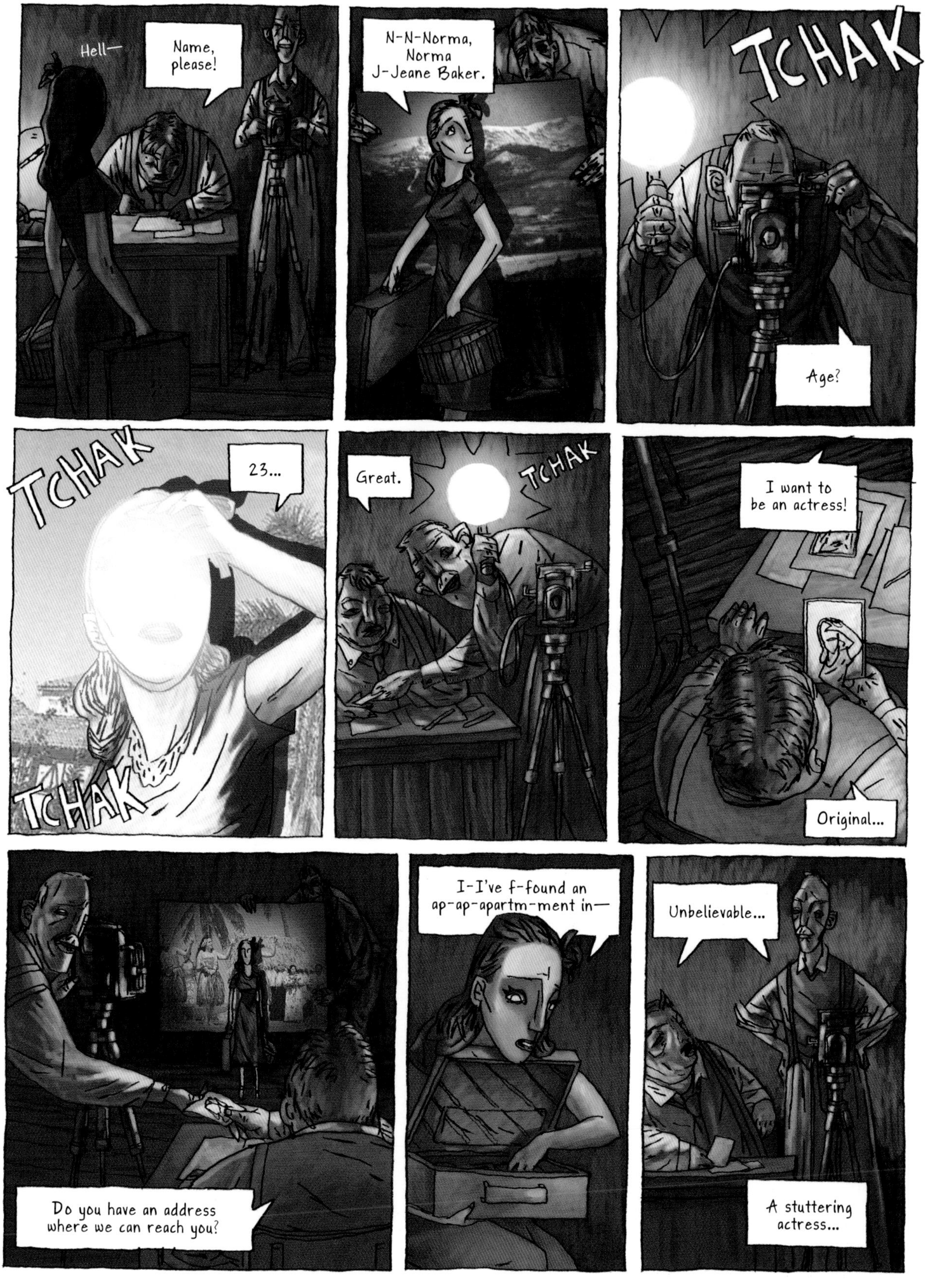
Hell—
Name, please!
N-N-Norma, Norma J-Jeane Baker.
TCHAK
Age?
TCHAK
23...
TCHAK
Great.
TCHAK
I want to be an actress!
Original...
Do you have an address where we can reach you?
I-I've f-found an ap-ap-apartm-ment in—
Unbelievable...
A stuttering actress...

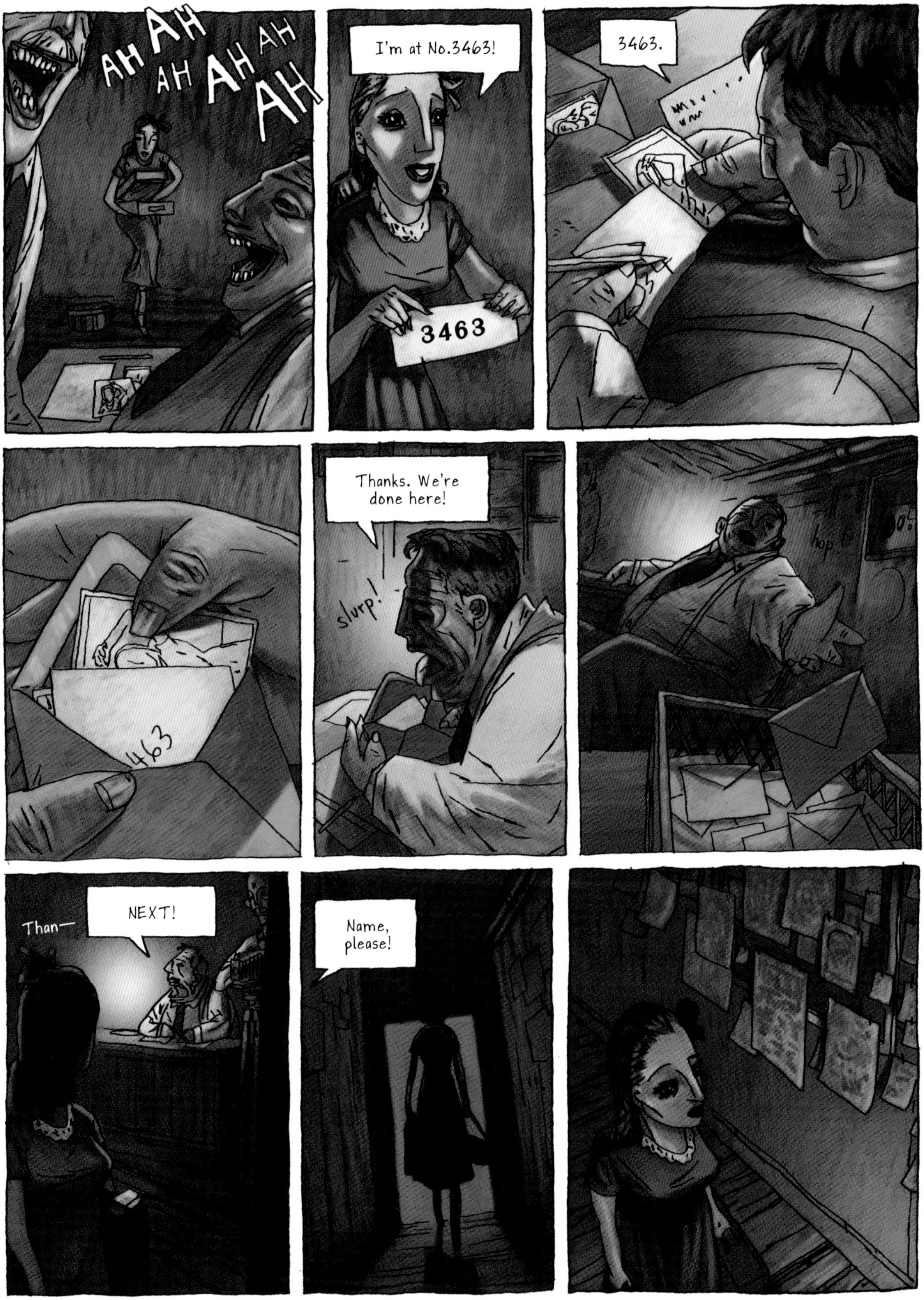
AH AH AH AH AH AH AH
I'm at No.3463!
3463
3463.
463
Thanks. We're done here!
slurp!
hop
Than—
NEXT!
Name, please!

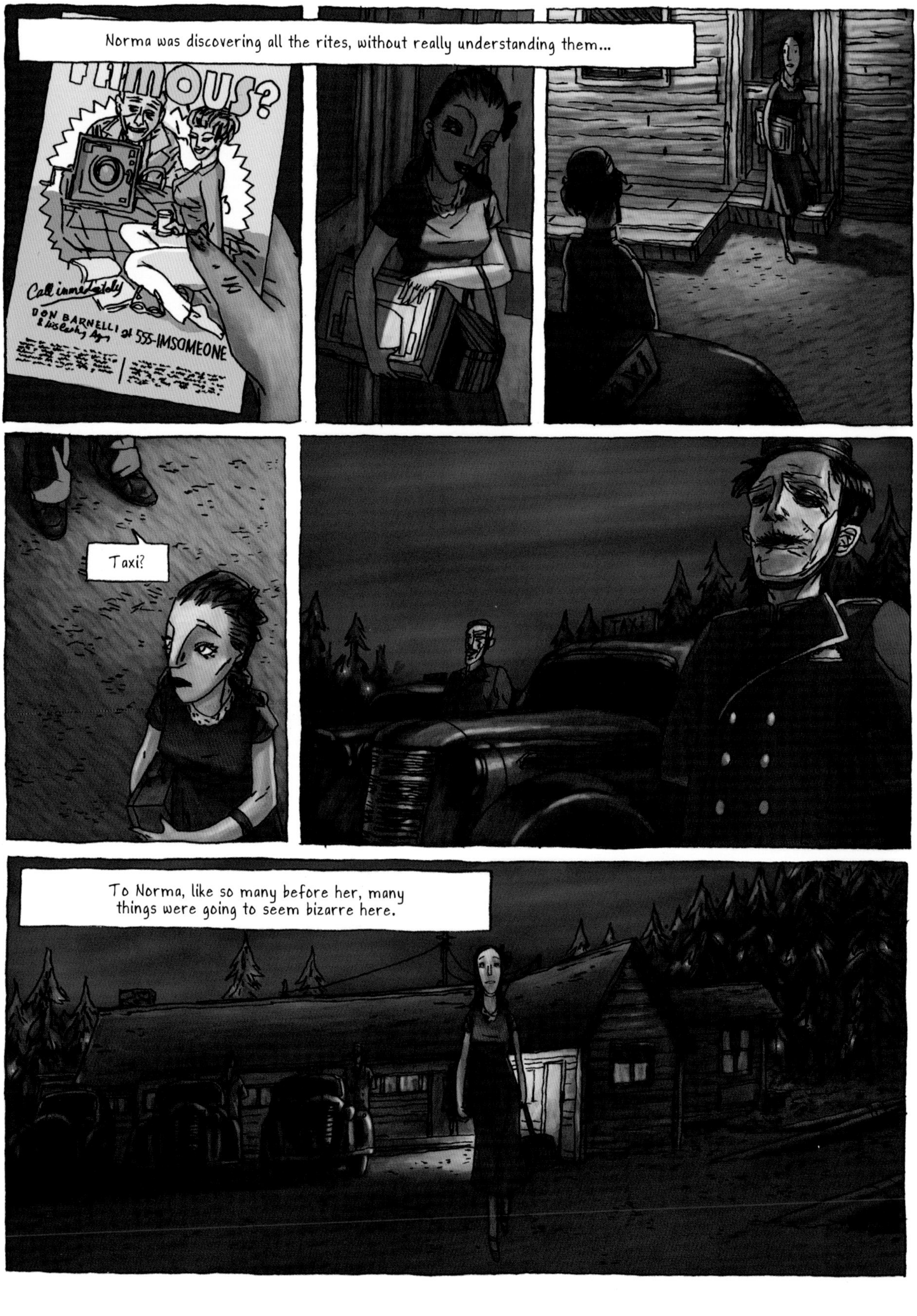
Norma was discovering all the rites, without really understanding them...
Call immediately
DON BARNELLI
555-IMSOMEONE
Taxi?
To Norma, like so many before her, many things were going to seem bizarre here.

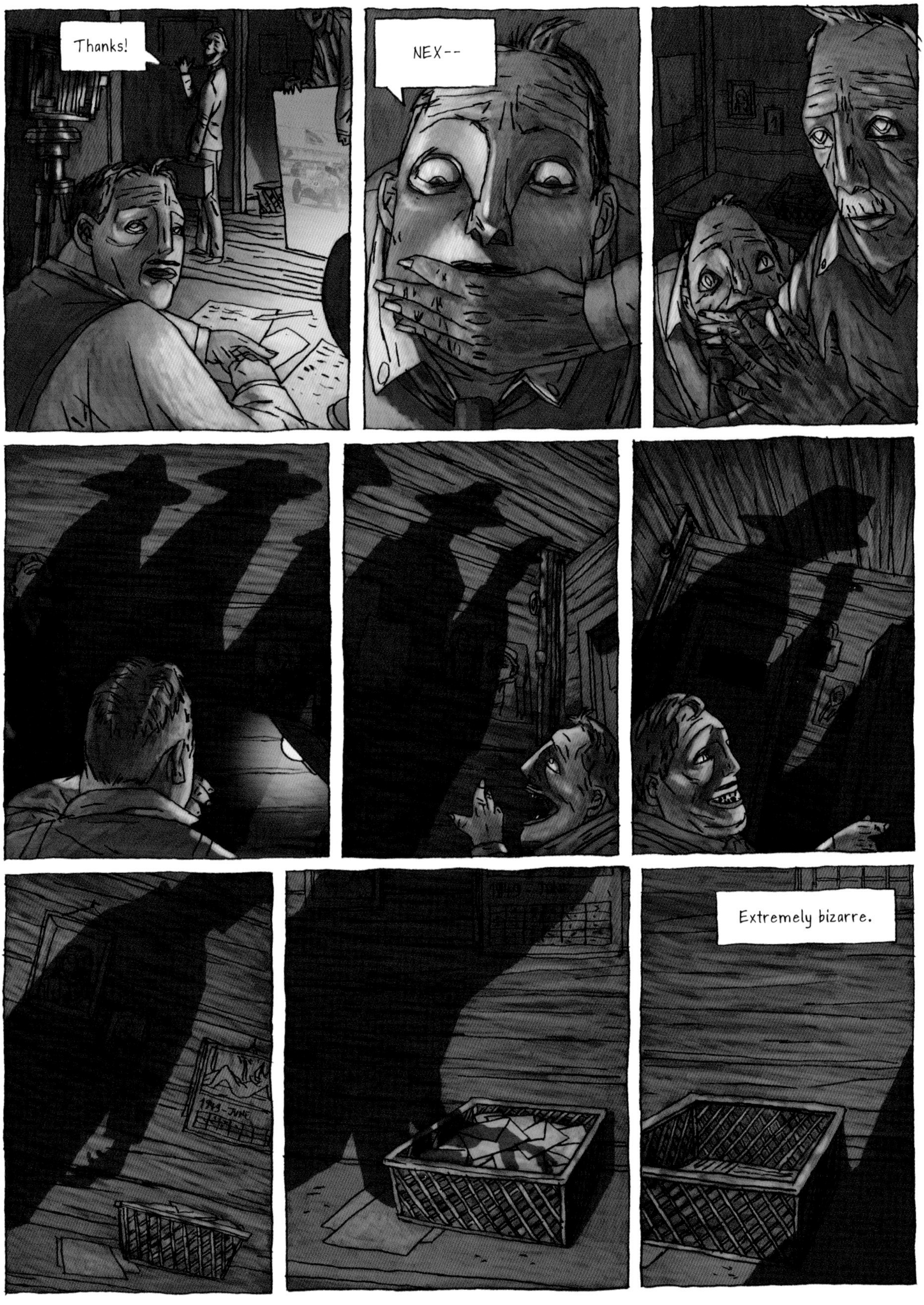
Thanks!
NEX--
Extremely bizarre.

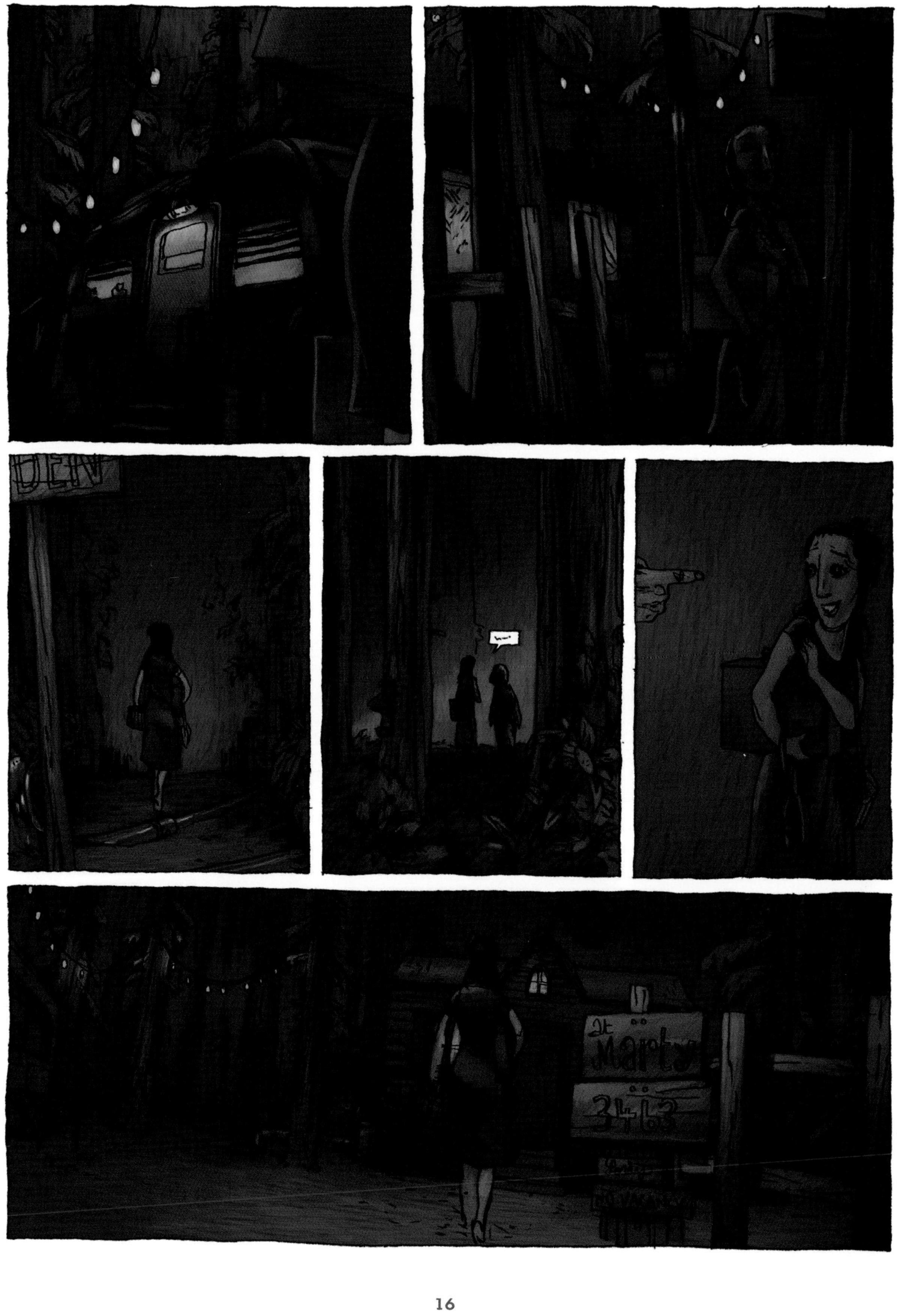
Marty
3463

CHAPTER 1
BLURRED

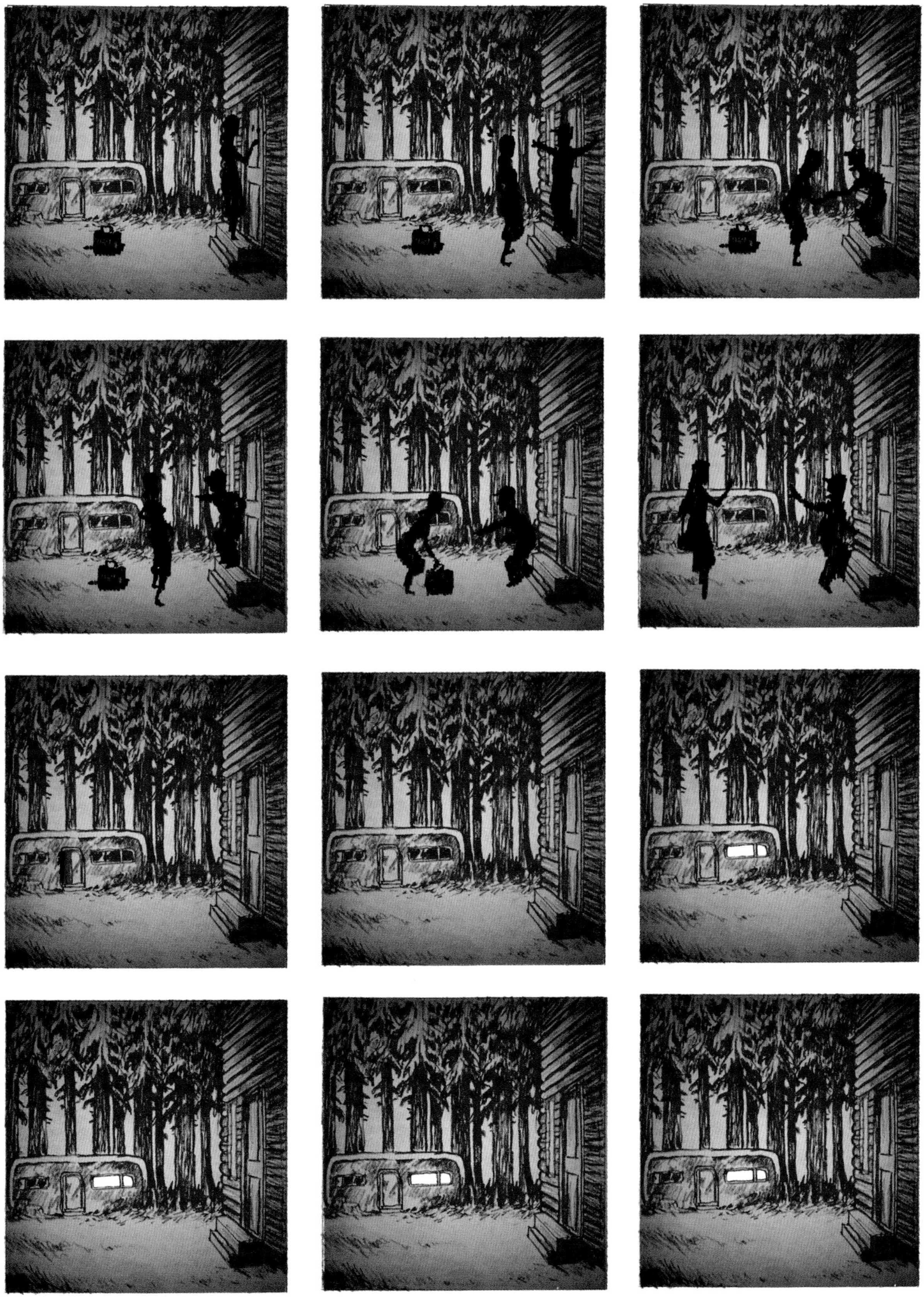

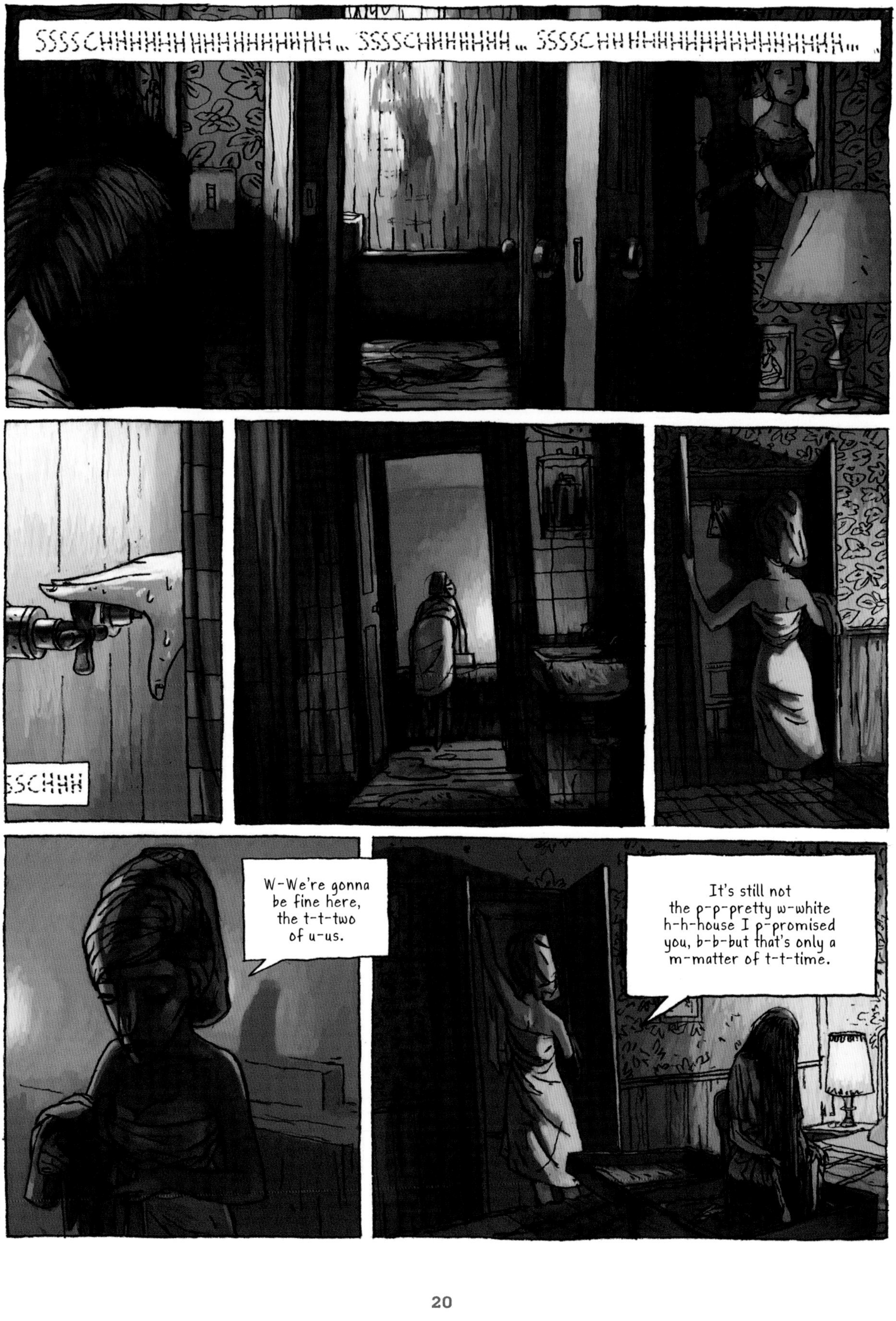

SSSSCHHHHHHHHHHHHHHHH... SSSSCHHHHHHH... SSSSCHHHHHHHHHHHHHHHHHH...
SCHHH
W-We're gonna be fine here, the t-t-two of u-us.
It's still not the p-p-pretty w-white h-h-house I p-promised you, b-b-but that's only a m-matter of t-t-time.

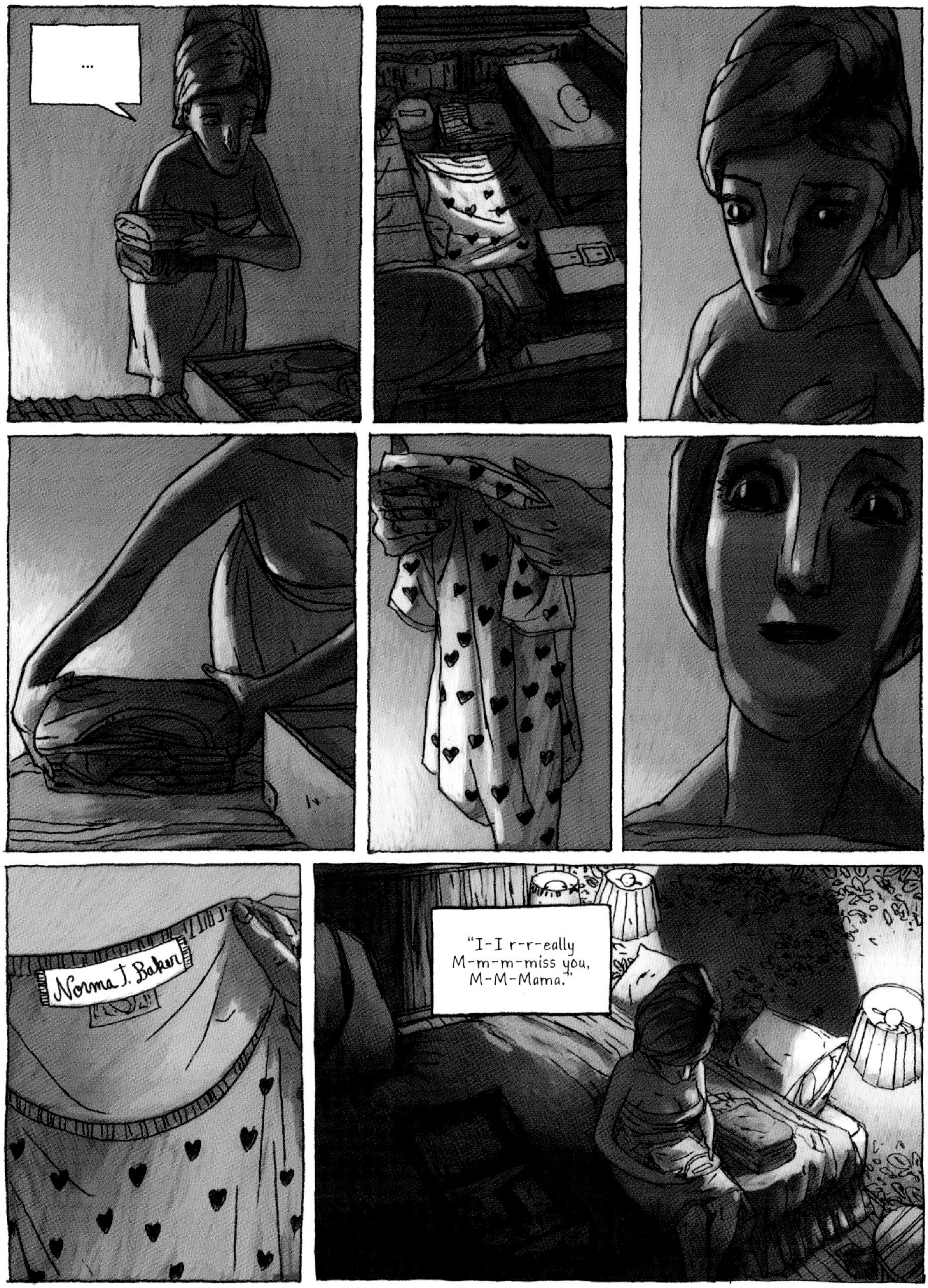
...
Norma J. Baker
"I-I r-r-eally M-m-m-miss you, M-M-Mama."

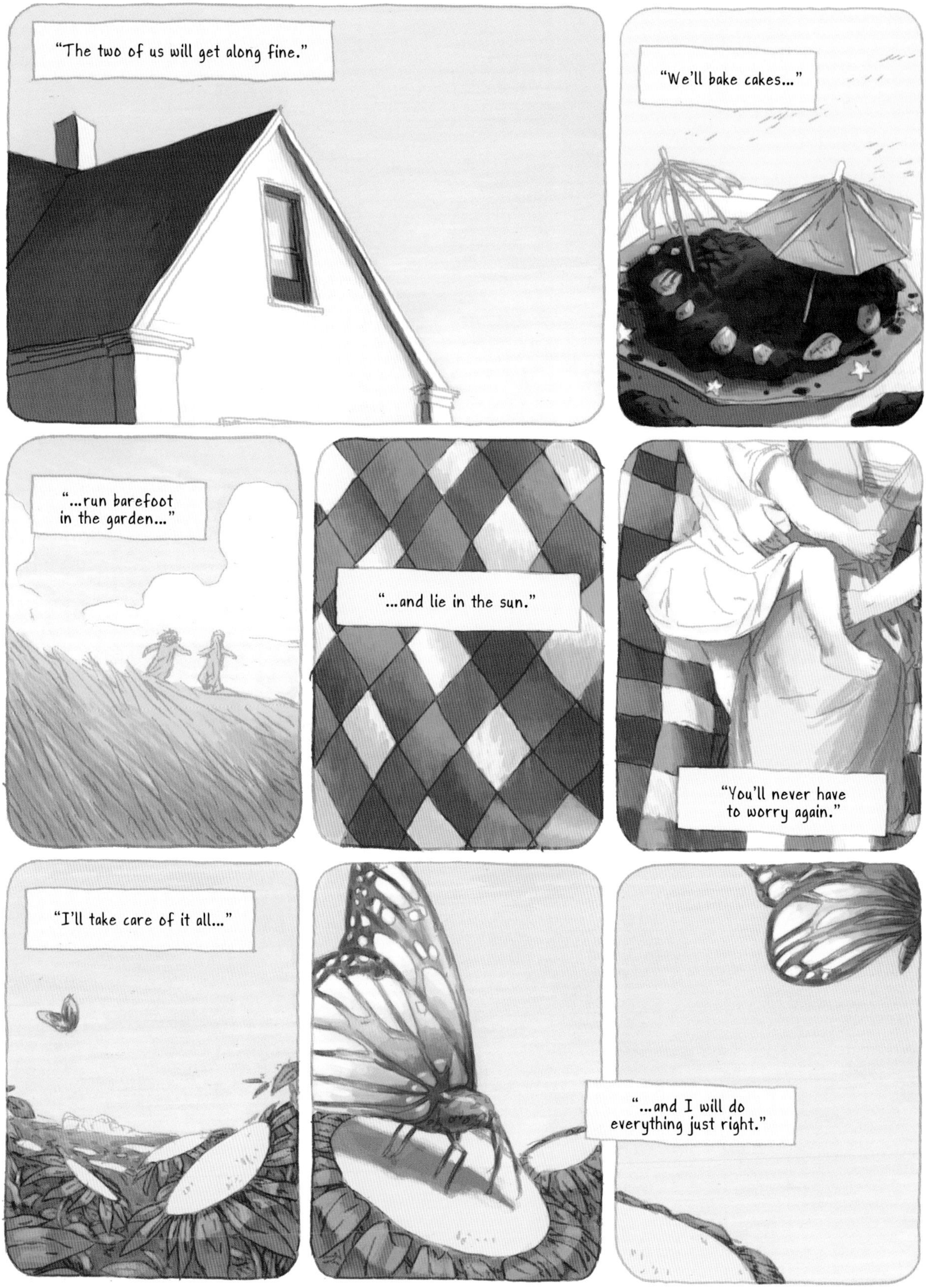
"The two of us will get along fine."
"We'll bake cakes..."
"...run barefoot in the garden..."
"...and lie in the sun."
"You'll never have to worry again."
"I'll take care of it all..."
"...and I will do everything just right."

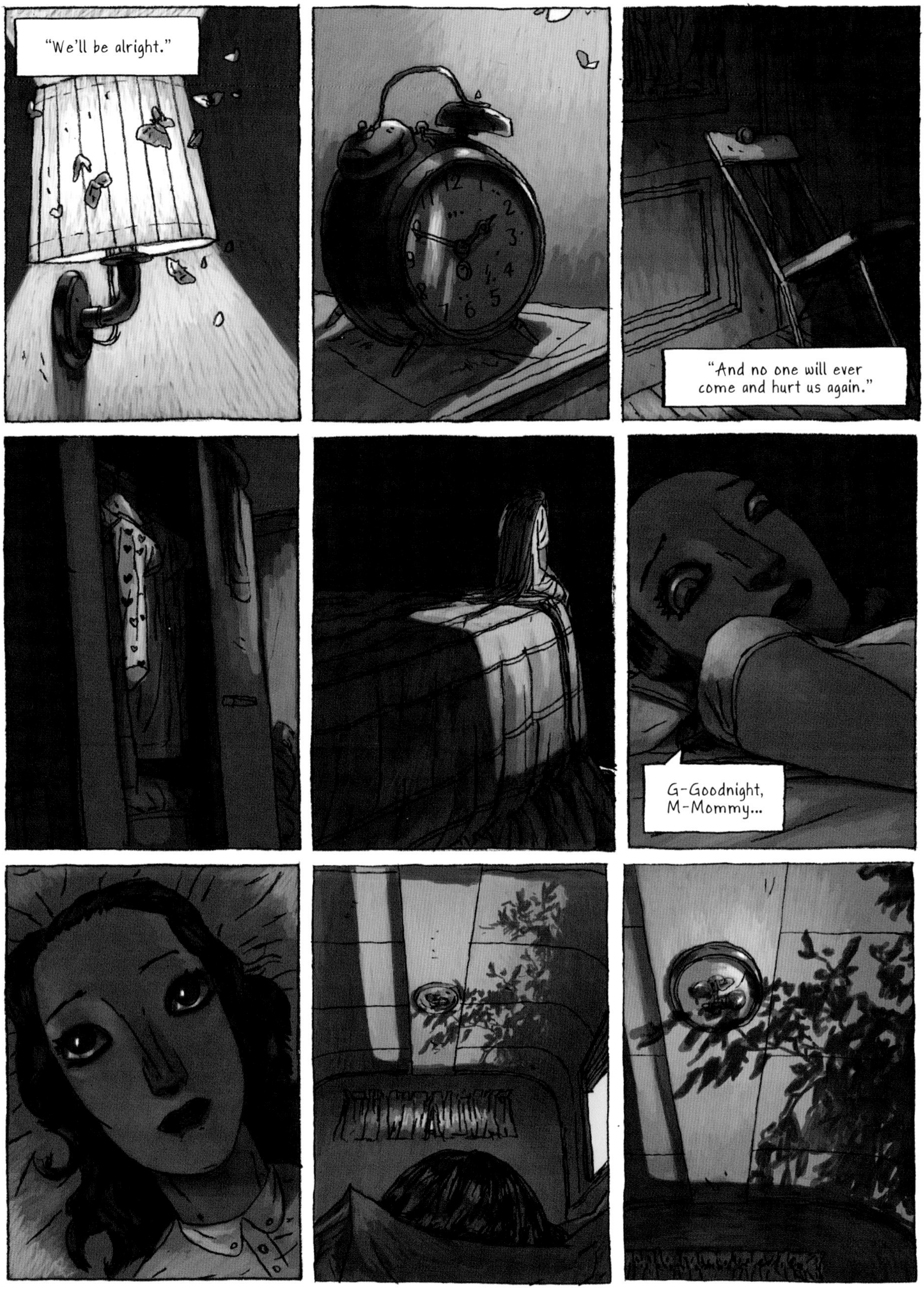
"We'll be alright."
"And no one will ever come and hurt us again."
G-Goodnight, M-Mommy...

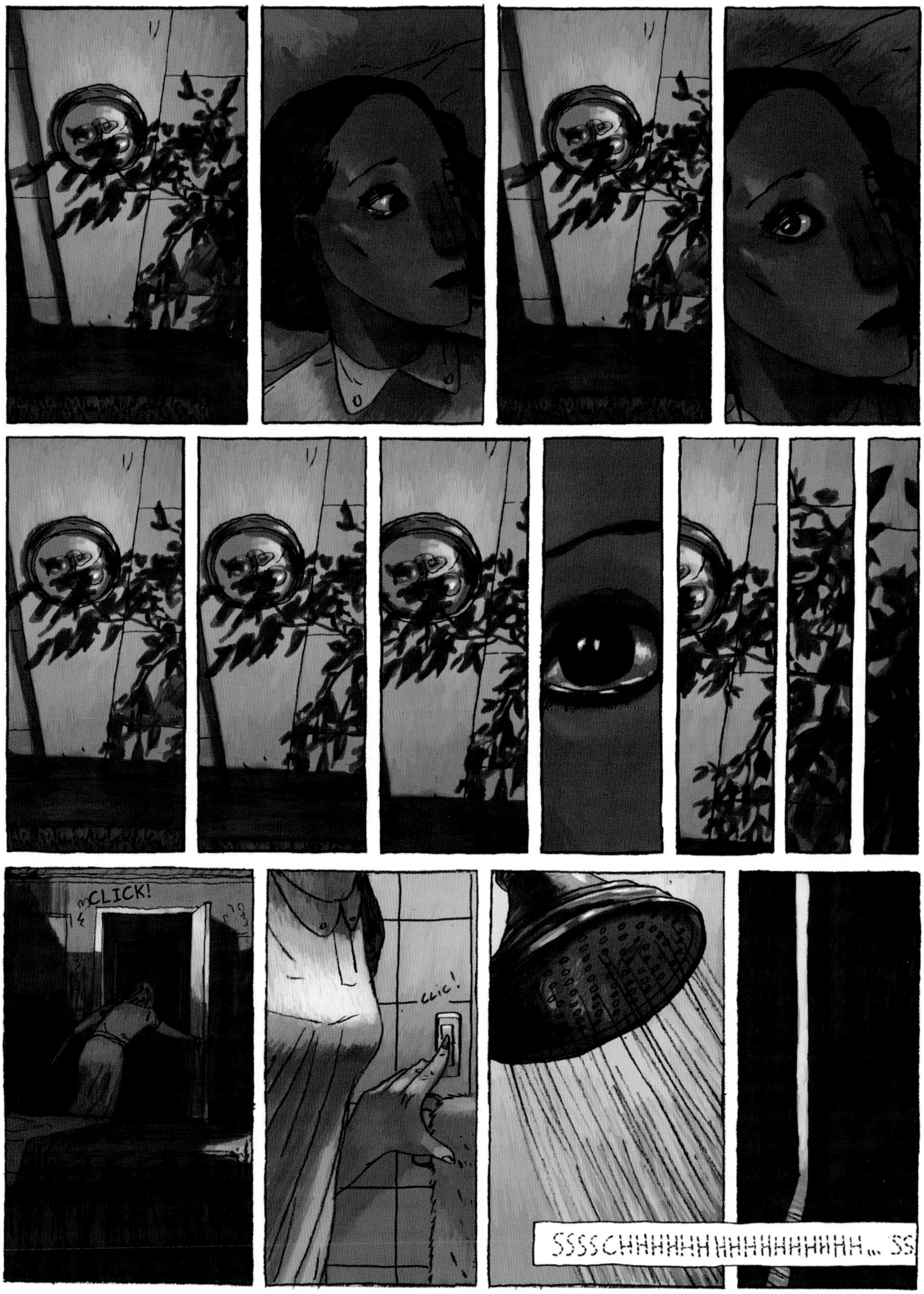
CLICK!
CLIC!
SSSSCHHHHHH HHHHHHHHHH... SS

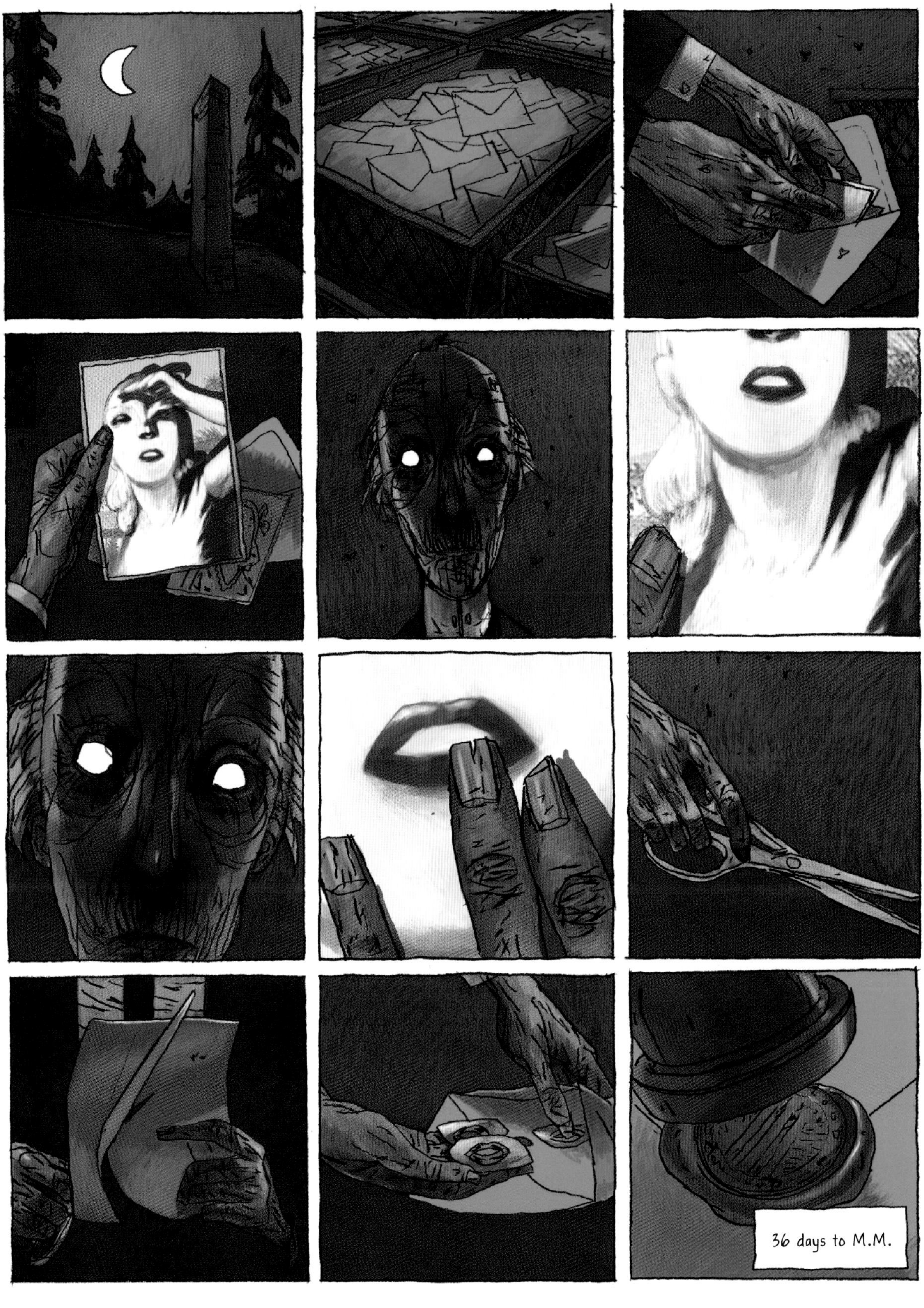
36 days to M.M.

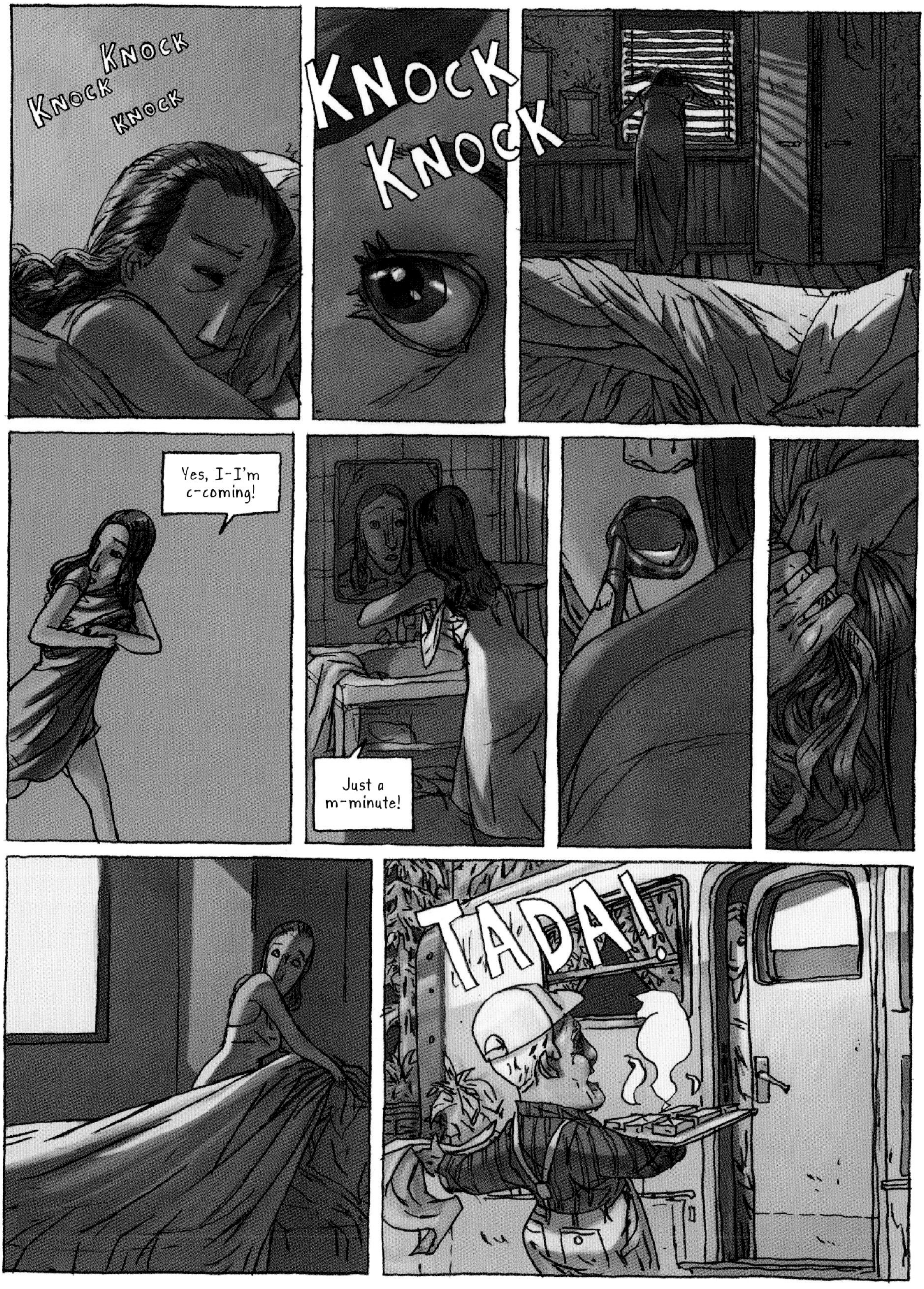
Knock
Knock
knock
Knock
Knock
Yes, I-I'm c-coming!
Just a m-minute!
TADA!

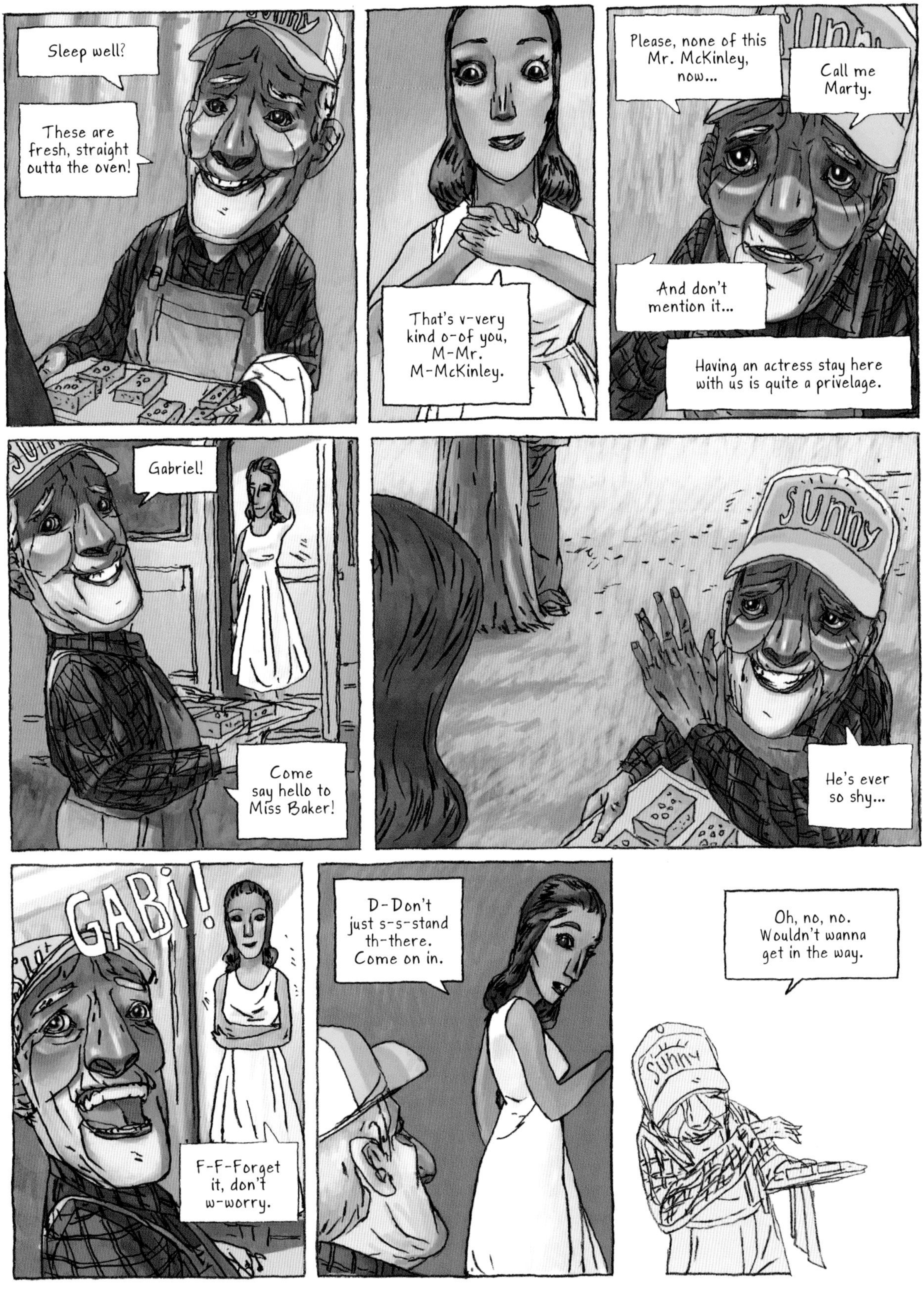
Sleep well?
These are fresh, straight outta the oven!
That's v-very kind o-of you, M-Mr. M-McKinley.
SUNNY
Please, none of this Mr. McKinley, now...
Call me Marty.
And don't mention it...
Having an actress stay here with us is quite a privelage.
Gabriel!
Come say hello to Miss Baker!
SUNNY
He's ever so shy...
GABI!
F-F-Forget it, don't w-worry.
D-Don't just s-s-stand th-there. Come on in.
Oh, no, no. Wouldn't wanna get in the way.
SUNNY

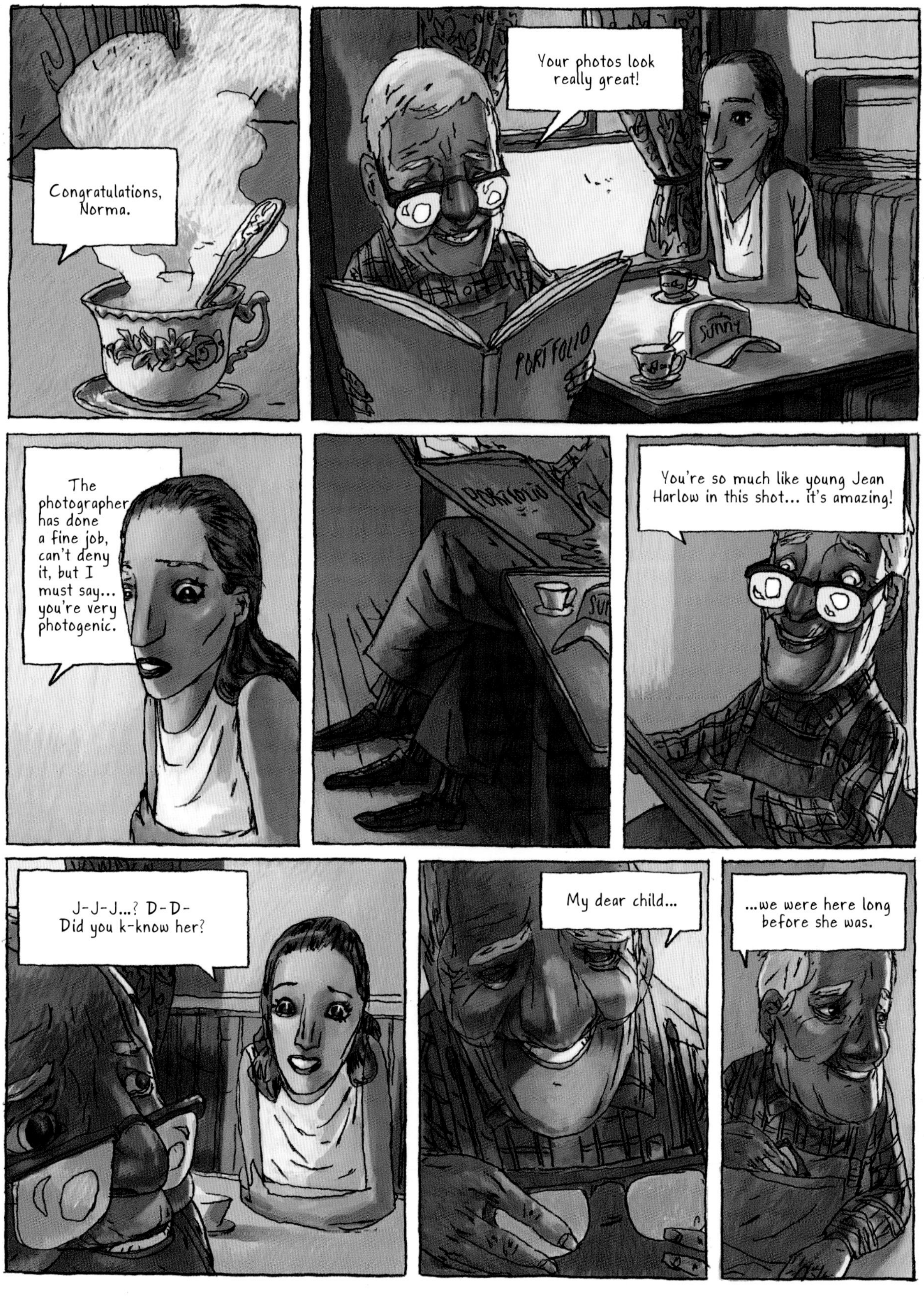
Congratulations, Norma.
Your photos look really great!
PORTFOLIO
SUNNY
The photographer has done a fine job, can't deny it, but I must say... you're very photogenic.
You're so much like young Jean Harlow in this shot... it's amazing!
J-J-J...? D-D- Did you k-know her?
My dear child...
...we were here long before she was.

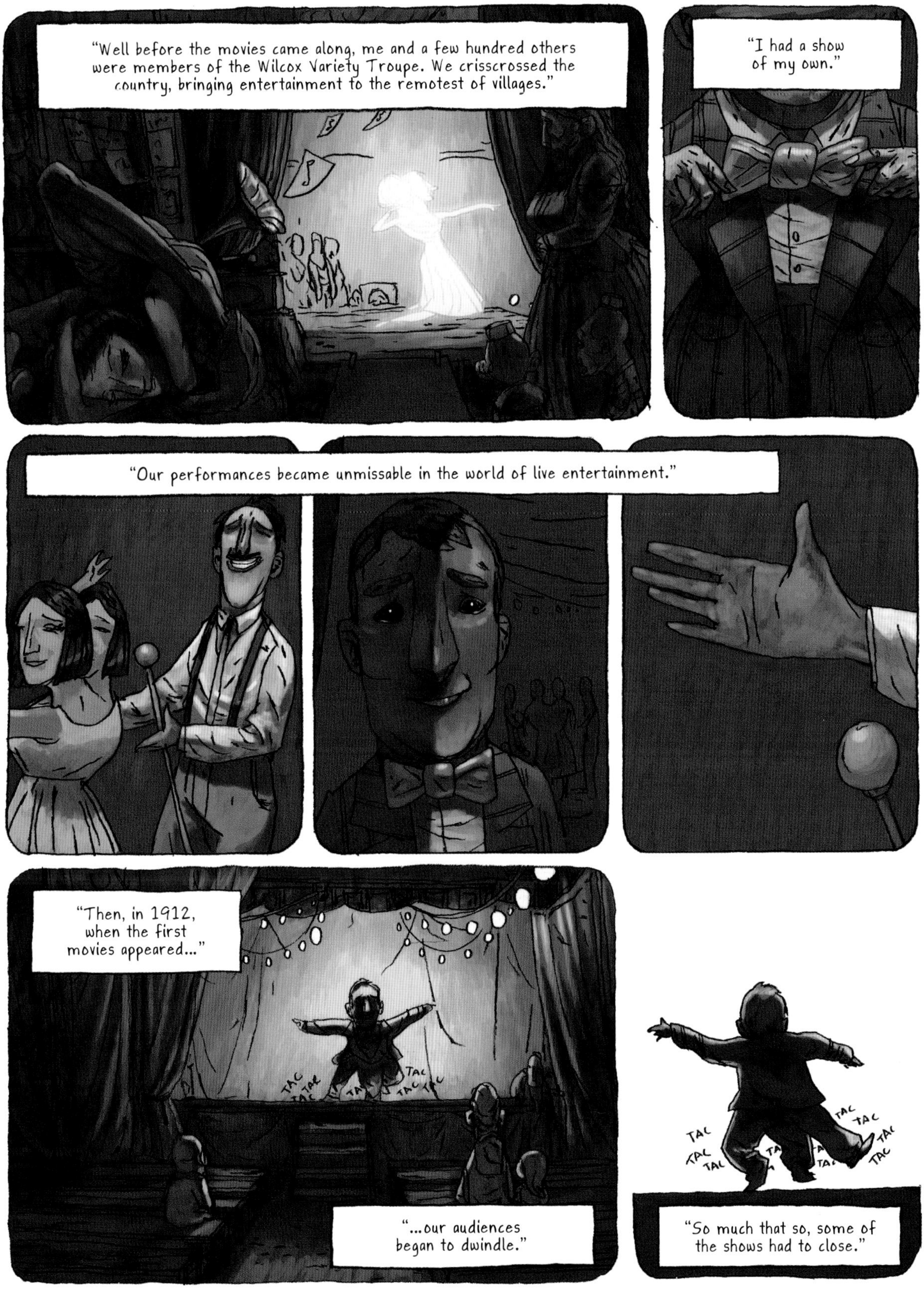
"Well before the movies came along, me and a few hundred others were members of the Wilcox Variety Troupe. We crisscrossed the country, bringing entertainment to the remotest of villages."
"I had a show of my own."
"Our performances became unmissable in the world of live entertainment."
"Then, in 1912, when the first movies appeared..."
TAC TAC TAC
"...our audiences began to dwindle."
TAC TAC TAC TAC TAC TAC
"So much that so, some of the shows had to close."

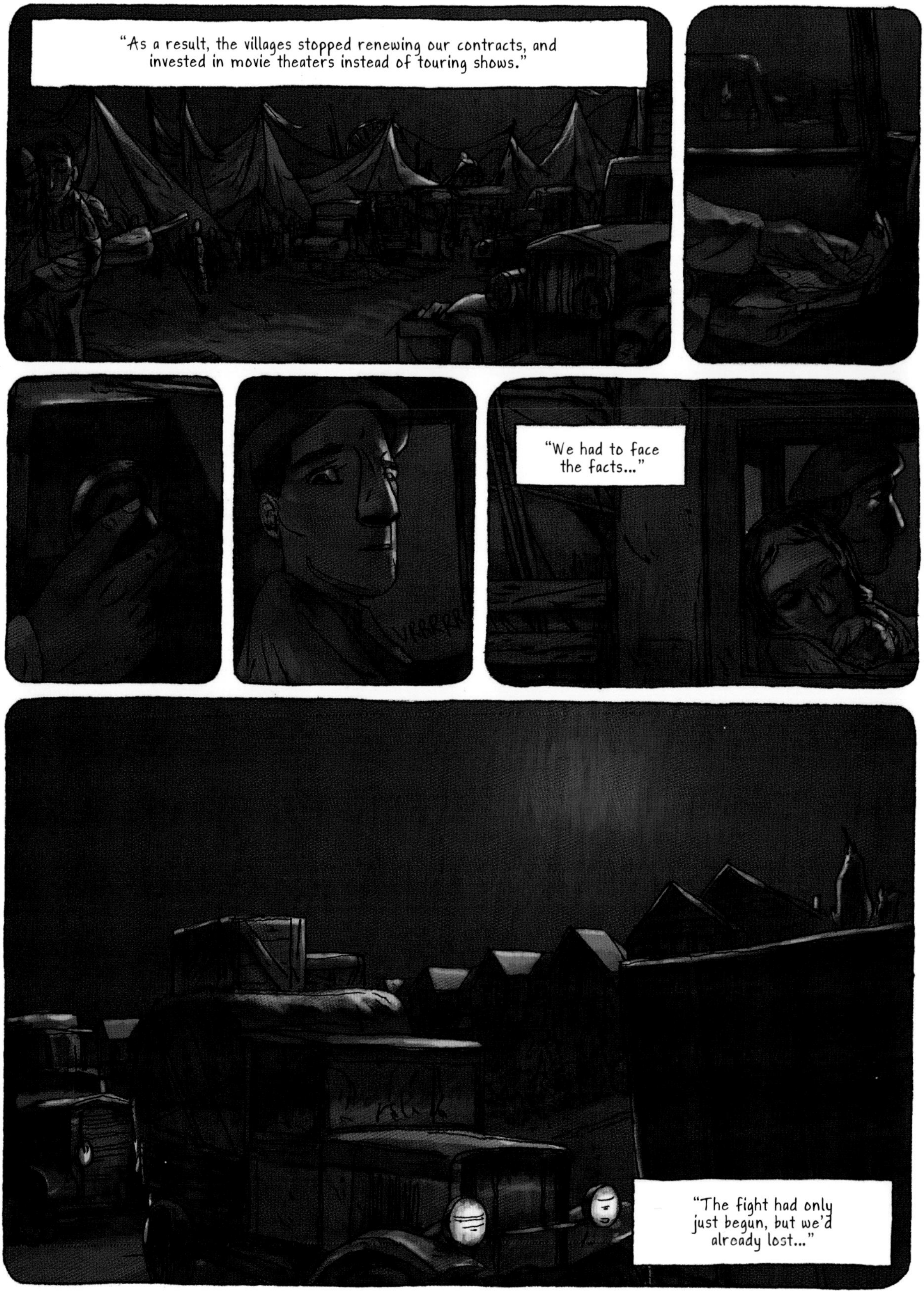
"As a result, the villages stopped renewing our contracts, and invested in movie theaters instead of touring shows."
"We had to face the facts..."
"The fight had only just begun, but we'd already lost..."

"Eventually, in September 1912, Harvey and Daieda Wilcox decided to stop in this wood, for reasons we couldn't quite understand."

"Because of the 'waves', they said."

"(Although I've never felt anything myself...)"

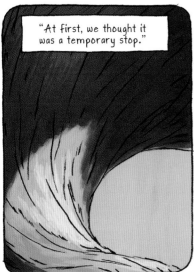

"At first, we thought it was a temporary stop."

"But the months slipped by..."

"...then the years..."

"...until 'temporary' gradually turned into 'permanent.'"

W-Who are Harvey and D-D-D-D, D-Da--

Harvey and Daieda.

"Here, we call 'em The Founders."

"Harvey must be around 190, and his wife's about the same age."

Without them, we might all be dead by now.

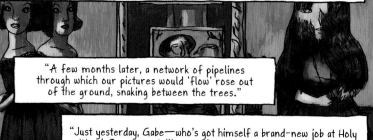

"We had to face it, our shows just couldn't pull a crowd any more. To make sure that the troupe didn't fall apart altogether, The Founders decided to get into the cinematographic industry. From then on, every picture you could possibly imagine would be made right here. 'Homegrown,' as folks used to say."

"A few months later, a network of pipelines through which our pictures would 'flow' rose out of the ground, snaking between the trees."

"Just yesterday, Gabe—who's got himself a brand-new job at Holy Wood, Inc.—was telling me there are now over 750 miles of pipes, and nearly twice as many movies flowing beneath our feet."

"That's how it is..."

Times have changed... Our profession's evolved. Once it was us in the spotlight, but now we shine the lights on you.

... Never mind. We're all still here. That's the important thing.

Like in any stepfamily, there's a place for everybody. You just need to find your own.

Do you have family?

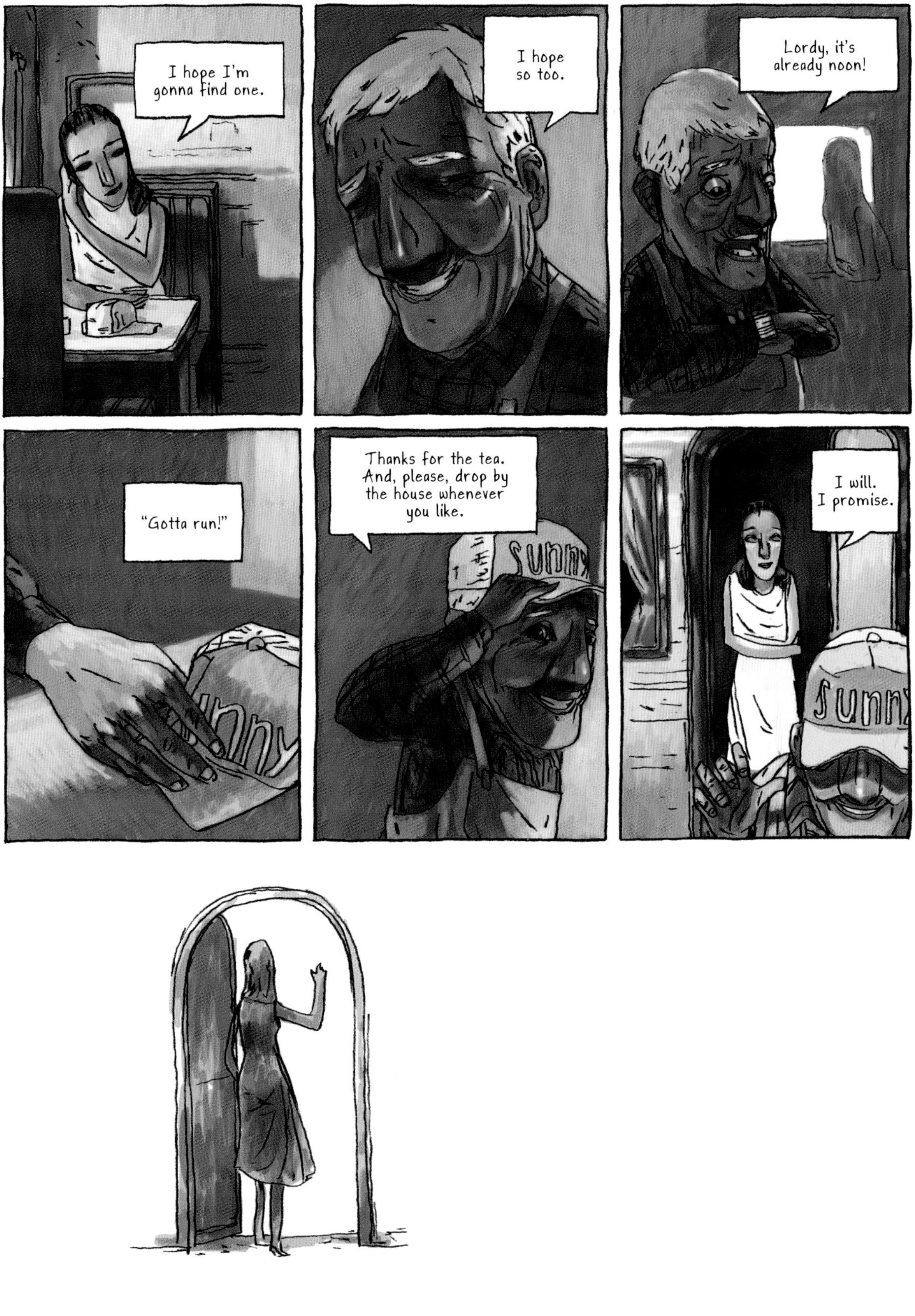
I hope I'm gonna find one.
I hope so too.
Lordy, it's already noon!
"Gotta run!"
Thanks for the tea. And, please, drop by the house whenever you like.
I will. I promise.

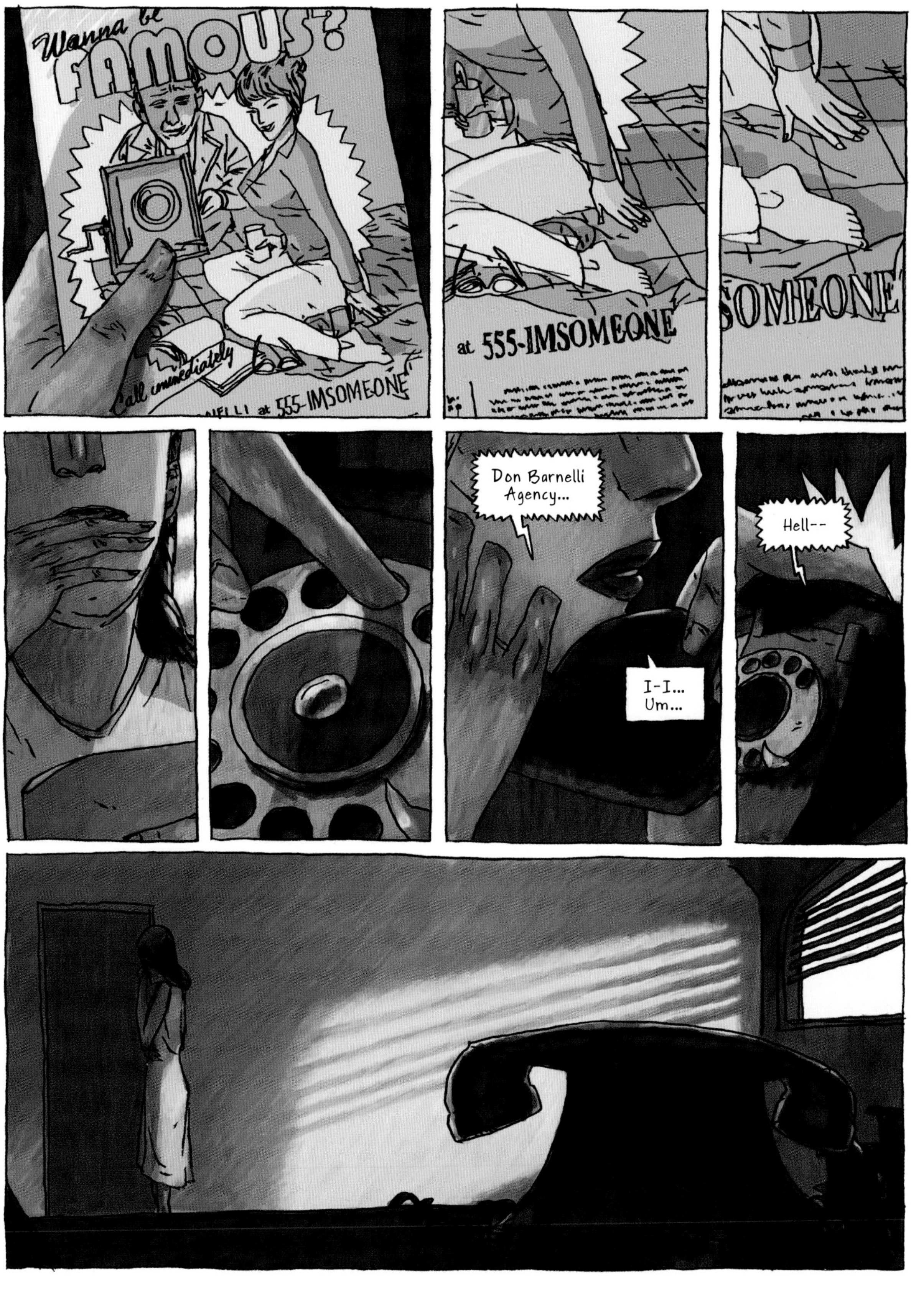
Wanna be FAMOUS?
Call immediately
...NELLI at 555-IMSOMEONE
at 555-IMSOMEONE
SOMEONE
Don Barnelli Agency...
I-I... Um...
Hell--

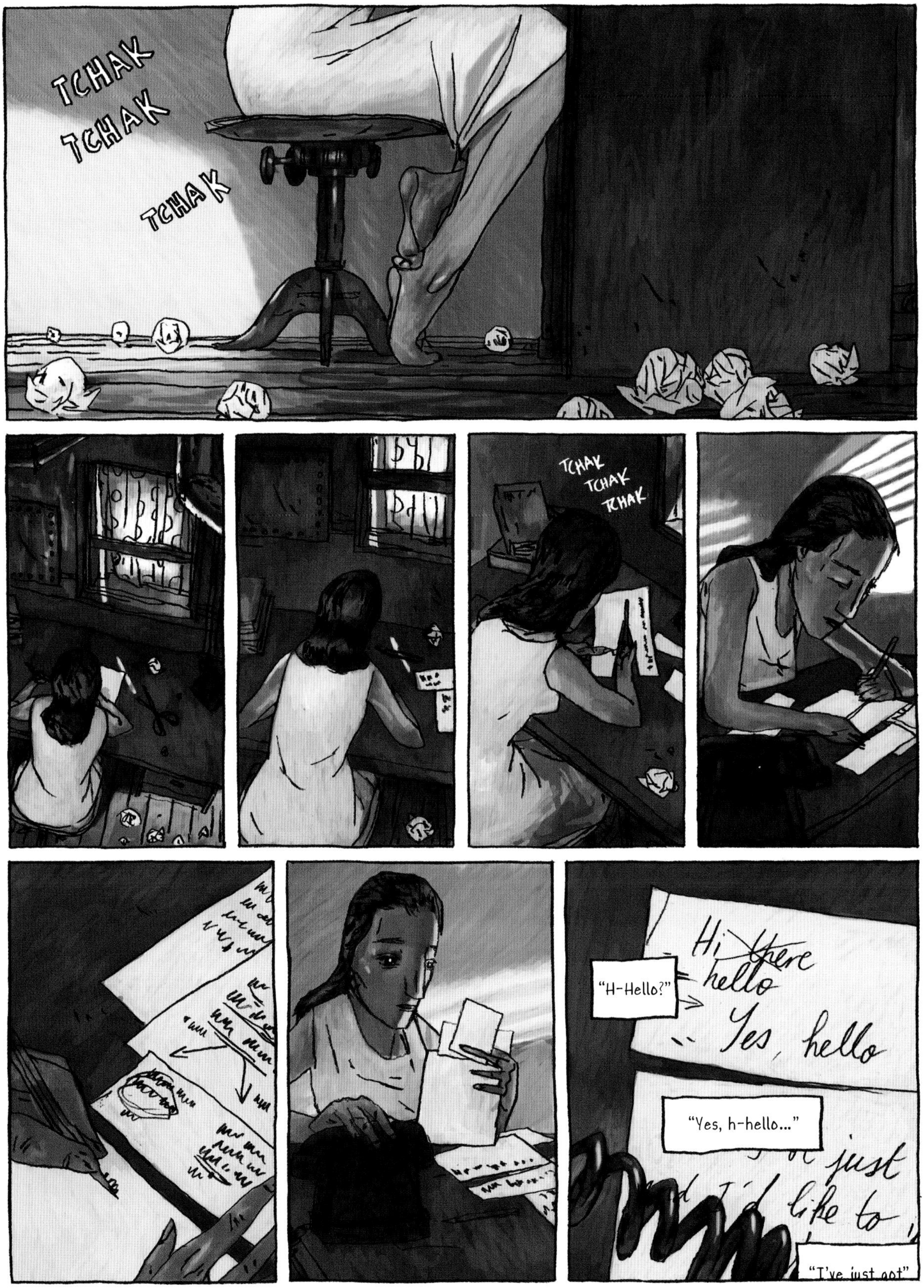
TCHAK
TCHAK
TCHAK
TCHAK
TCHAK
TCHAK
Hi there
hello
Yes, hello
"H-Hello?"
"Yes, h-hello..."
just
I'd like to
"I've just got"

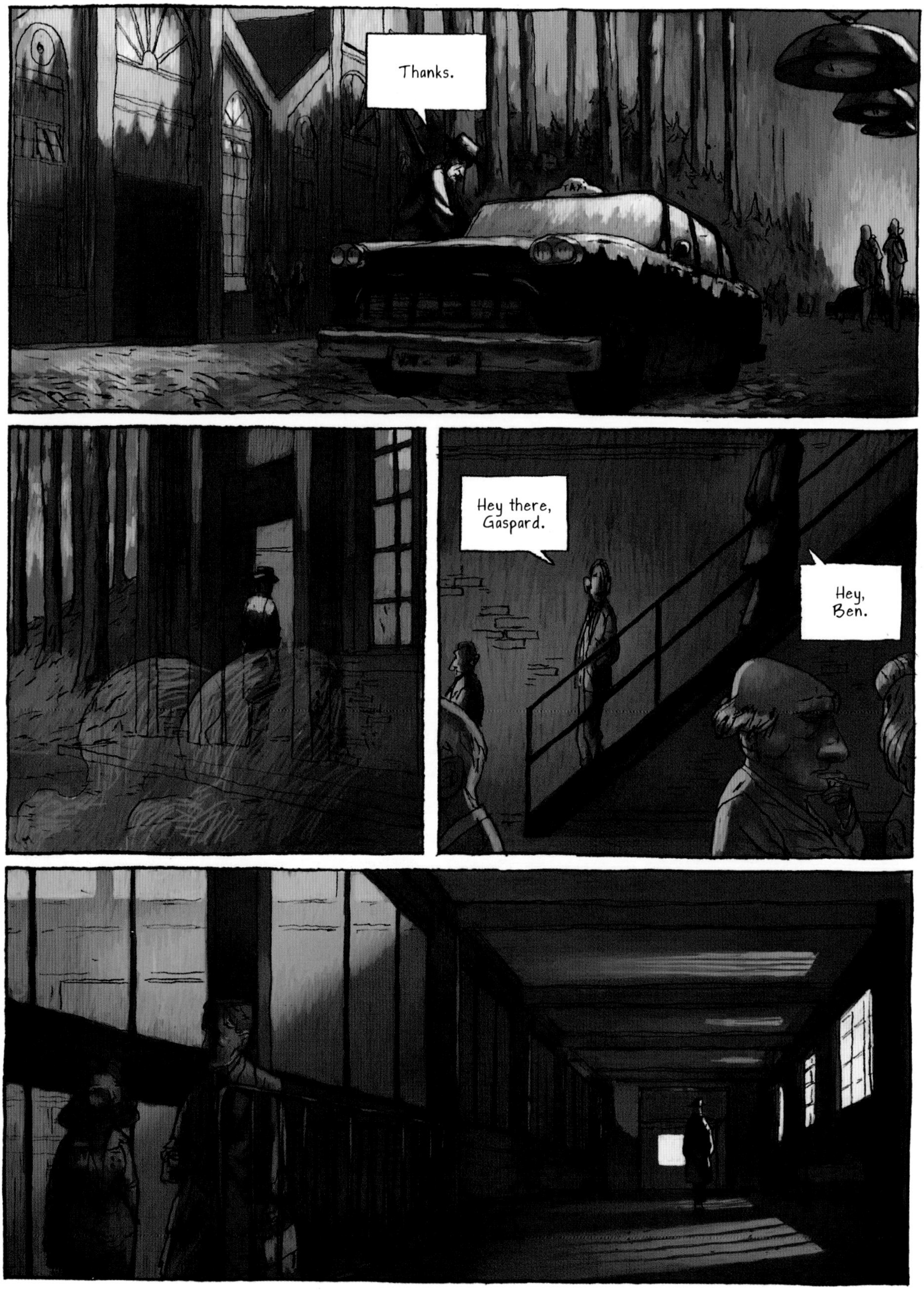
Thanks.
Hey there, Gaspard.
Hey, Ben.

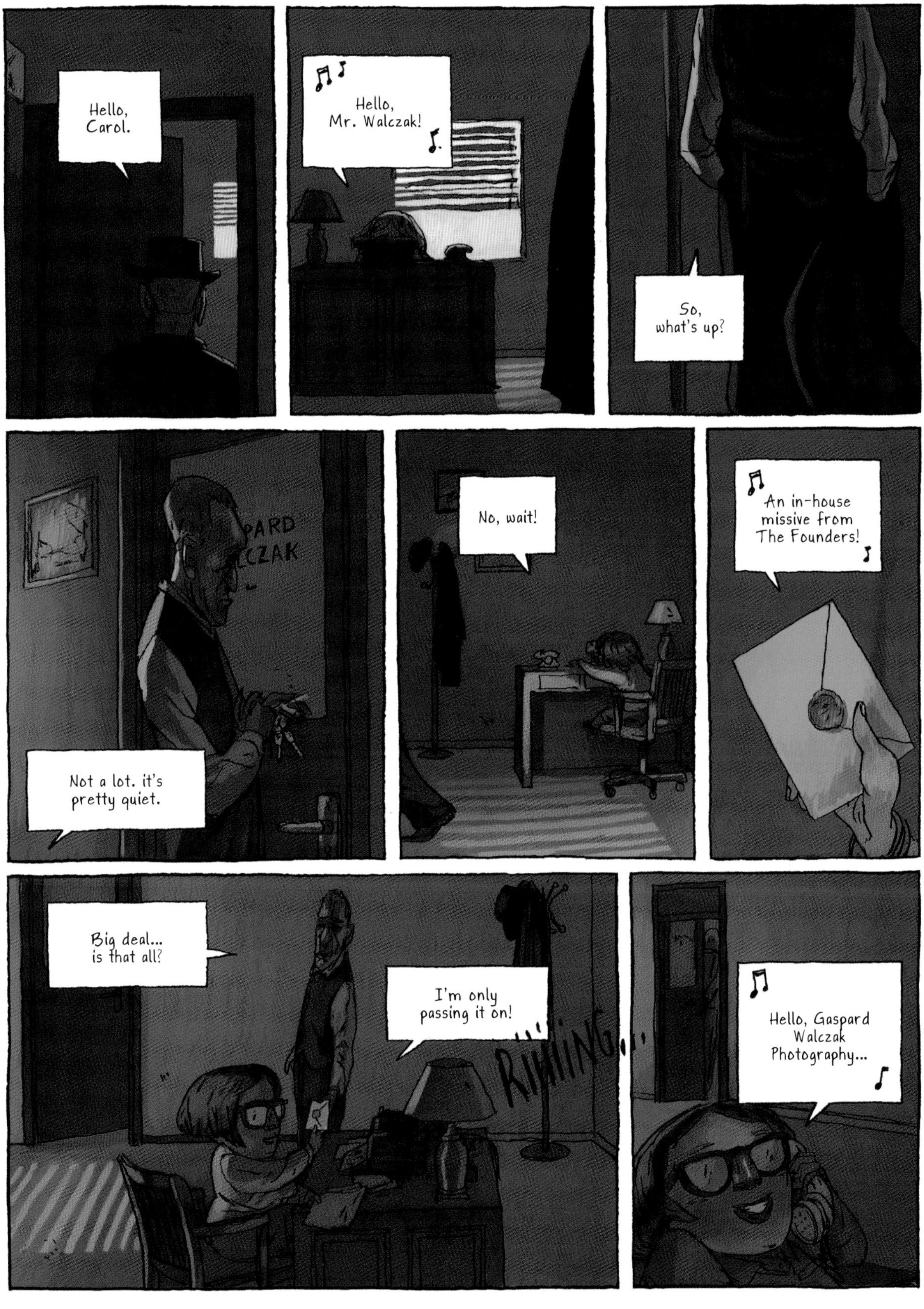
Hello, Carol.
Hello, Mr. Walczak!
So, what's up?
Not a lot. it's pretty quiet.
No, wait!
An in-house missive from The Founders!
Big deal... is that all?
I'm only passing it on!
RIIIING...
Hello, Gaspard Walczak Photography...

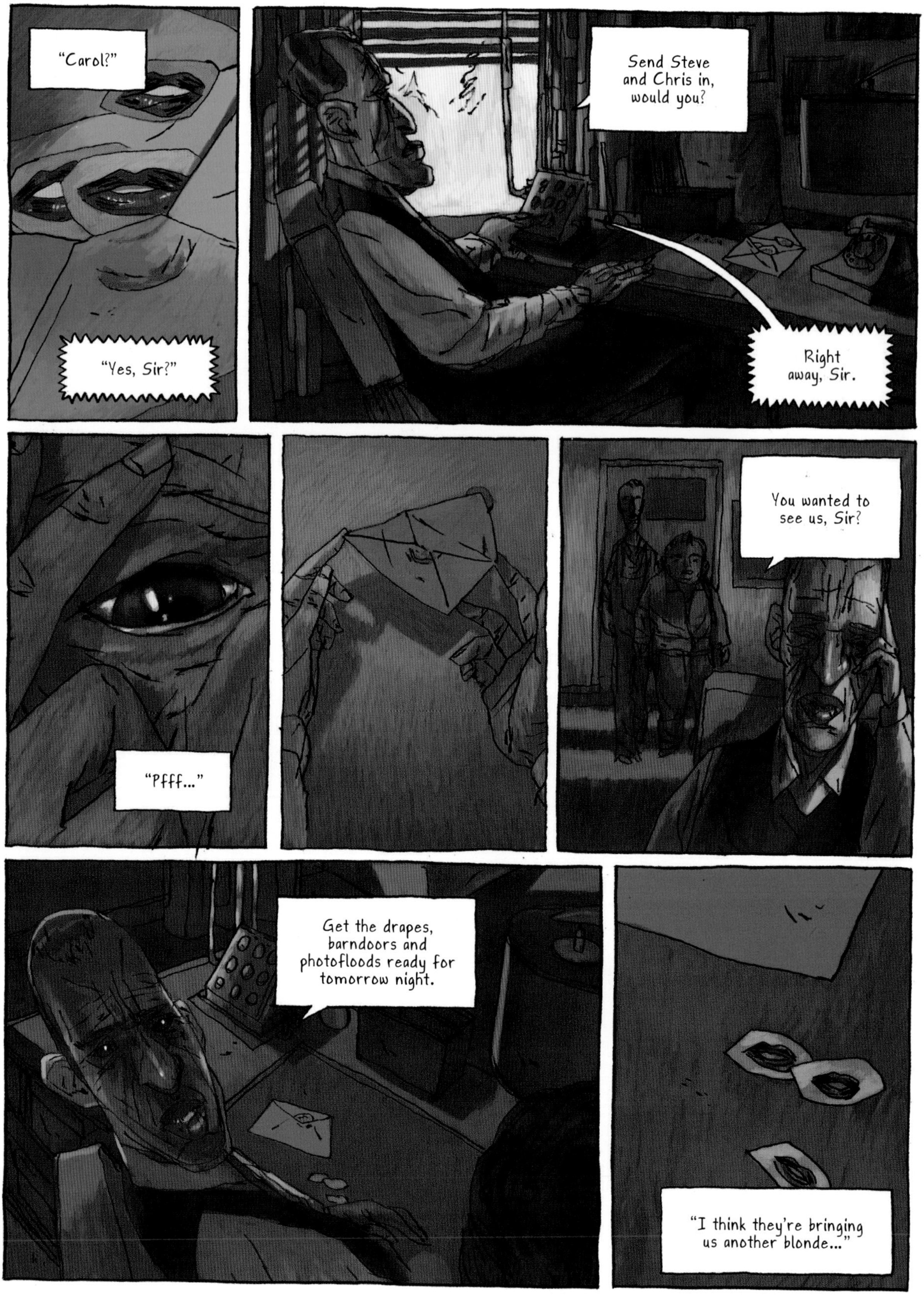
"Carol?"
"Yes, Sir?"
Send Steve and Chris in, would you?
Right away, Sir.
"Pfff..."
You wanted to see us, Sir?
Get the drapes, barndoors and photofloods ready for tomorrow night.
"I think they're bringing us another blonde..."

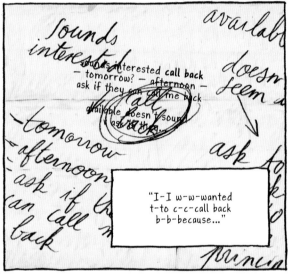

"I-I w-w-wanted t-to c-c-call back b-b-because..."

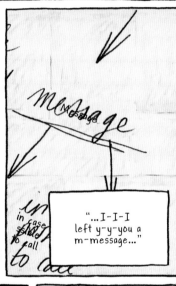

"...I-I-I left y-y-you a m-message..."

"L-L-Later, y-you say?"

"A-Alright, th-thanks."

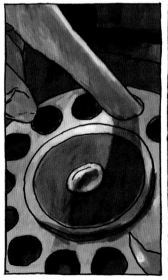

"F-Famous?"

"N-N-No, n-not y-y-y..."

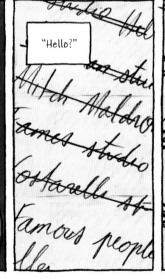

"Hello?"

"Yes, hello..."

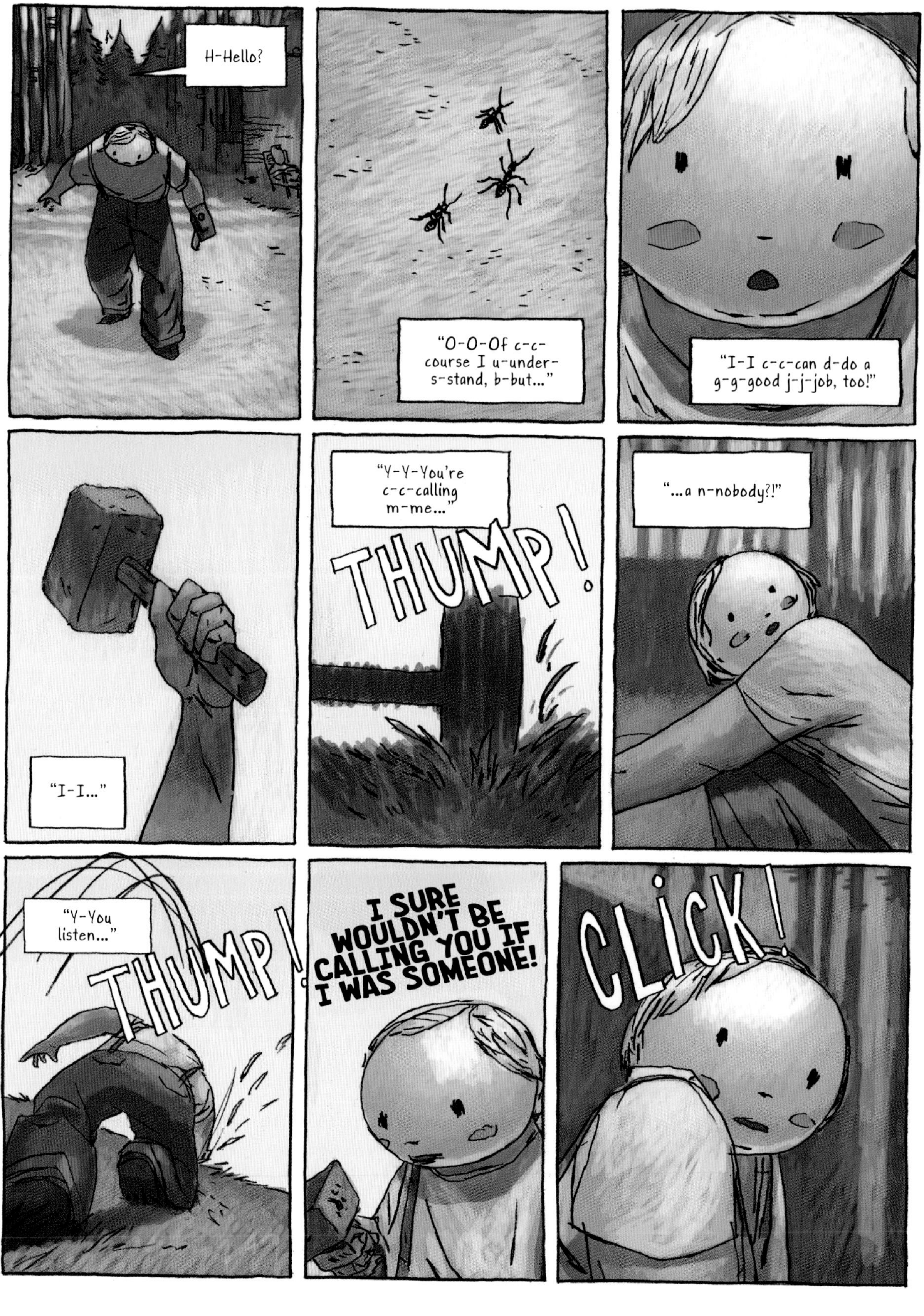
H-Hello?
"O-O-Of c-c-course I u-under-s-stand, b-but..."
"I-I c-c-can d-do a g-g-good j-j-job, too!"
"I-I..."
"Y-Y-You're c-c-calling m-me..."
THUMP!
"...a n-nobody?!"
"Y-You listen..."
THUMP!
I SURE WOULDN'T BE CALLING YOU IF I WAS SOMEONE!
CLICK!

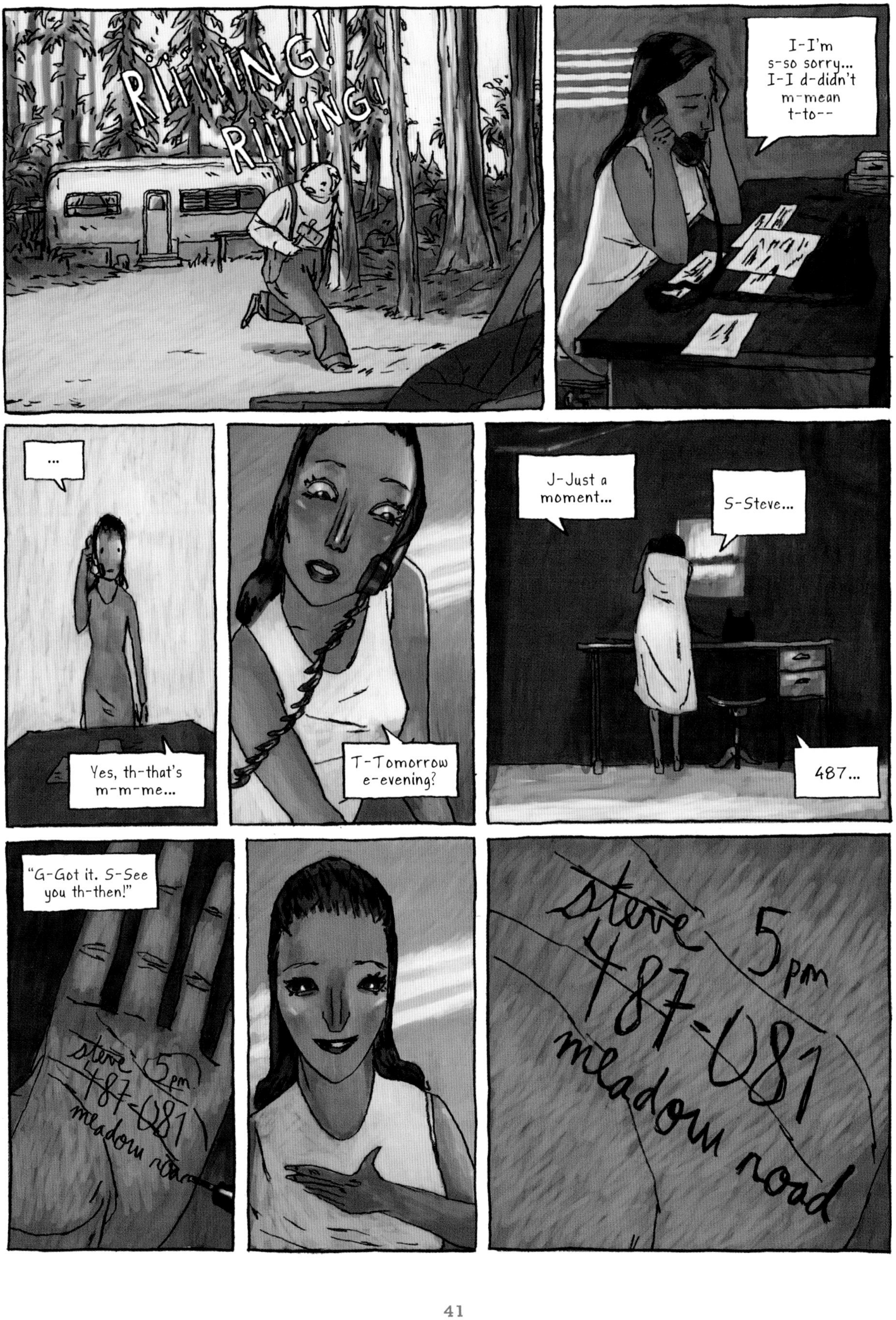
RIIIING! RIIIING!
I-I'm s-so sorry... I-I d-didn't m-mean t-to--
...
Yes, th-that's m-m-me...
T-Tomorrow e-evening?
J-Just a moment...
S-Steve...
487...
"G-Got it. S-See you th-then!"
steve 5 pm 487-081 meadow road
steve 5 pm 487-081 meadow road

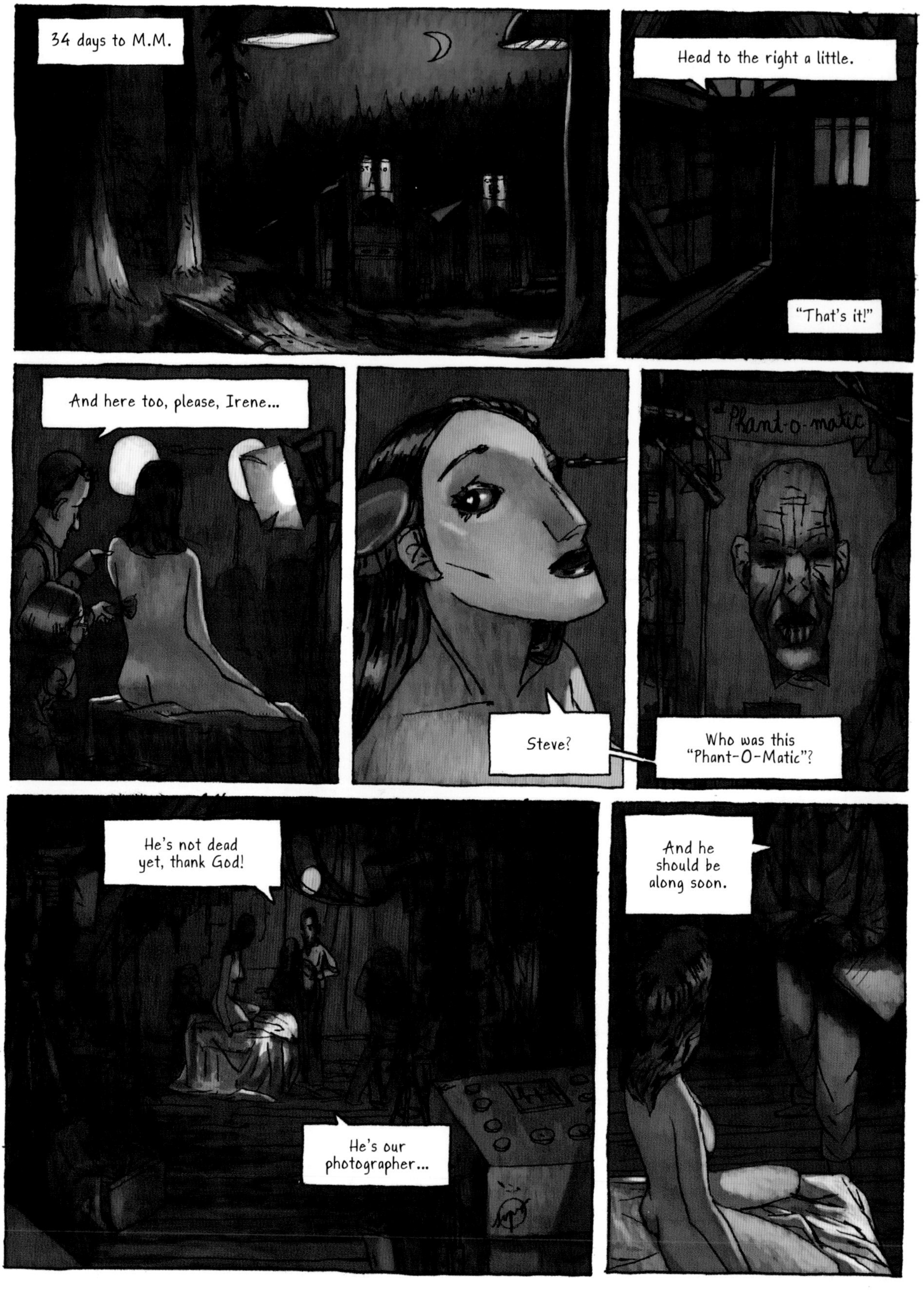
34 days to M.M.
Head to the right a little.
"That's it!"
And here too, please, Irene...
Phant-o-matic
Steve?
Who was this "Phant-O-Matic"?
He's not dead yet, thank God!
He's our photographer...
And he should be along soon.

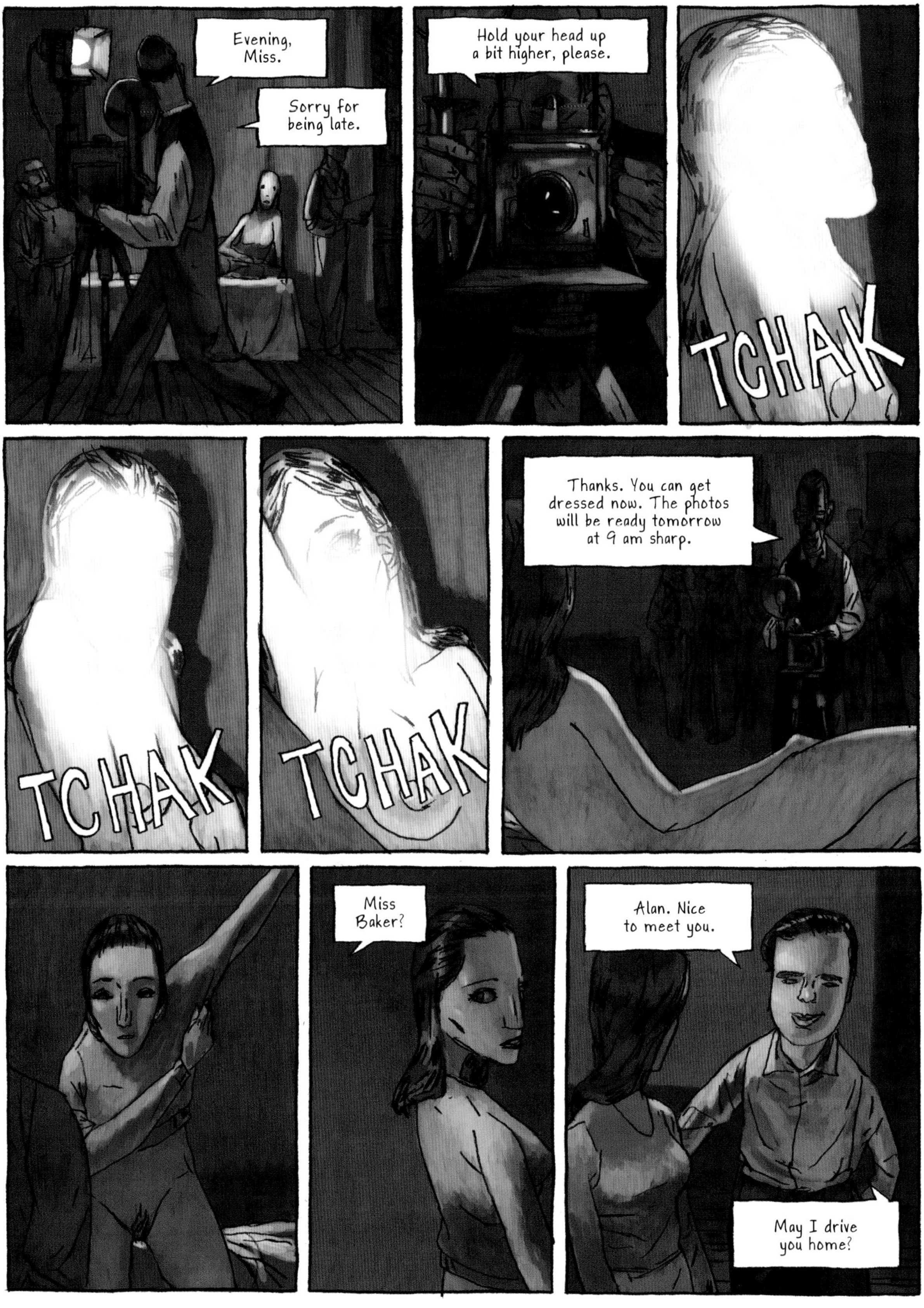
Evening, Miss.
Sorry for being late.
Hold your head up a bit higher, please.
TCHAK
TCHAK
TCHAK
Thanks. You can get dressed now. The photos will be ready tomorrow at 9 am sharp.
Miss Baker?
Alan. Nice to meet you.
May I drive you home?

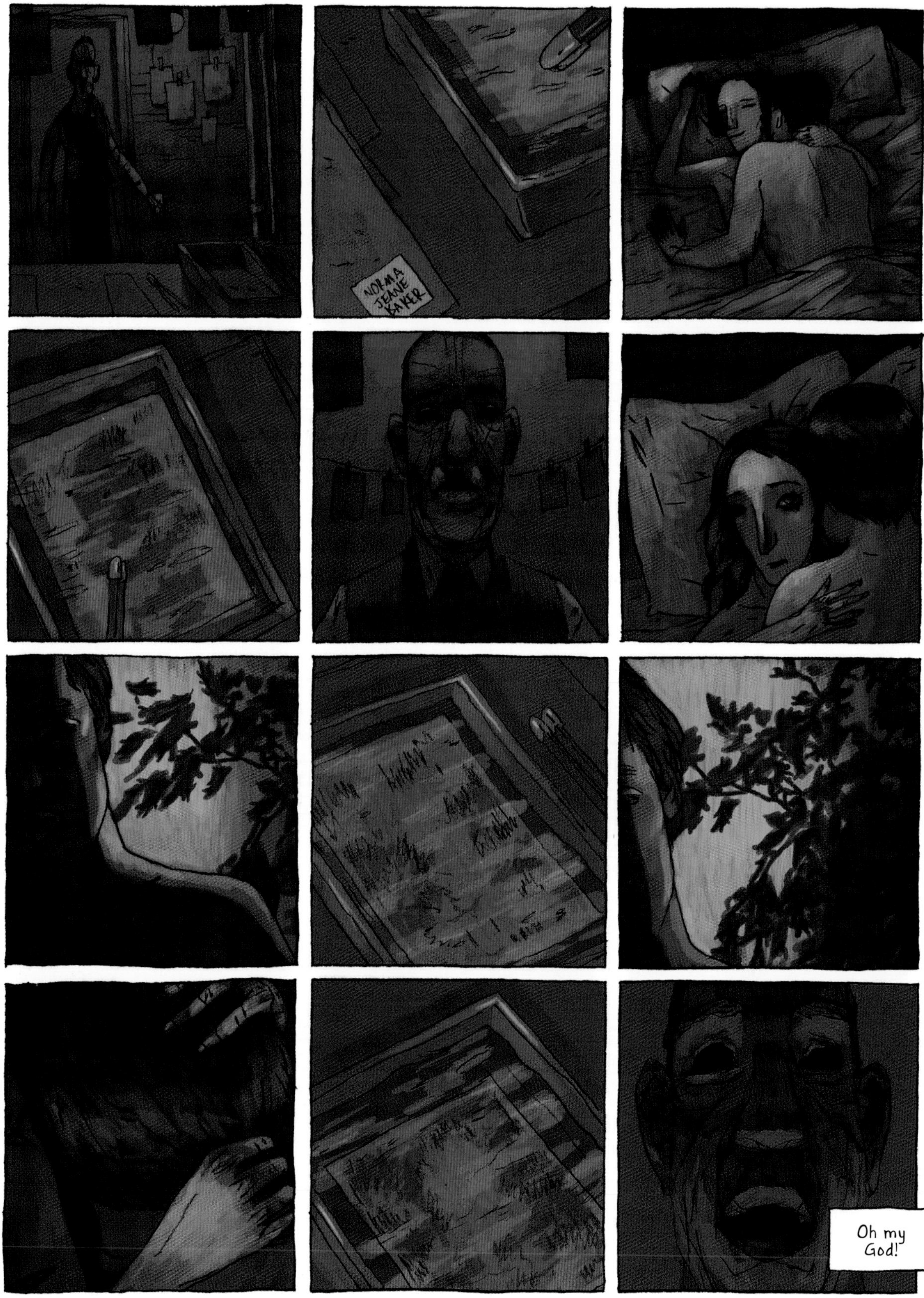
NORMA JEANE BAKER
Oh my God!

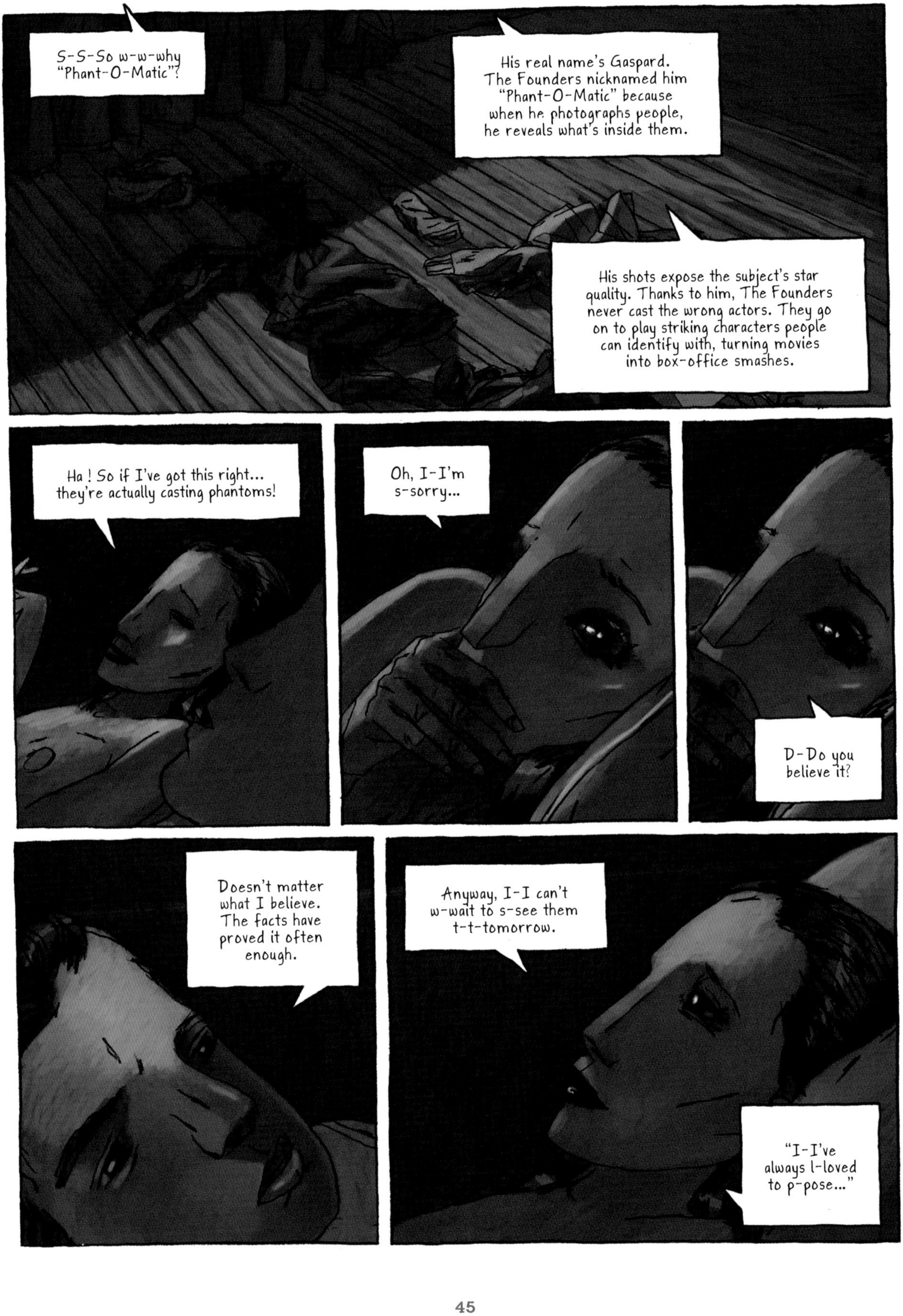

S-S-So w-w-why "Phant-O-Matic"?
His real name's Gaspard. The Founders nicknamed him "Phant-O-Matic" because when he photographs people, he reveals what's inside them.
His shots expose the subject's star quality. Thanks to him, The Founders never cast the wrong actors. They go on to play striking characters people can identify with, turning movies into box-office smashes.
Ha ! So if I've got this right... they're actually casting phantoms!
Oh, I-I'm s-sorry...
D-Do you believe it?
Doesn't matter what I believe. The facts have proved it often enough.
Anyway, I-I can't w-wait to s-see them t-t-tomorrow.
"I-I've always l-loved to p-pose..."

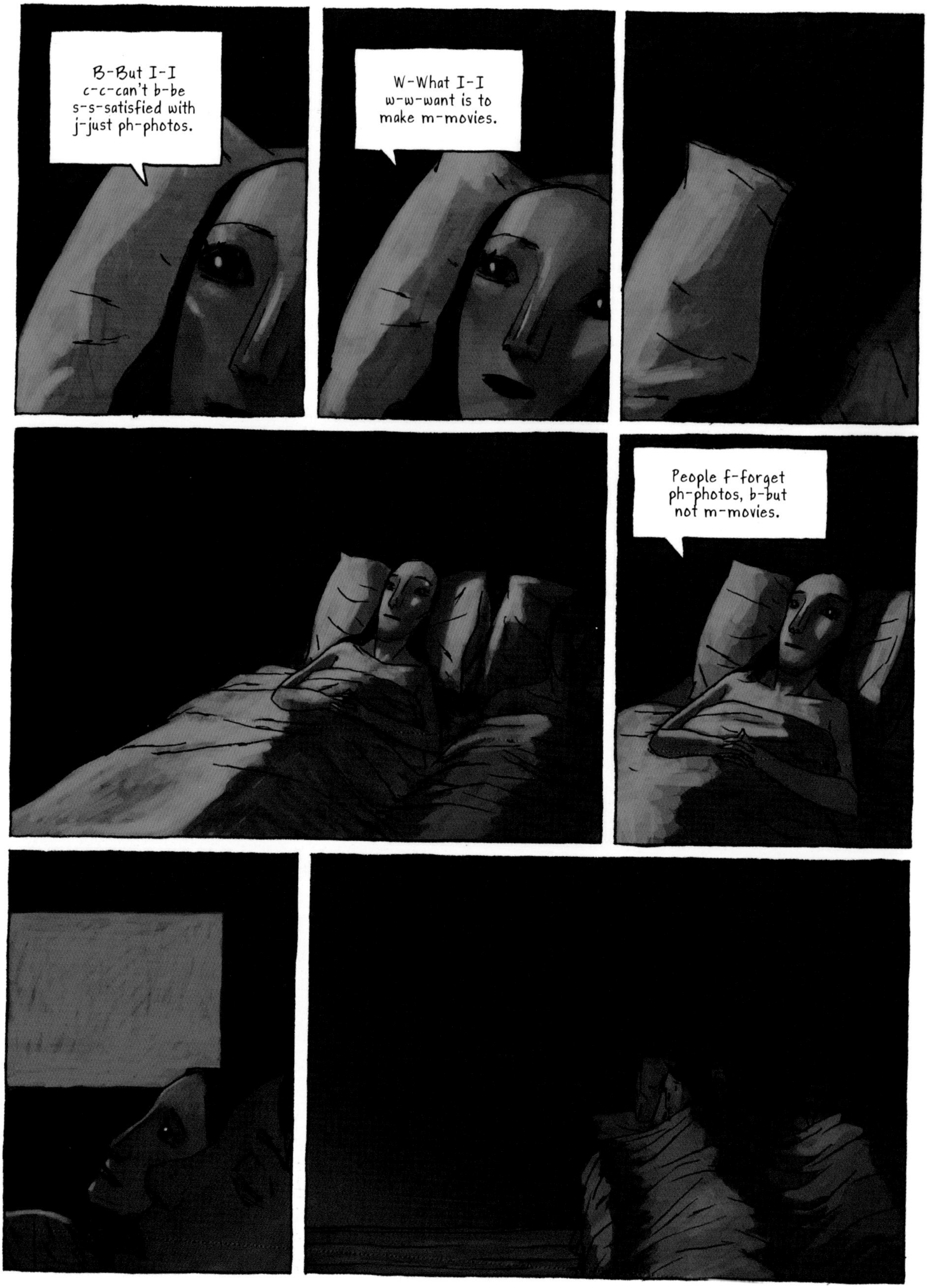
B-But I-I c-c-can't b-be s-s-satisfied with j-just ph-photos.
W-What I-I w-w-want is to make m-movies.
People f-forget ph-photos, b-but not m-movies.

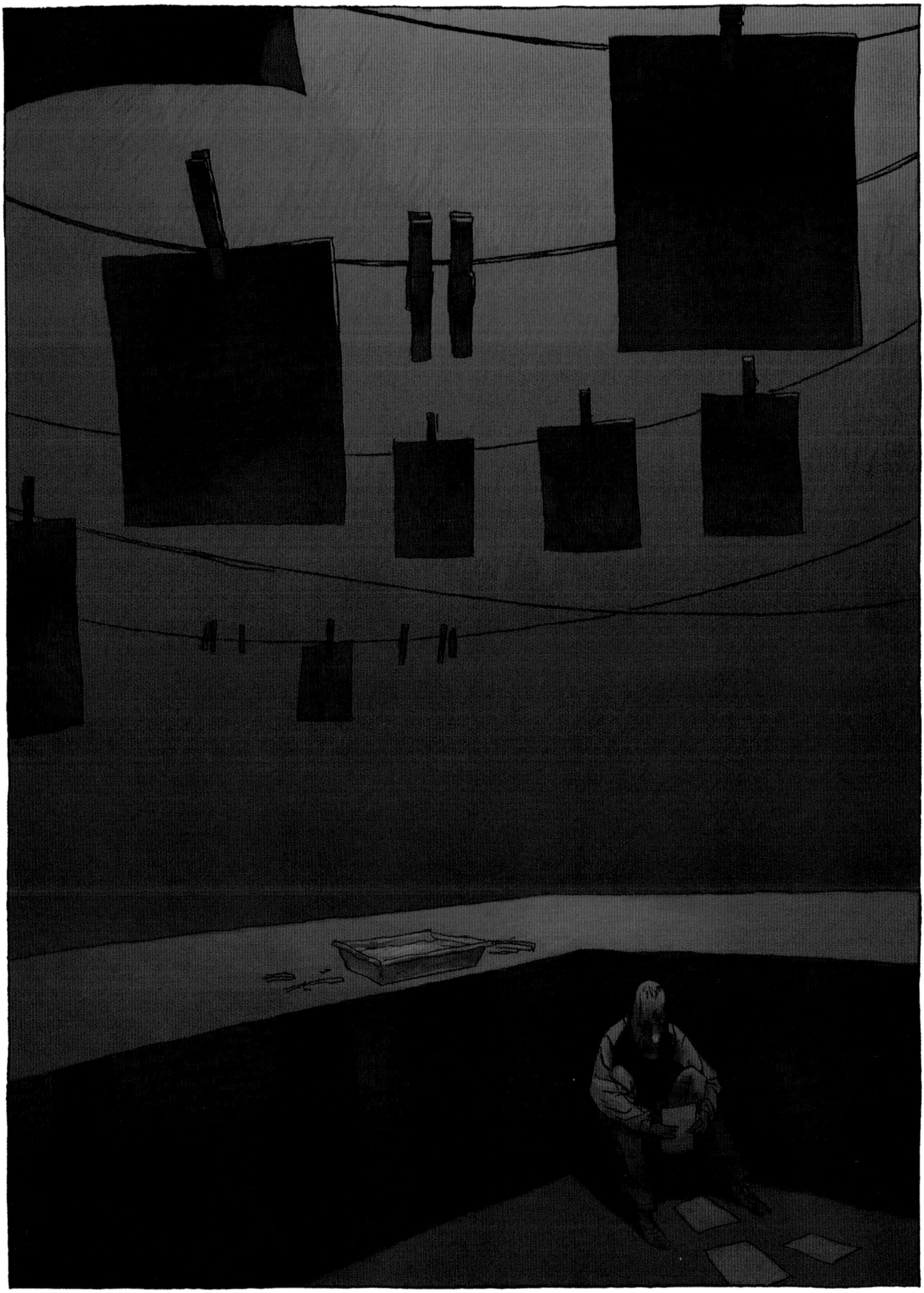

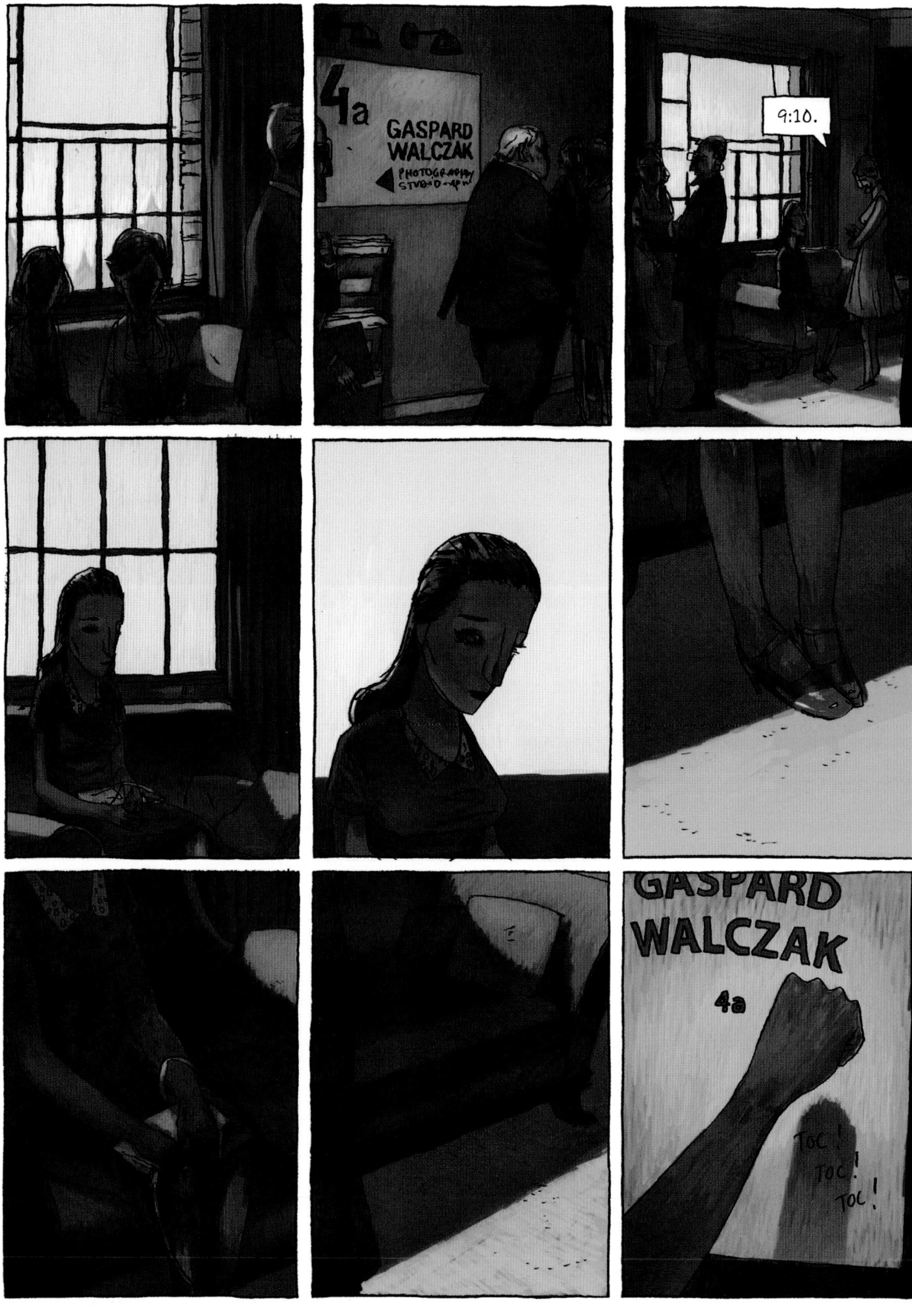
4a
GASPARD
WALCZAK
9:10.
GASPARD
WALCZAK
4a
TOC!
TOC!
TOC!

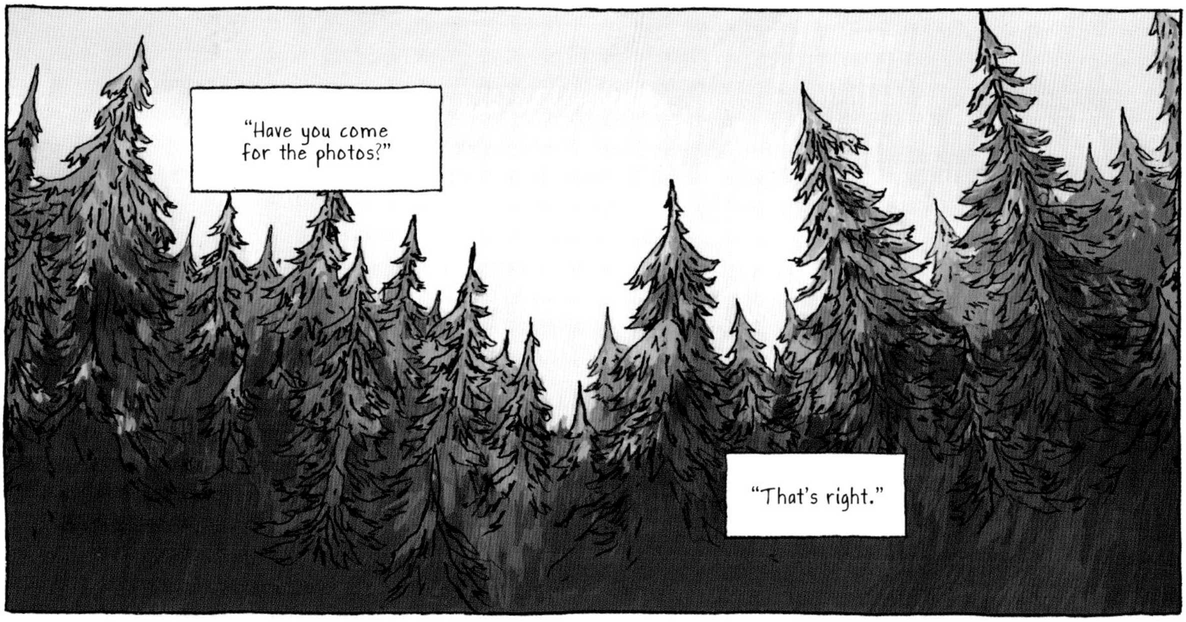
"Have you come for the photos?"
"That's right."

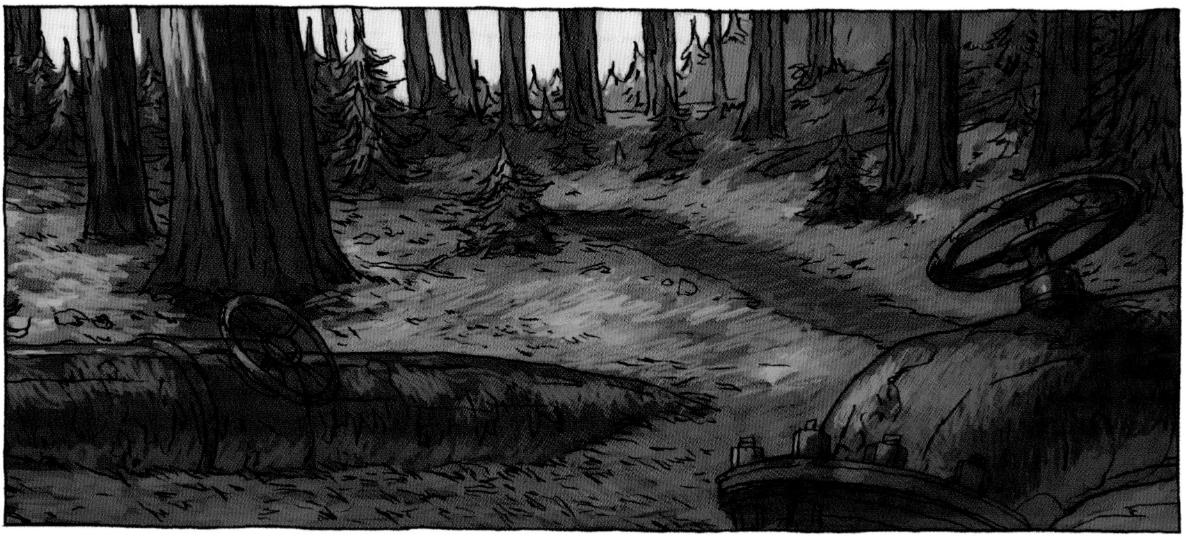

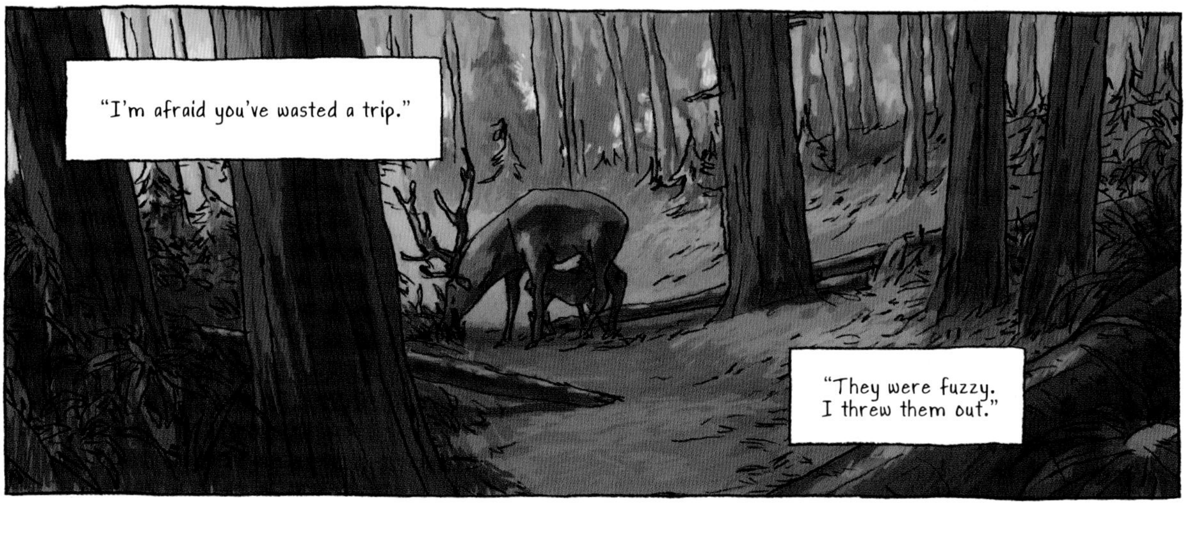
"I'm afraid you've wasted a trip."
"They were fuzzy. I threw them out."

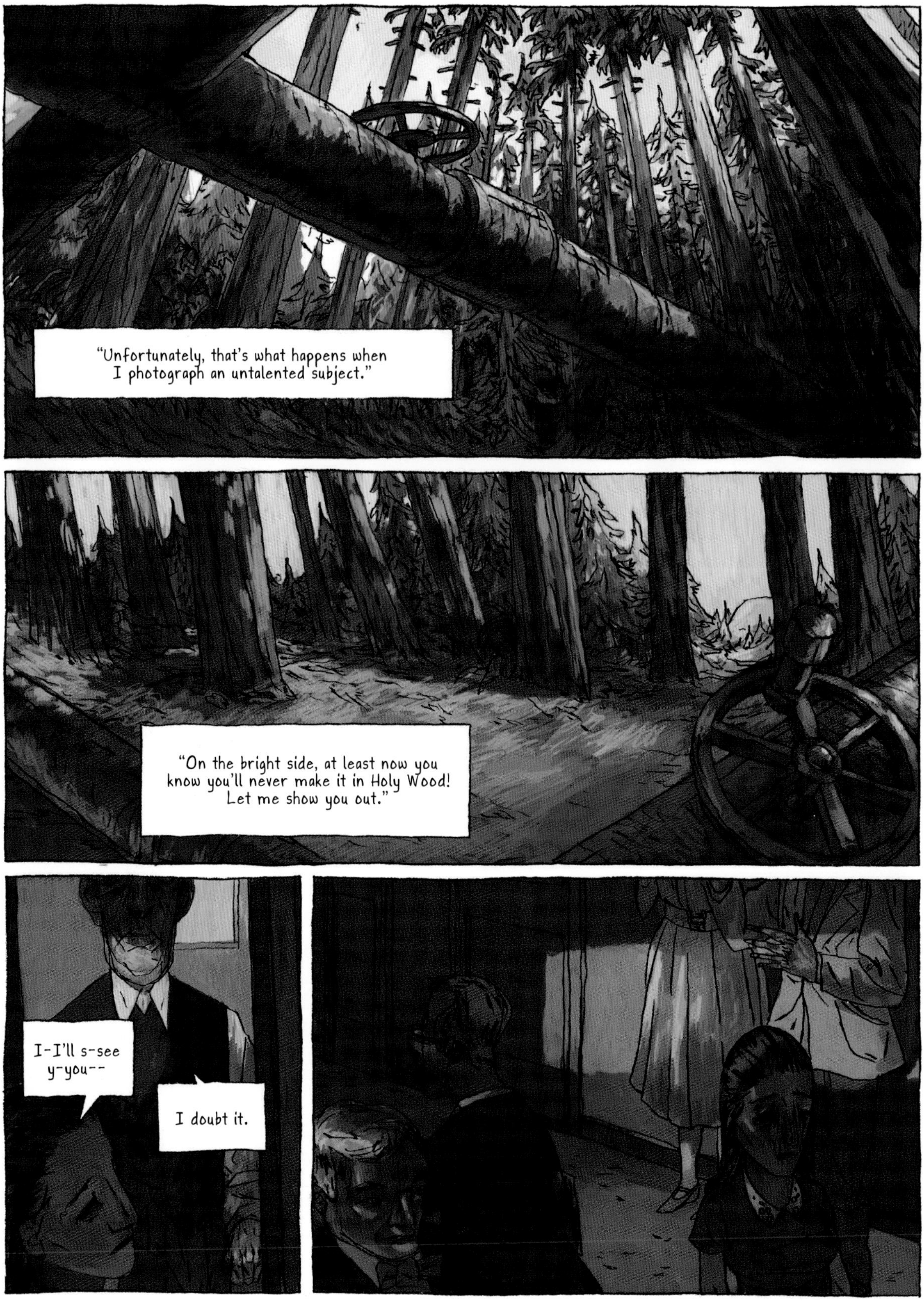
"Unfortunately, that's what happens when I photograph an untalented subject."
"On the bright side, at least now you know you'll never make it in Holy Wood! Let me show you out."
I-I'll s-see y-you--
I doubt it.

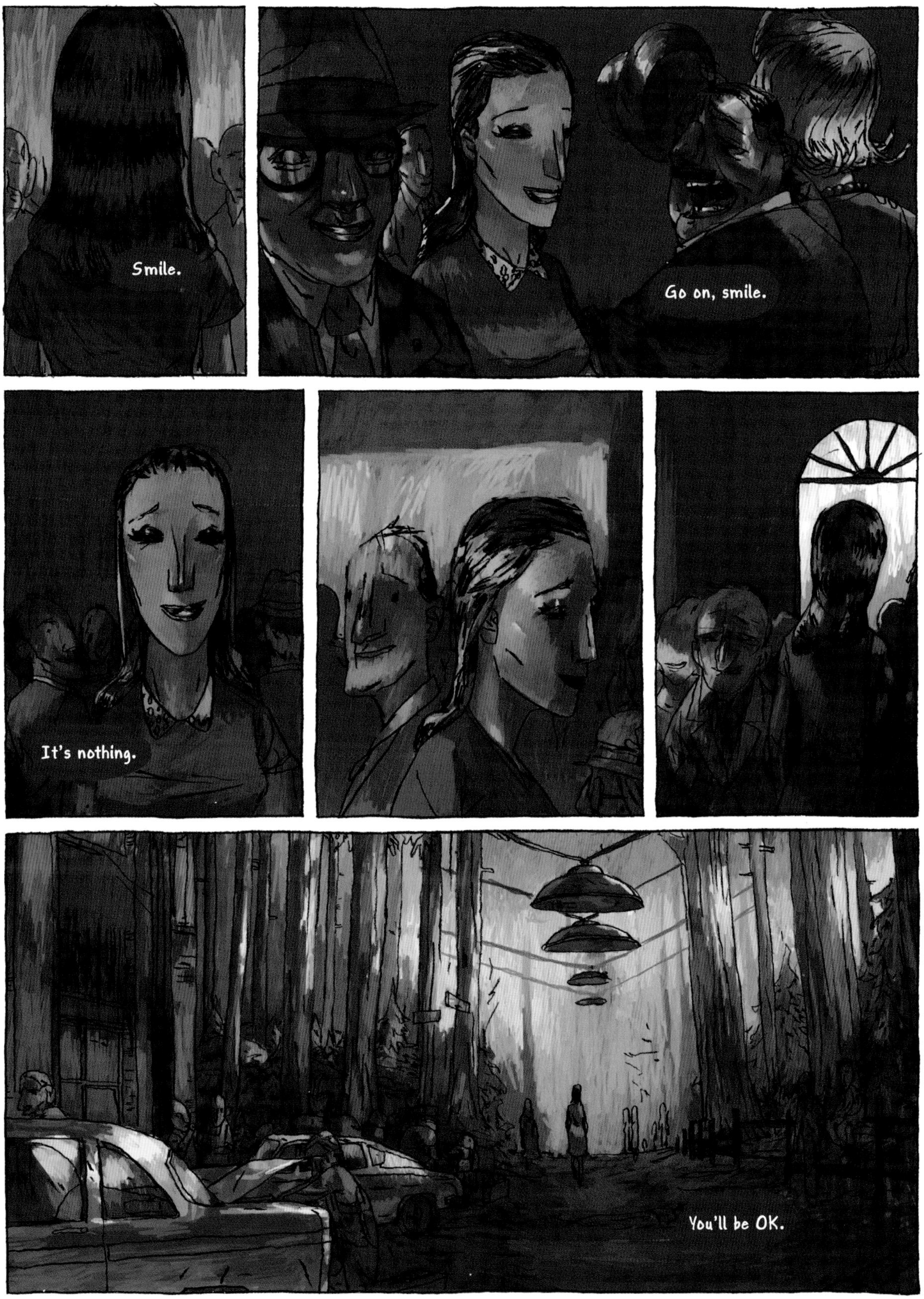
Smile.
Go on, smile.
It's nothing.
You'll be OK.

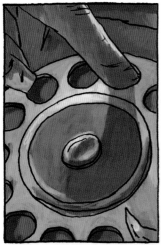

Authorization 1.3.9.37.5.

[Mr. and Mrs. Wilcox are listening, Mr. Walczak.]

Case report on 3463-B.A.K.E.R. The photos are fuzzy. "The Mouth" is fuzzy. Zero artistic potential. Case closed.

...

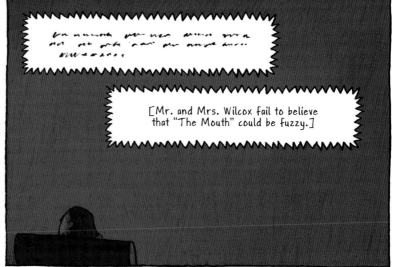

[Mr. and Mrs. Wilcox fail to believe that "The Mouth" could be fuzzy.]

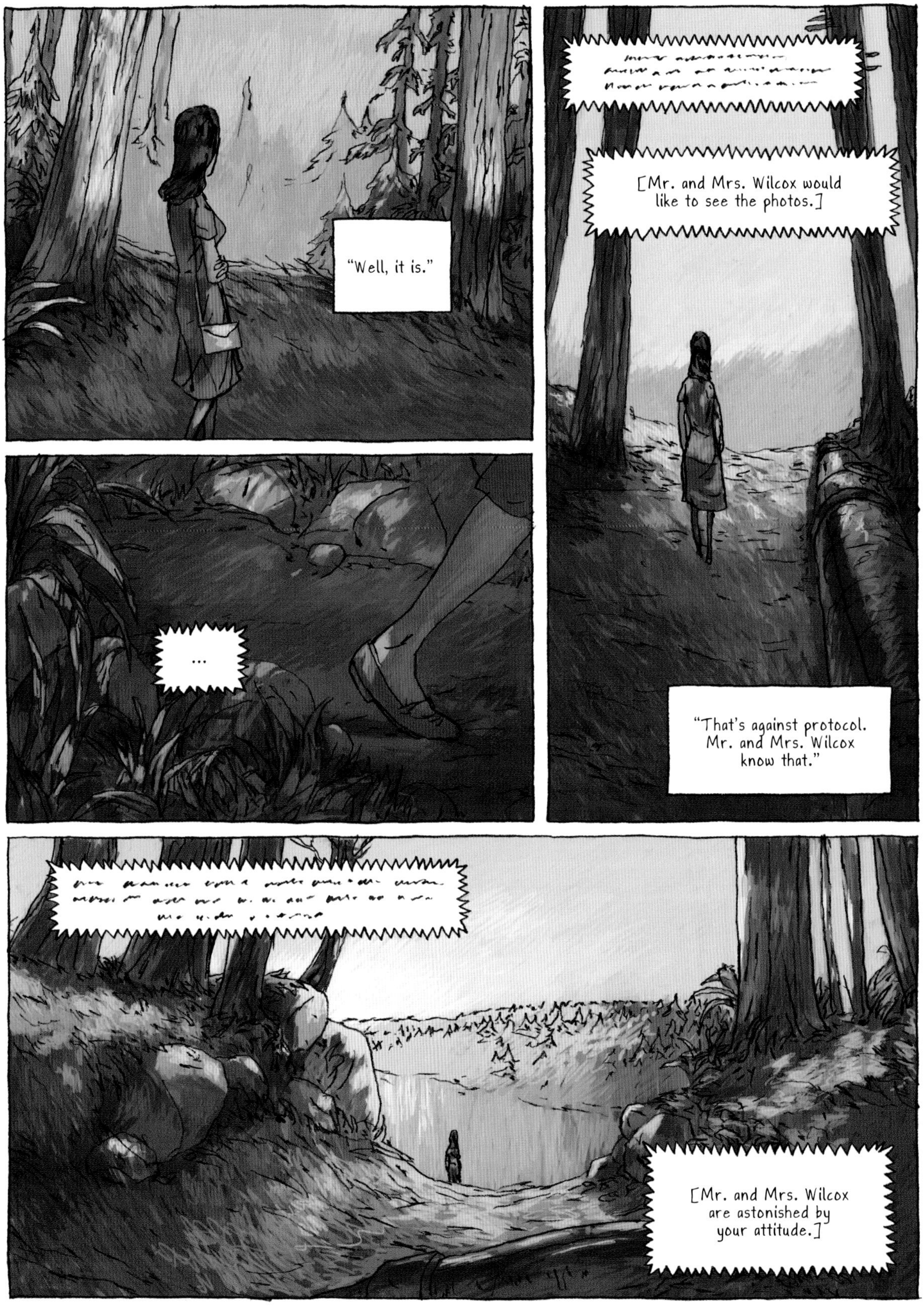
"Well, it is."
[Mr. and Mrs. Wilcox would like to see the photos.]
...
"That's against protocol. Mr. and Mrs. Wilcox know that."
[Mr. and Mrs. Wilcox are astonished by your attitude.]

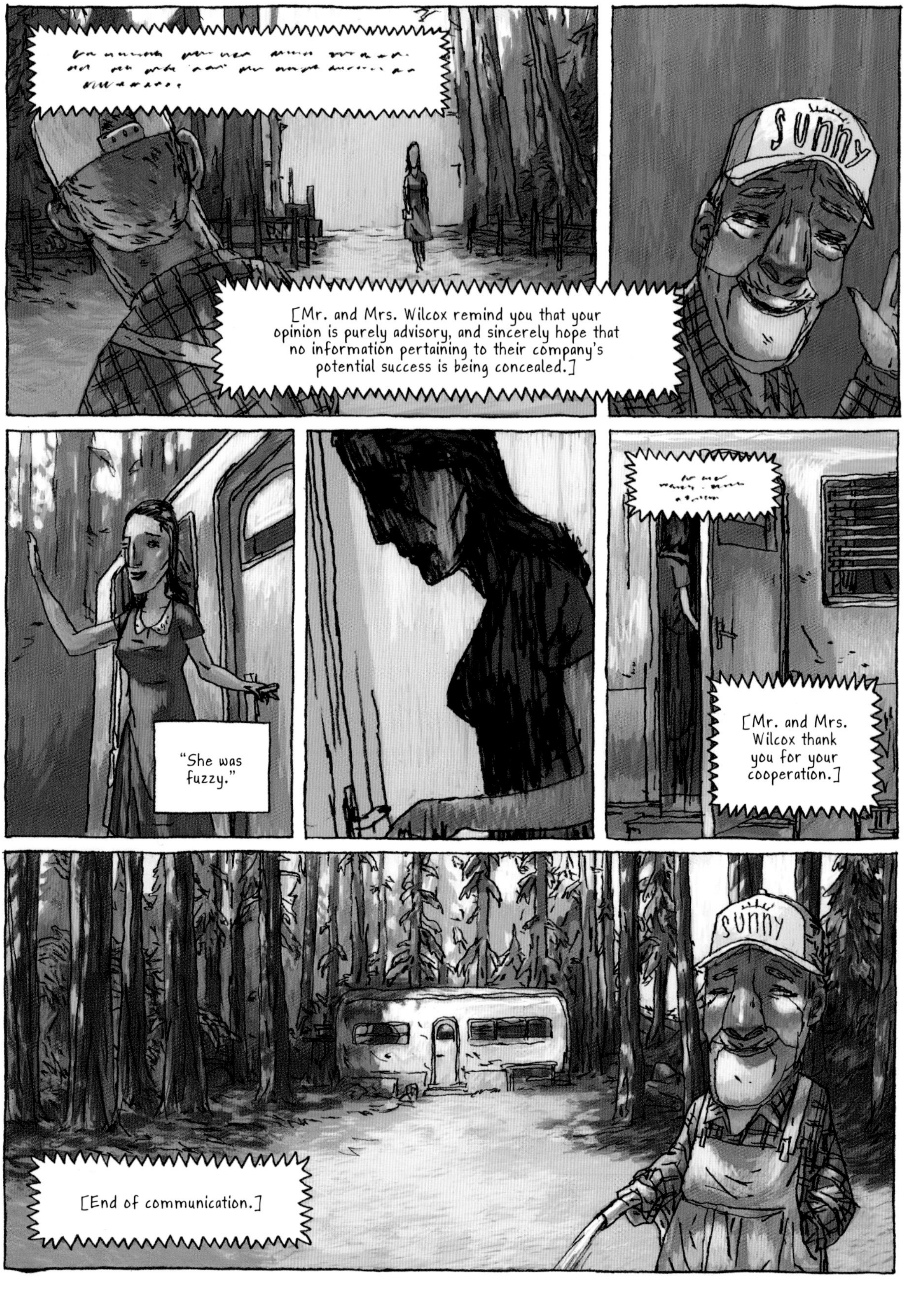
[Mr. and Mrs. Wilcox remind you that your opinion is purely advisory, and sincerely hope that no information pertaining to their company's potential success is being concealed.]
SUNNY
"She was fuzzy."
[Mr. and Mrs. Wilcox thank you for your cooperation.]
SUNNY
[End of communication.]

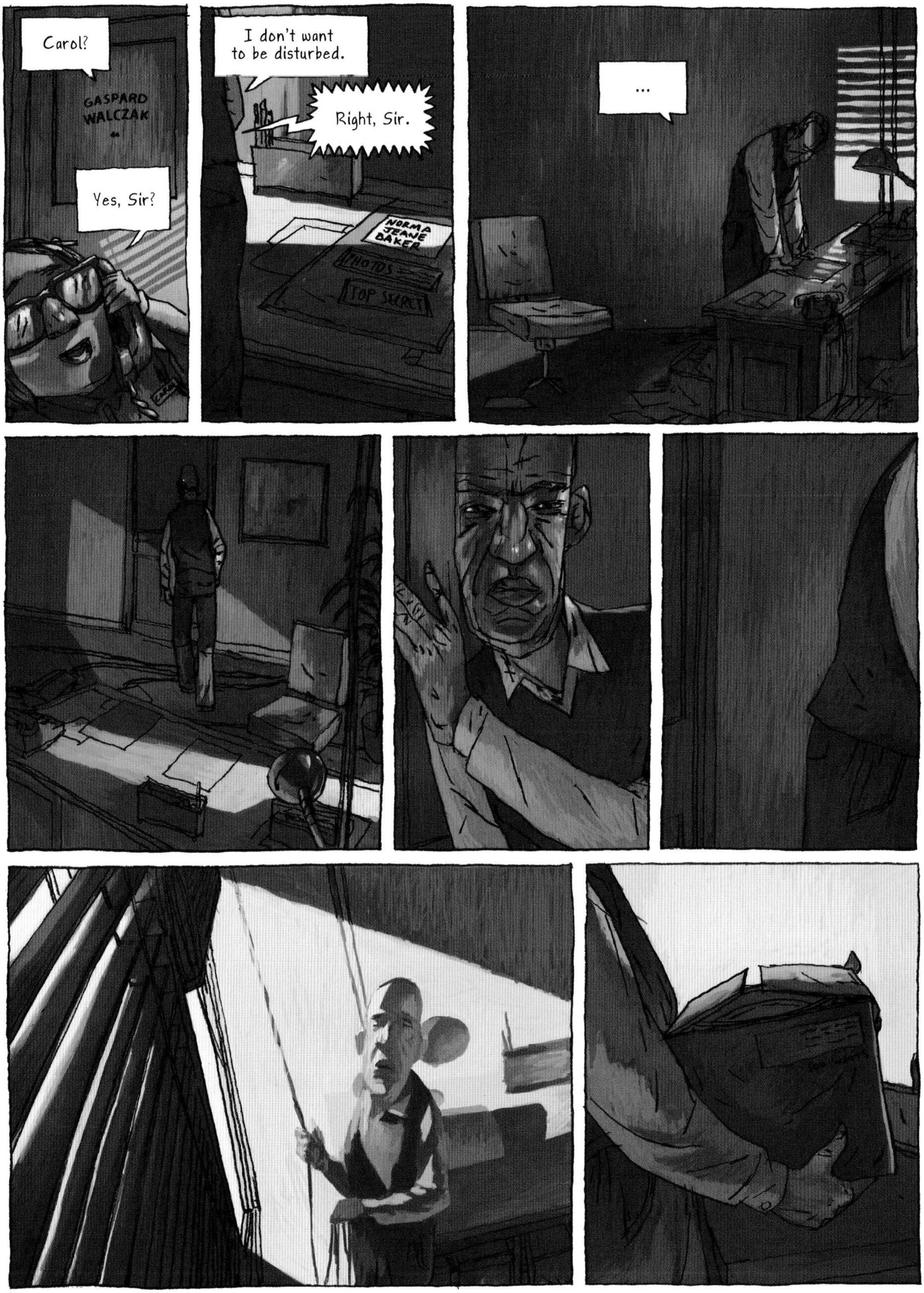
Carol?
GASPARD WALCZAK
Yes, Sir?
I don't want to be disturbed.
Right, Sir.
NORMA JEANE BAKER
PHOTOS
TOP SECRET
...

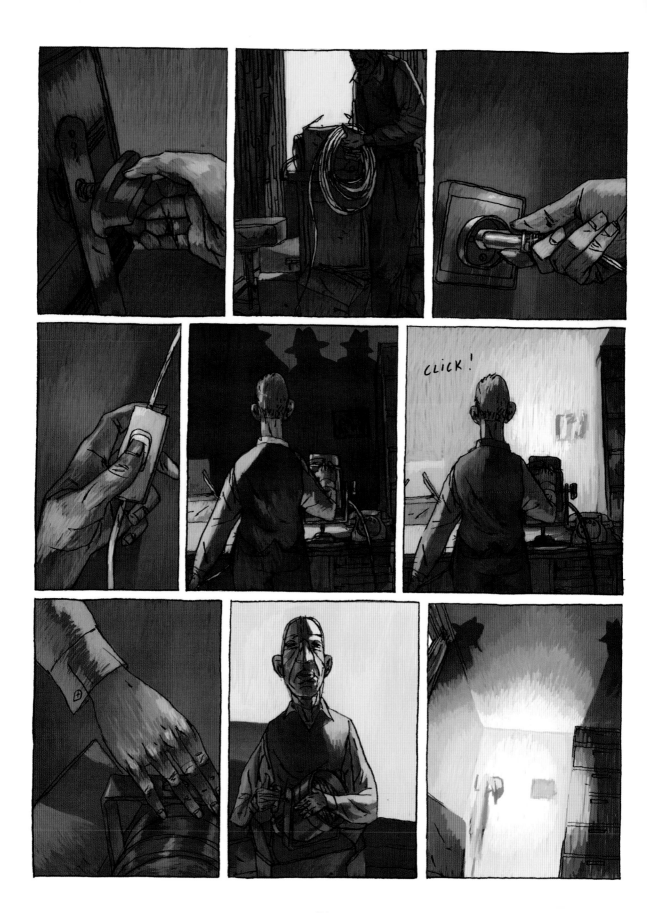

CLICK!

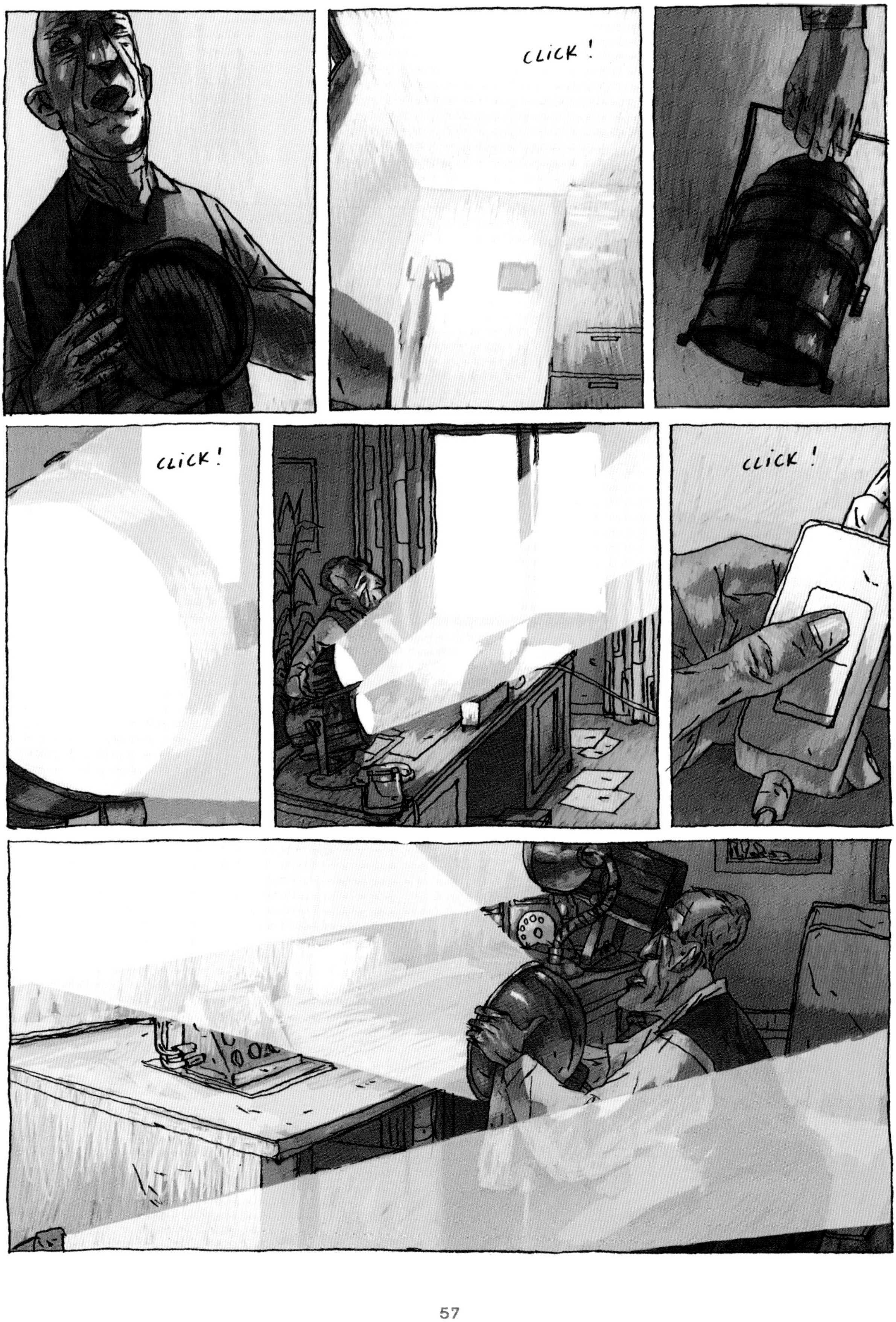
CLICK!
CLICK!
CLICK!

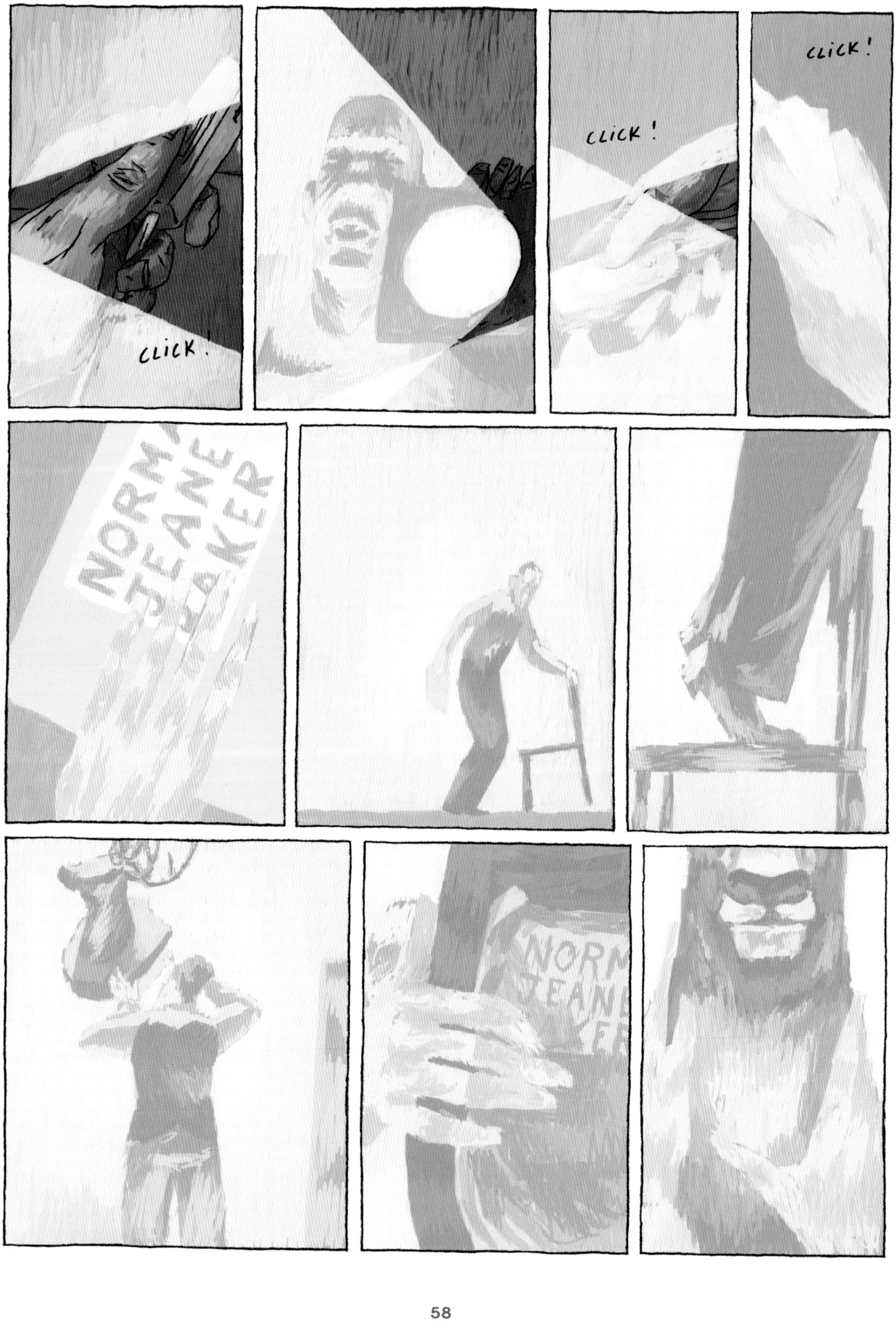
CLICK!
CLICK!
CLICK!
NORM
JEANE
AKER
NORM
JEAN

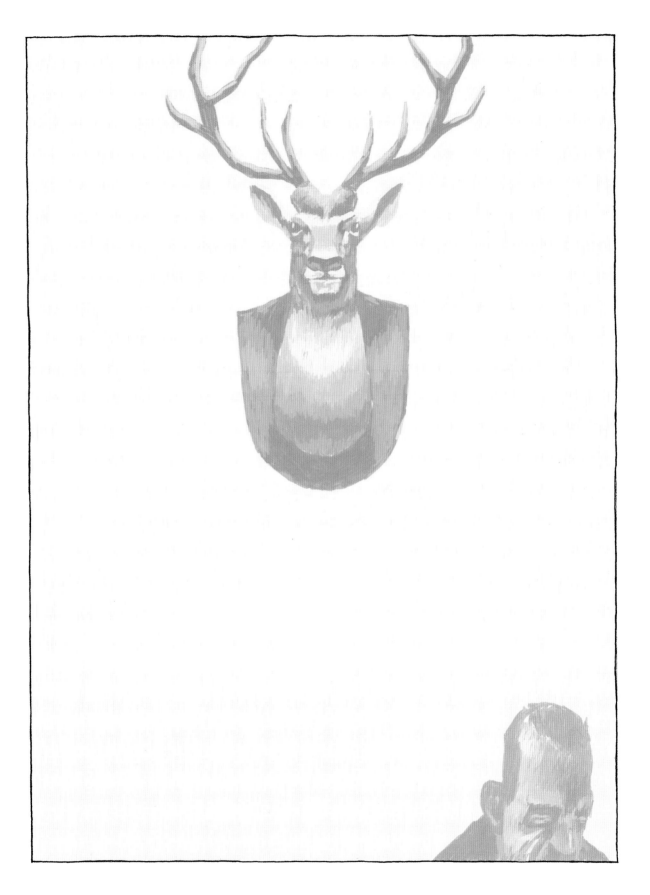

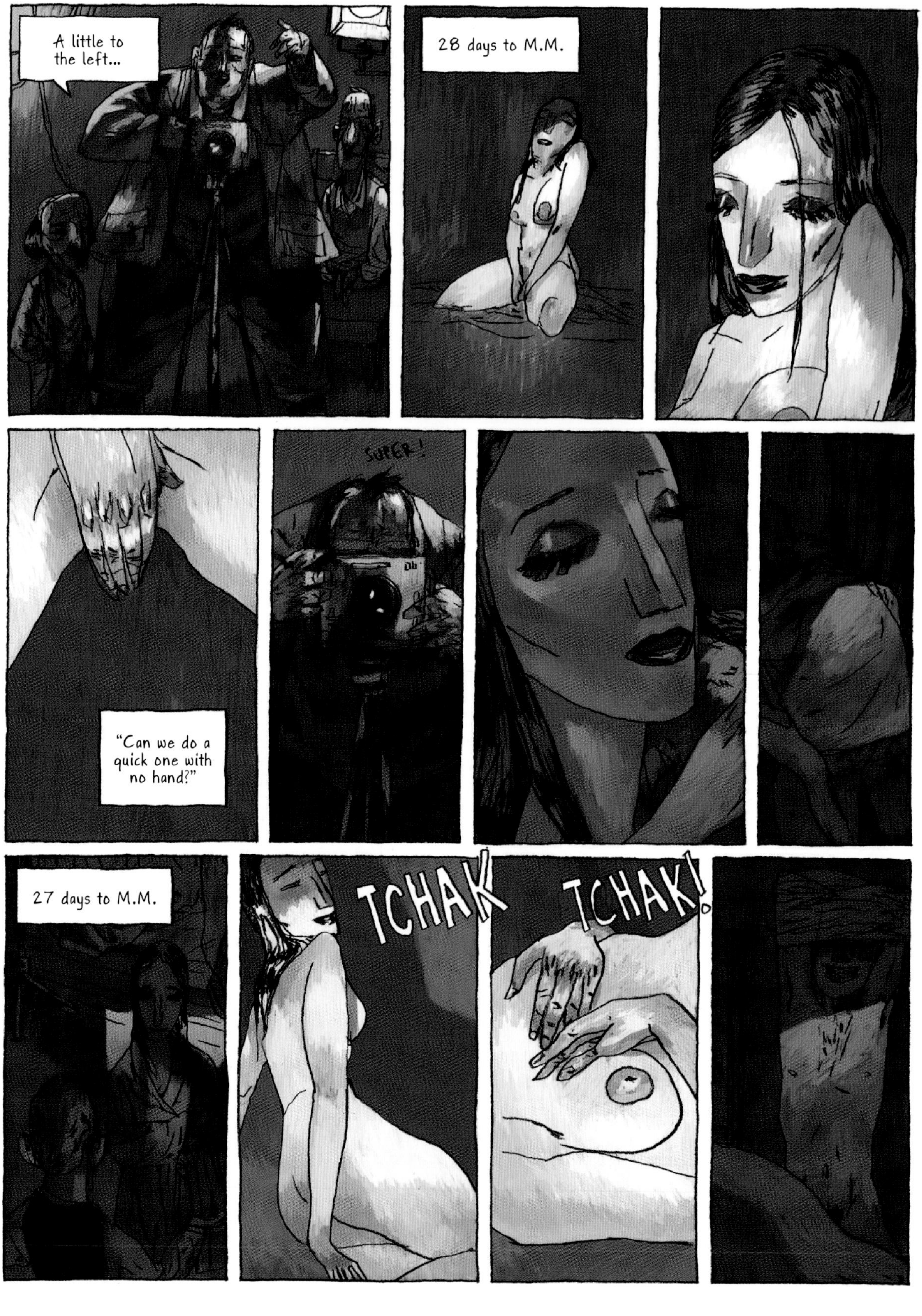
A little to the left...
28 days to M.M.
SUPER!
"Can we do a quick one with no hand?"
27 days to M.M.
TCHAK
TCHAK!

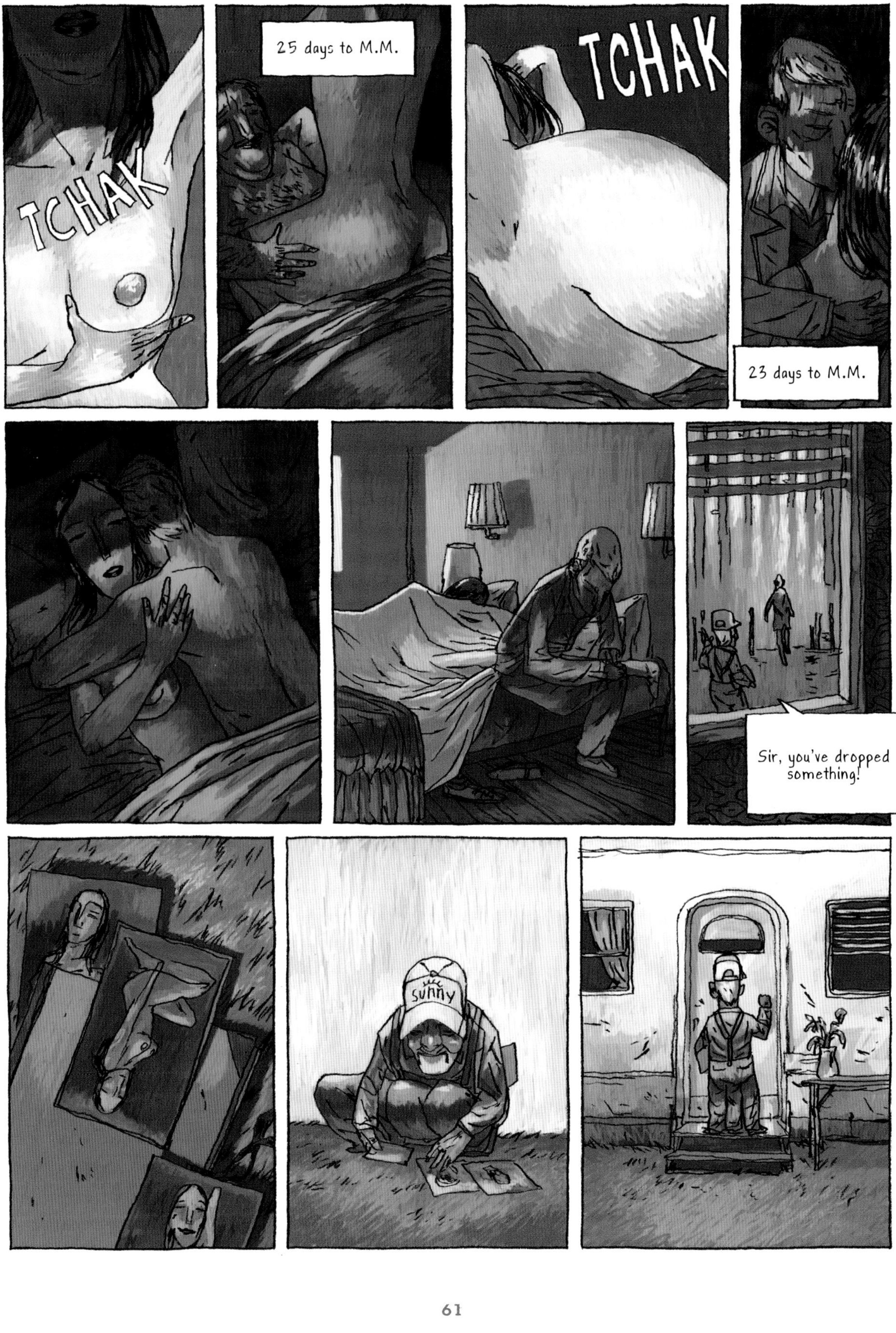
TCHAK
25 days to M.M.
TCHAK
23 days to M.M.
Sir, you've dropped something!
sunny

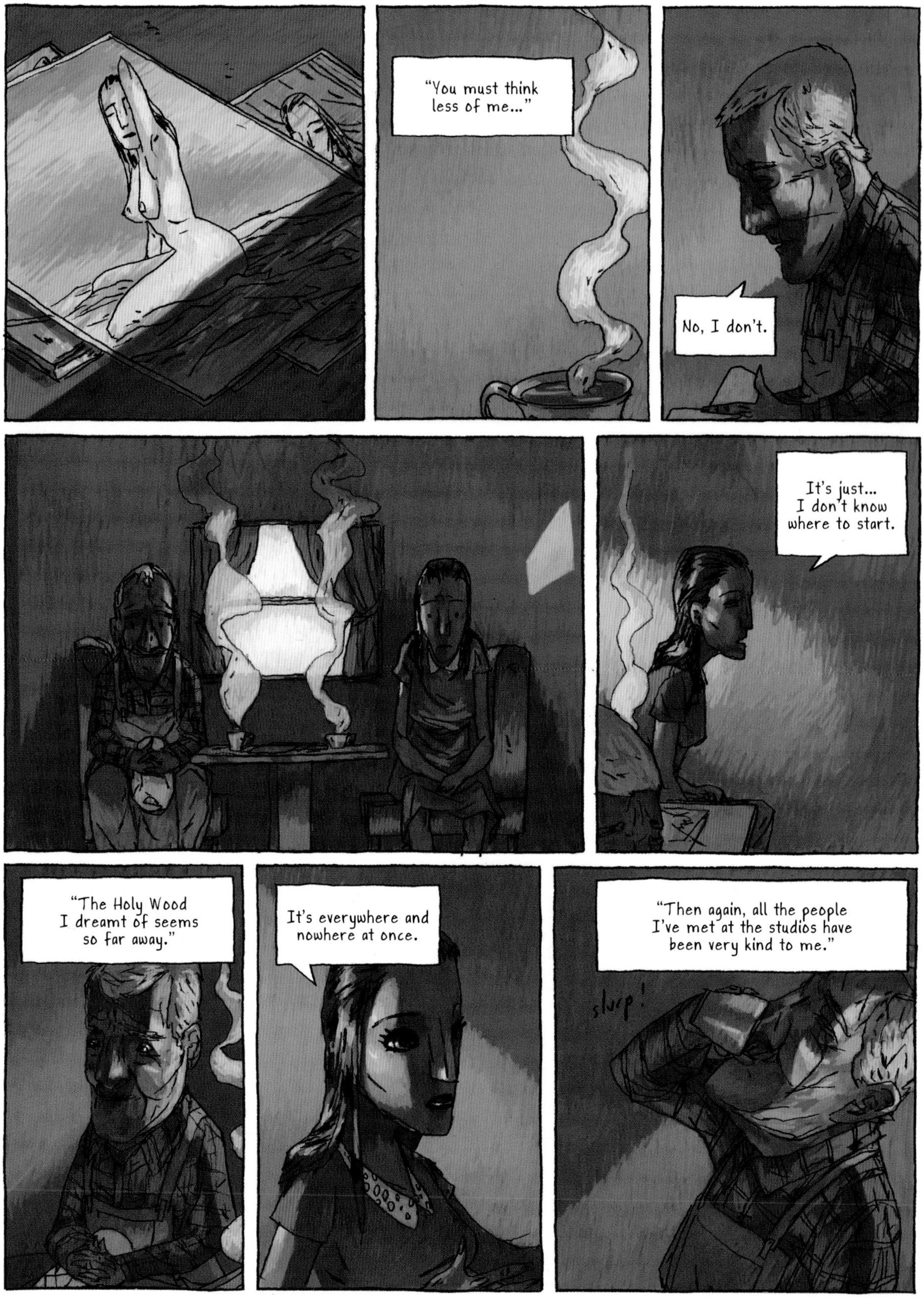
"You must think less of me..."
No, I don't.
It's just... I don't know where to start.
"The Holy Wood I dreamt of seems so far away."
It's everywhere and nowhere at once.
"Then again, all the people I've met at the studios have been very kind to me."
slurp!

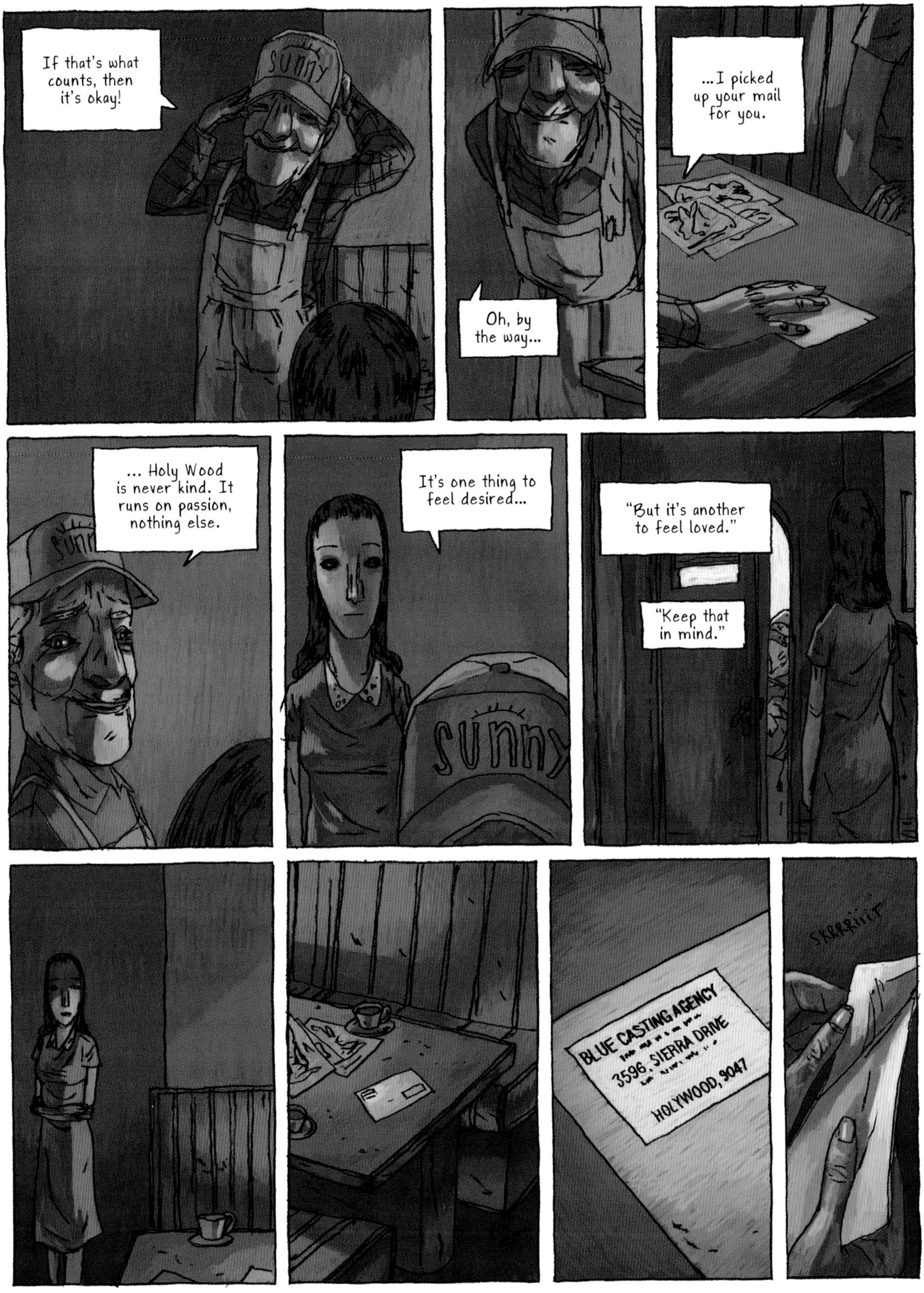
If that's what counts, then it's okay!
Oh, by the way...
...I picked up your mail for you.
... Holy Wood is never kind. It runs on passion, nothing else.
It's one thing to feel desired...
"But it's another to feel loved."
"Keep that in mind."
SUNNY
BLUE CASTING AGENCY
3596, SIERRA DRIVE
HOLYWOOD, 9047
SKRRRiiiiT

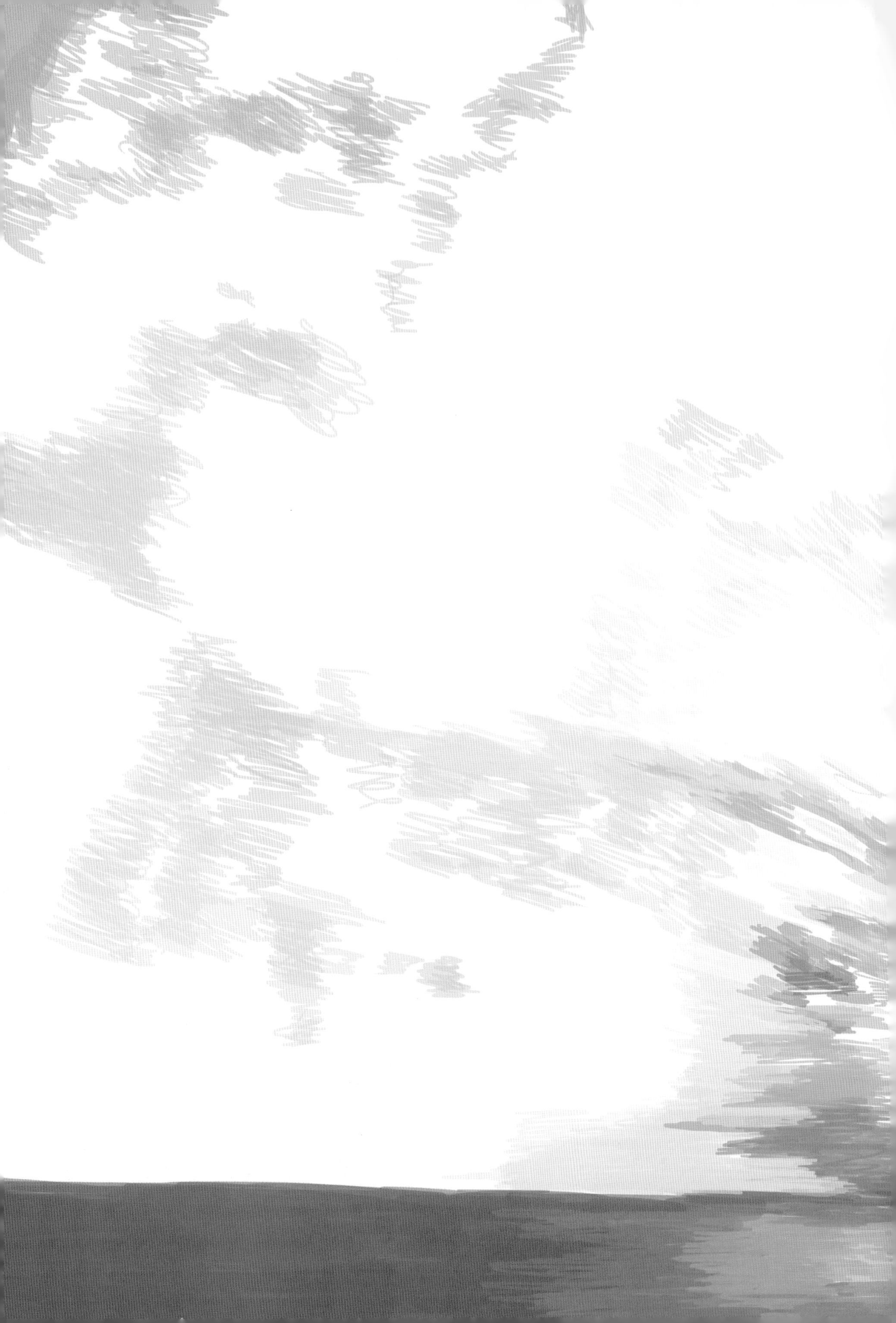

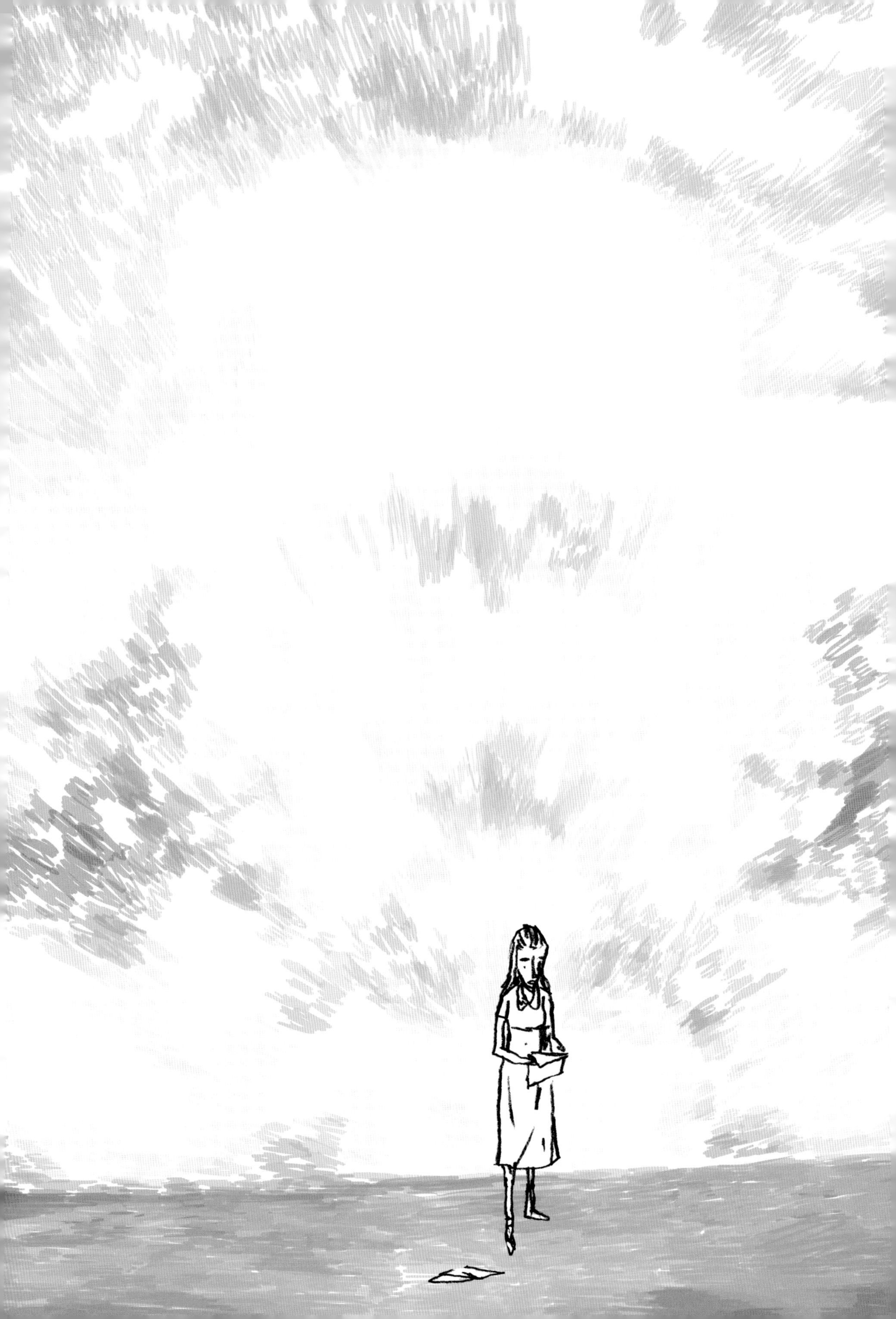

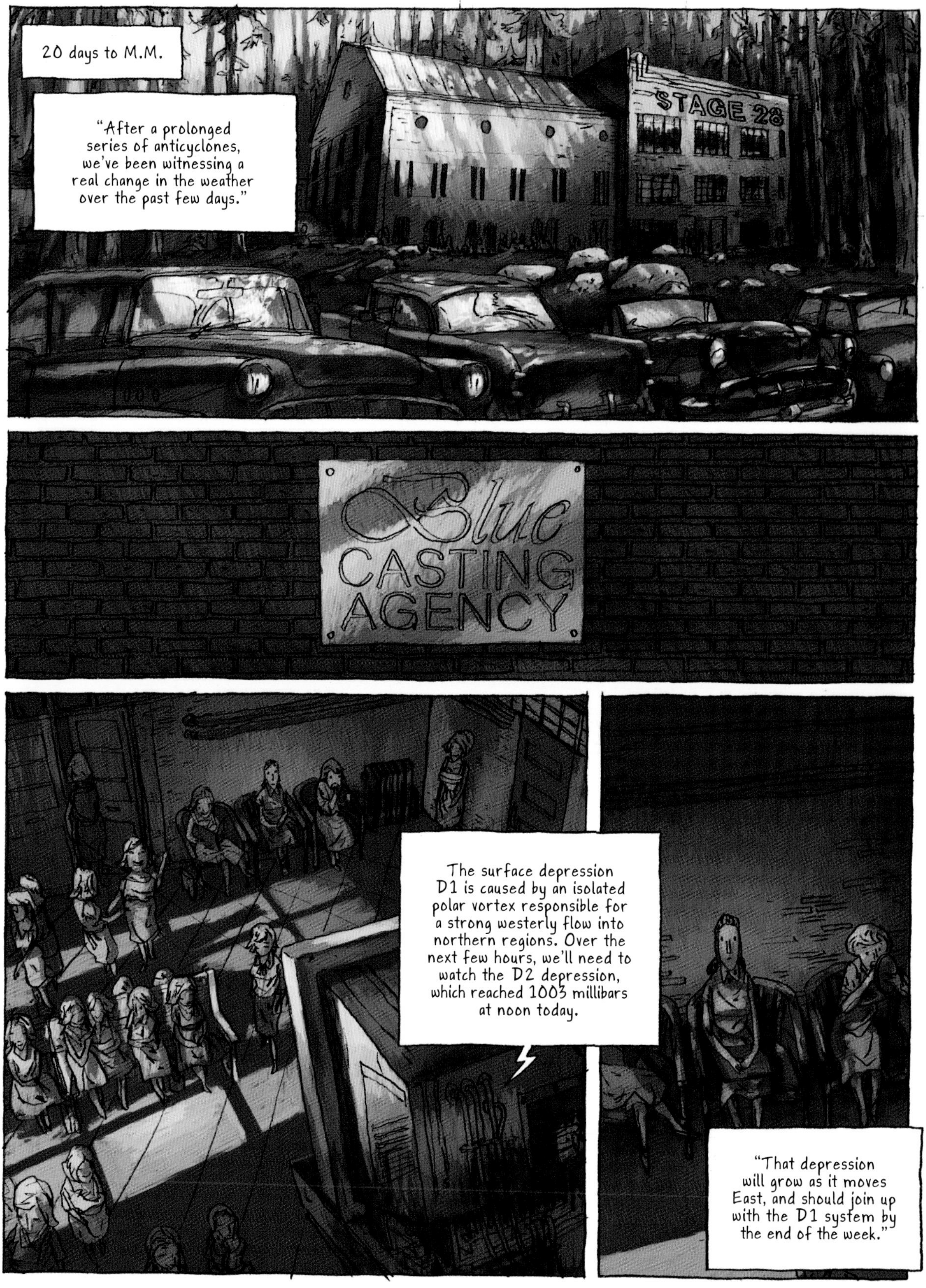
20 days to M.M.
"After a prolonged series of anticyclones, we've been witnessing a real change in the weather over the past few days."
STAGE 28
Blue CASTING AGENCY
The surface depression D1 is caused by an isolated polar vortex responsible for a strong westerly flow into northern regions. Over the next few hours, we'll need to watch the D2 depression, which reached 1003 millibars at noon today.
"That depression will grow as it moves East, and should join up with the D1 system by the end of the week."

The pressure gradient will drop sharply throughout Monday, then reach its peak overnight until Tuesday morning.

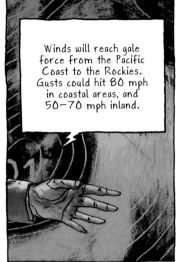

Winds will reach gale force from the Pacific Coast to the Rockies. Gusts could hit 80 mph in coastal areas, and 50–70 mph inland.

The depression responsible for these gales will be accompanied by an active cold front and heavy rain. Ahead of it—a strong southeast wind, bringing humidity and increasingly persistent rain.

This deterioration will spread by the end of the day, with rain possibly leading to scattered storms by Wednesday morning.

"Miss Baker?"

Subsequently, a new depression could generate high winds and heavy rainfall from Friday to Saturday. We'll probably be updating our forecast a little later on.

"Miss Baker?"

Miss Baker?

It's your turn.

SLAM!

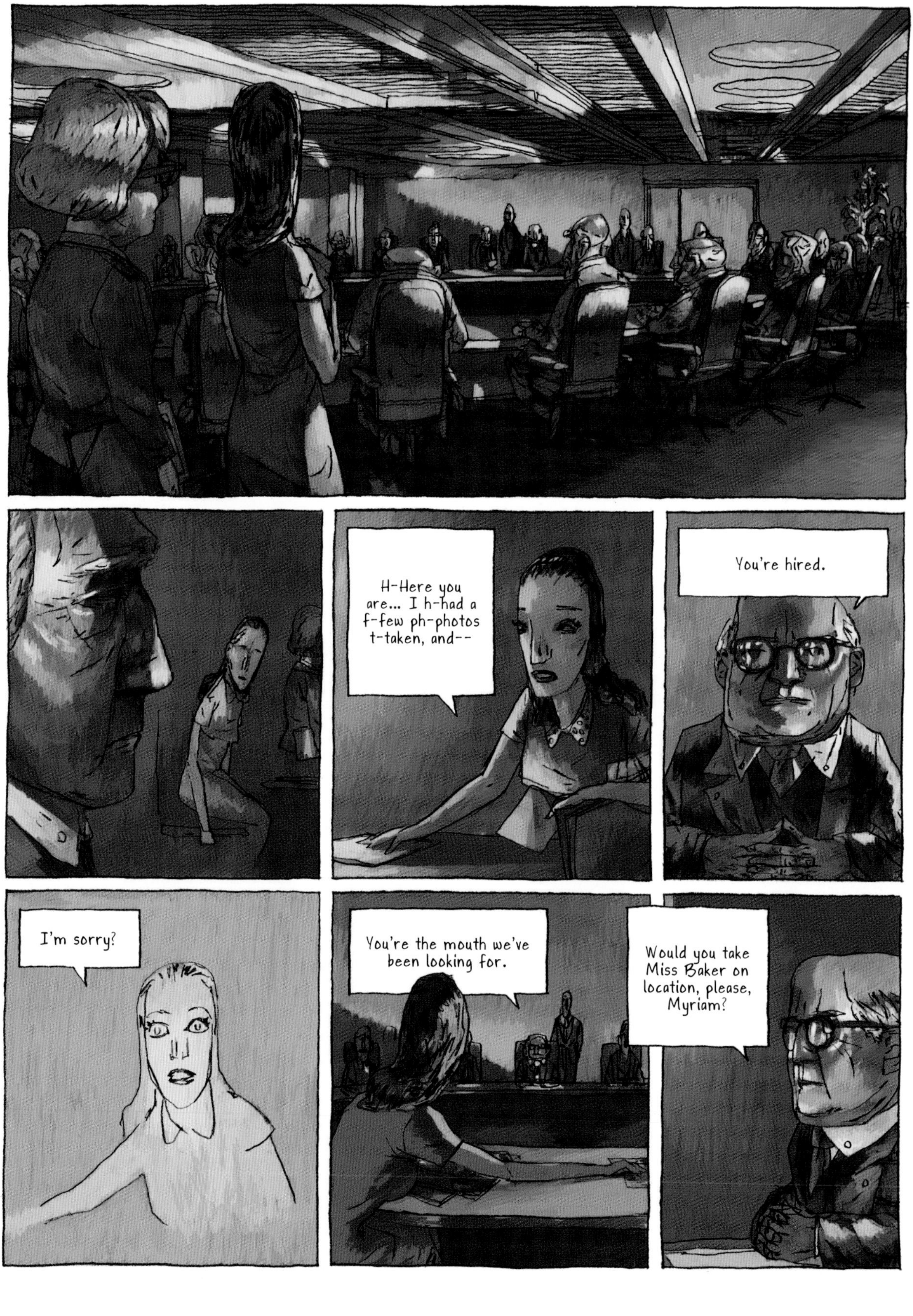
H-Here you are... I h-had a f-few ph-photos t-taken, and--
You're hired.
I'm sorry?
You're the mouth we've been looking for.
Would you take Miss Baker on location, please, Myriam?

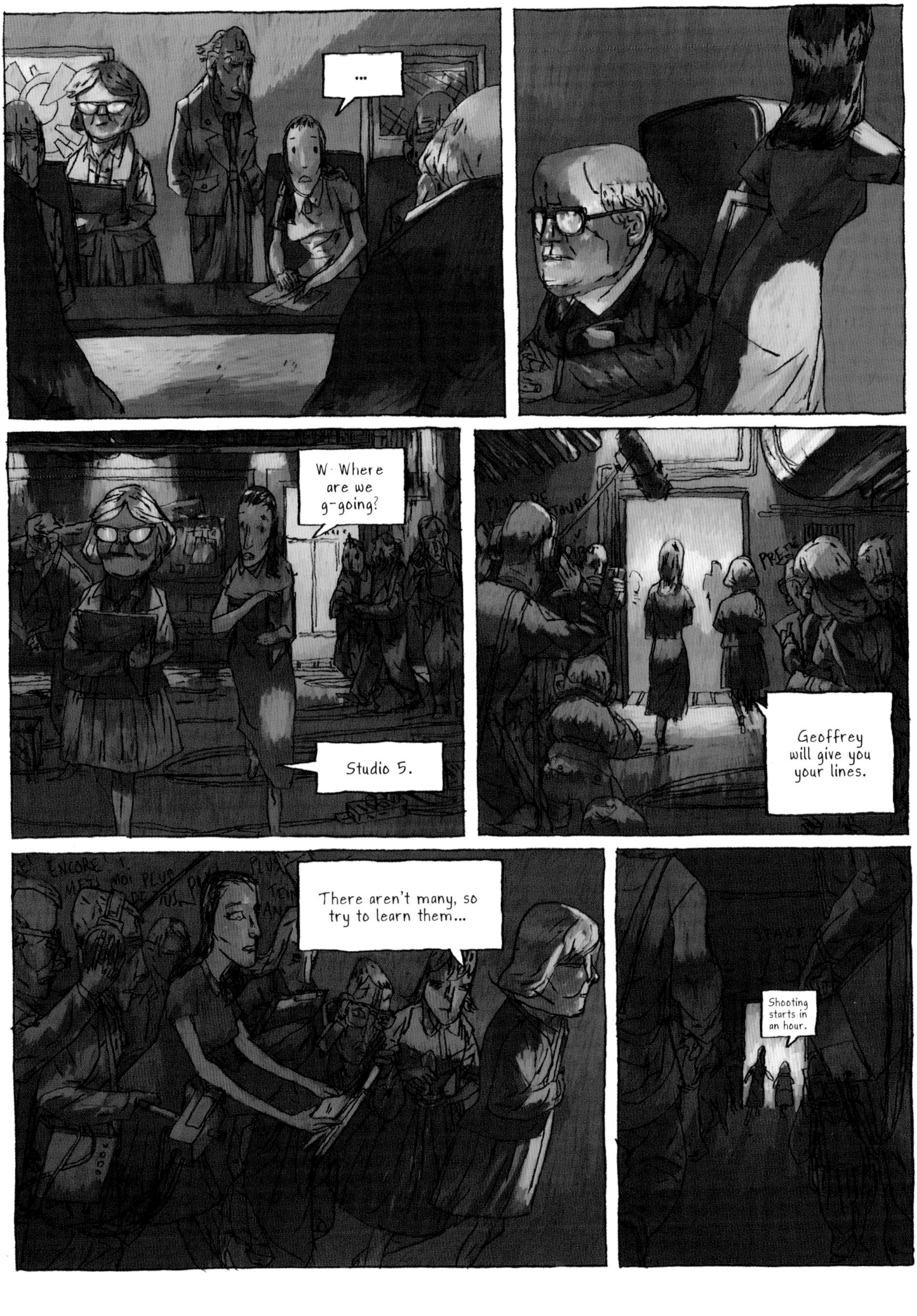
...
W- Where are we g-going?
Studio 5.
Geoffrey will give you your lines.
There aren't many, so try to learn them...
Shooting starts in an hour.

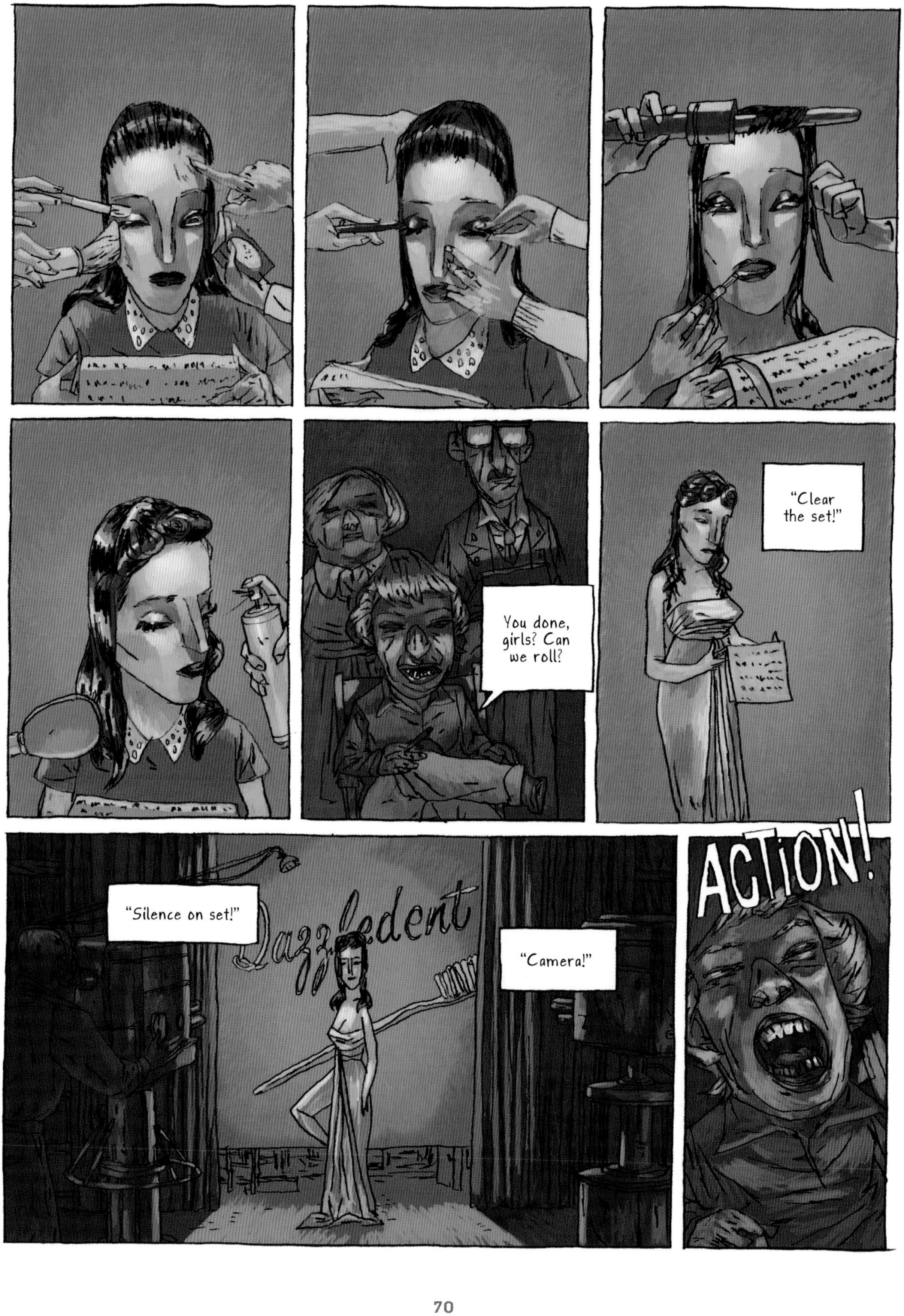
You done, girls? Can we roll?
"Clear the set!"
"Silence on set!"
Dazzledent
"Camera!"
ACTION!

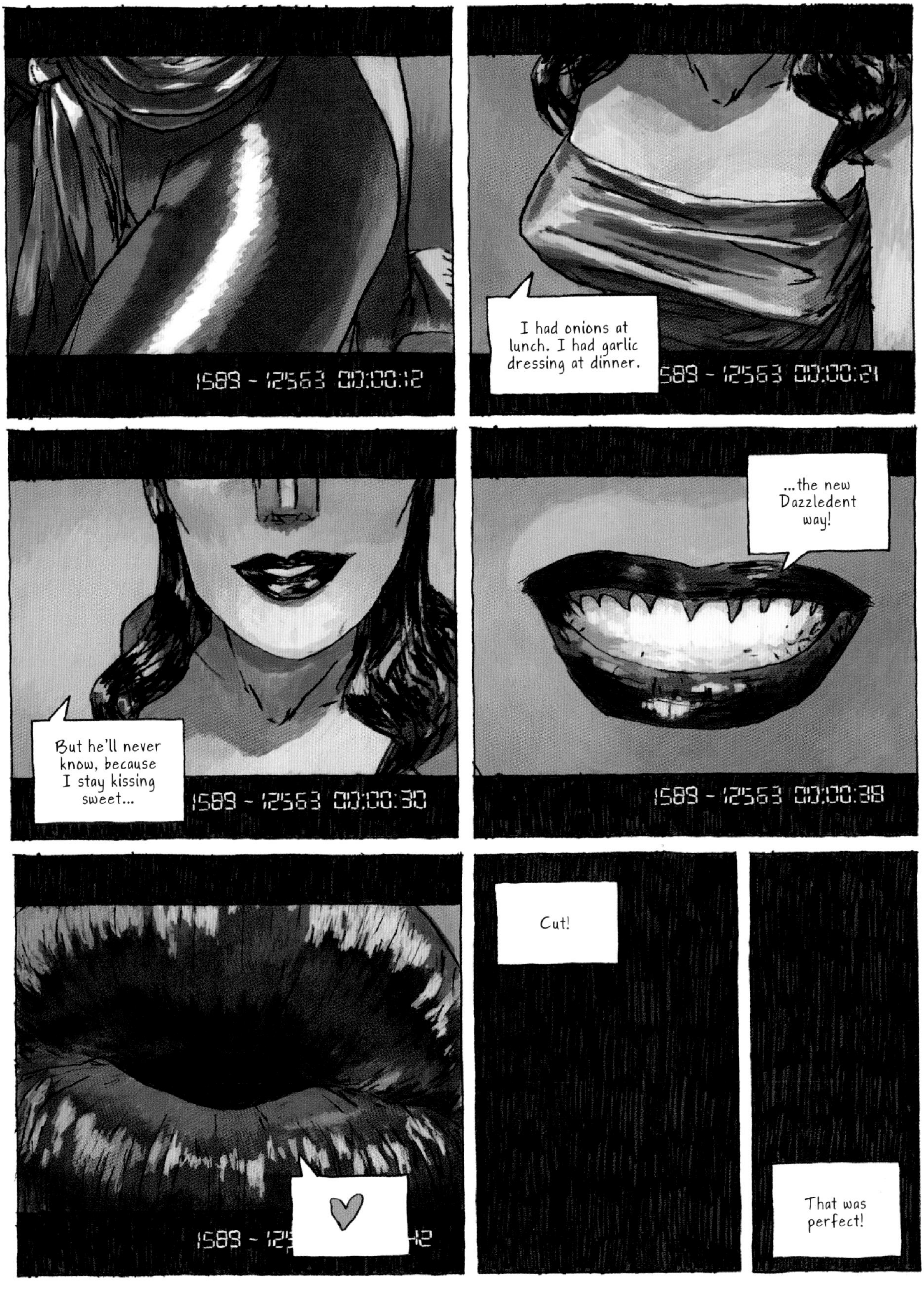
1589 - 12563 00:00:12
I had onions at lunch. I had garlic dressing at dinner.
589 - 12563 00:00:21
But he'll never know, because I stay kissing sweet...
1589 - 12563 00:00:30
...the new Dazzledent way!
1589 - 12563 00:00:38
1589 - 12
42
Cut!
That was perfect!

TOC
TOC
Marty
3463
Miss Baker?
Yes?
A letter for you, from the Ministry.
The Ministry?!

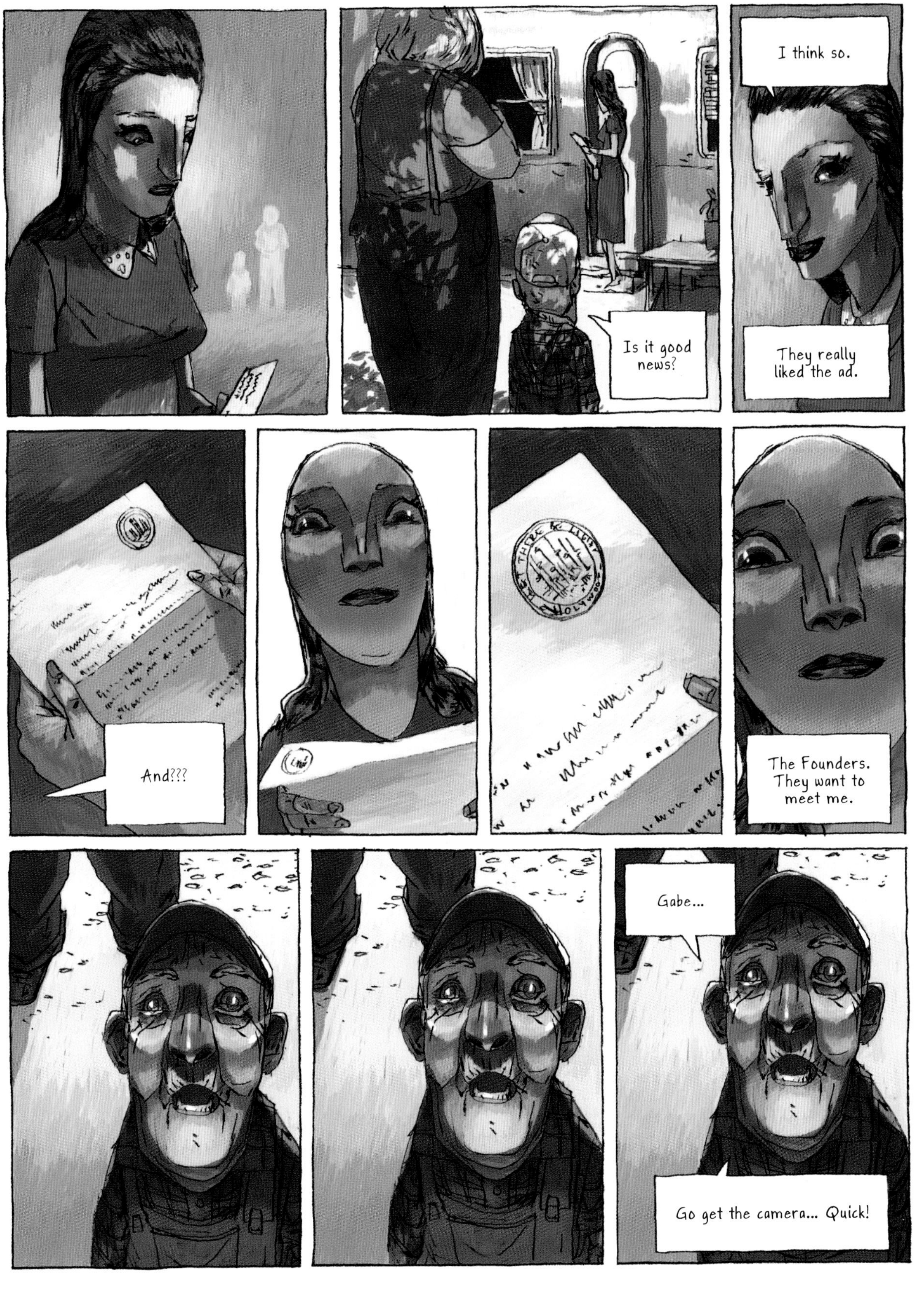
Is it good news?
I think so.
They really liked the ad.
And???
The Founders. They want to meet me.
Gabe...
Go get the camera... Quick!

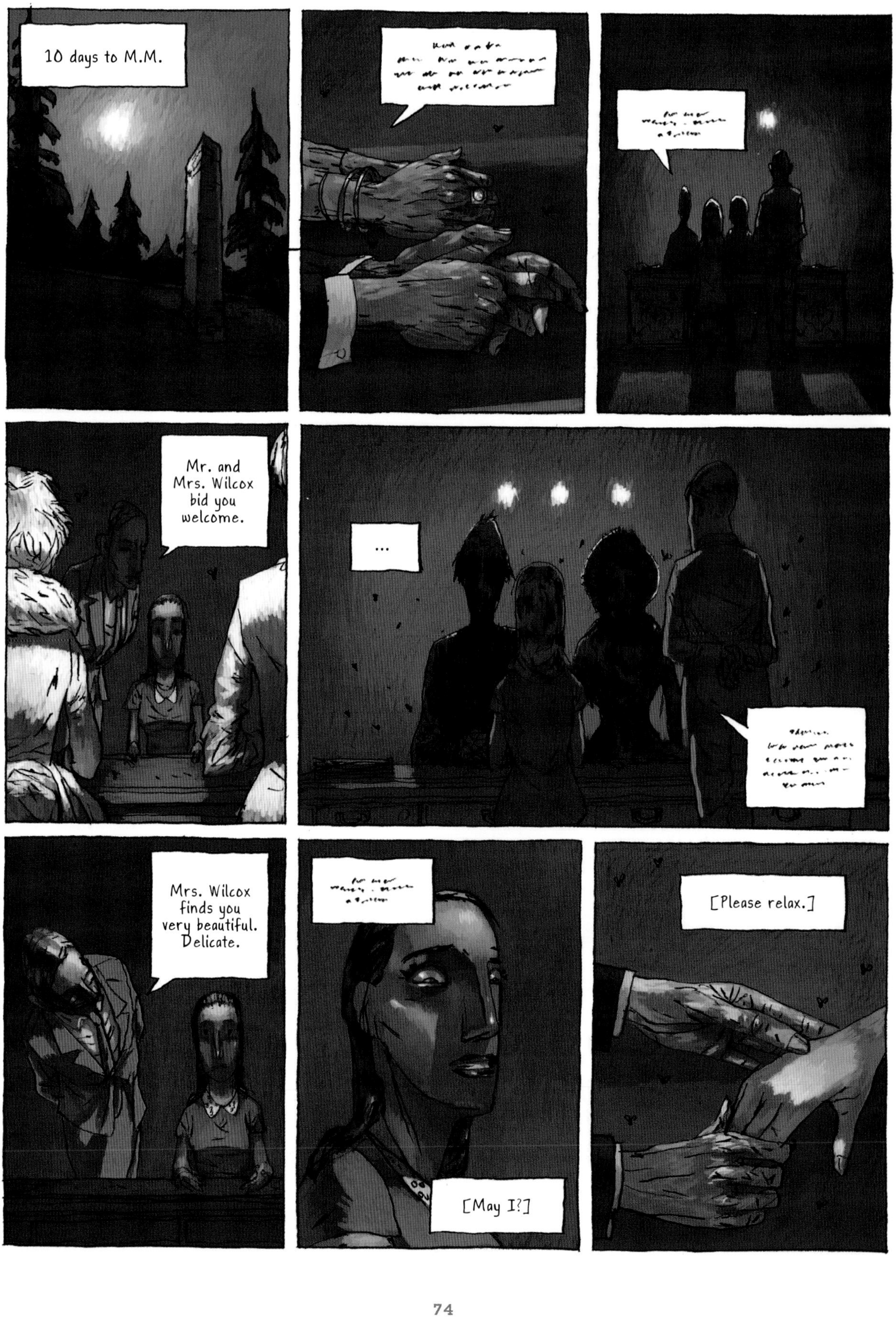
10 days to M.M.
Mr. and Mrs. Wilcox bid you welcome.
...
Mrs. Wilcox finds you very beautiful. Delicate.
[May I?]
[Please relax.]

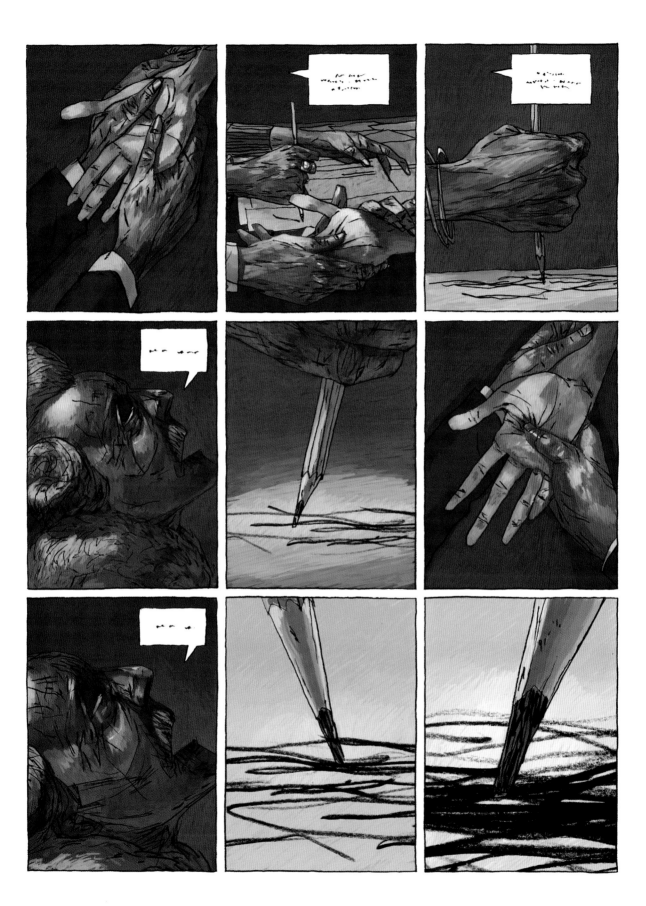

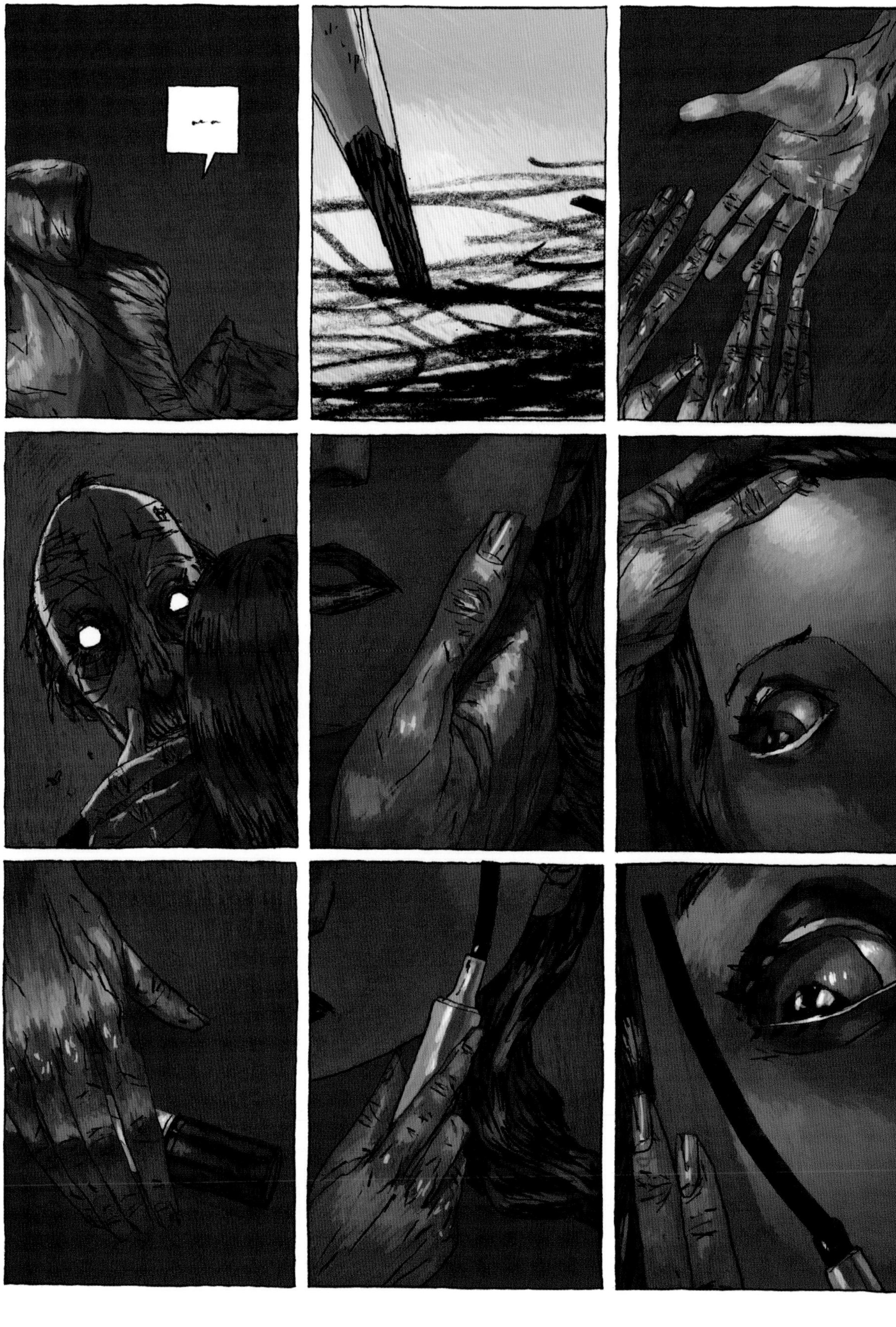
...

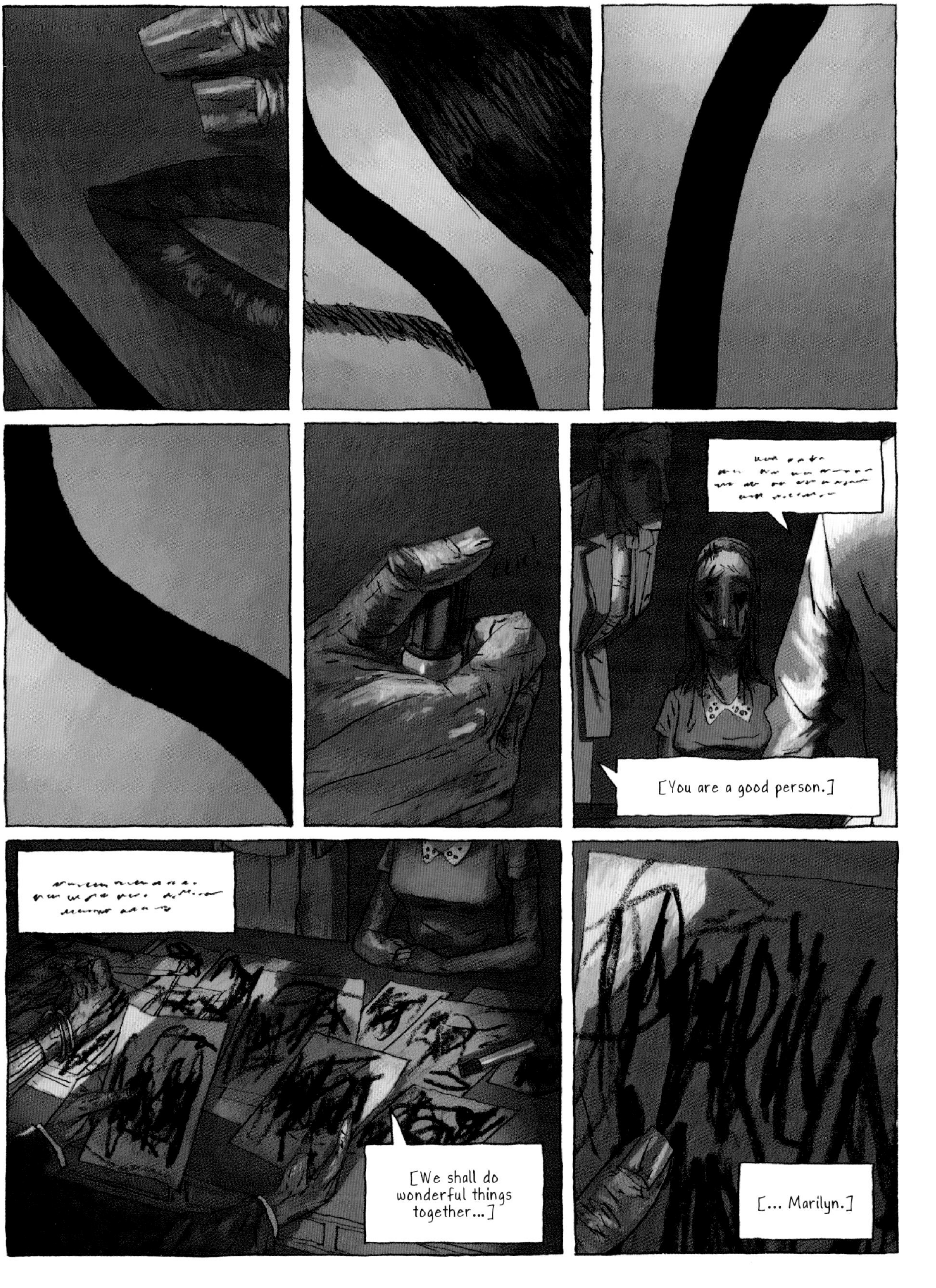

[You are a good person.]
[We shall do wonderful things together...]
[... Marilyn.]

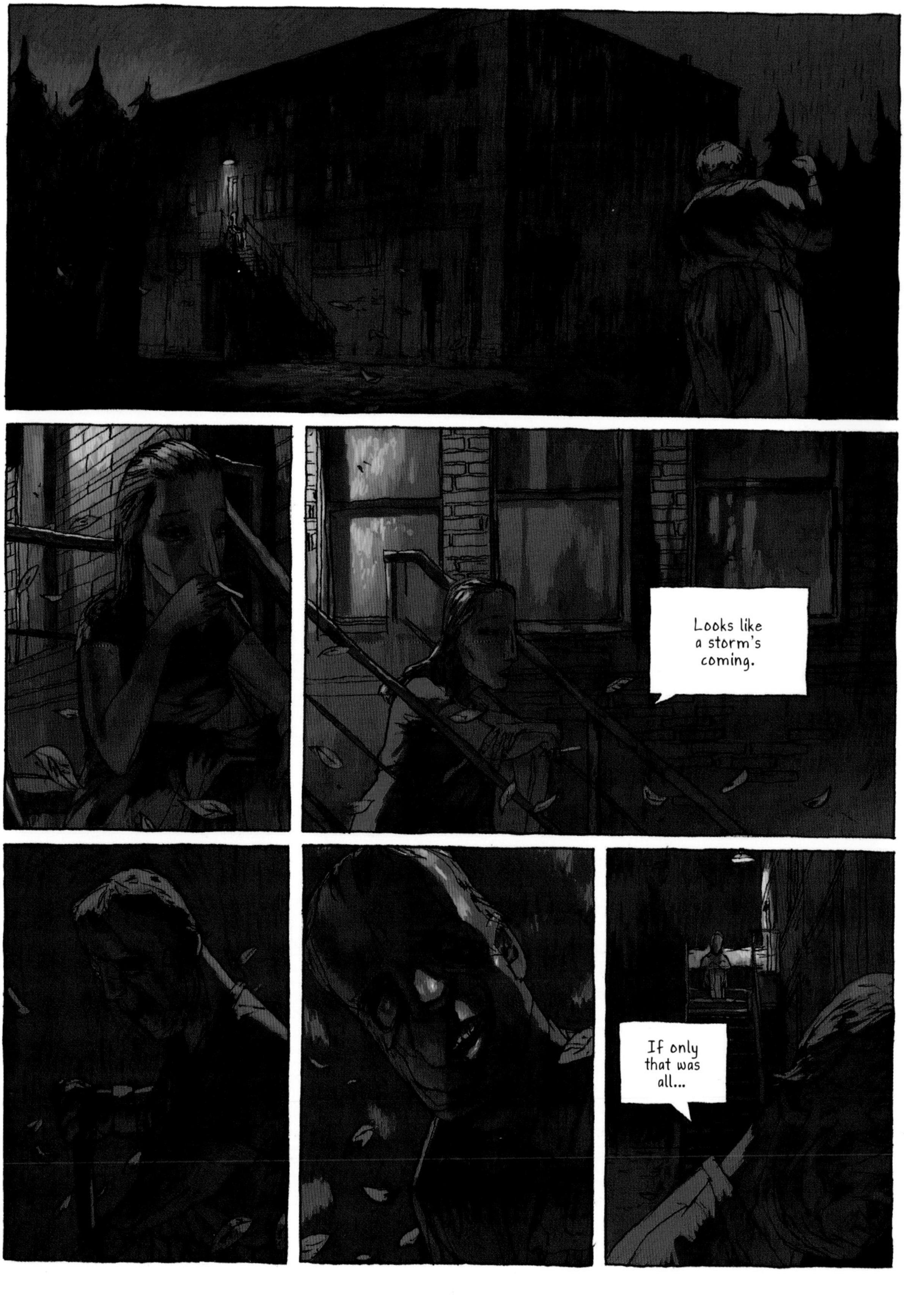
Looks like a storm's coming.
If only that was all...

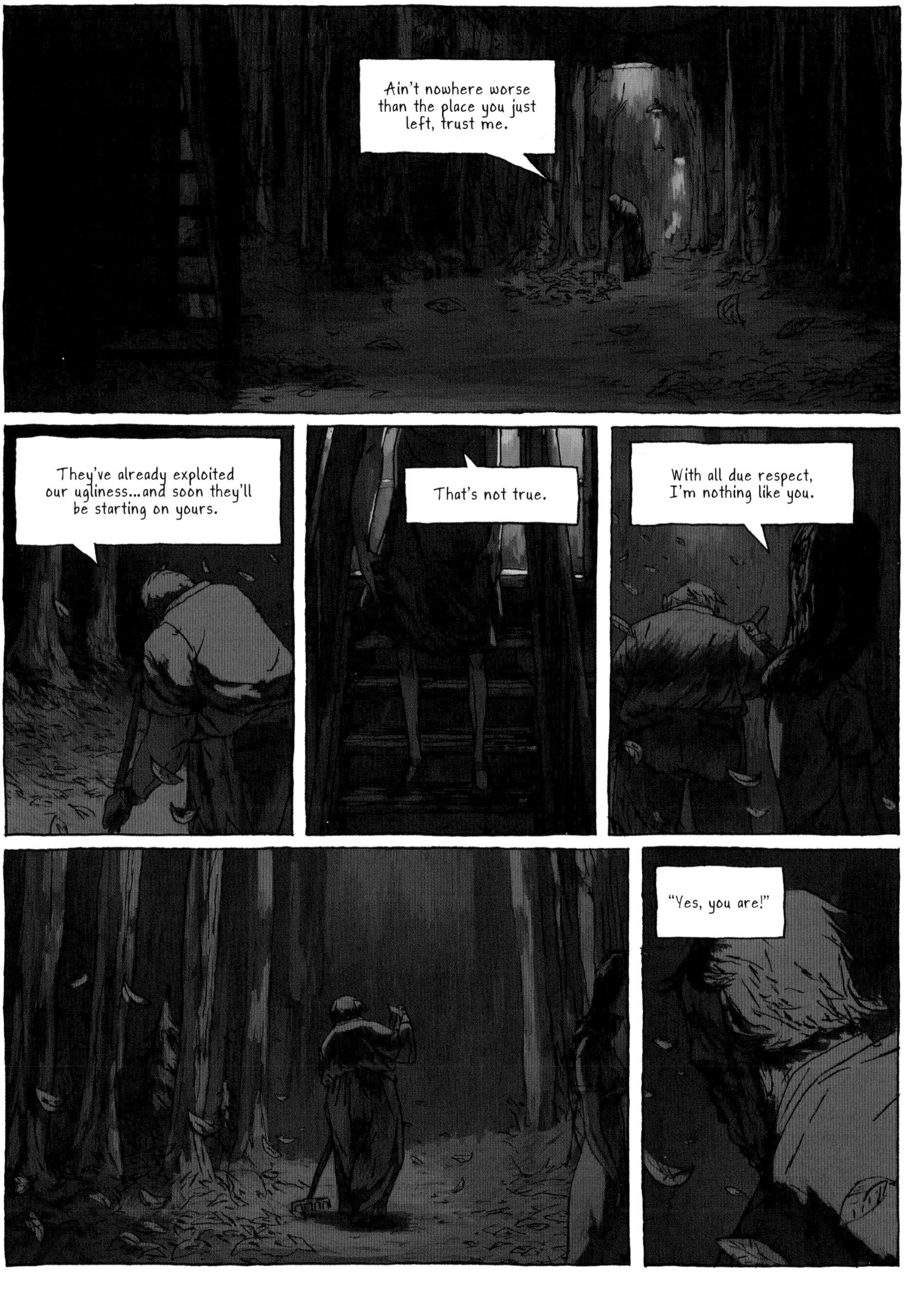
Ain't nowhere worse than the place you just left, trust me.
They've already exploited our ugliness...and soon they'll be starting on yours.
That's not true.
With all due respect, I'm nothing like you.
"Yes, you are!"

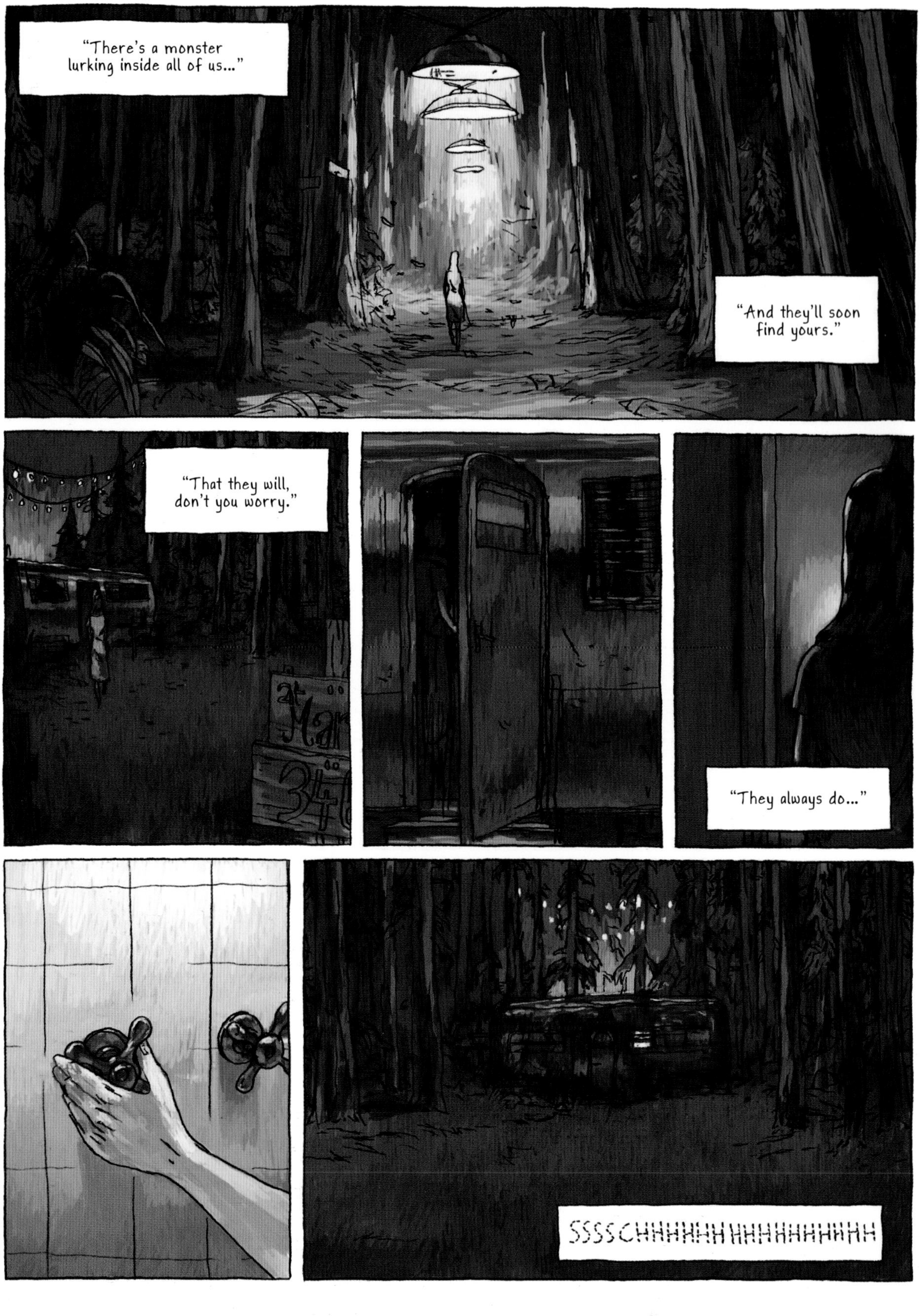
"There's a monster lurking inside all of us..."
"And they'll soon find yours."
"That they will, don't you worry."
"They always do..."
SSSSCHHHHHHHHHHHHHHHH

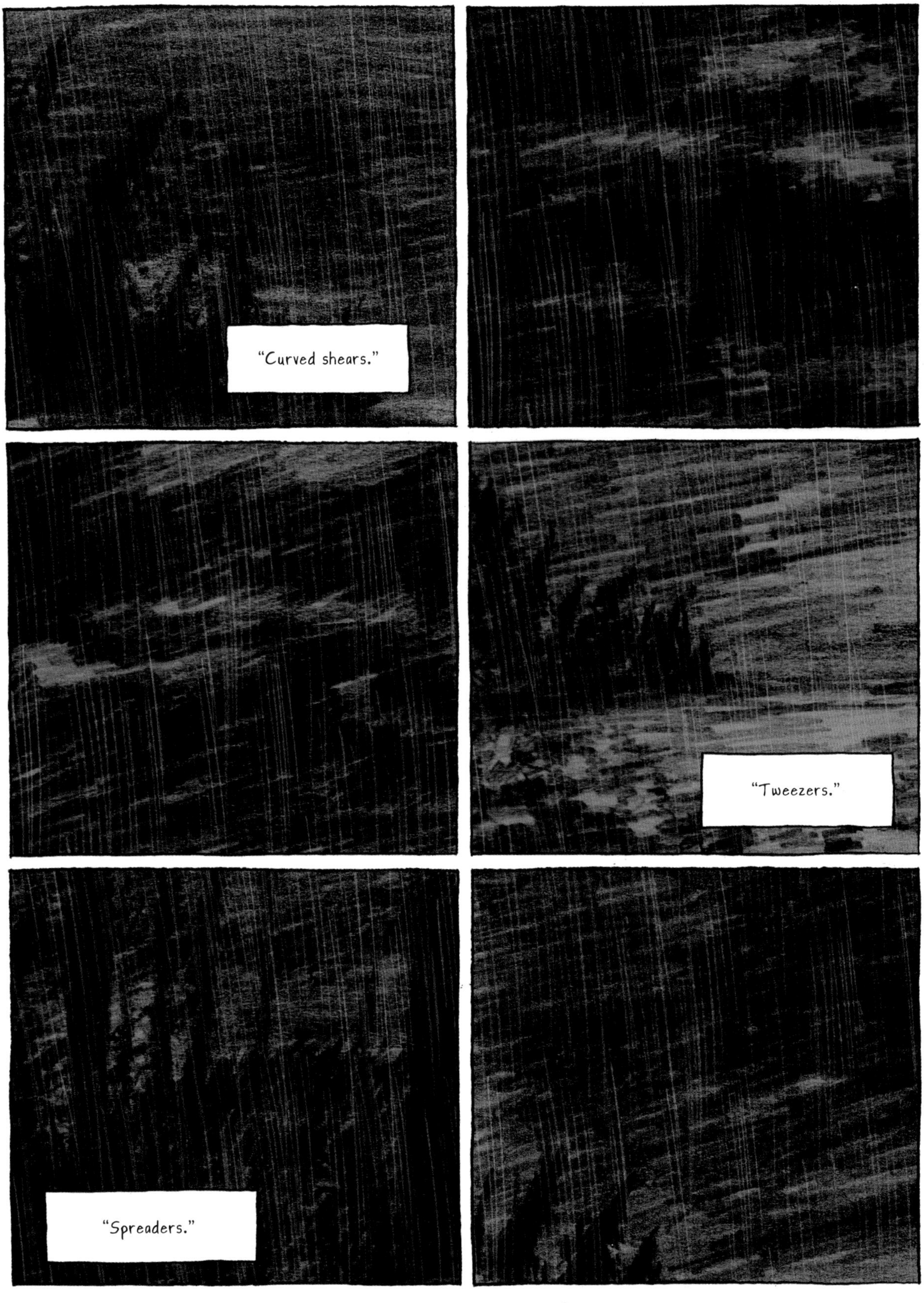
"Curved shears."
"Tweezers."
"Spreaders."

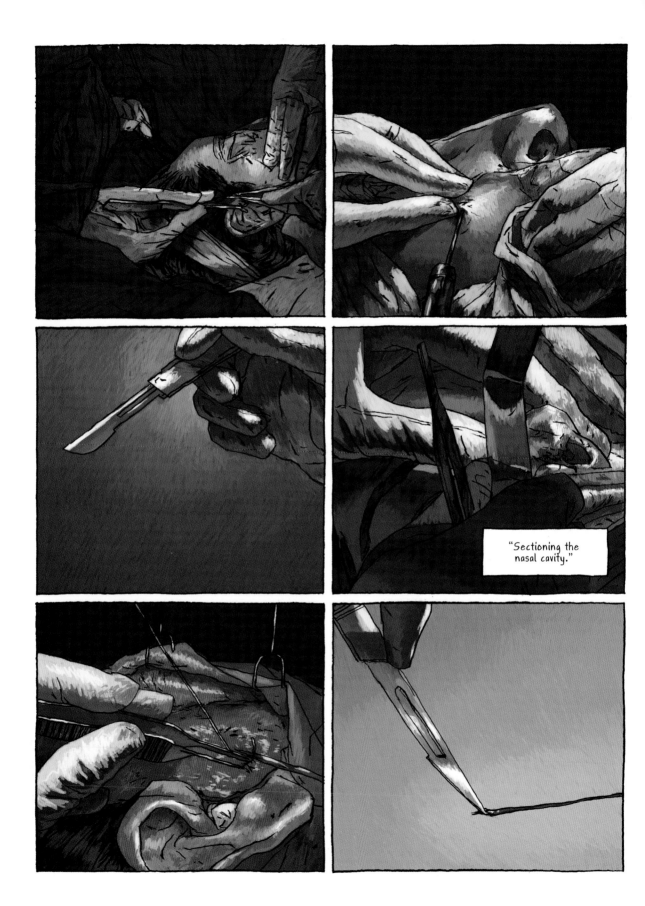

"Sectioning the nasal cavity."

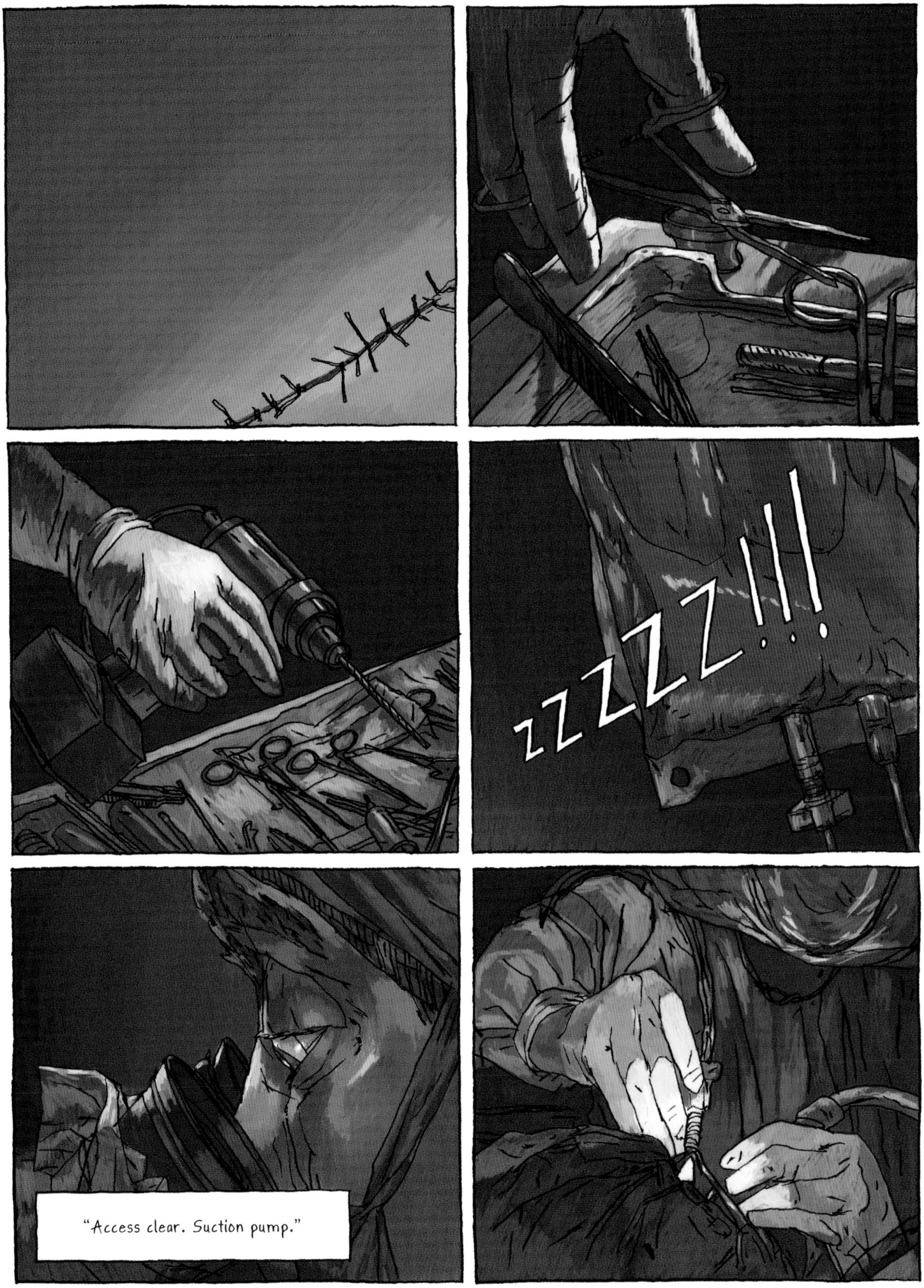
ZZZZZ!!!
"Access clear. Suction pump."

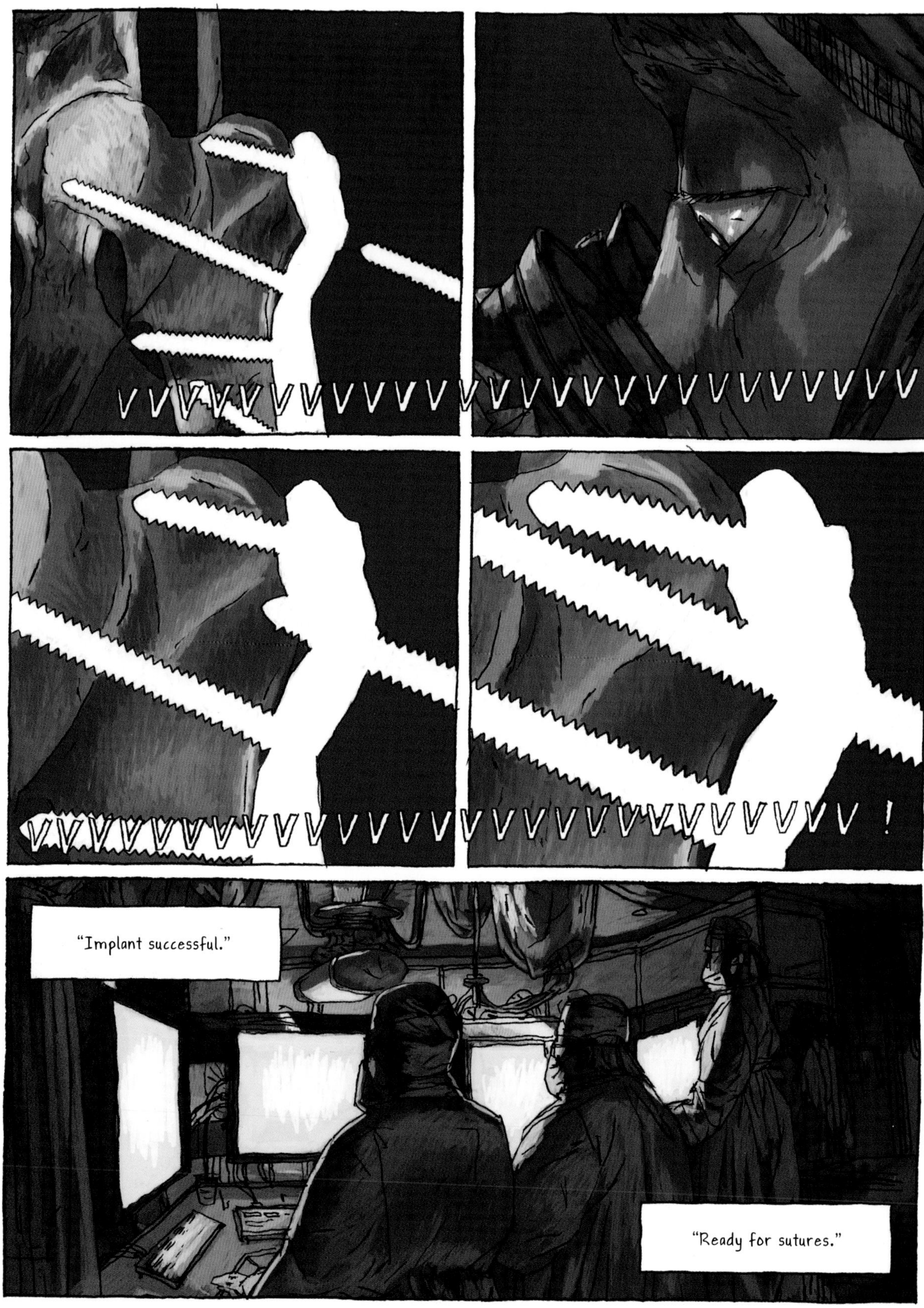
"Implant successful."
"Ready for sutures."

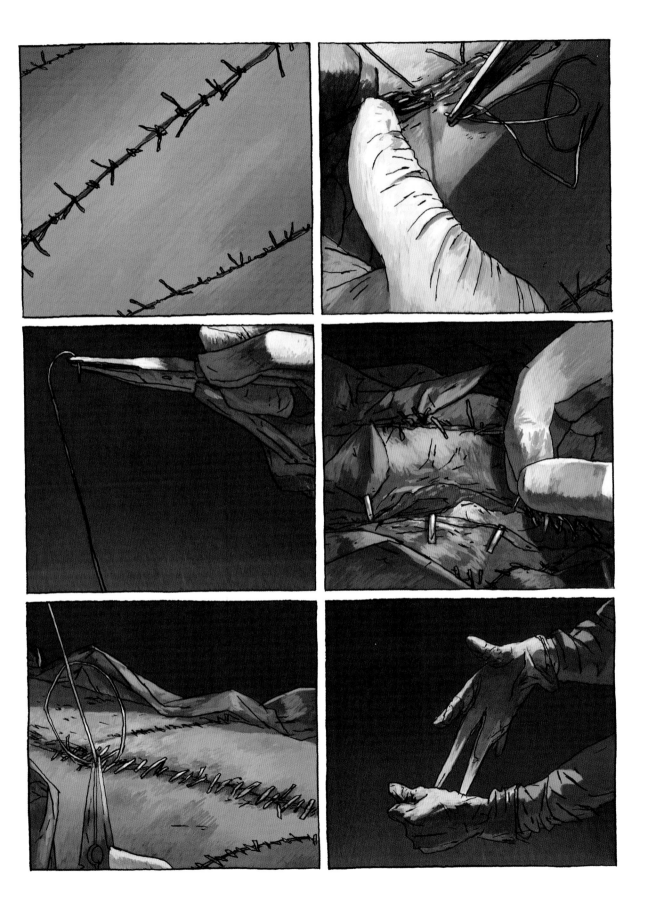

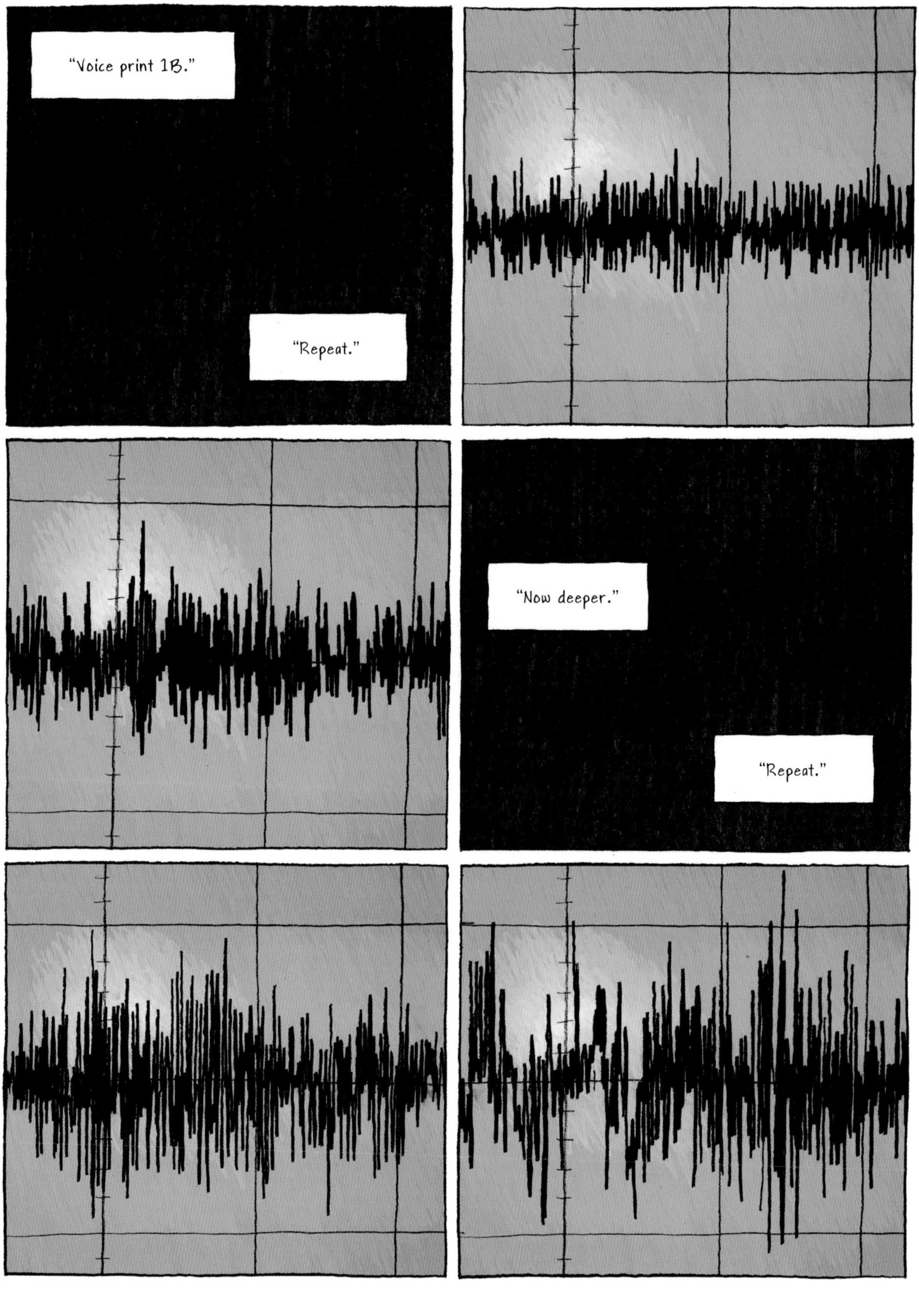
"Voice print 1B."
"Repeat."
"Now deeper."
"Repeat."

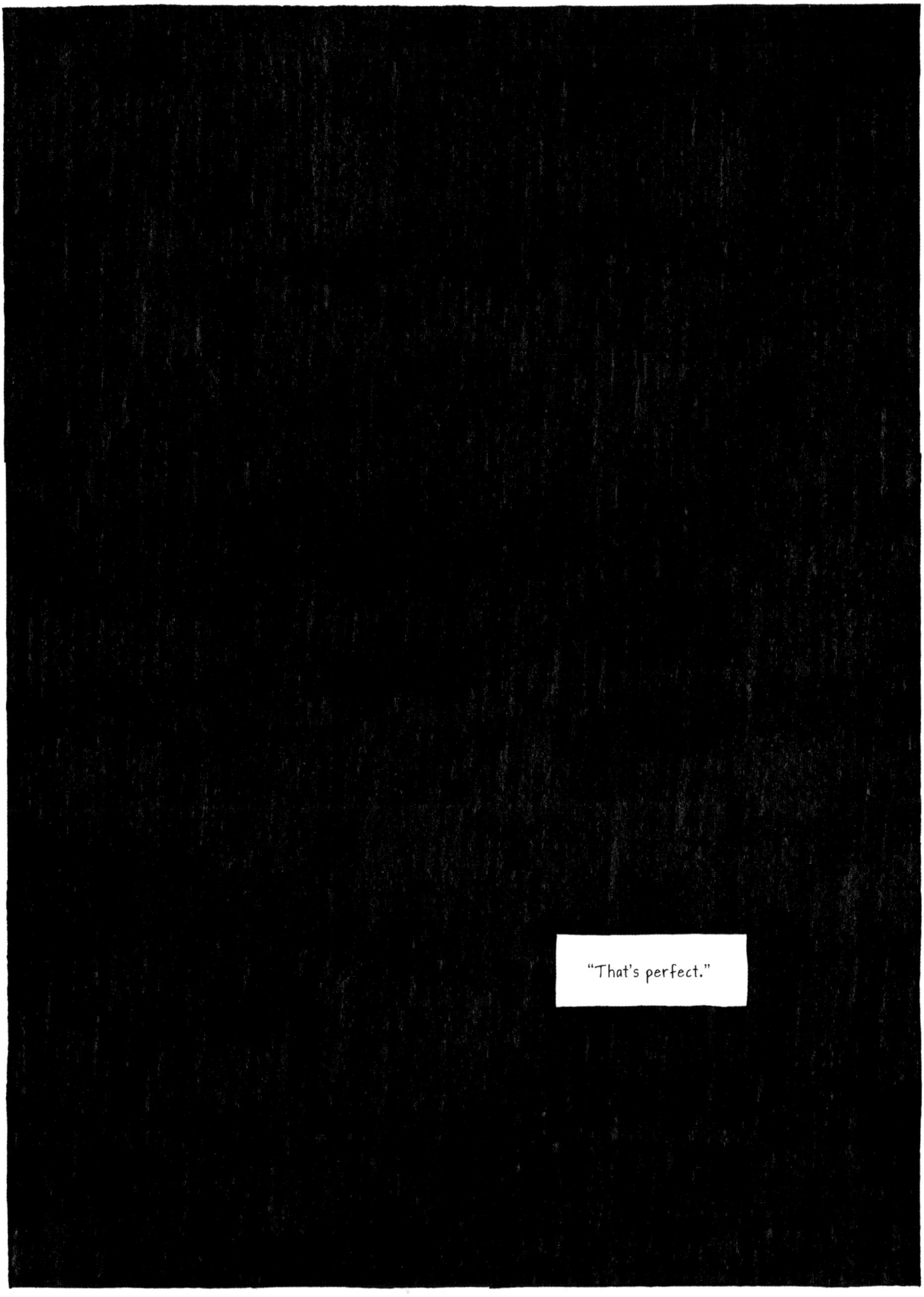
"That's perfect."

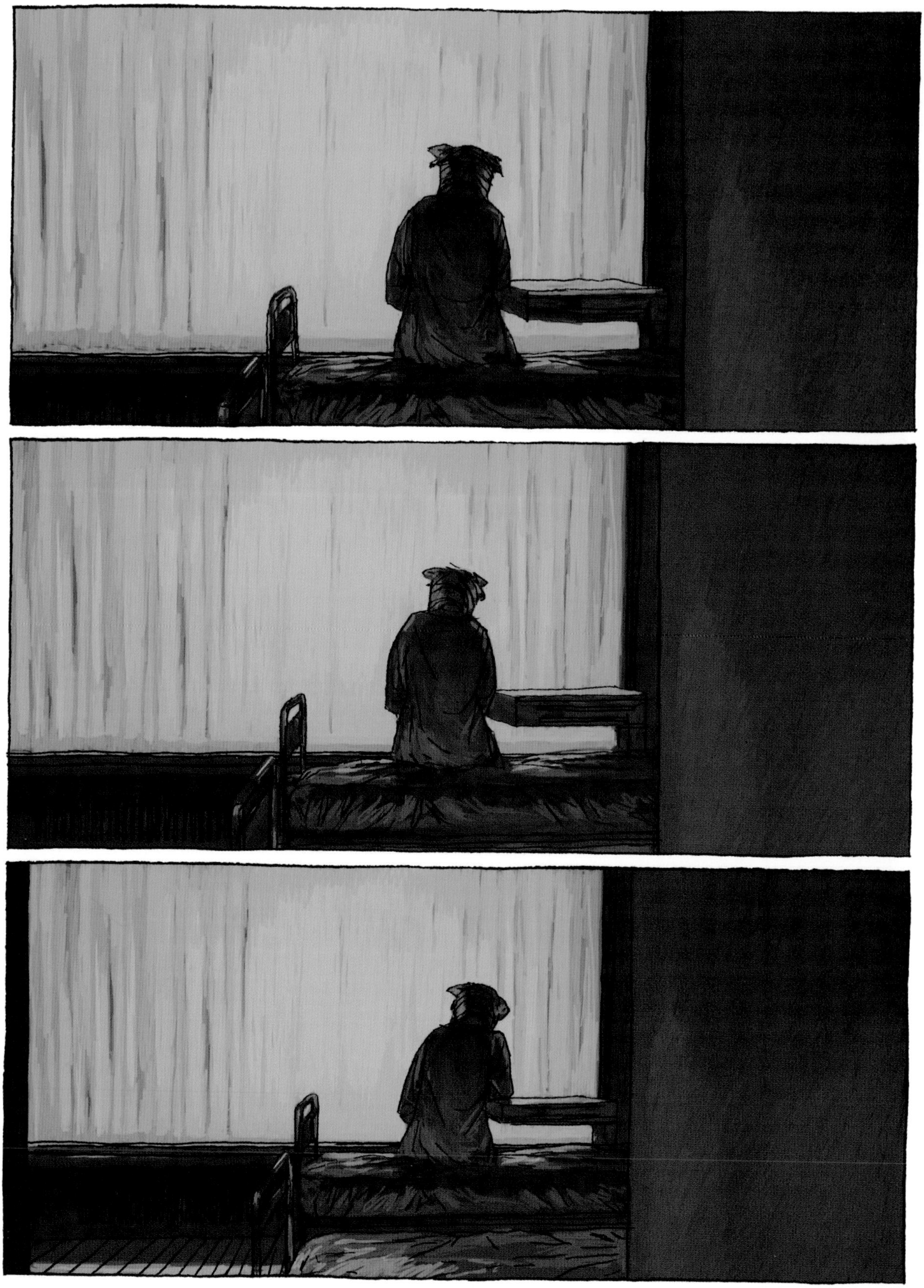

CHAPTER 2
/R(e)BiRTH/

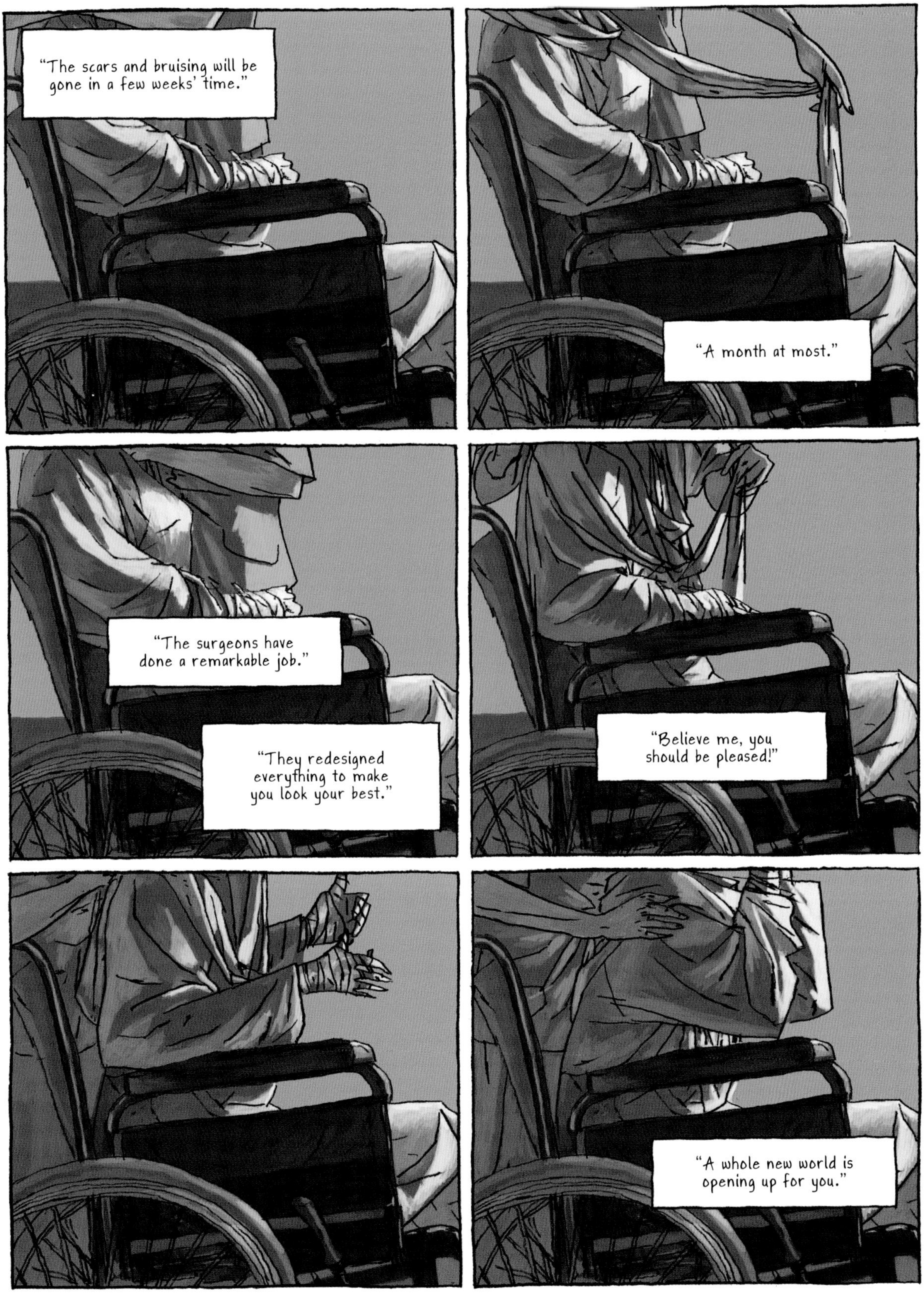
"The scars and bruising will be gone in a few weeks' time."
"A month at most."
"The surgeons have done a remarkable job."
"They redesigned everything to make you look your best."
"Believe me, you should be pleased!"
"A whole new world is opening up for you."

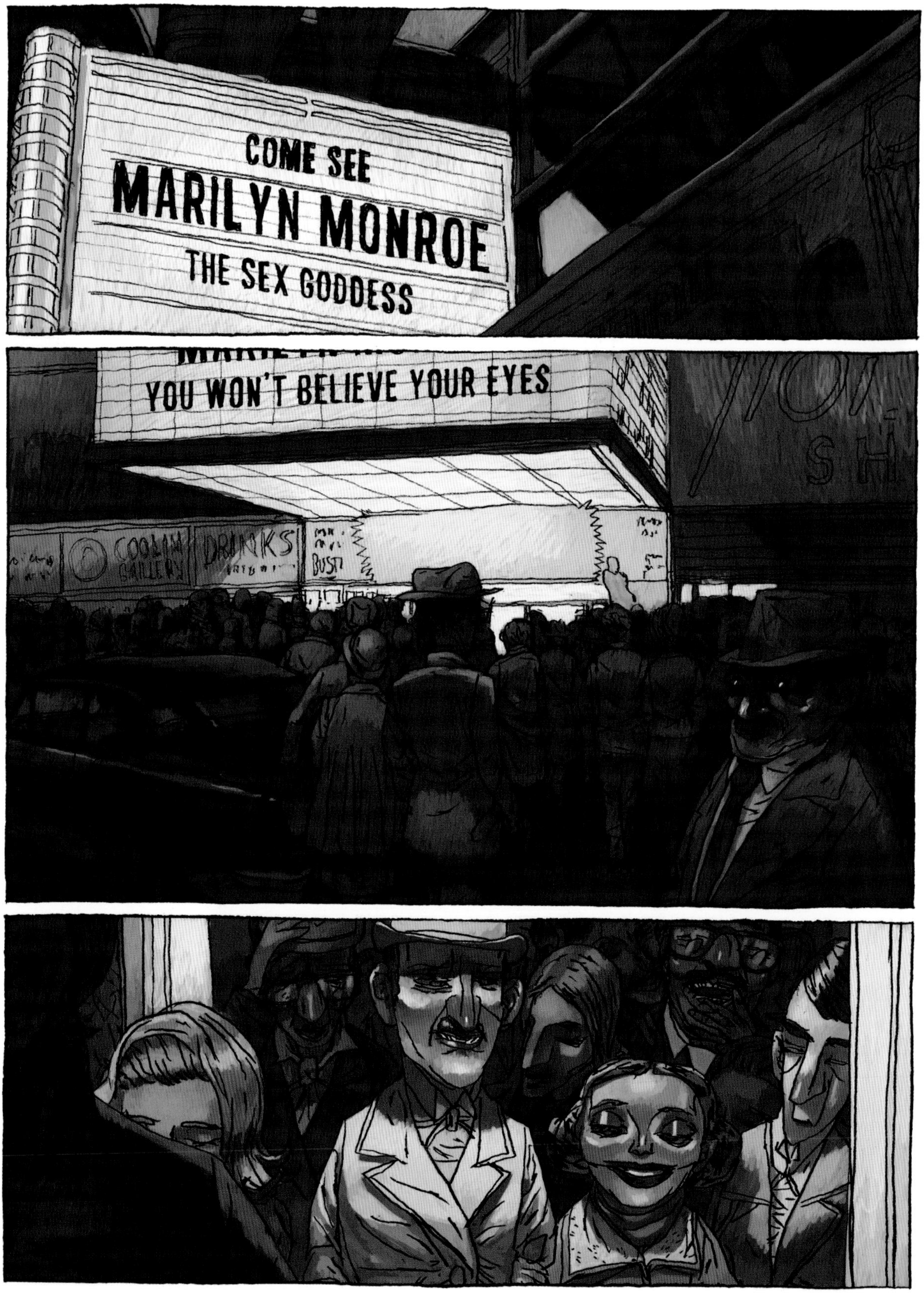
COME SEE
MARILYN MONROE
THE SEX GODDESS
YOU WON'T BELIEVE YOUR EYES
DRINKS

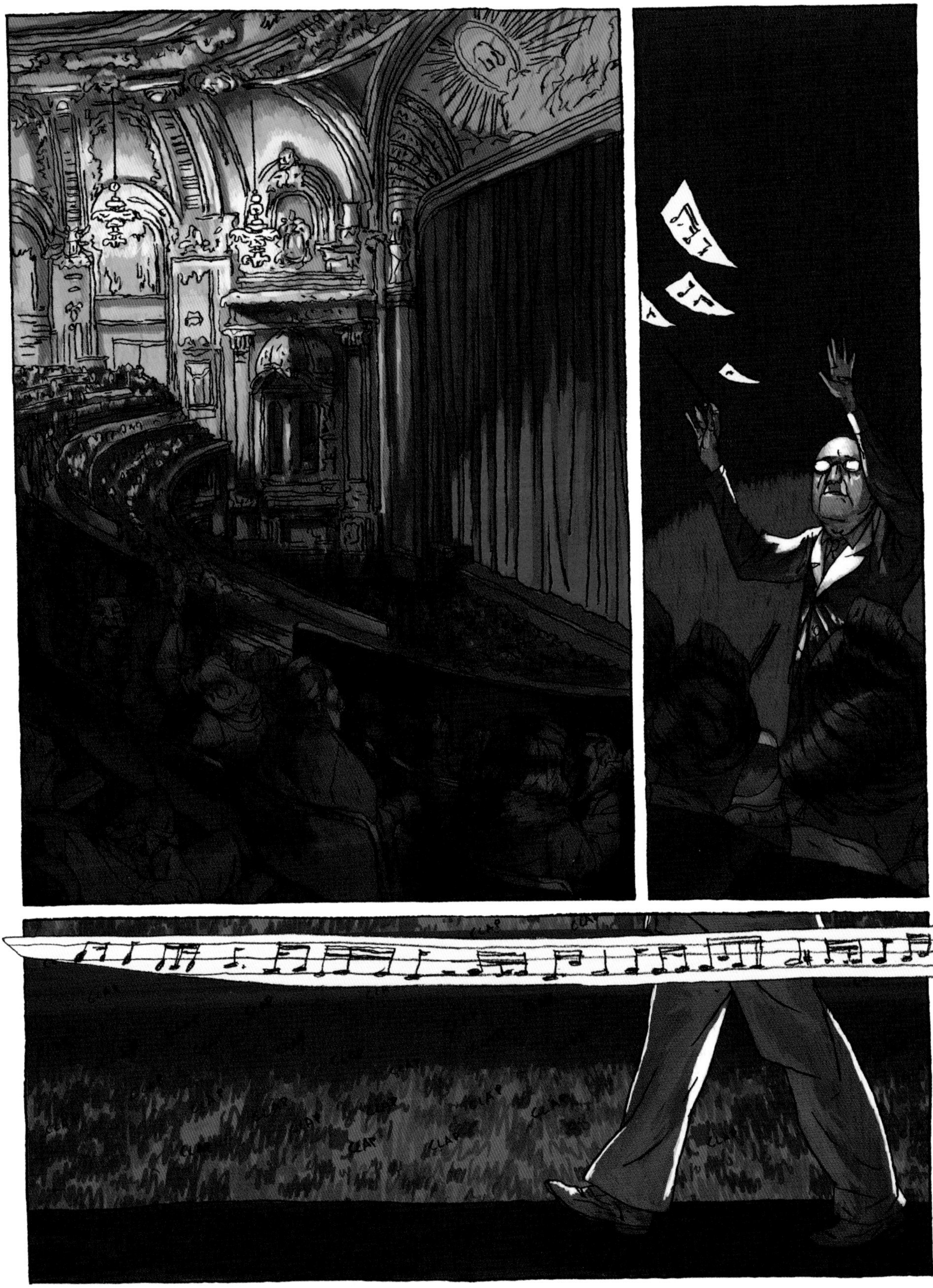

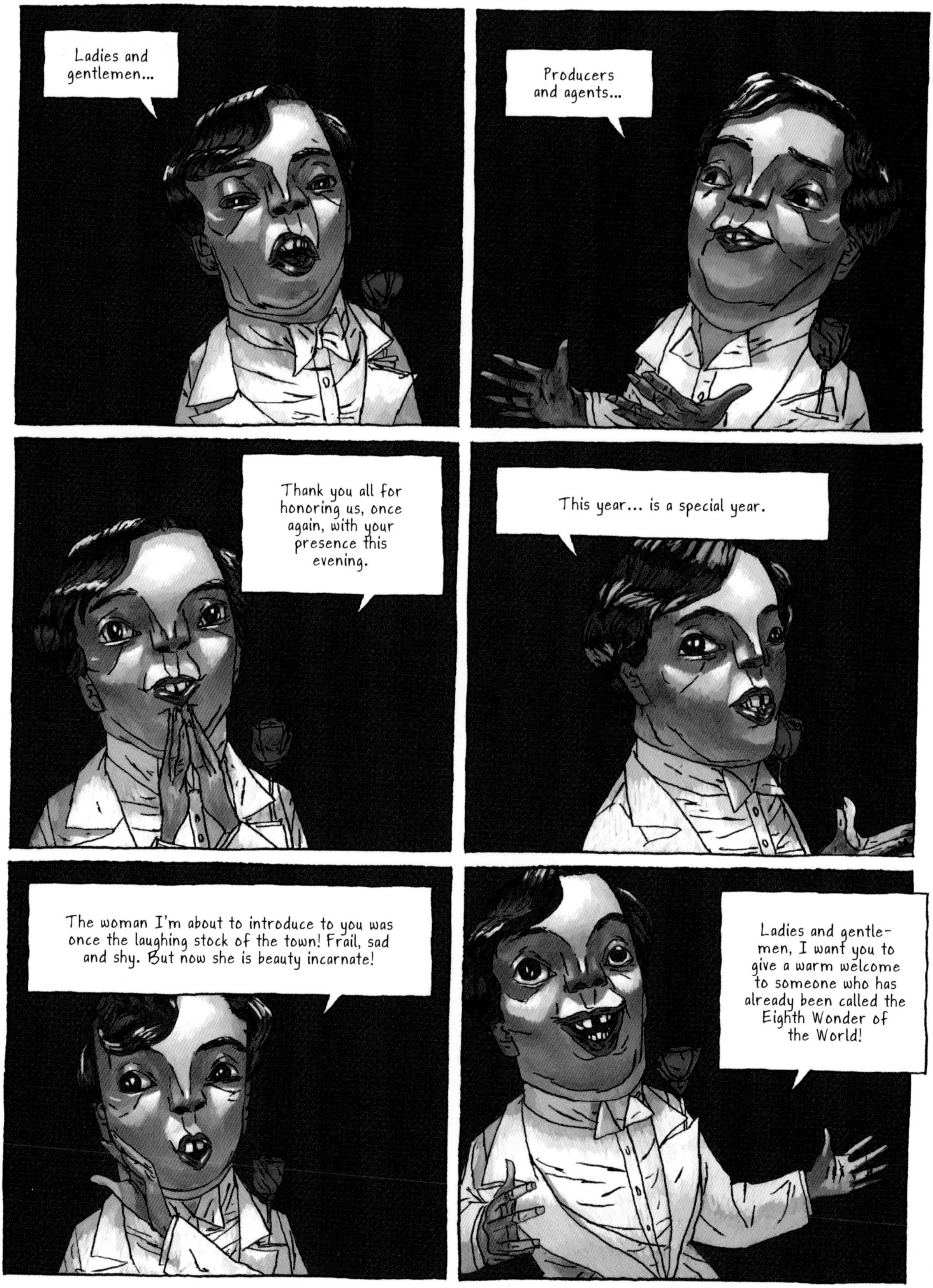
Ladies and gentlemen...
Producers and agents...
Thank you all for honoring us, once again, with your presence this evening.
This year... is a special year.
The woman I'm about to introduce to you was once the laughing stock of the town! Frail, sad and shy. But now she is beauty incarnate!
Ladies and gentle-men, I want you to give a warm welcome to someone who has already been called the Eighth Wonder of the World!

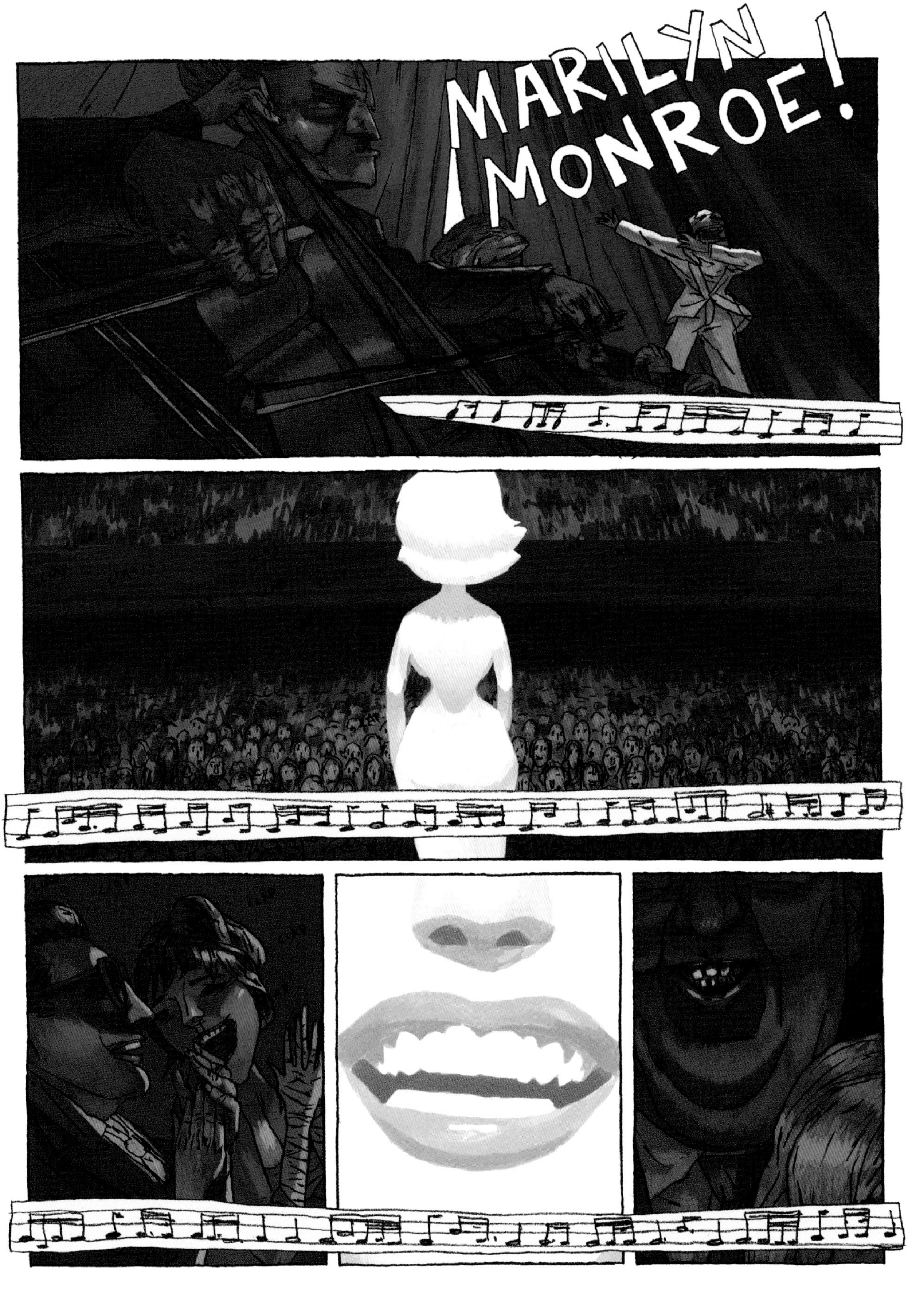
MARILYN MONROE!

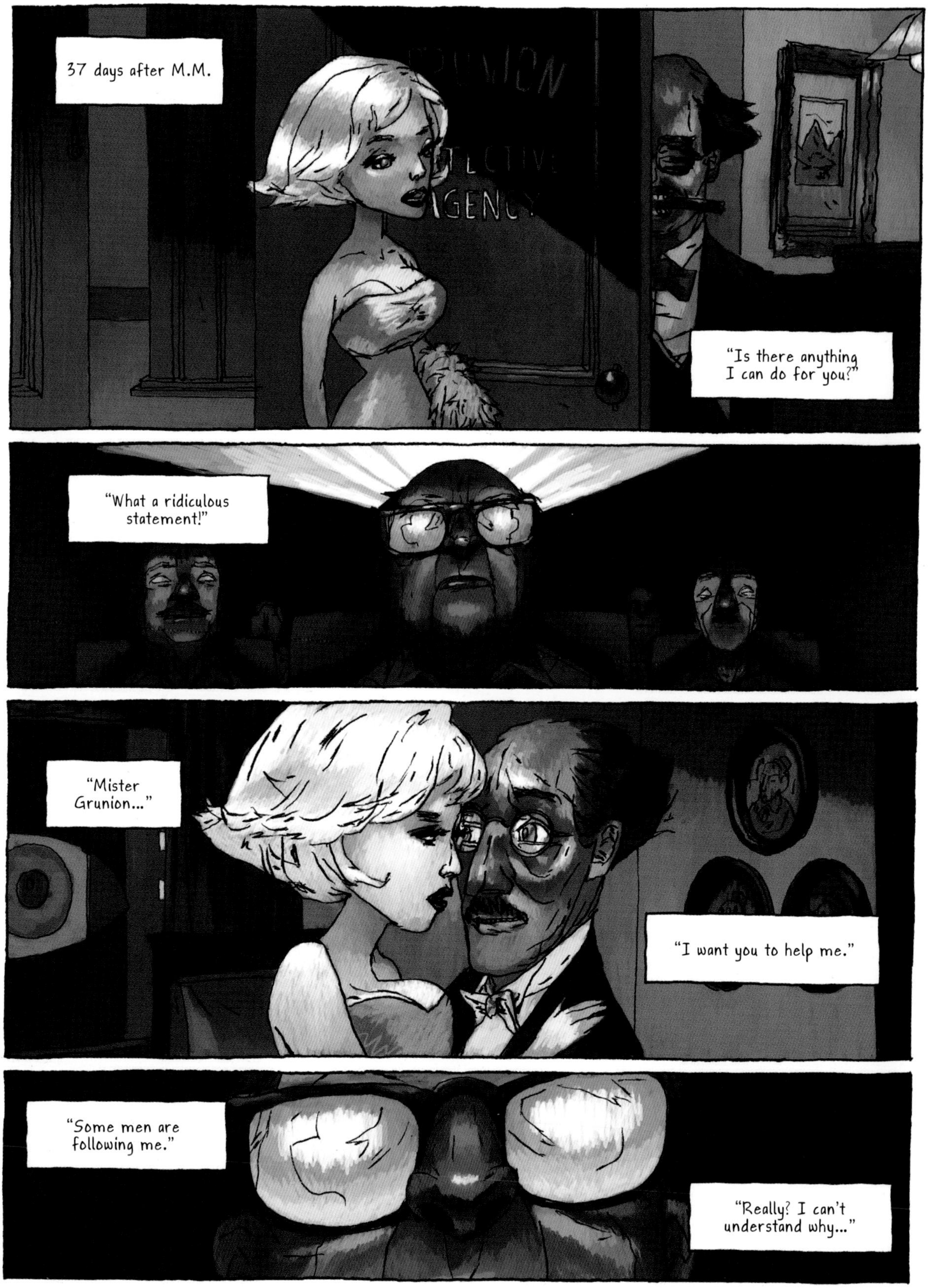
37 days after M.M.
"Is there anything I can do for you?"
"What a ridiculous statement!"
"Mister Grunion..."
"I want you to help me."
"Some men are following me."
"Really? I can't understand why..."

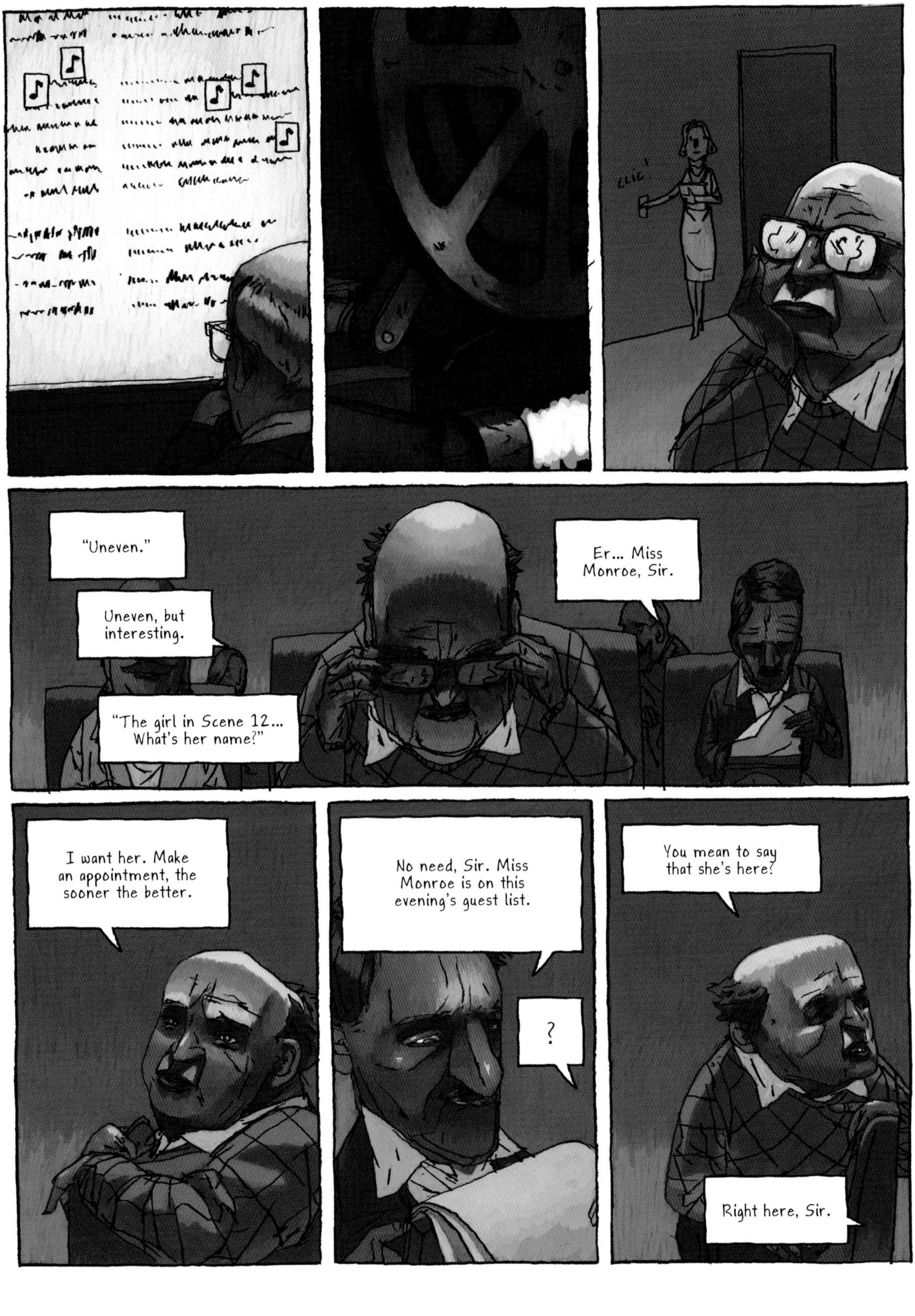
CLIC!
"Uneven."
Uneven, but interesting.
"The girl in Scene 12... What's her name?"
Er... Miss Monroe, Sir.
I want her. Make an appointment, the sooner the better.
No need, Sir. Miss Monroe is on this evening's guest list.
?
You mean to say that she's here?
Right here, Sir.

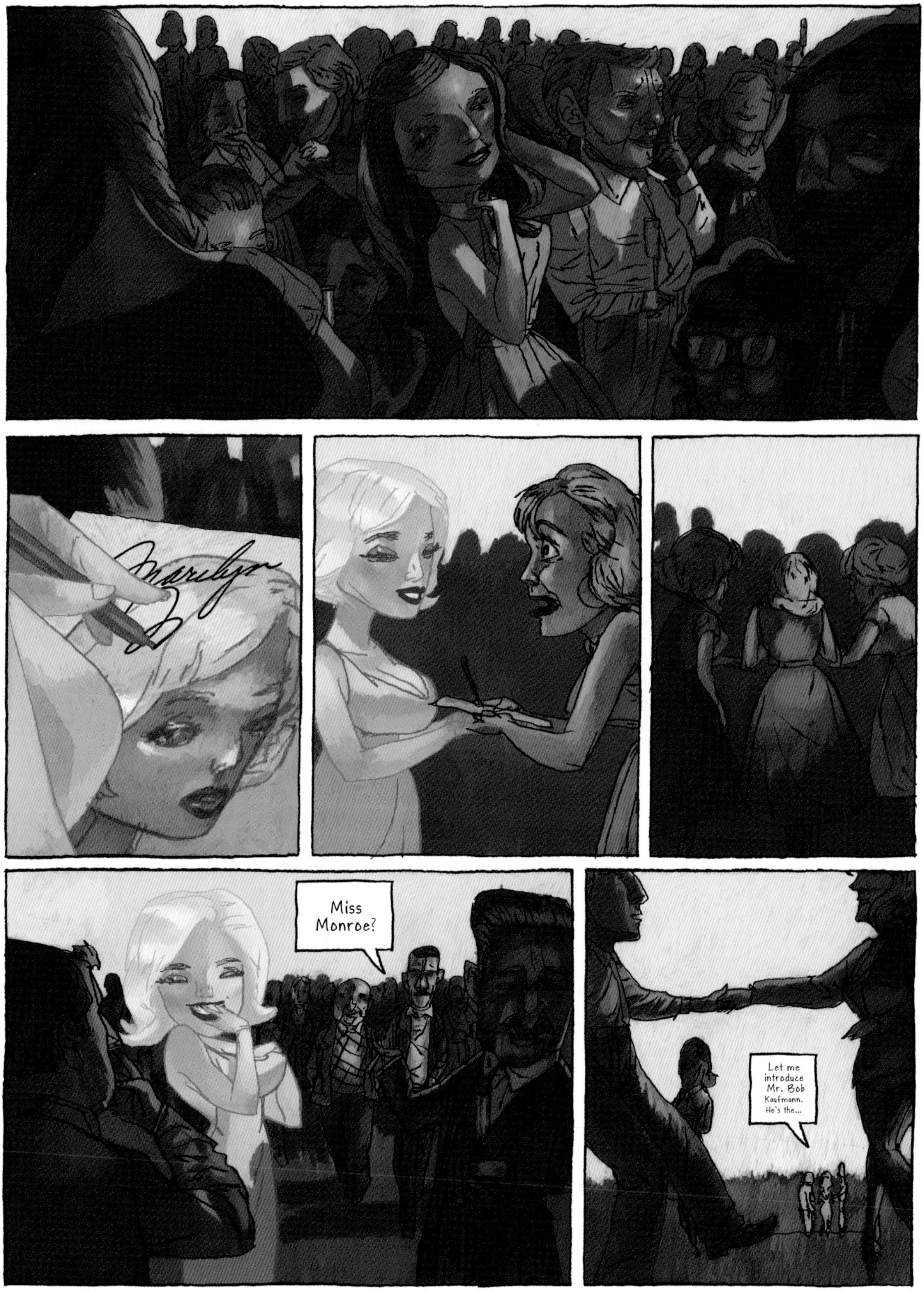
Marilyn
Miss Monroe?
Let me introduce Mr. Bob Kaufmann. He's the...

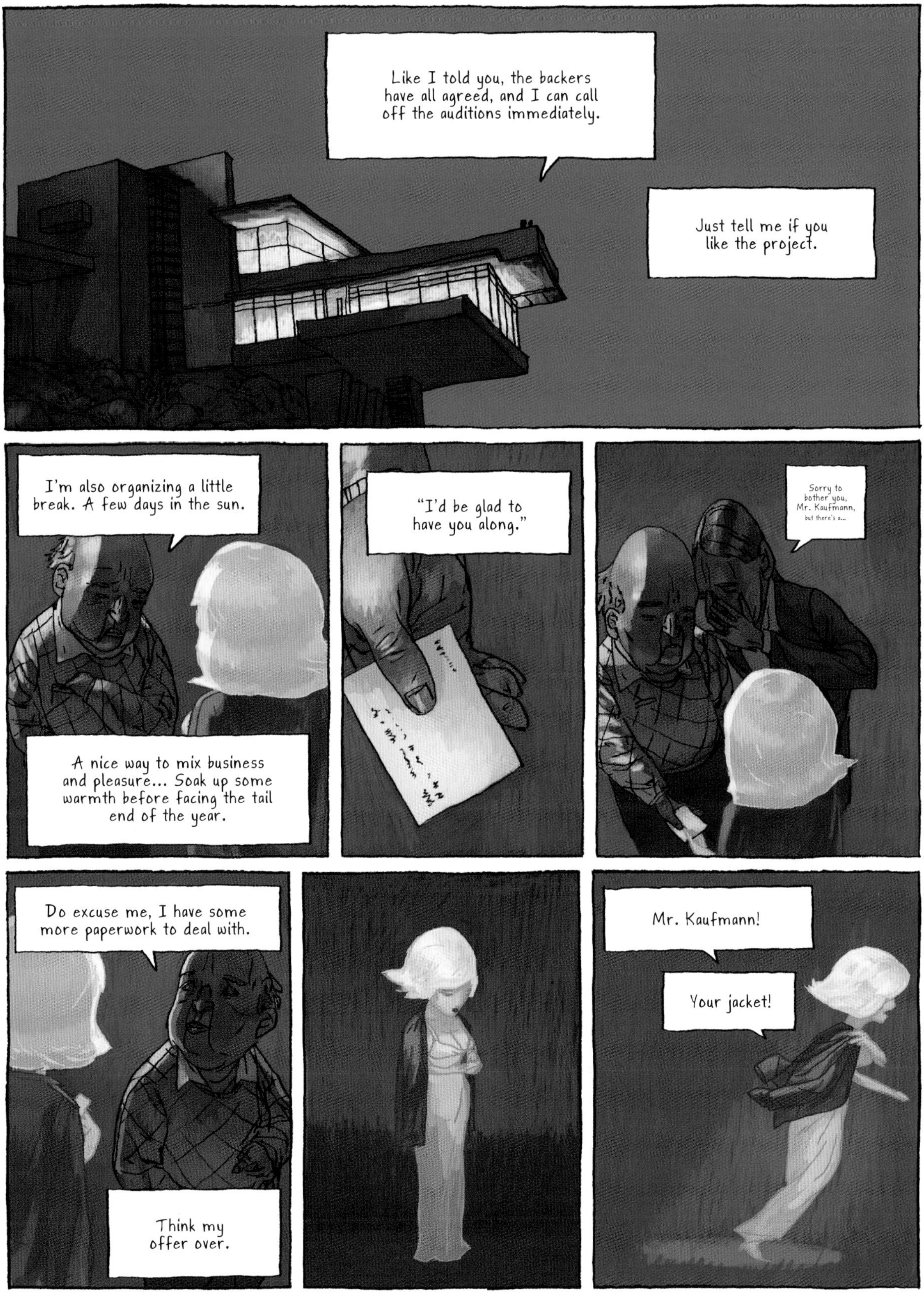
Like I told you, the backers have all agreed, and I can call off the auditions immediately.
Just tell me if you like the project.
I'm also organizing a little break. A few days in the sun.
A nice way to mix business and pleasure... Soak up some warmth before facing the tail end of the year.
"I'd be glad to have you along."
Sorry to bother you, Mr. Kaufmann, but there's a...
Do excuse me, I have some more paperwork to deal with.
Think my offer over.
Mr. Kaufmann!
Your jacket!

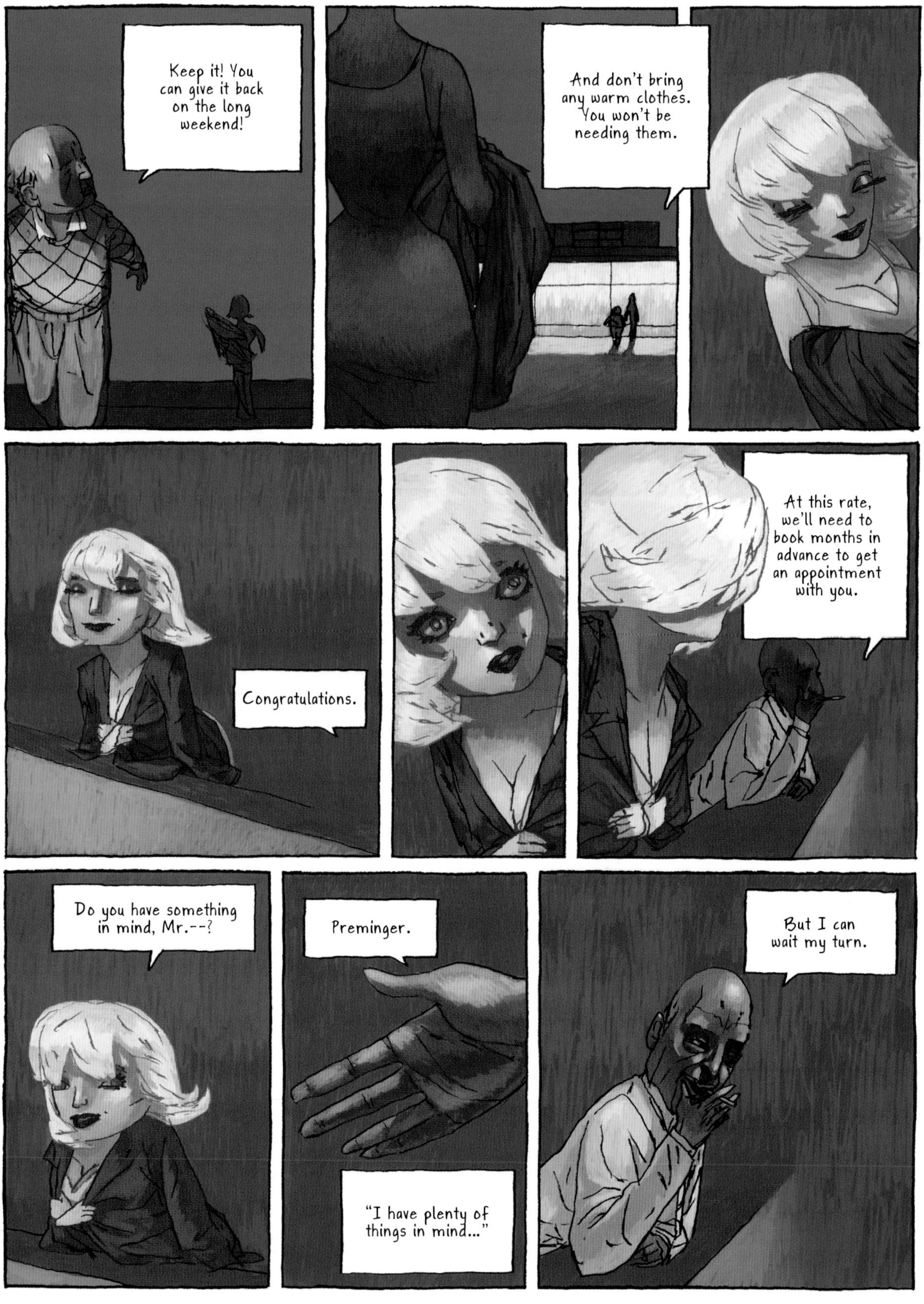
Keep it! You can give it back on the long weekend!
And don't bring any warm clothes. You won't be needing them.
Congratulations.
At this rate, we'll need to book months in advance to get an appointment with you.
Do you have something in mind, Mr.--?
Preminger.
"I have plenty of things in mind..."
But I can wait my turn.

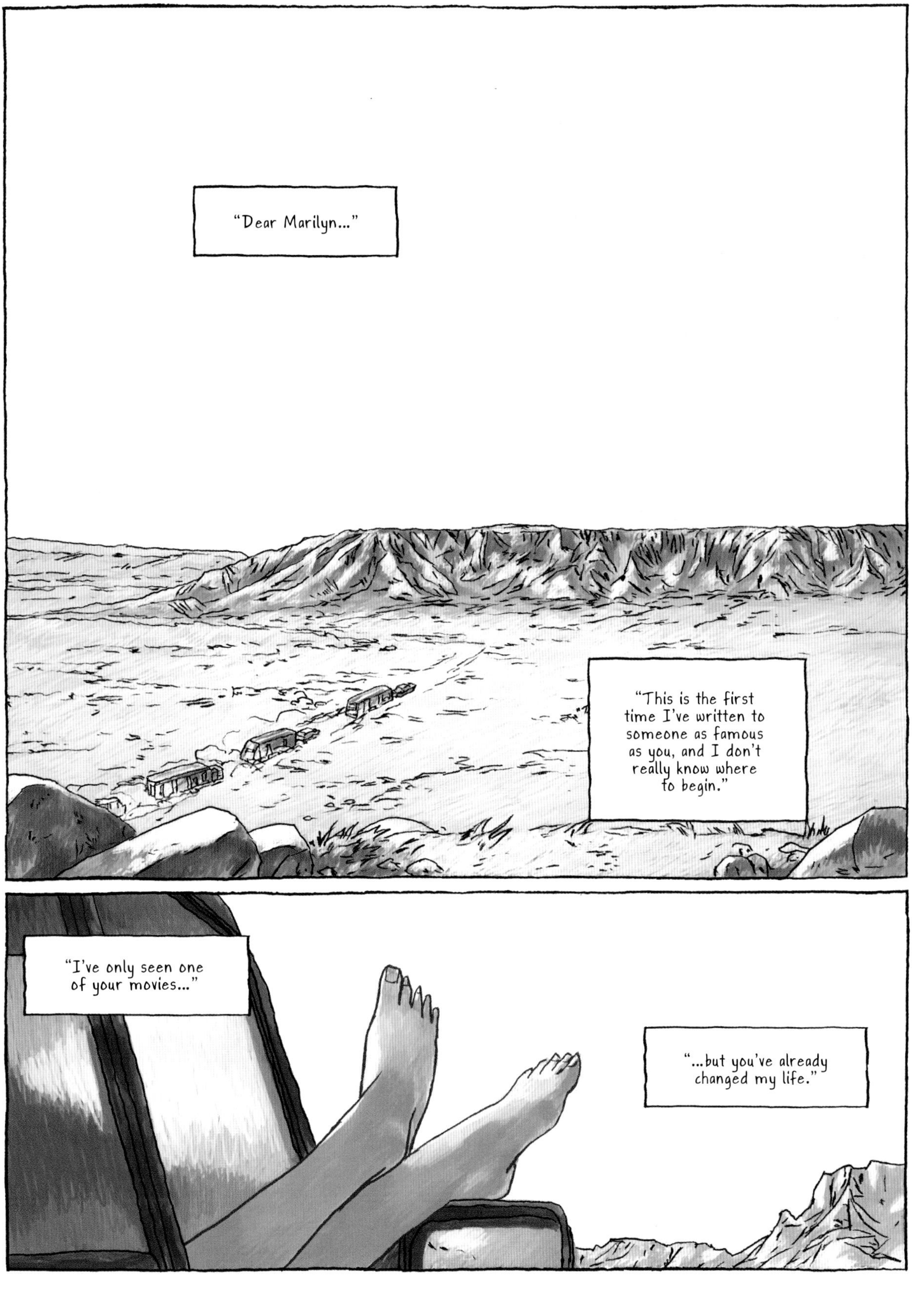
"Dear Marilyn..."
"This is the first time I've written to someone as famous as you, and I don't really know where to begin."
"I've only seen one of your movies..."
"...but you've already changed my life."

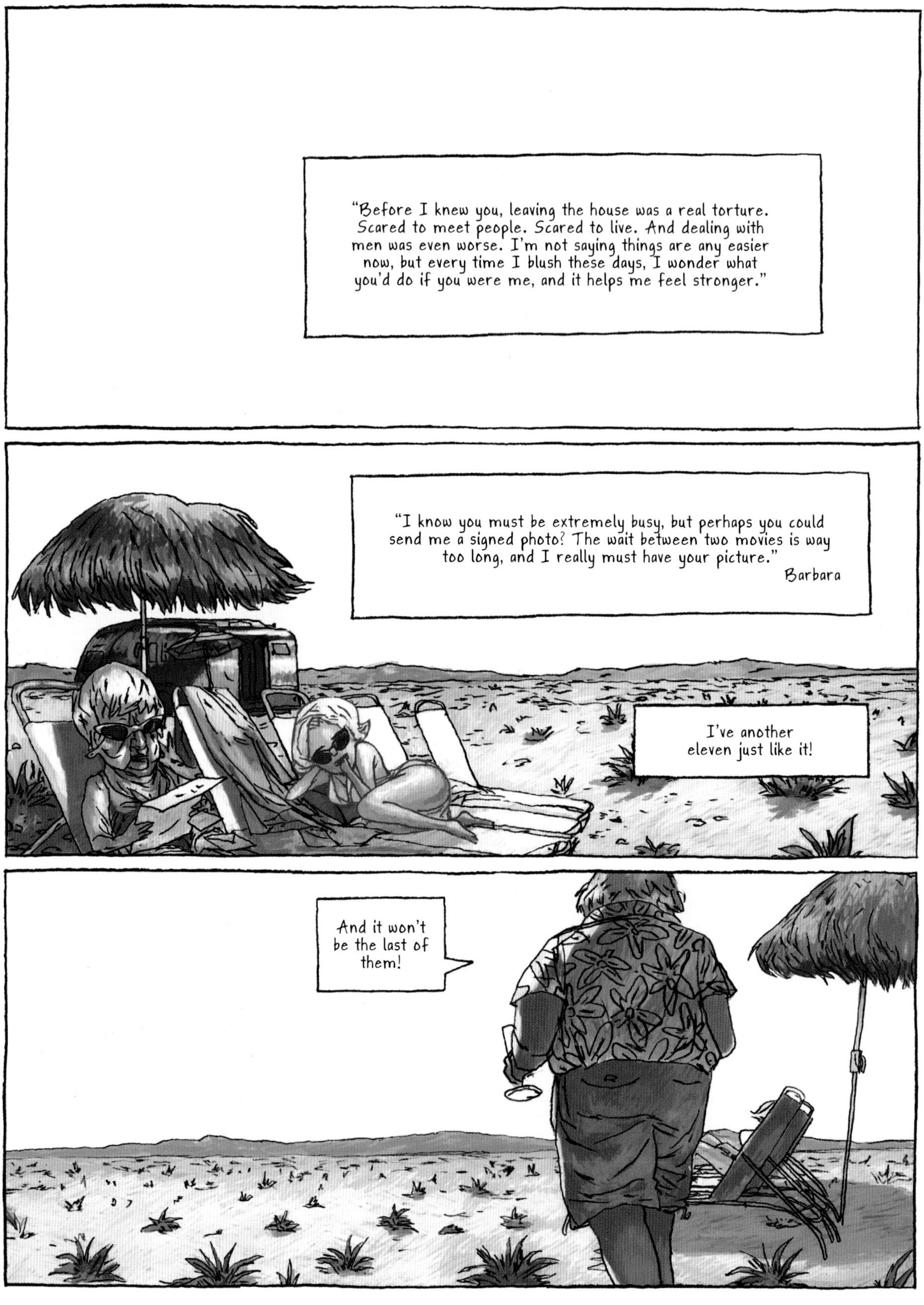
"Before I knew you, leaving the house was a real torture. Scared to meet people. Scared to live. And dealing with men was even worse. I'm not saying things are any easier now, but every time I blush these days, I wonder what you'd do if you were me, and it helps me feel stronger."
"I know you must be extremely busy, but perhaps you could send me a signed photo? The wait between two movies is way too long, and I really must have your picture."
Barbara
I've another eleven just like it!
And it won't be the last of them!

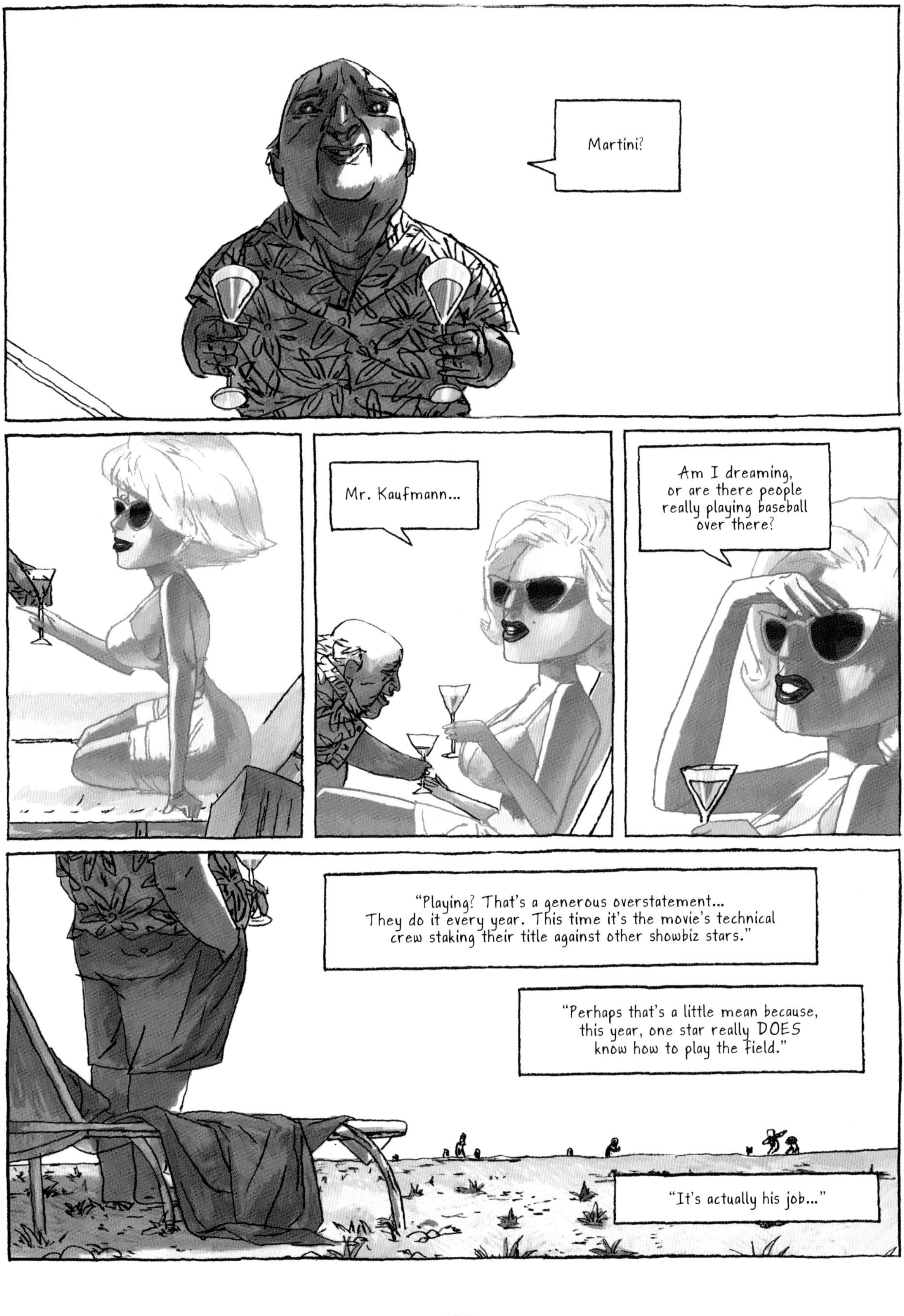
Martini?
Mr. Kaufmann...
Am I dreaming, or are there people really playing baseball over there?
"Playing? That's a generous overstatement... They do it every year. This time it's the movie's technical crew staking their title against other showbiz stars."
"Perhaps that's a little mean because, this year, one star really DOES know how to play the field."
"It's actually his job..."

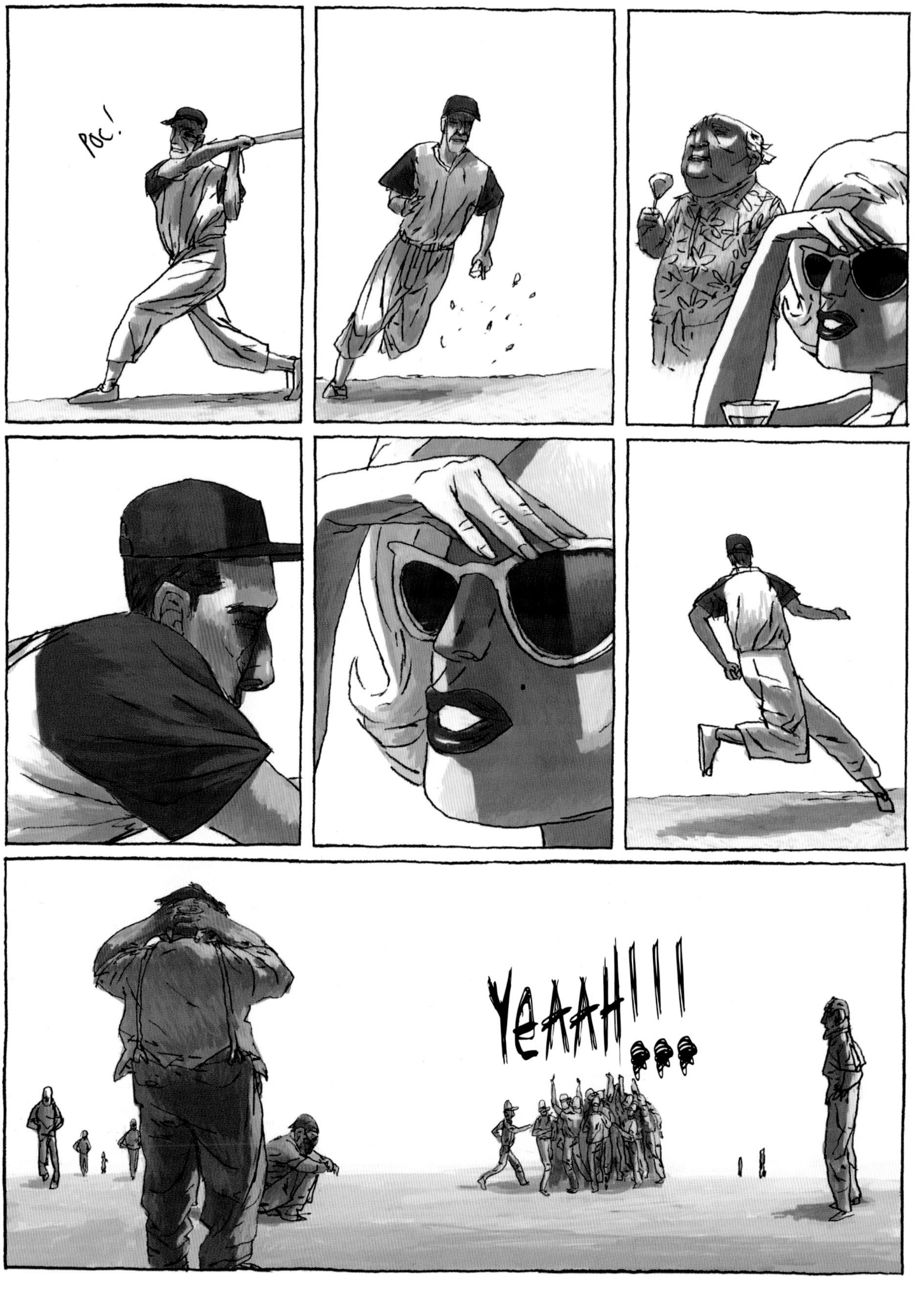
Poc!
YEAHHH!!!

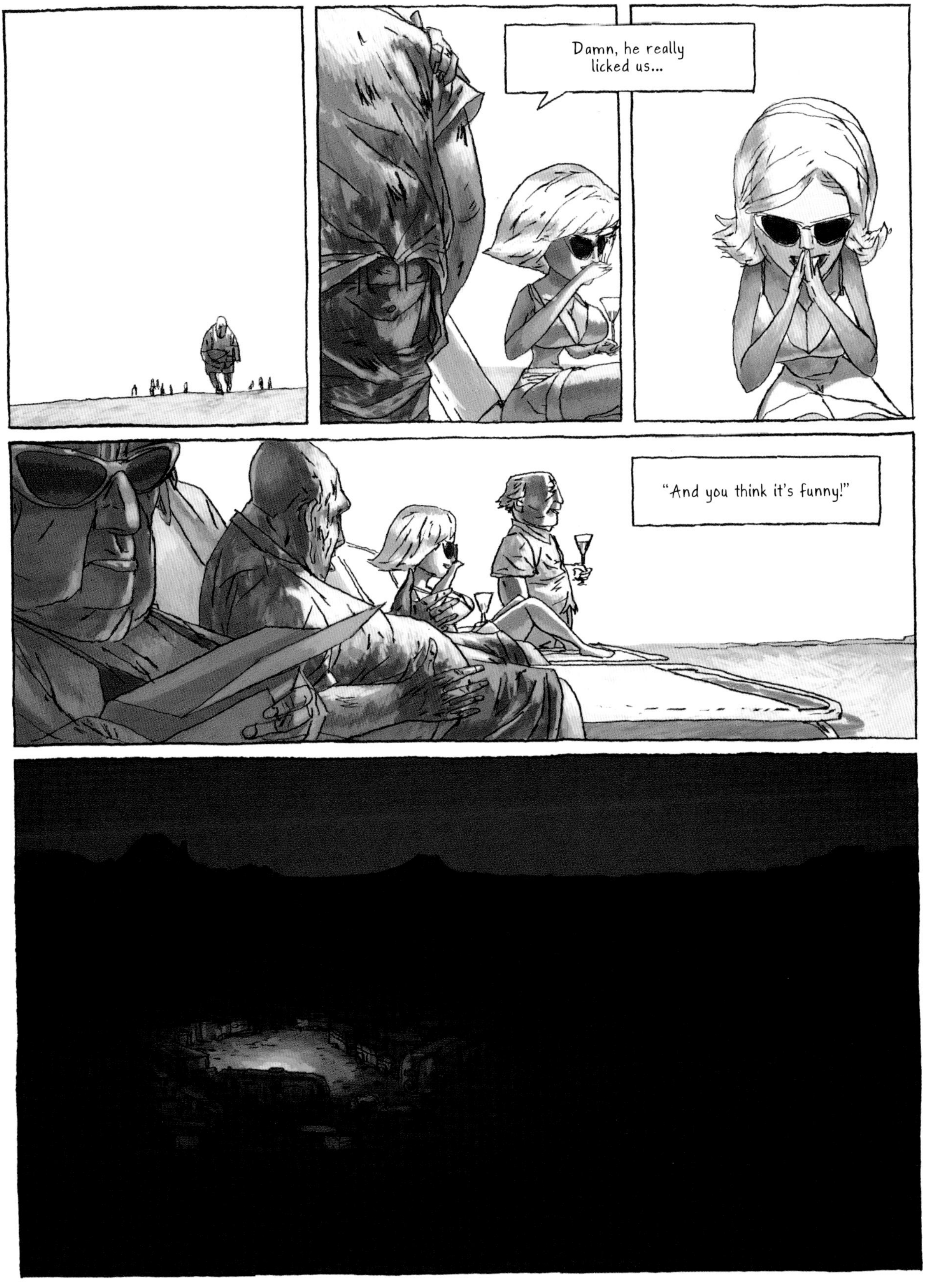
Damn, he really licked us...
"And you think it's funny!"

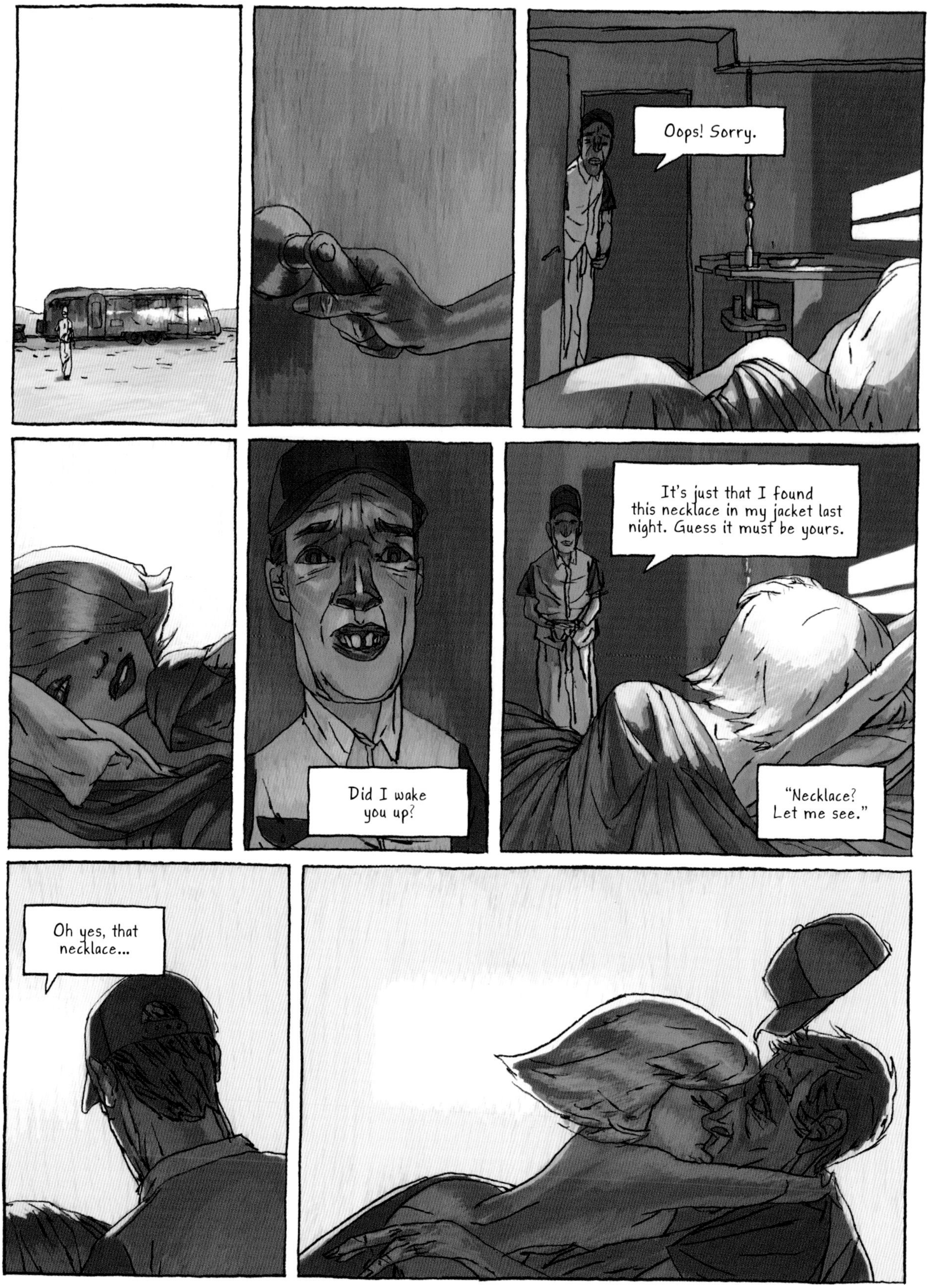
Oops! Sorry.
Did I wake you up?
It's just that I found this necklace in my jacket last night. Guess it must be yours.
"Necklace? Let me see."
Oh yes, that necklace...

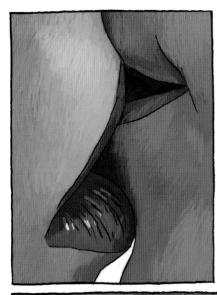
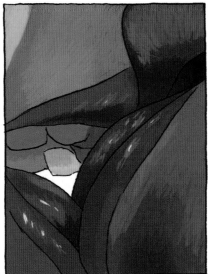
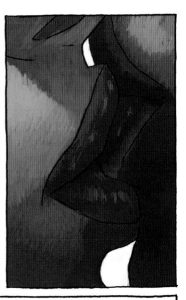

I guess I can officially say that professional baseballers aren't too good at reading between the lines!

"Let me tell you, girl, professional baseballers don't get paid to think, just to play and win..."

"...and make a stack of money."

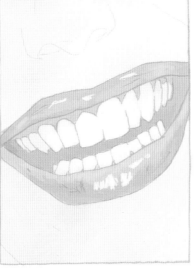

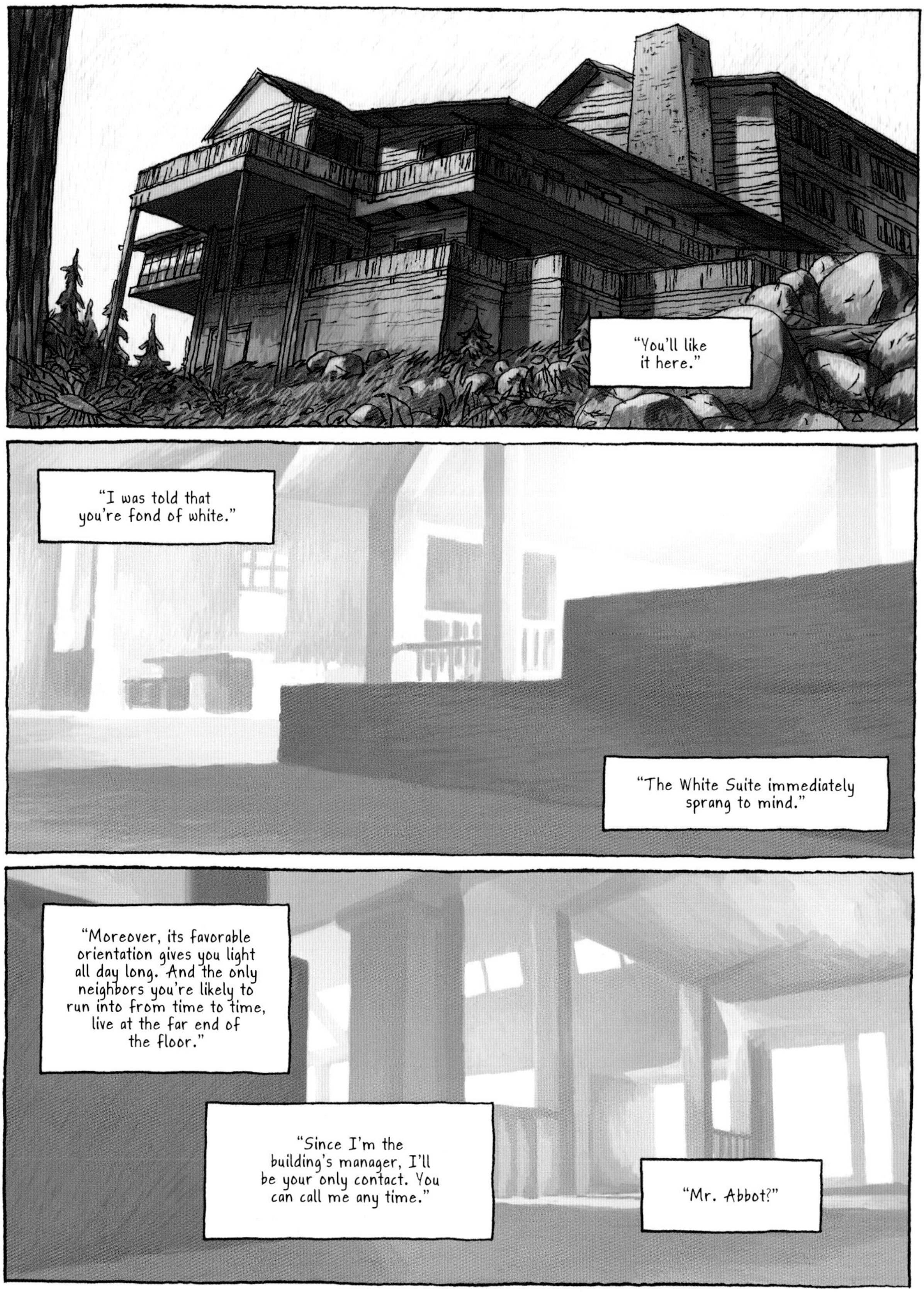
"You'll like it here."
"I was told that you're fond of white."
"The White Suite immediately sprang to mind."
"Moreover, its favorable orientation gives you light all day long. And the only neighbors you're likely to run into from time to time, live at the far end of the floor."
"Since I'm the building's manager, I'll be your only contact. You can call me any time."
"Mr. Abbot?"

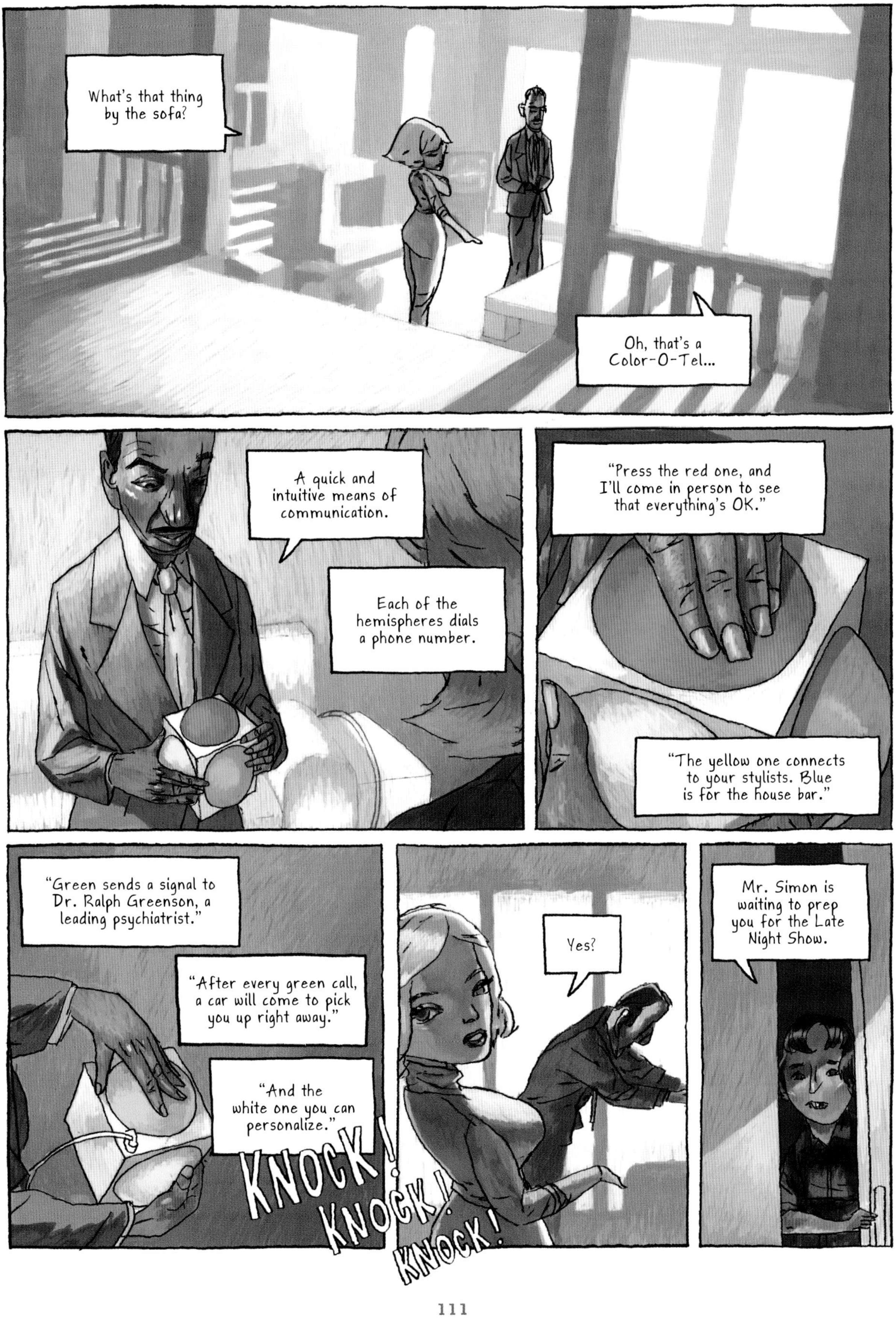
What's that thing by the sofa?
Oh, that's a Color-O-Tel...
A quick and intuitive means of communication.
Each of the hemispheres dials a phone number.
"Press the red one, and I'll come in person to see that everything's OK."
"The yellow one connects to your stylists. Blue is for the house bar."
"Green sends a signal to Dr. Ralph Greenson, a leading psychiatrist."
"After every green call, a car will come to pick you up right away."
"And the white one you can personalize."
KNOCK! KNOCK! KNOCK!
Yes?
Mr. Simon is waiting to prep you for the Late Night Show.

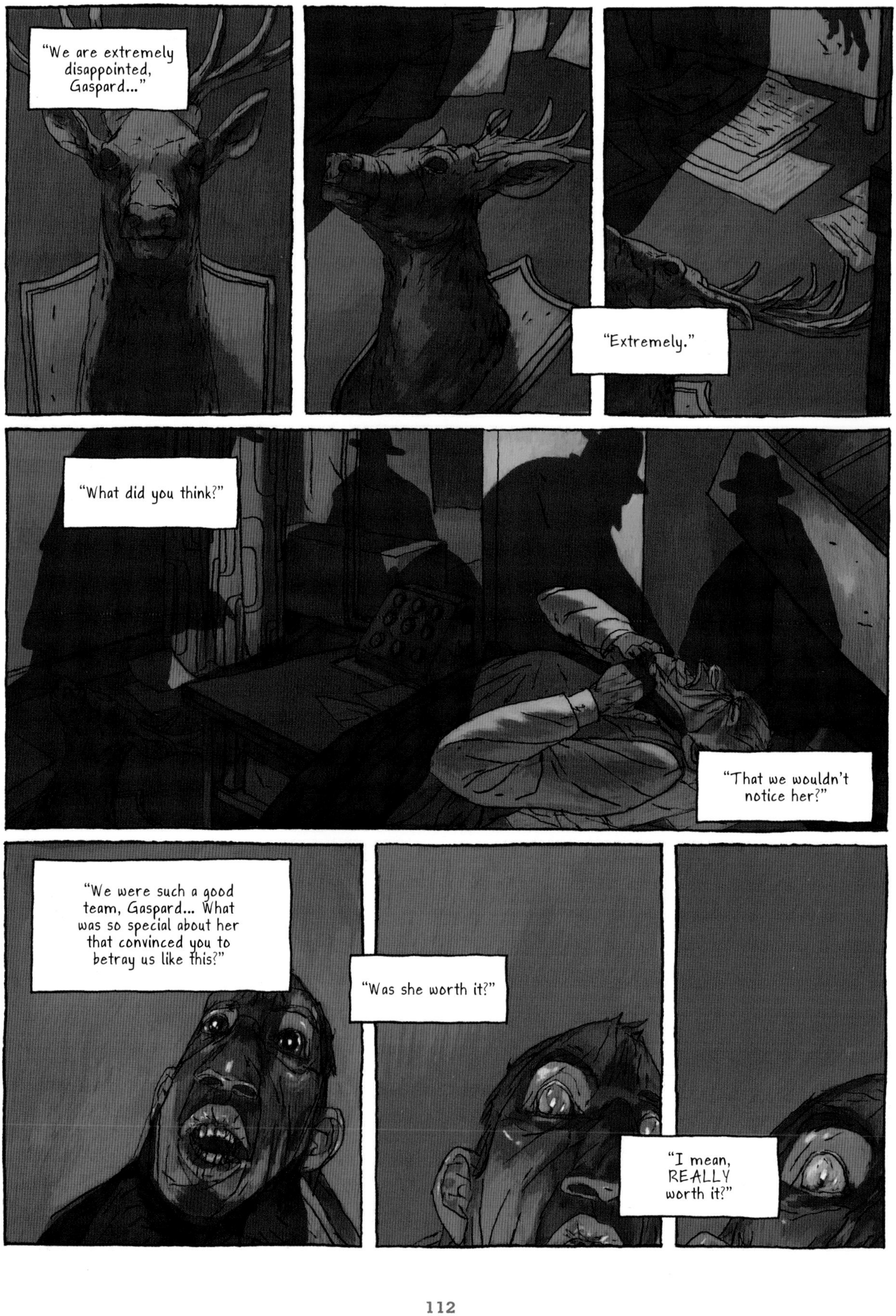
"We are extremely disappointed, Gaspard..."
"Extremely."
"What did you think?"
"That we wouldn't notice her?"
"We were such a good team, Gaspard... What was so special about her that convinced you to betray us like this?"
"Was she worth it?"
"I mean, REALLY worth it?"

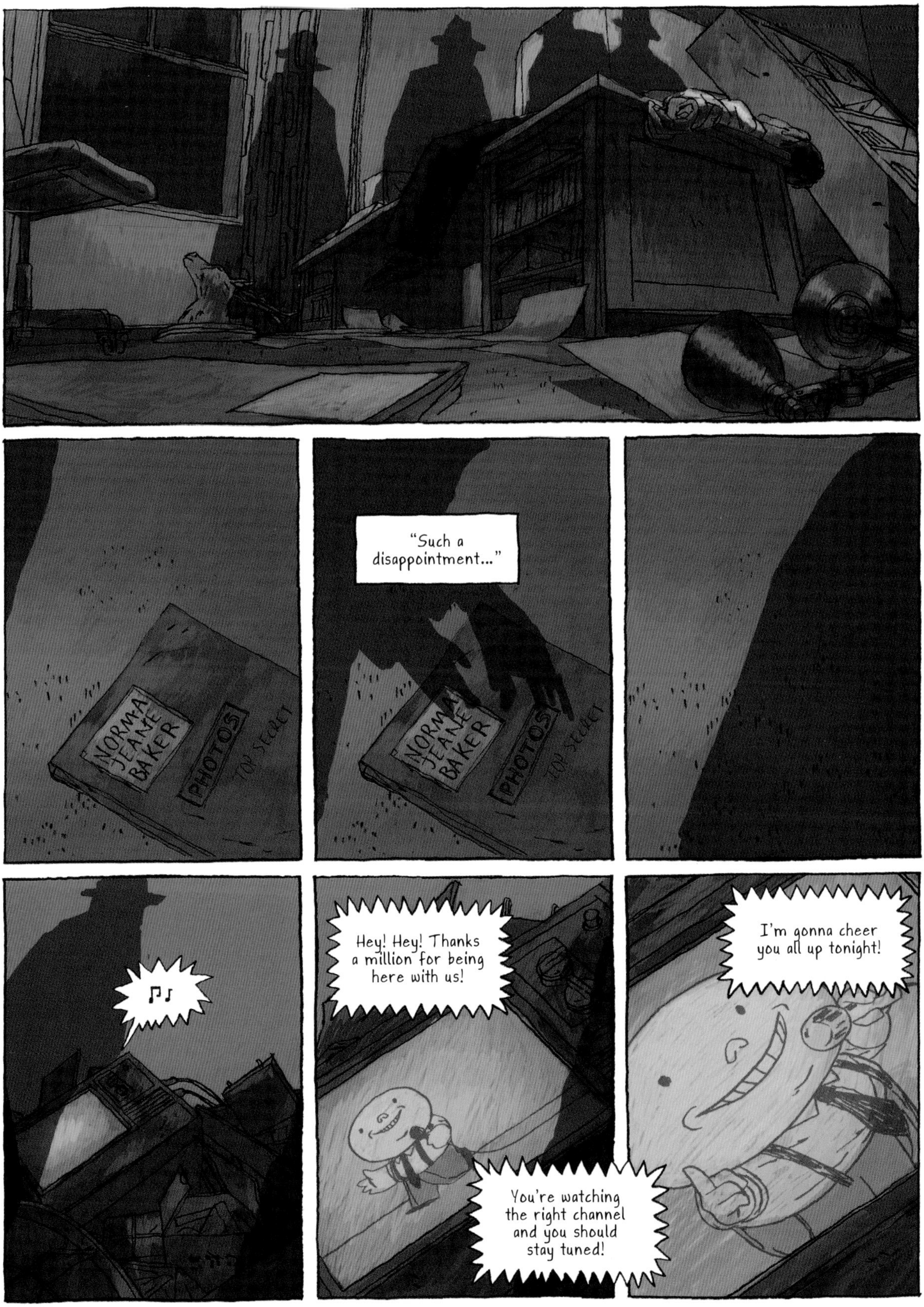

NORMA JEANE BAKER
PHOTOS
TOP SECRET
"Such a disappointment..."
NORMA JEANE BAKER
PHOTOS
TOP SECRET
♫♪
Hey! Hey! Thanks a million for being here with us!
You're watching the right channel and you should stay tuned!
I'm gonna cheer you all up tonight!

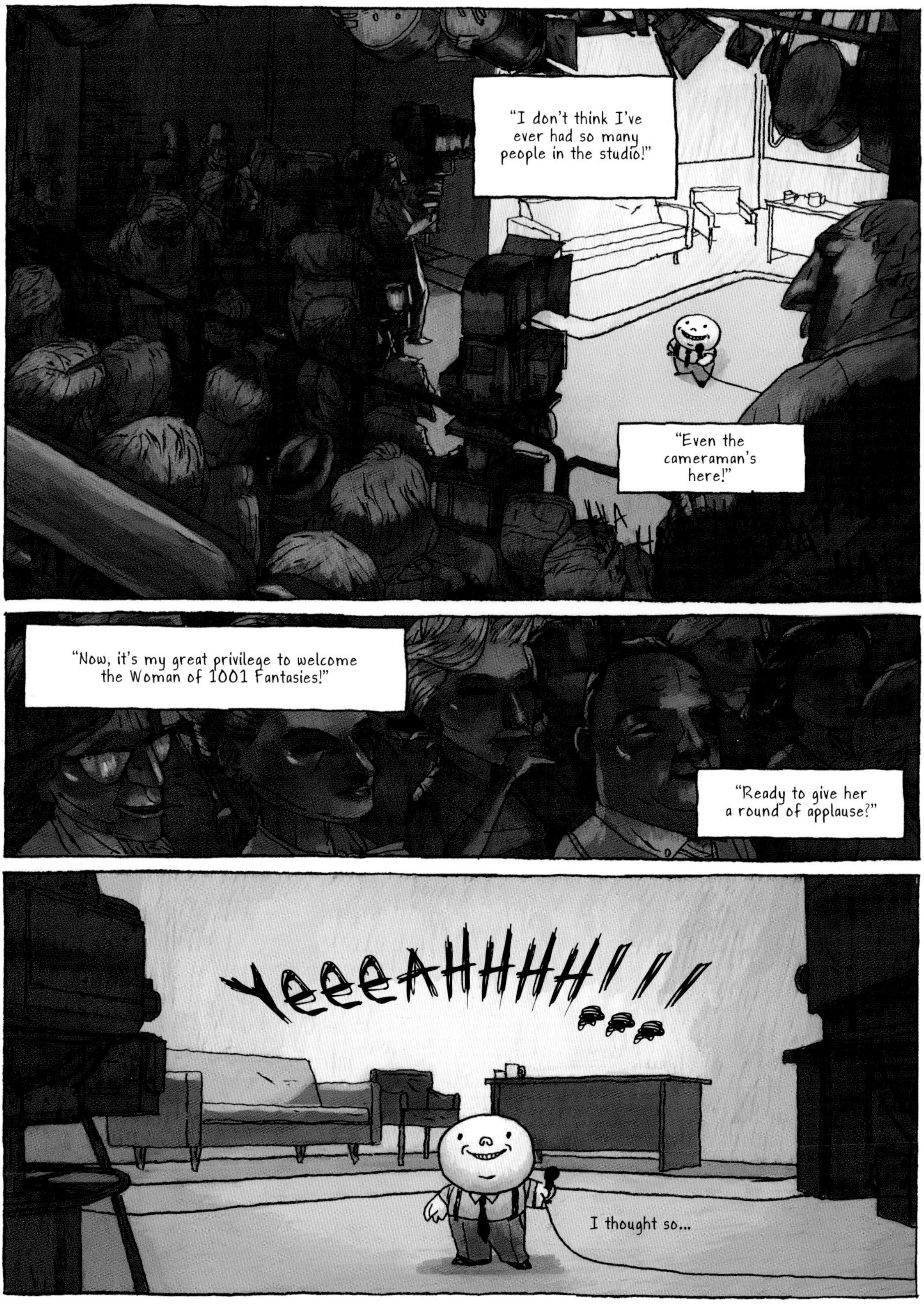
"I don't think I've ever had so many people in the studio!"
"Even the cameraman's here!"
"Now, it's my great privilege to welcome the Woman of 1001 Fantasies!"
"Ready to give her a round of applause?"
YEEEAHHHH!!!!
I thought so...

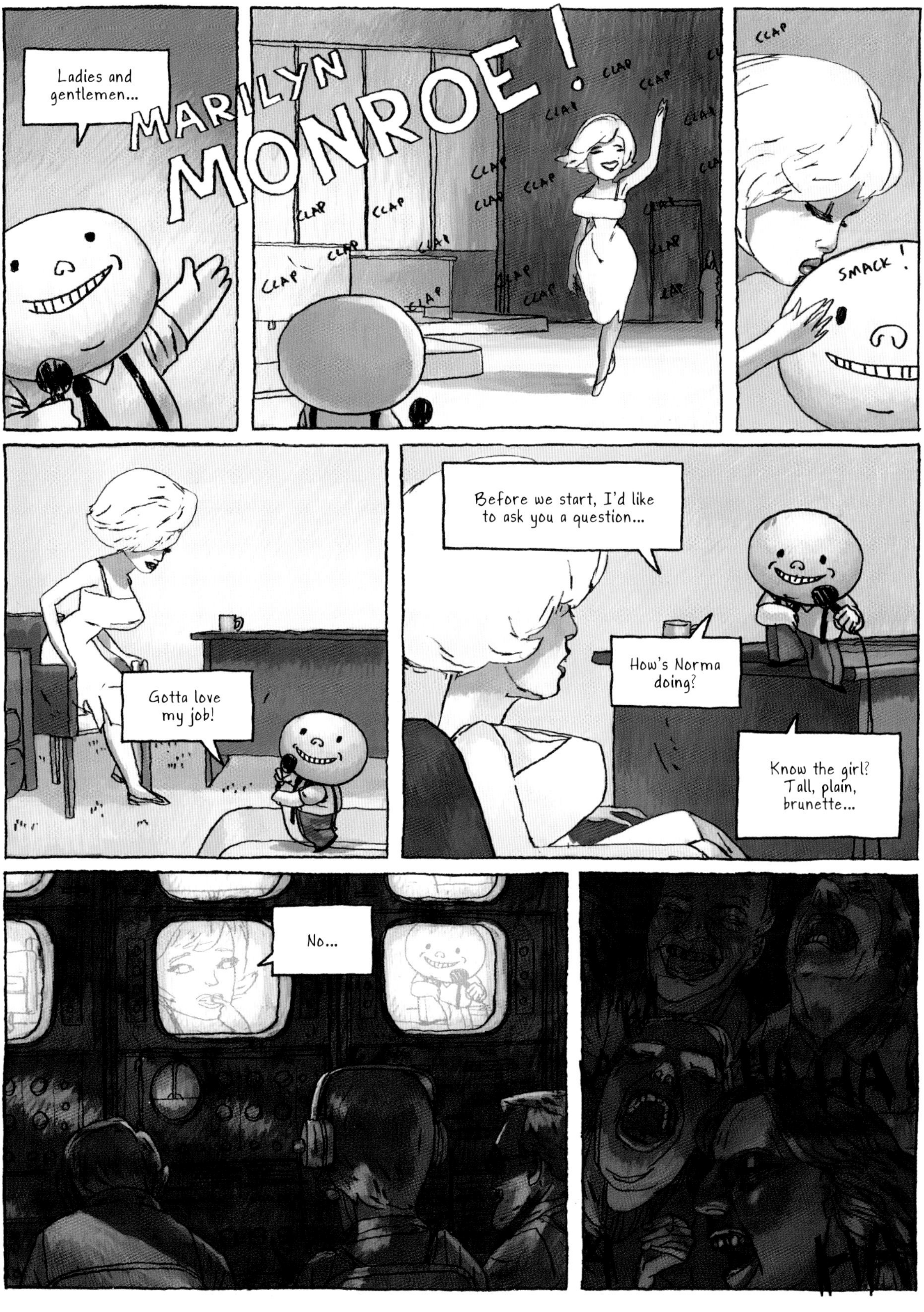
Ladies and gentlemen...
MARILYN MONROE!
CLAP CLAP CLAP CLAP CLAP CLAP CLAP CLAP CLAP CLAP CLAP CLAP CLAP CLAP CLAP CLAP CLAP
CLAP
SMACK!
Gotta love my job!
Before we start, I'd like to ask you a question...
How's Norma doing?
Know the girl? Tall, plain, brunette...
No...

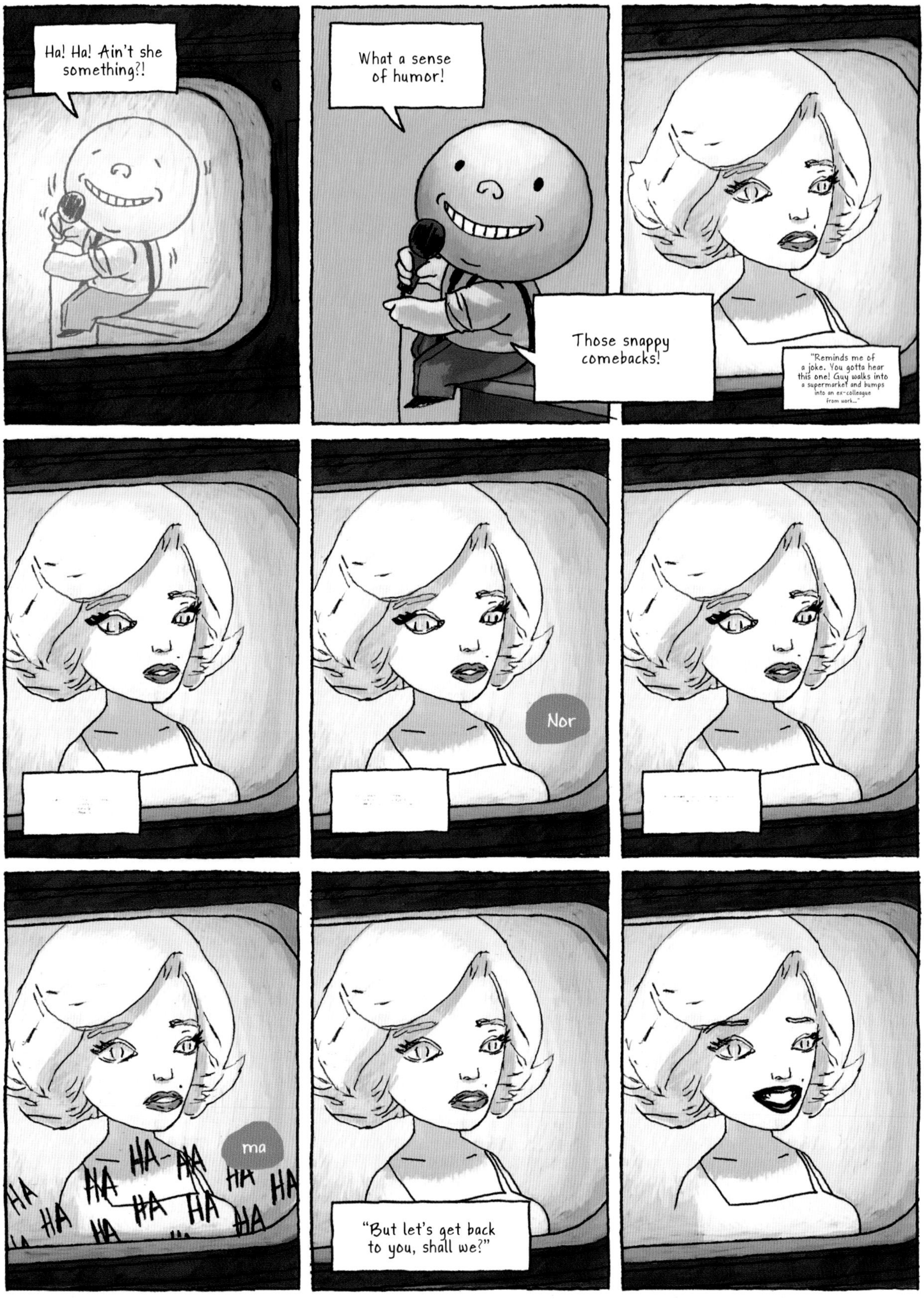
Ha! Ha! Ain't she something?!
What a sense of humor!
Those snappy comebacks!
"Reminds me of a joke. You gotta hear this one! Guy walks into a supermarket and bumps into an ex-colleague from work..."
Nor
ma
HA HA HA HA HA HA HA HA HA HA HA HA
"But let's get back to you, shall we?"

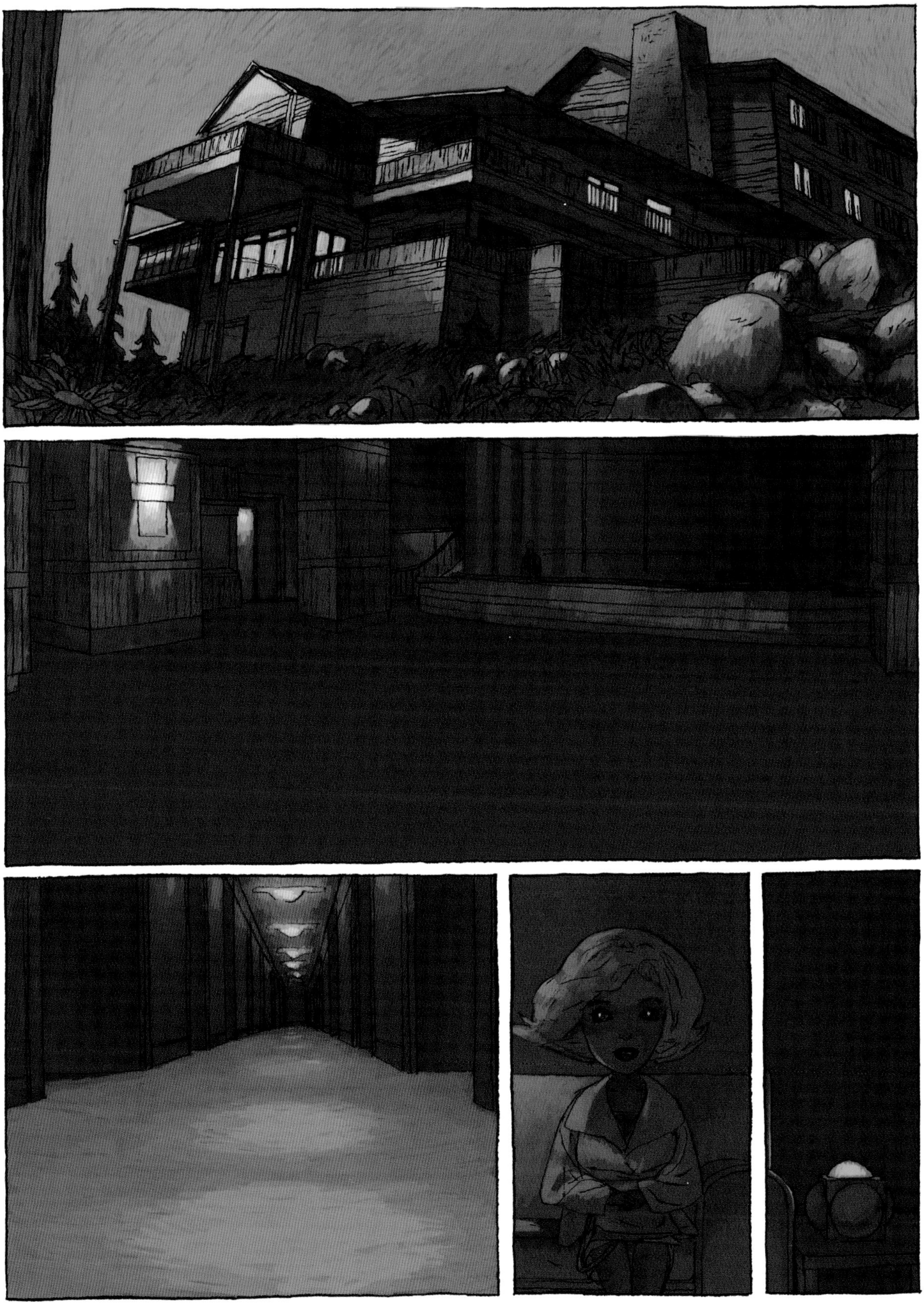

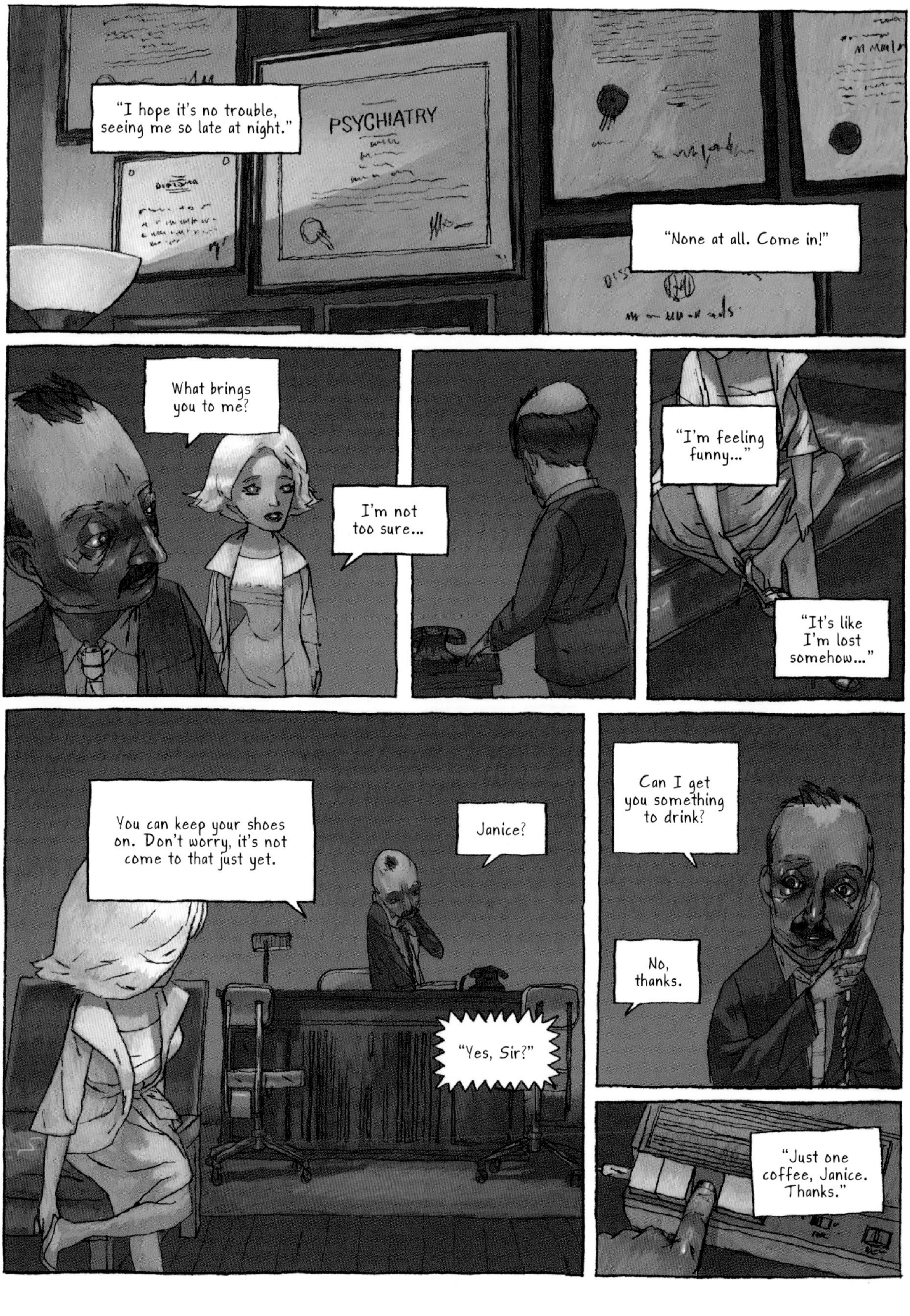
"I hope it's no trouble, seeing me so late at night."
PSYCHIATRY
"None at all. Come in!"
What brings you to me?
I'm not too sure...
"I'm feeling funny..."
"It's like I'm lost somehow..."
You can keep your shoes on. Don't worry, it's not come to that just yet.
Janice?
"Yes, Sir?"
Can I get you something to drink?
No, thanks.
"Just one coffee, Janice. Thanks."

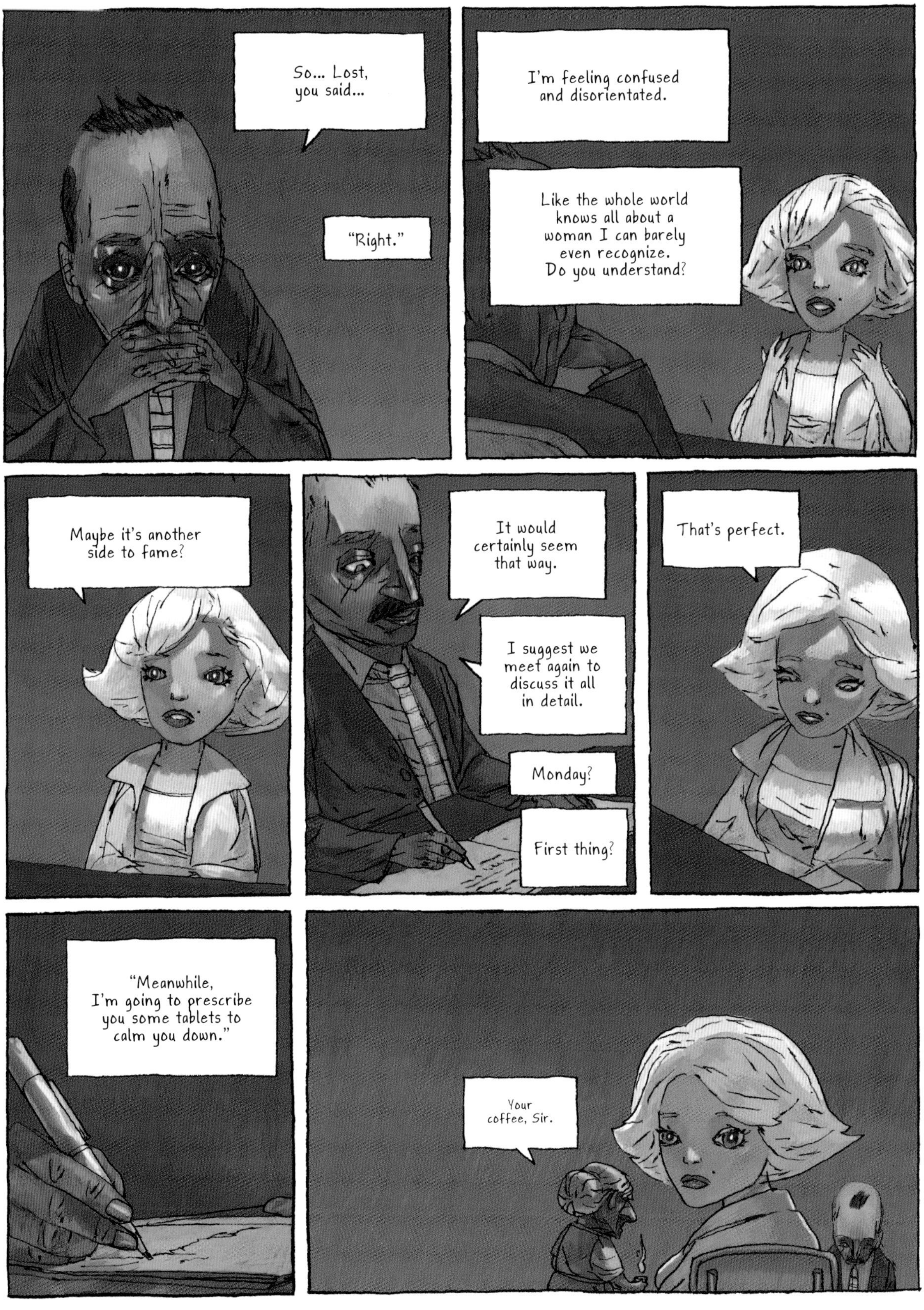
So... Lost, you said...
"Right."
I'm feeling confused and disorientated.
Like the whole world knows all about a woman I can barely even recognize. Do you understand?
Maybe it's another side to fame?
It would certainly seem that way.
I suggest we meet again to discuss it all in detail.
Monday?
First thing?
That's perfect.
"Meanwhile, I'm going to prescribe you some tablets to calm you down."
Your coffee, Sir.

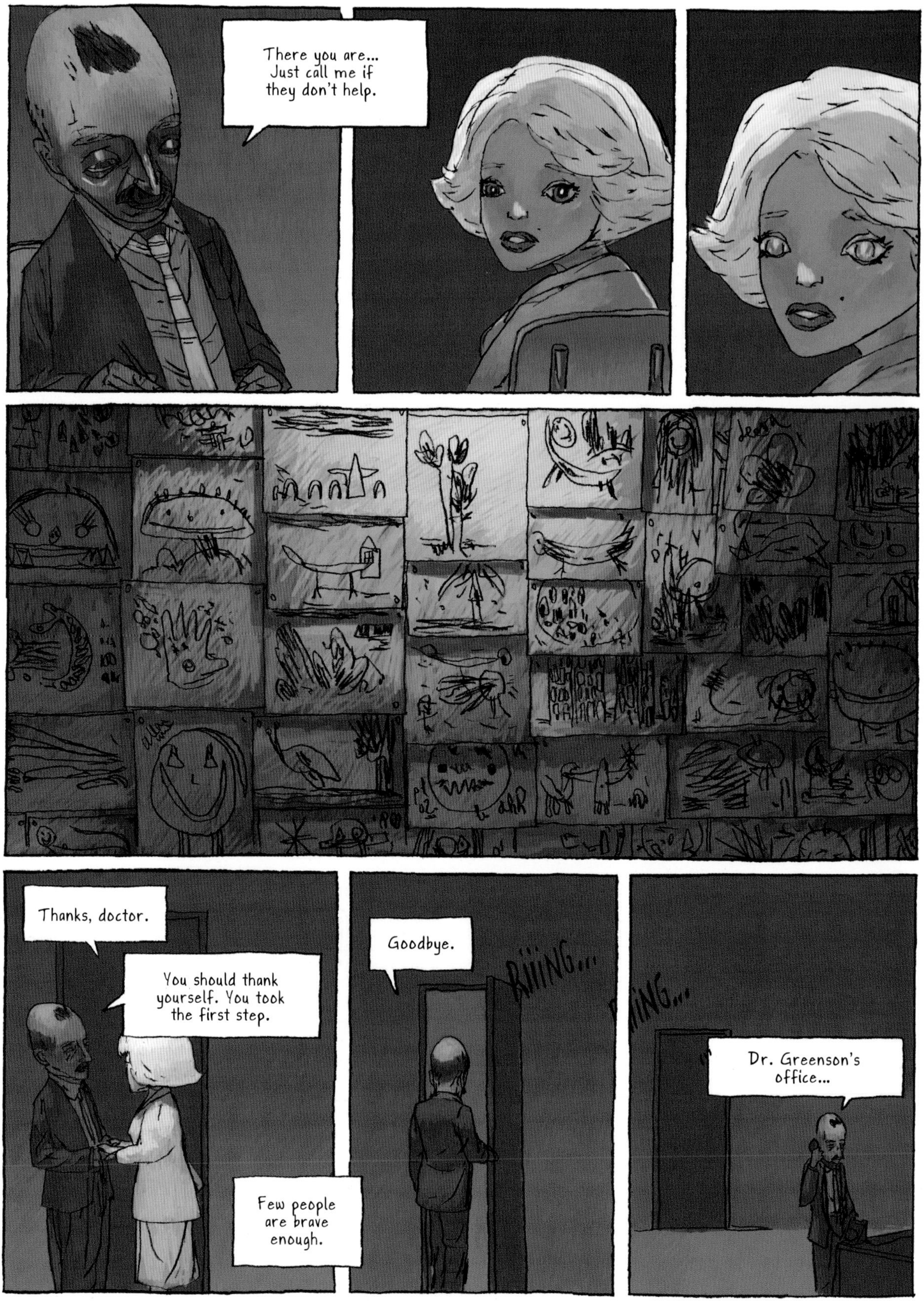
There you are... Just call me if they don't help.
Thanks, doctor.
You should thank yourself. You took the first step.
Few people are brave enough.
Goodbye.
RIIING...
RIIING...
Dr. Greenson's office...

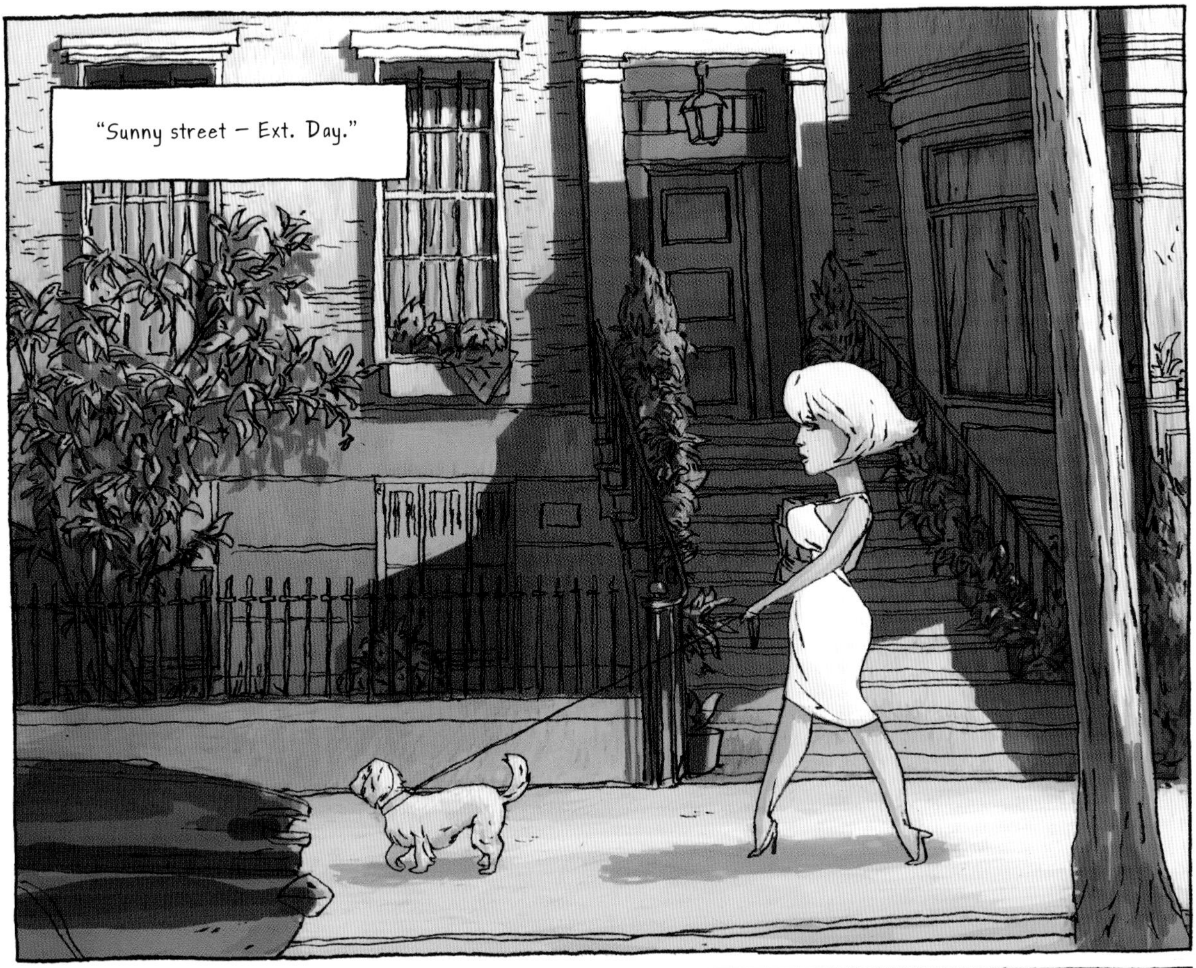
"Sunny street – Ext. Day."

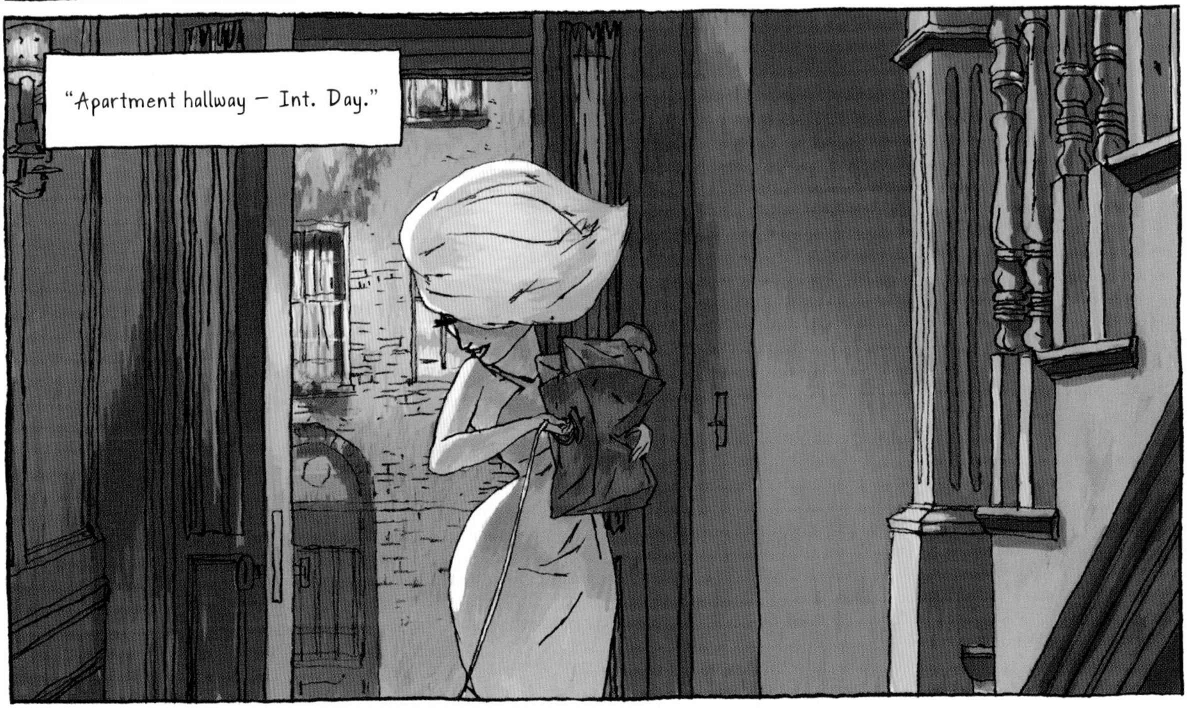
"Apartment hallway – Int. Day."

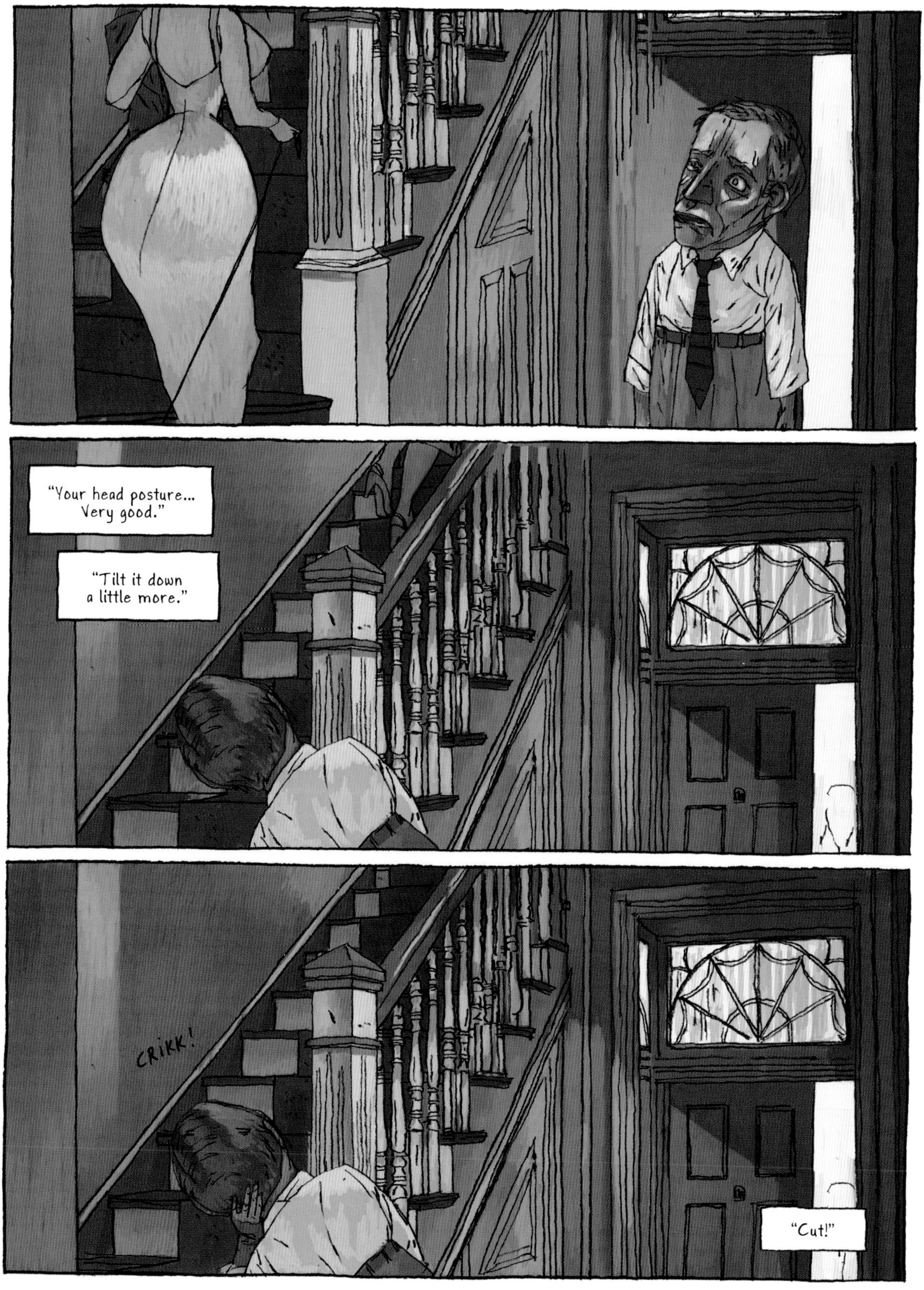
"Your head posture...
Very good."
"Tilt it down
a little more."
CRIKK!
"Cut!"

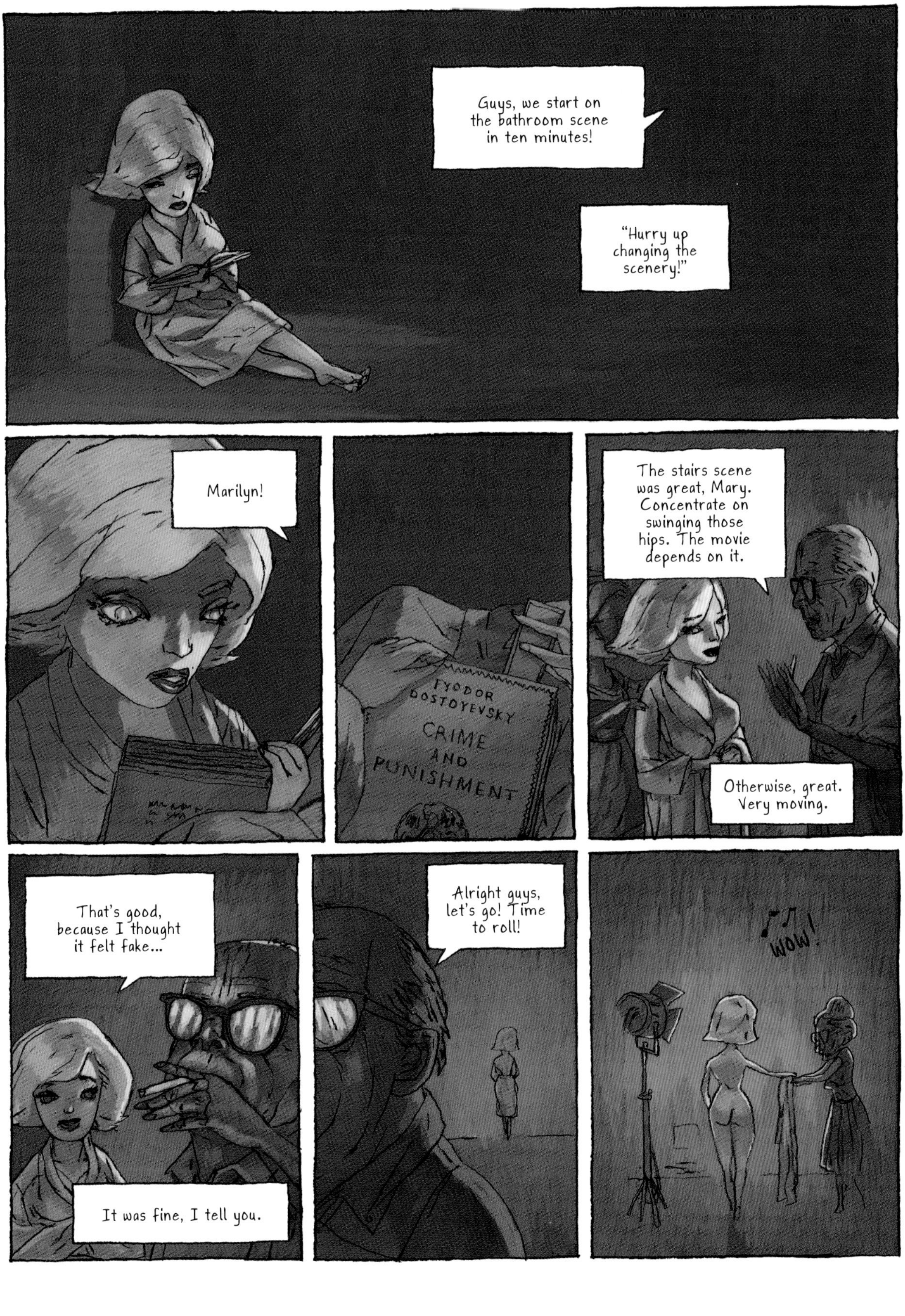
Guys, we start on the bathroom scene in ten minutes!
"Hurry up changing the scenery!"
Marilyn!
FYODOR DOSTOYEVSKY CRIME AND PUNISHMENT
The stairs scene was great, Mary. Concentrate on swinging those hips. The movie depends on it.
Otherwise, great. Very moving.
That's good, because I thought it felt fake...
It was fine, I tell you.
Alright guys, let's go! Time to roll!
WOW!

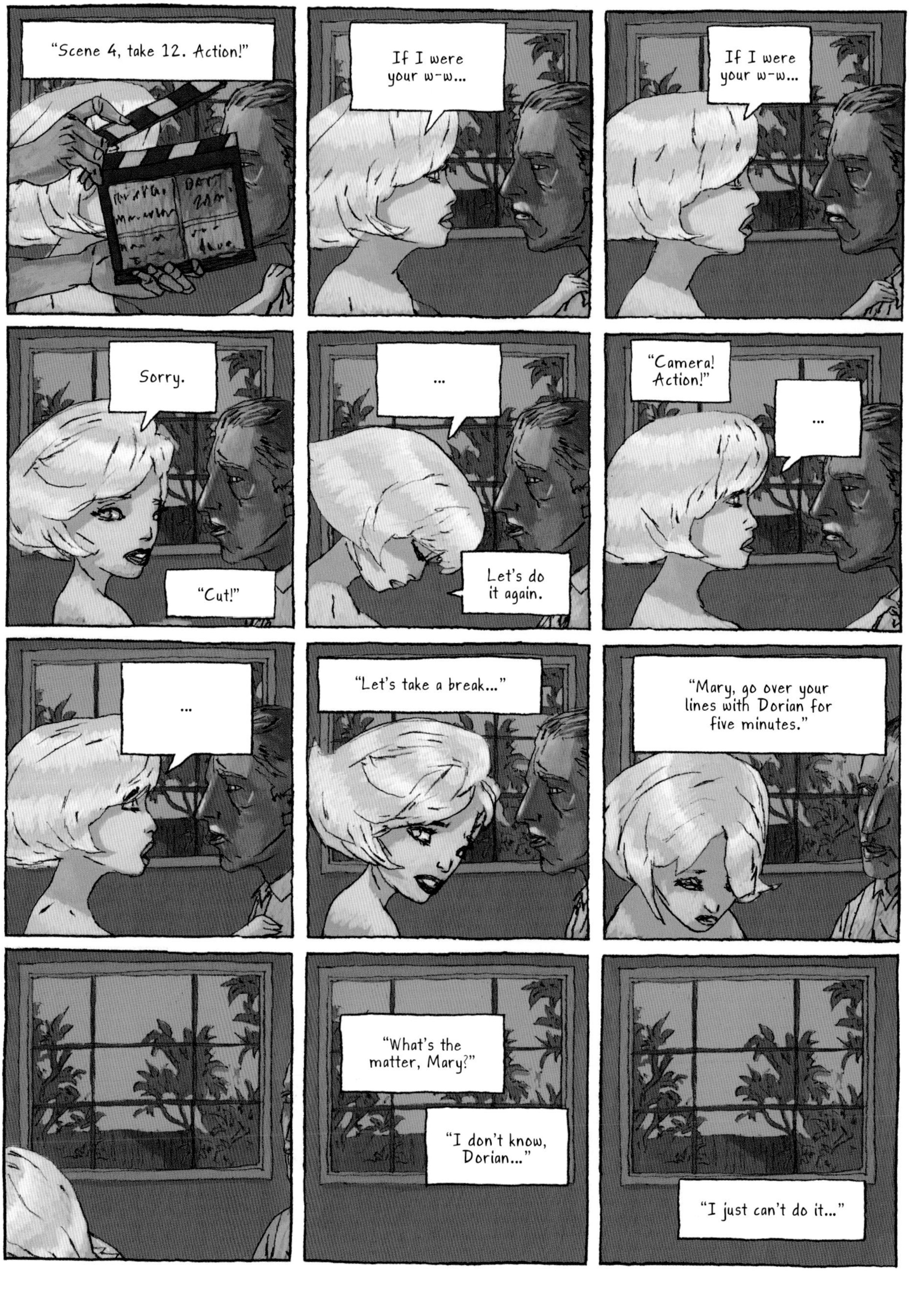
"Scene 4, take 12. Action!"
If I were your w-w...
If I were your w-w...
Sorry.
"Cut!"
...
Let's do it again.
"Camera! Action!"
...
...
"Let's take a break..."
"Mary, go over your lines with Dorian for five minutes."
"What's the matter, Mary?"
"I don't know, Dorian..."
"I just can't do it..."

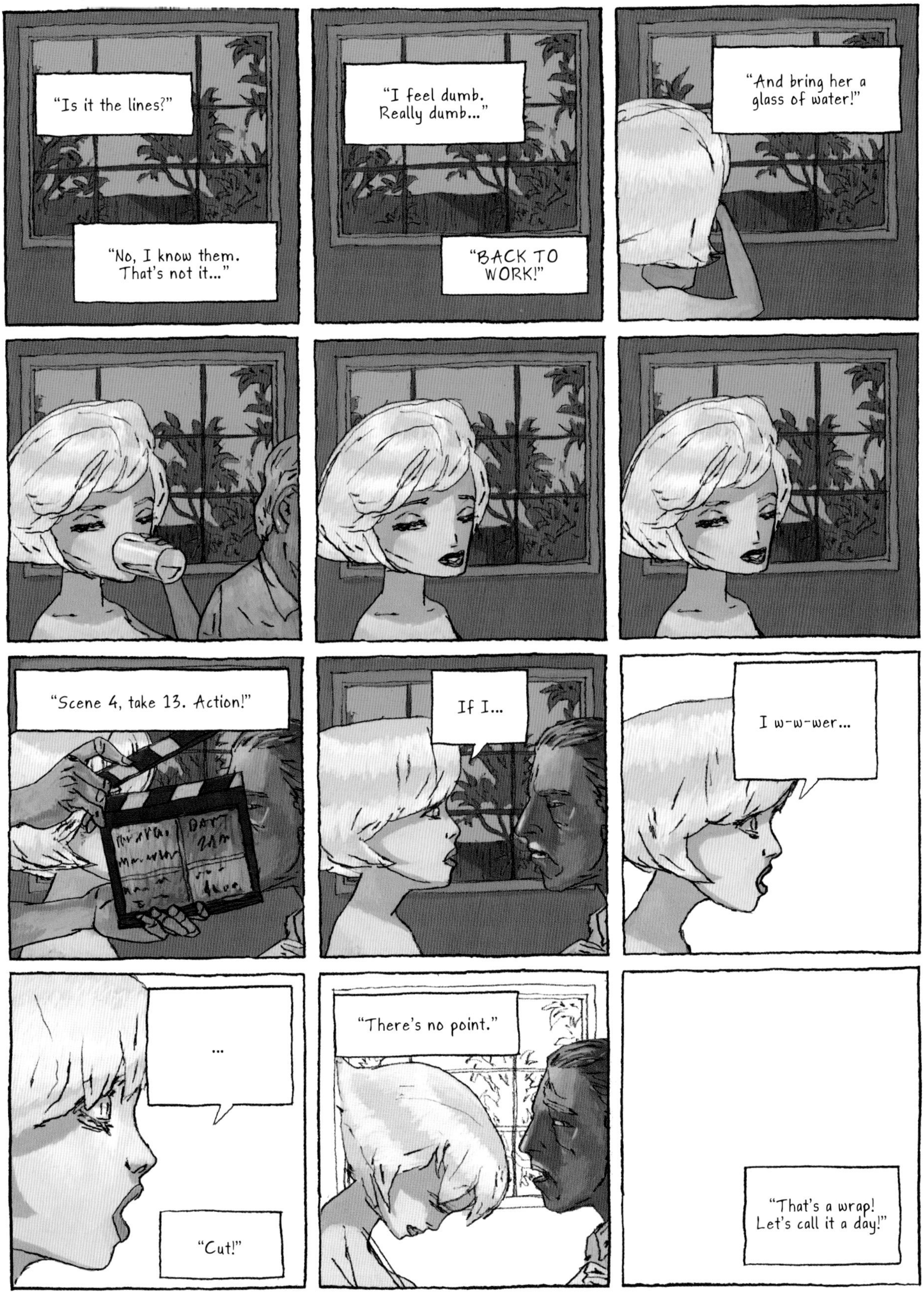
"Is it the lines?"
"No, I know them. That's not it..."
"I feel dumb. Really dumb..."
"BACK TO WORK!"
"And bring her a glass of water!"
"Scene 4, take 13. Action!"
If I...
I w-w-wer...
...
"Cut!"
"There's no point."
"That's a wrap! Let's call it a day!"

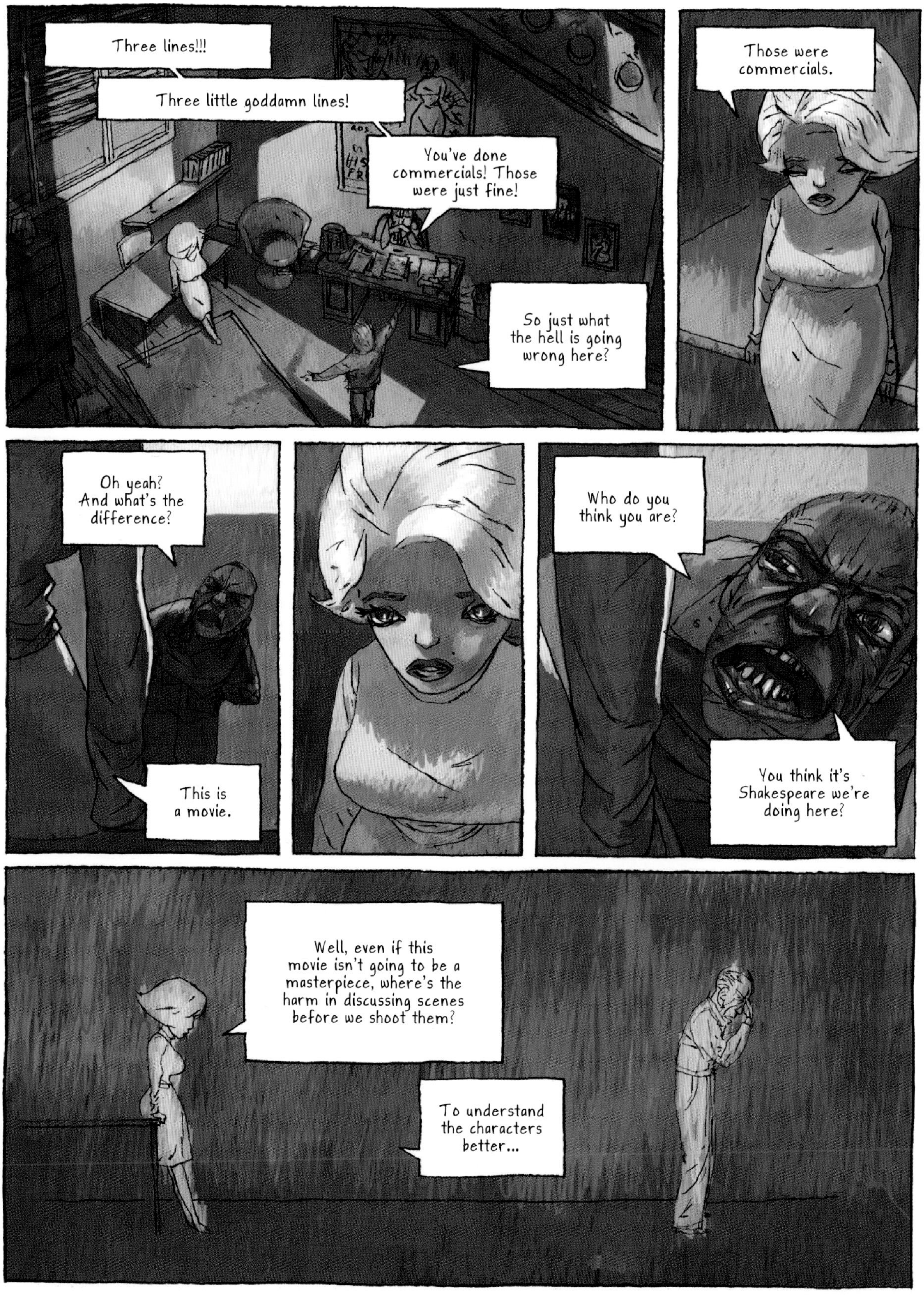
Three lines!!!
Three little goddamn lines!
You've done commercials! Those were just fine!
So just what the hell is going wrong here?
Those were commercials.
Oh yeah? And what's the difference?
This is a movie.
Who do you think you are?
You think it's Shakespeare we're doing here?
Well, even if this movie isn't going to be a masterpiece, where's the harm in discussing scenes before we shoot them?
To understand the characters better...

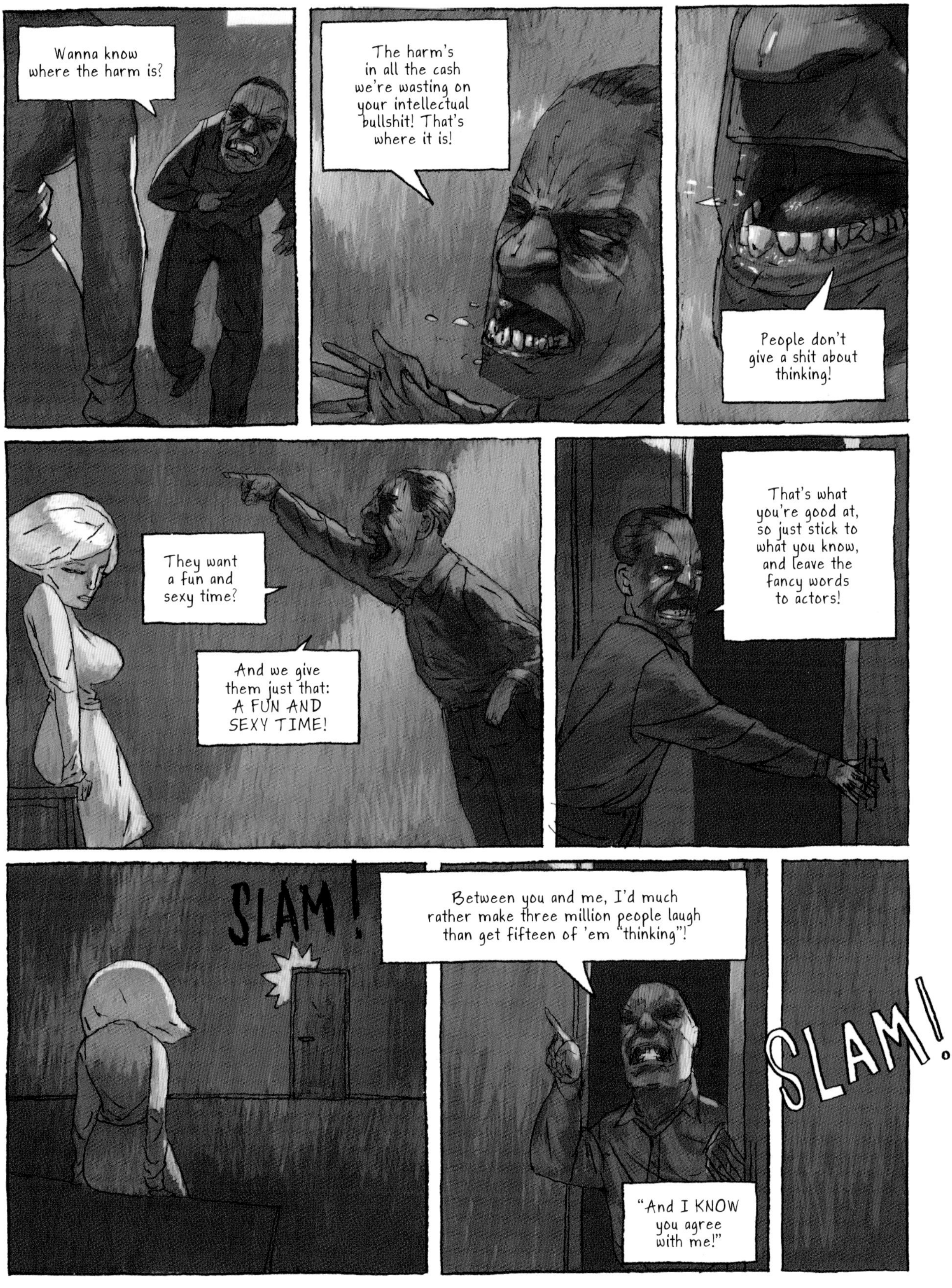
Wanna know where the harm is?
The harm's in all the cash we're wasting on your intellectual bullshit! That's where it is!
People don't give a shit about thinking!
They want a fun and sexy time?
And we give them just that: A FUN AND SEXY TIME!
That's what you're good at, so just stick to what you know, and leave the fancy words to actors!
SLAM!
Between you and me, I'd much rather make three million people laugh than get fifteen of 'em "thinking"!
"And I KNOW you agree with me!"
SLAM!

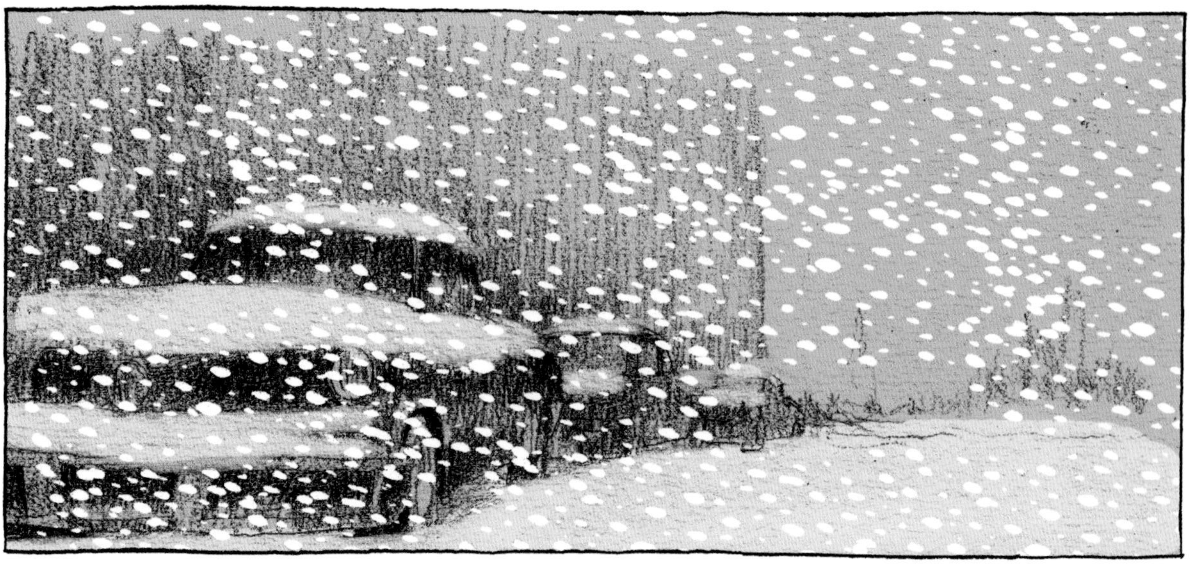

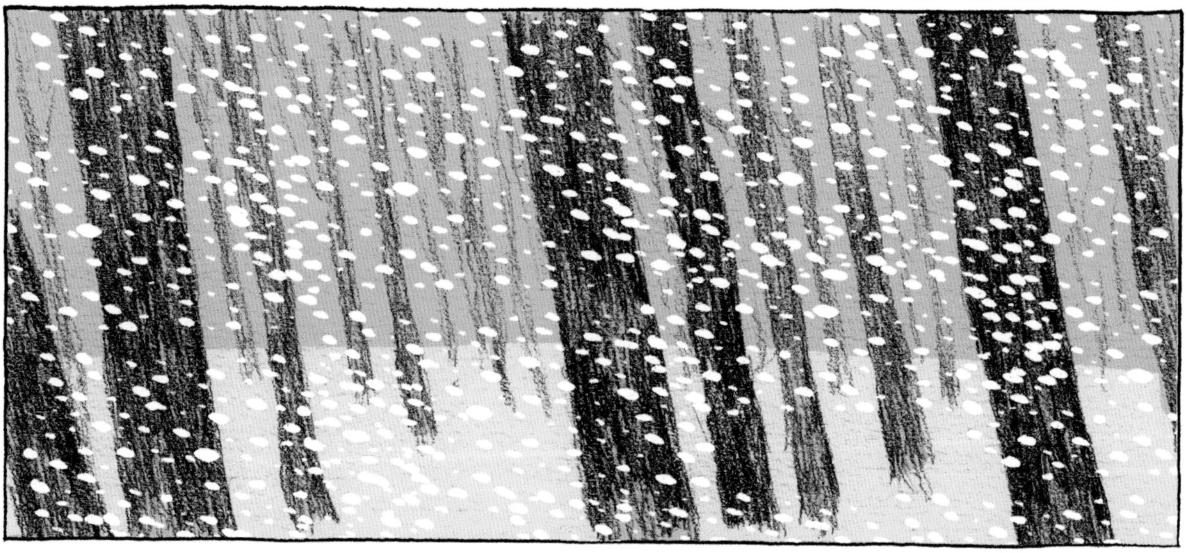

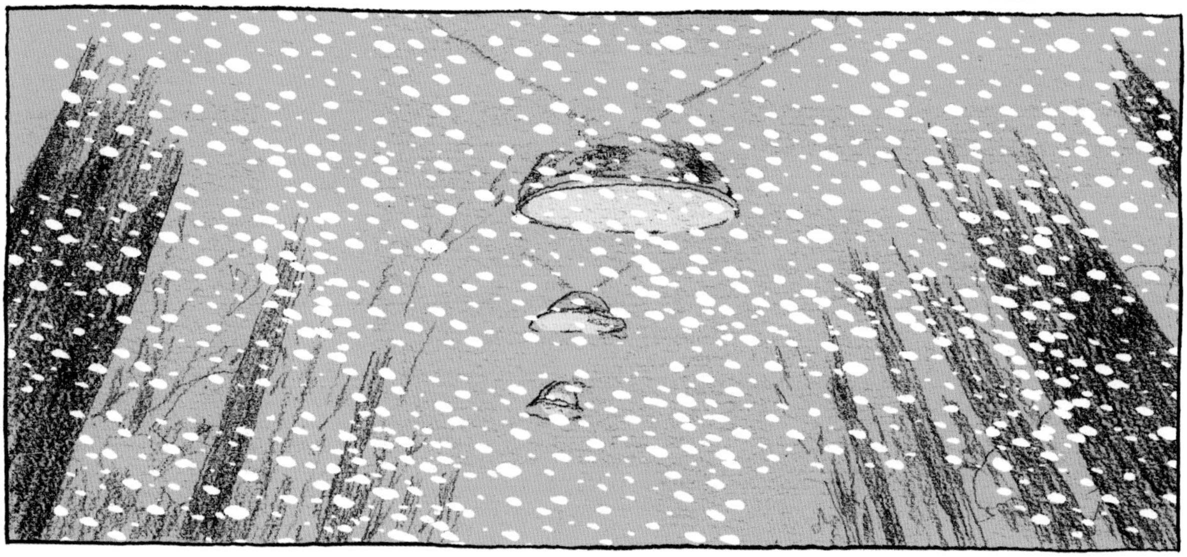

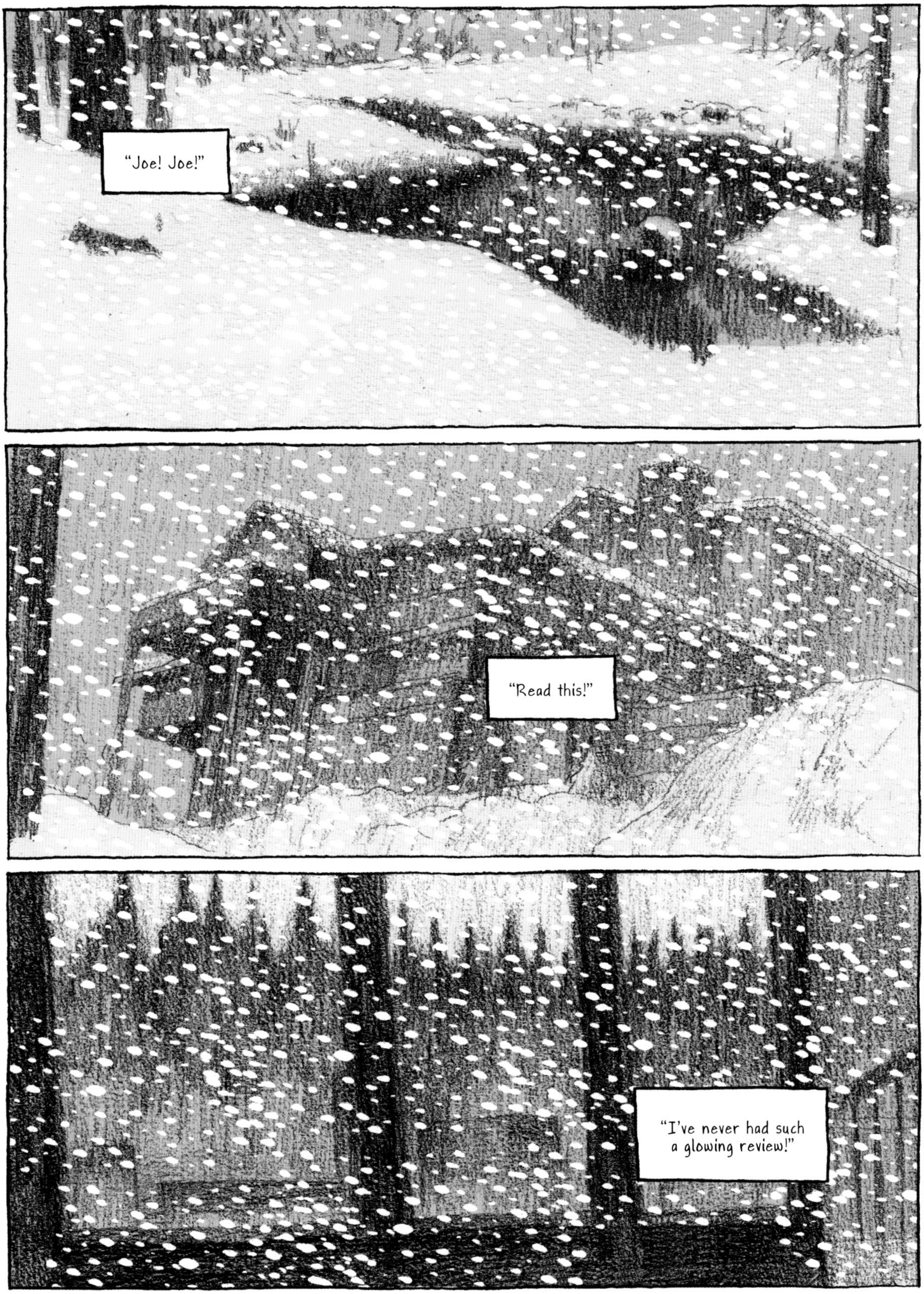
"Joe! Joe!"
"Read this!"
"I've never had such a glowing review!"

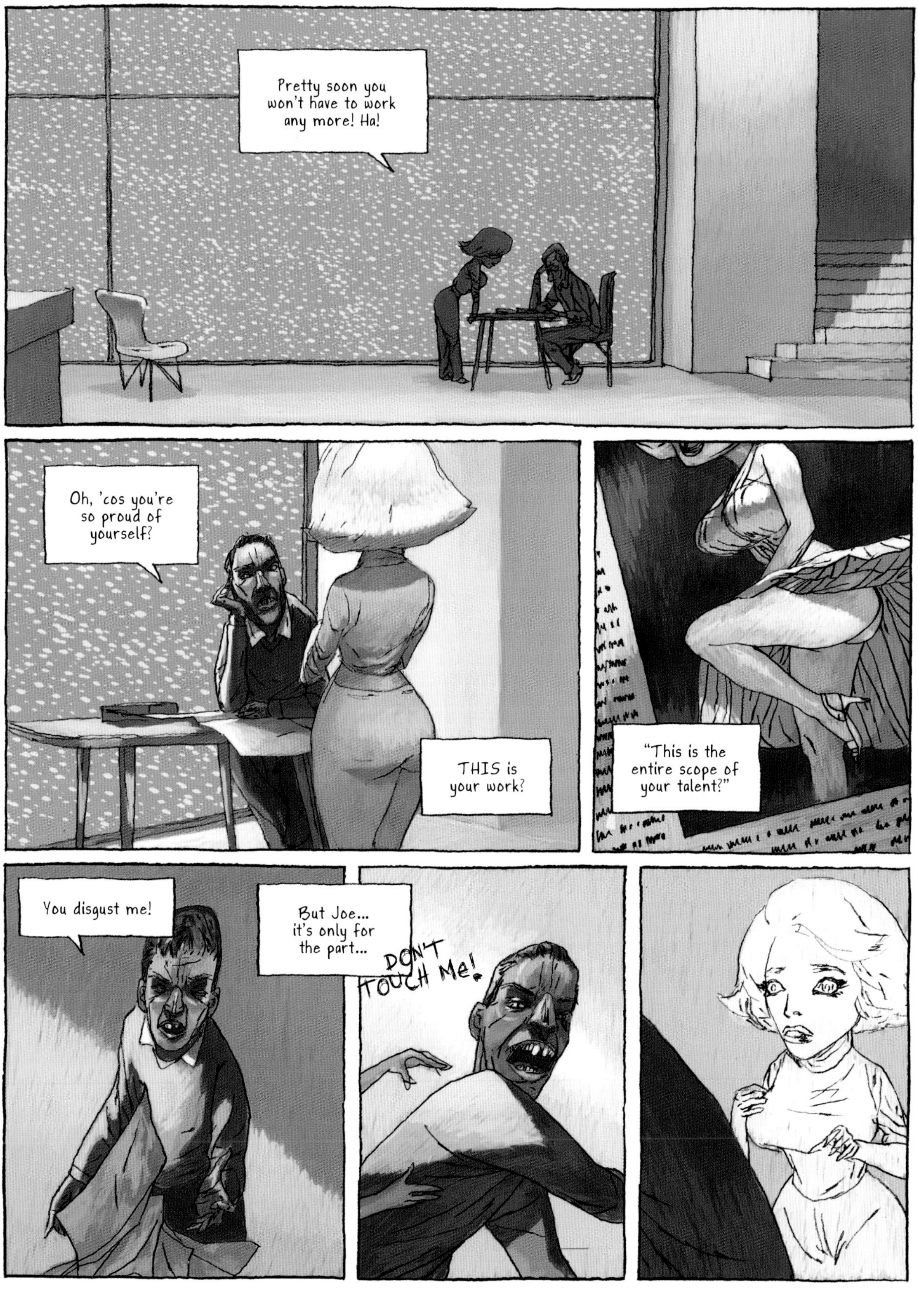

Pretty soon you won't have to work any more! Ha!
Oh, 'cos you're so proud of yourself?
THIS is your work?
"This is the entire scope of your talent?"
You disgust me!
But Joe... it's only for the part...
DON'T TOUCH ME!

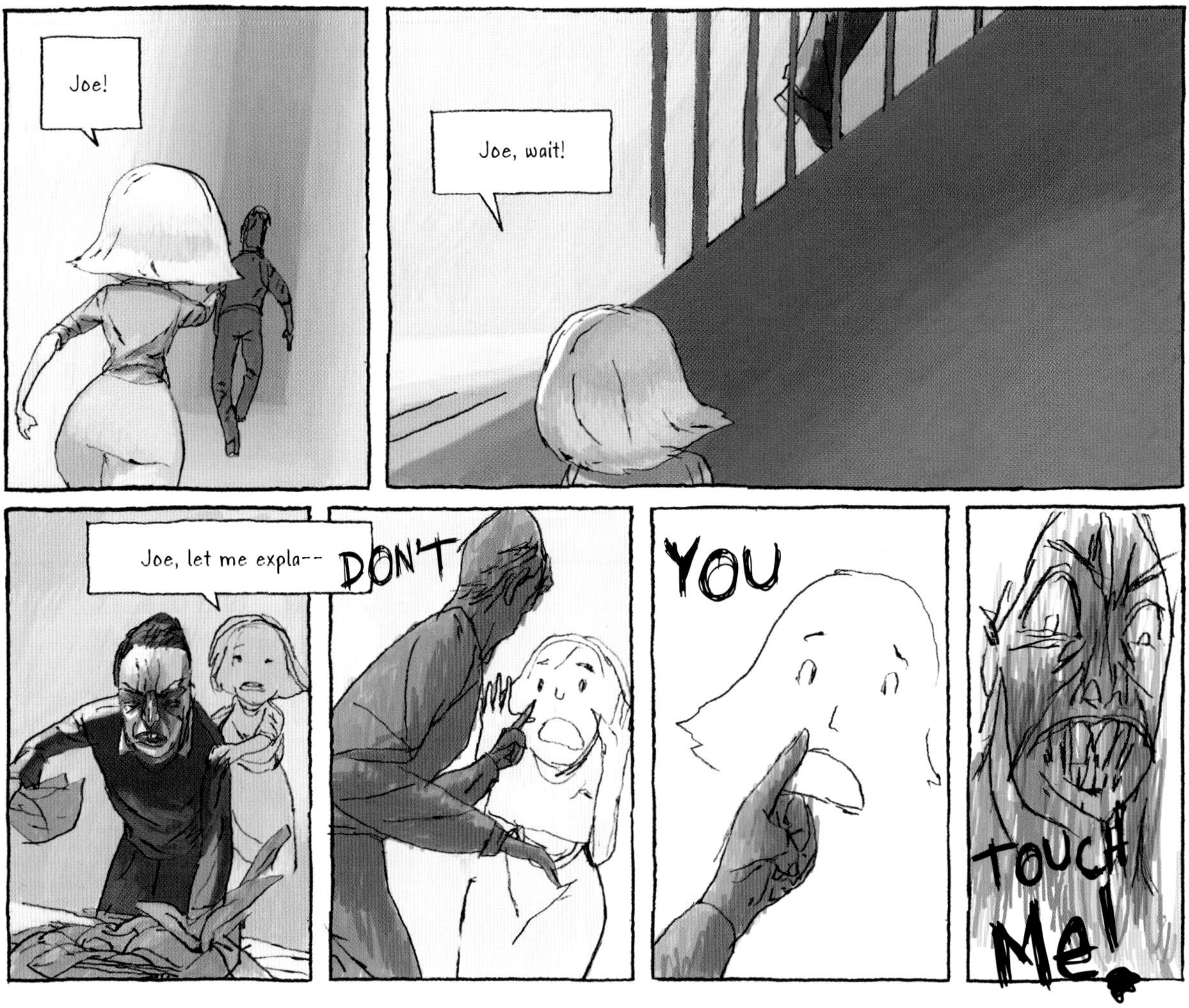
Joe!
Joe, wait!
Joe, let me expla--
DON'T
YOU
TOUCH
Me!

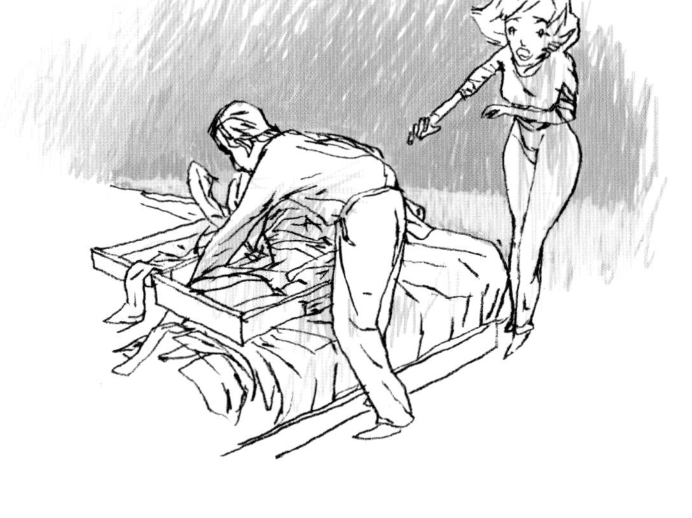
Don't do this to me, Joe!

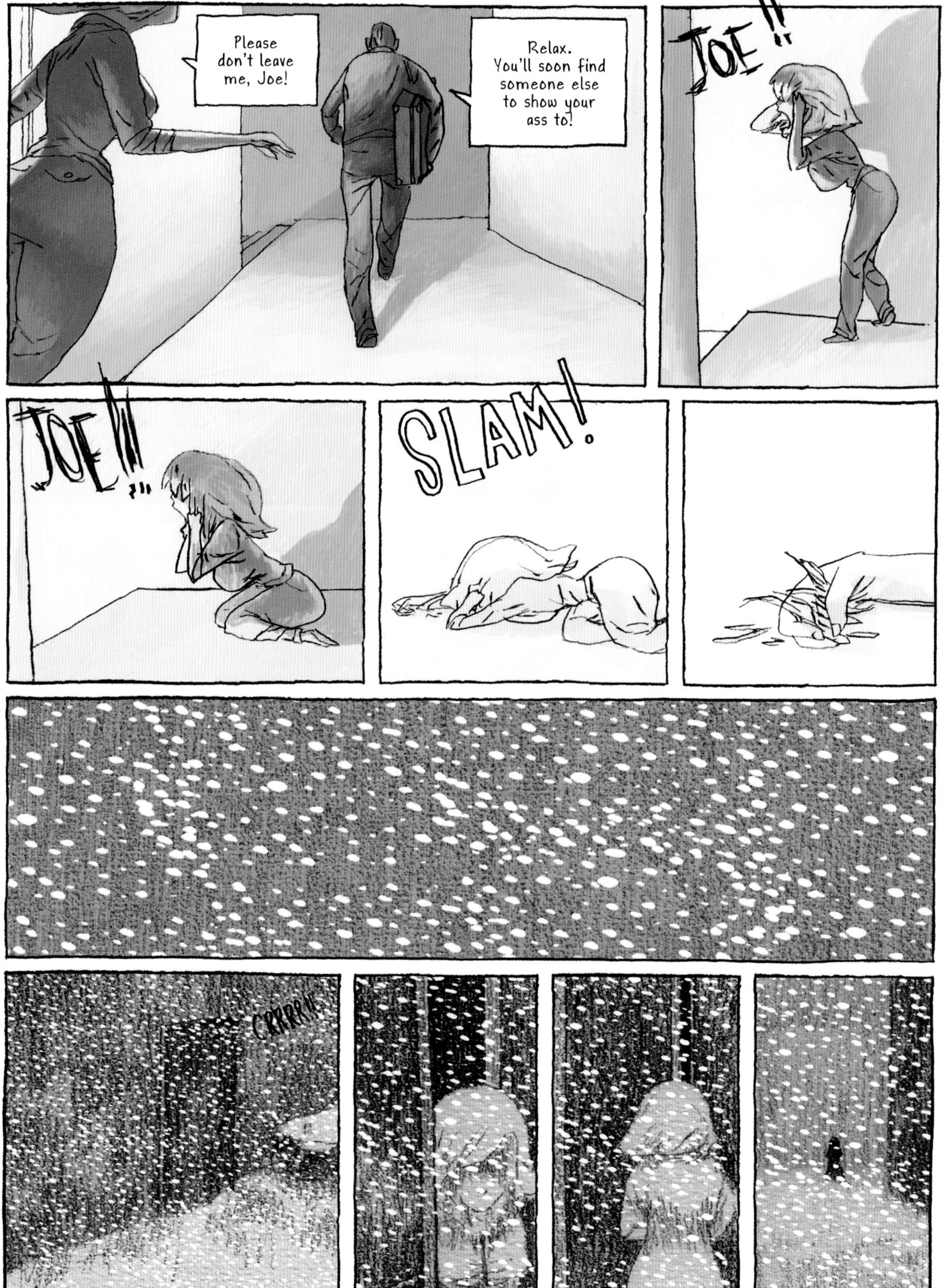
Please don't leave me, Joe!
Relax. You'll soon find someone else to show your ass to!
JOE!!
JOE!!!
SLAM!
CRRRR!!

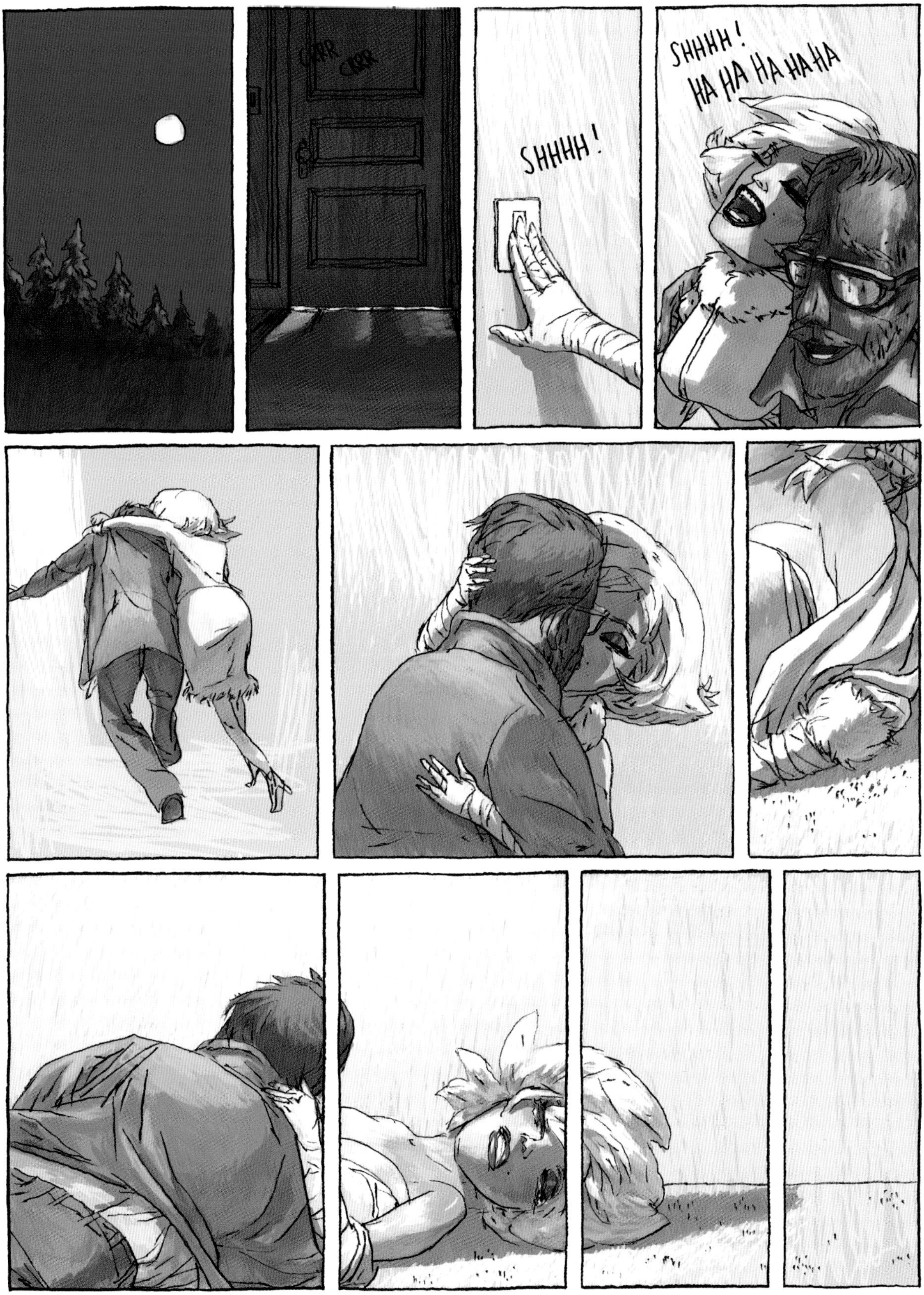
CRRR CRRR
SHHHH!
SHHHH!
HA HA HA HA HA

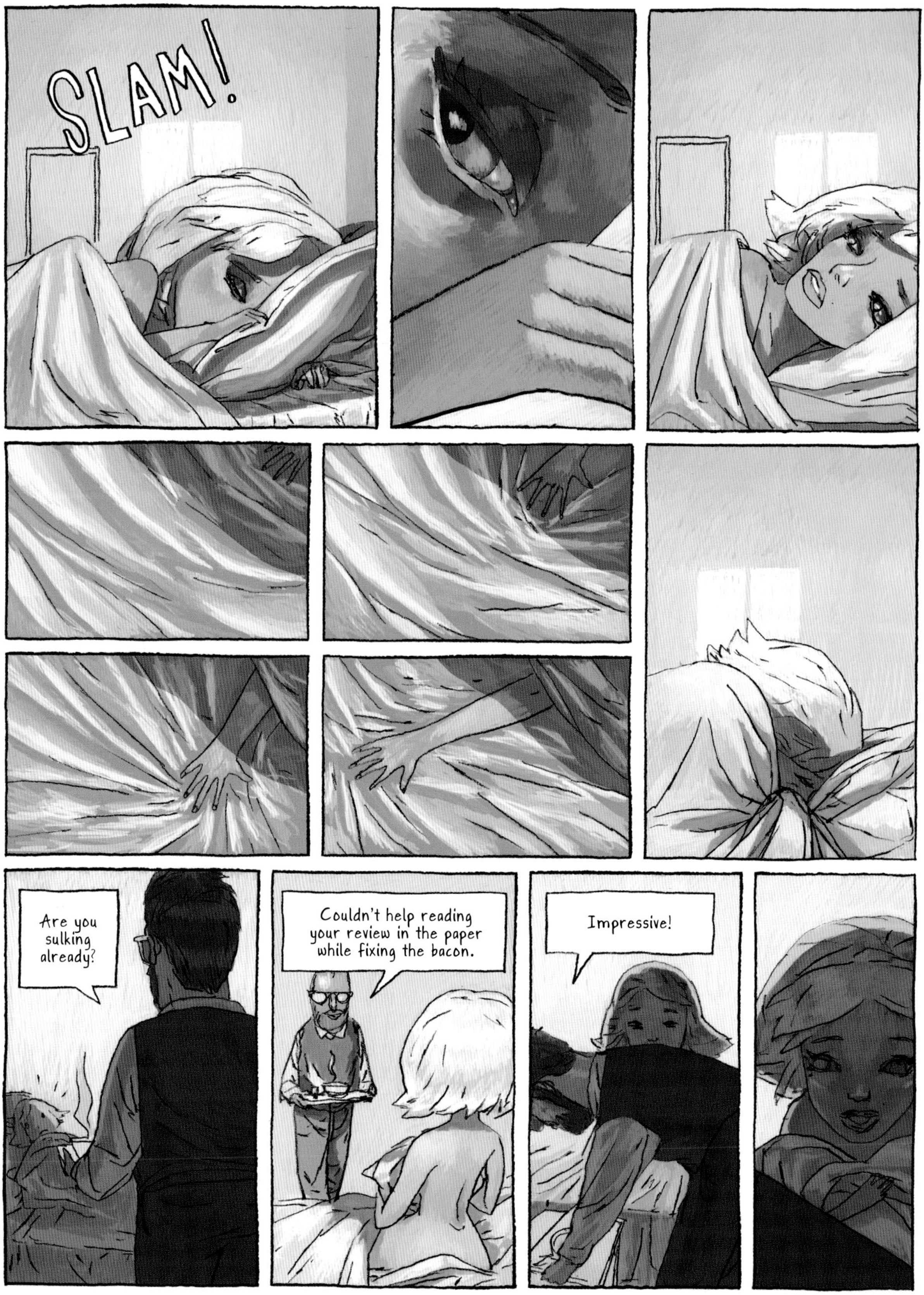
SLAM!
Are you sulking already?
Couldn't help reading your review in the paper while fixing the bacon.
Impressive!

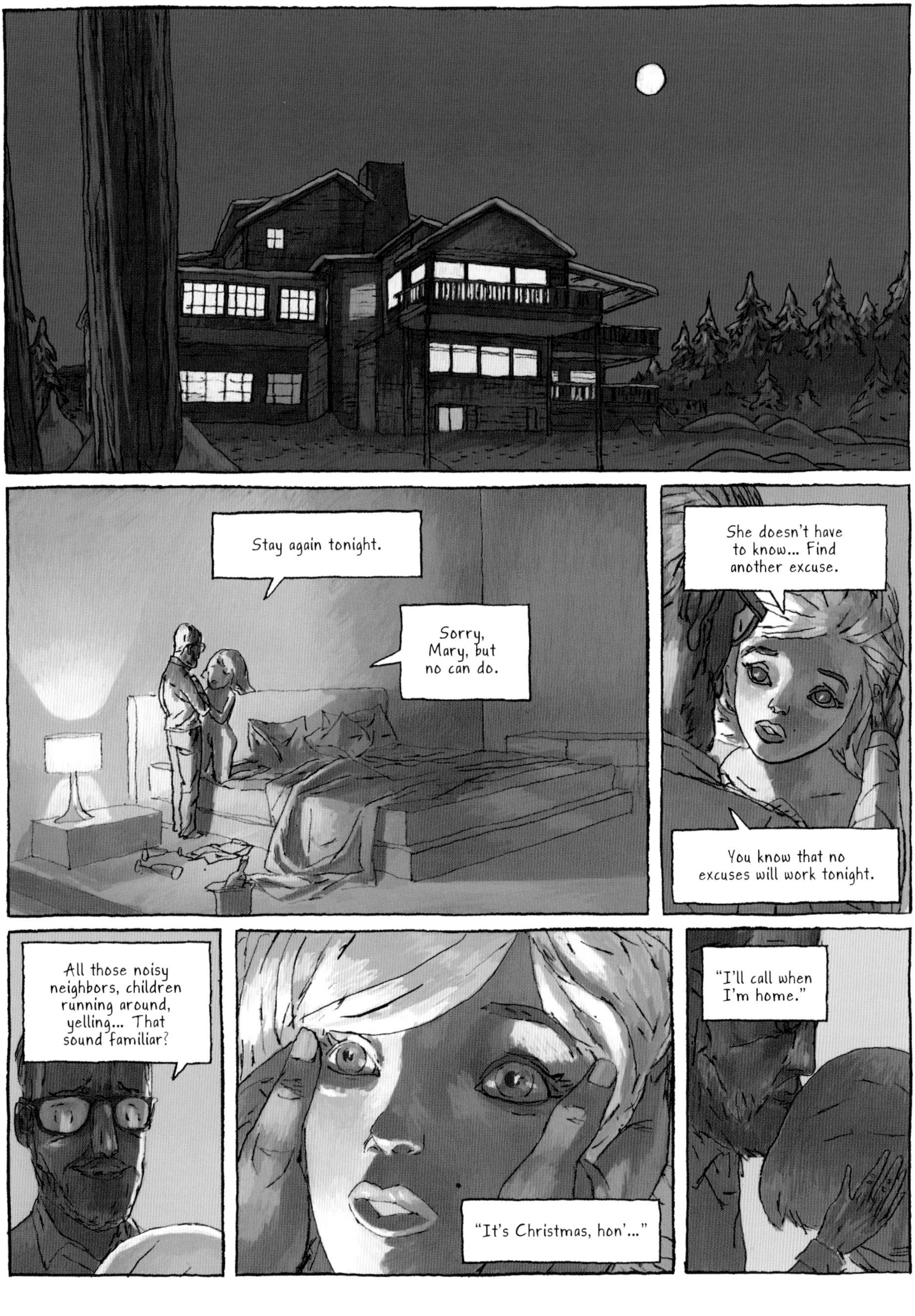

Stay again tonight.
Sorry, Mary, but no can do.
She doesn't have to know... Find another excuse.
You know that no excuses will work tonight.
All those noisy neighbors, children running around, yelling... That sound familiar?
"It's Christmas, hon'..."
"I'll call when I'm home."

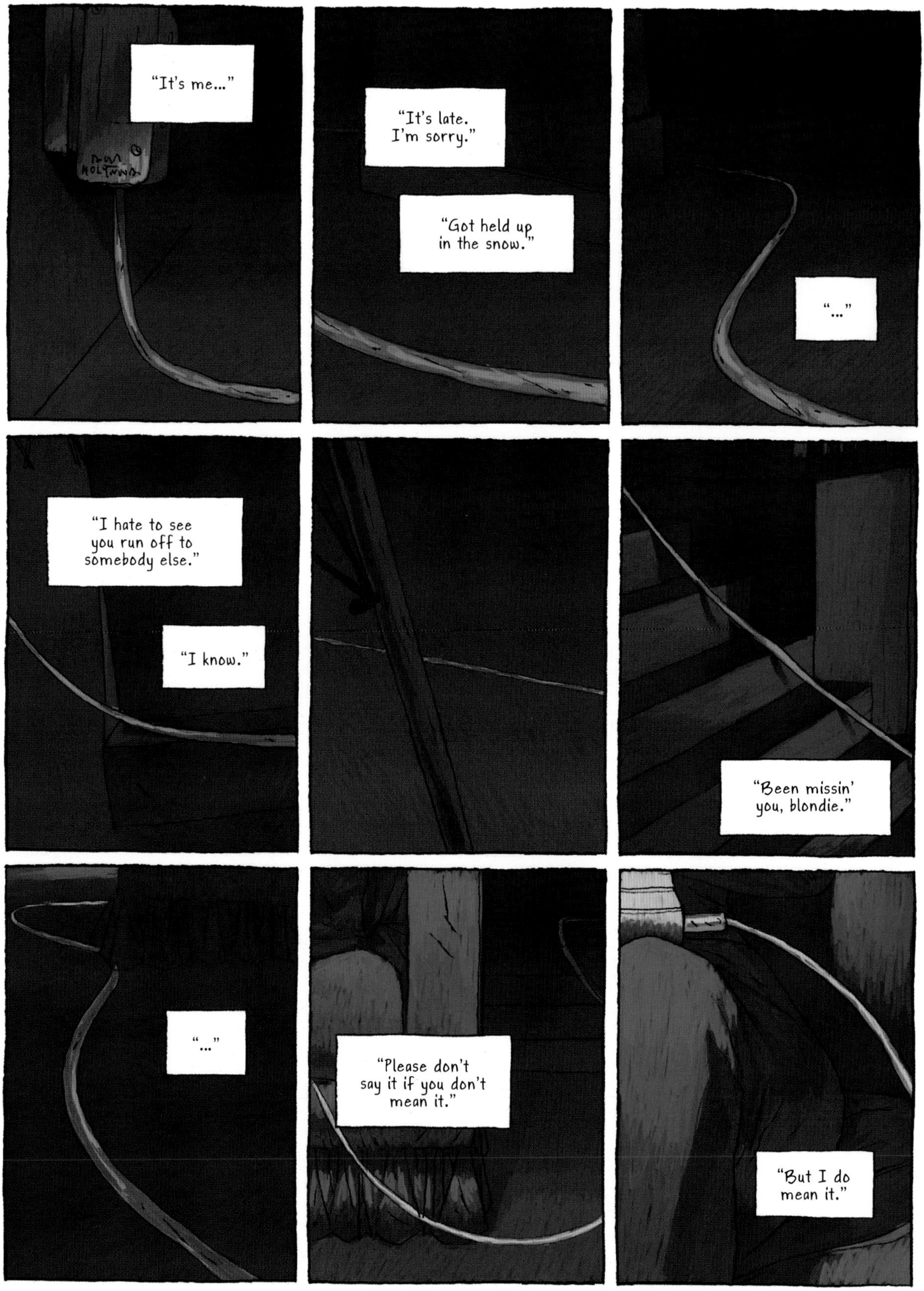
"It's me..."
"It's late. I'm sorry."
"Got held up in the snow."
"..."
"I hate to see you run off to somebody else."
"I know."
"Been missin' you, blondie."
"..."
"Please don't say it if you don't mean it."
"But I do mean it."

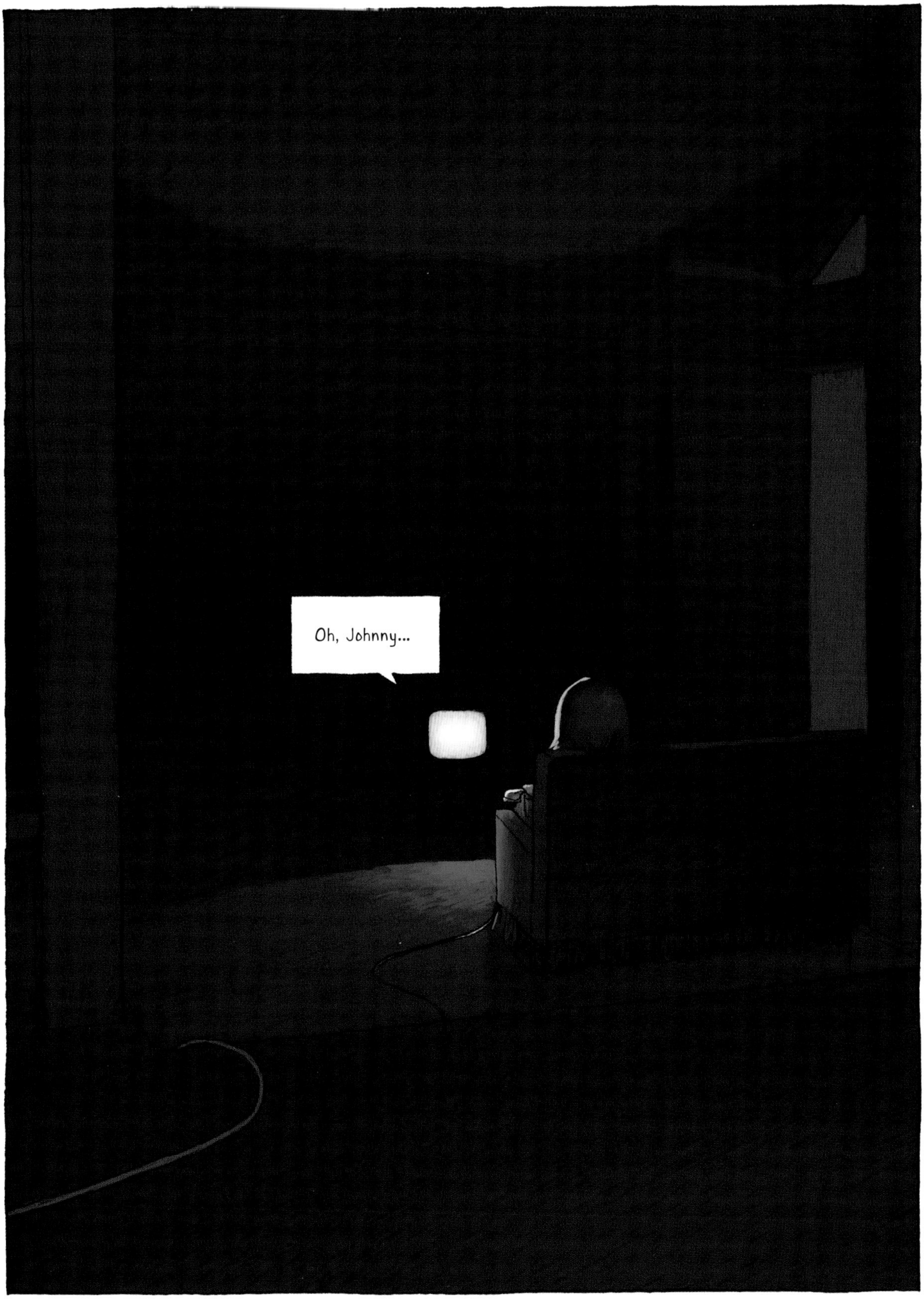
Oh, Johnny...

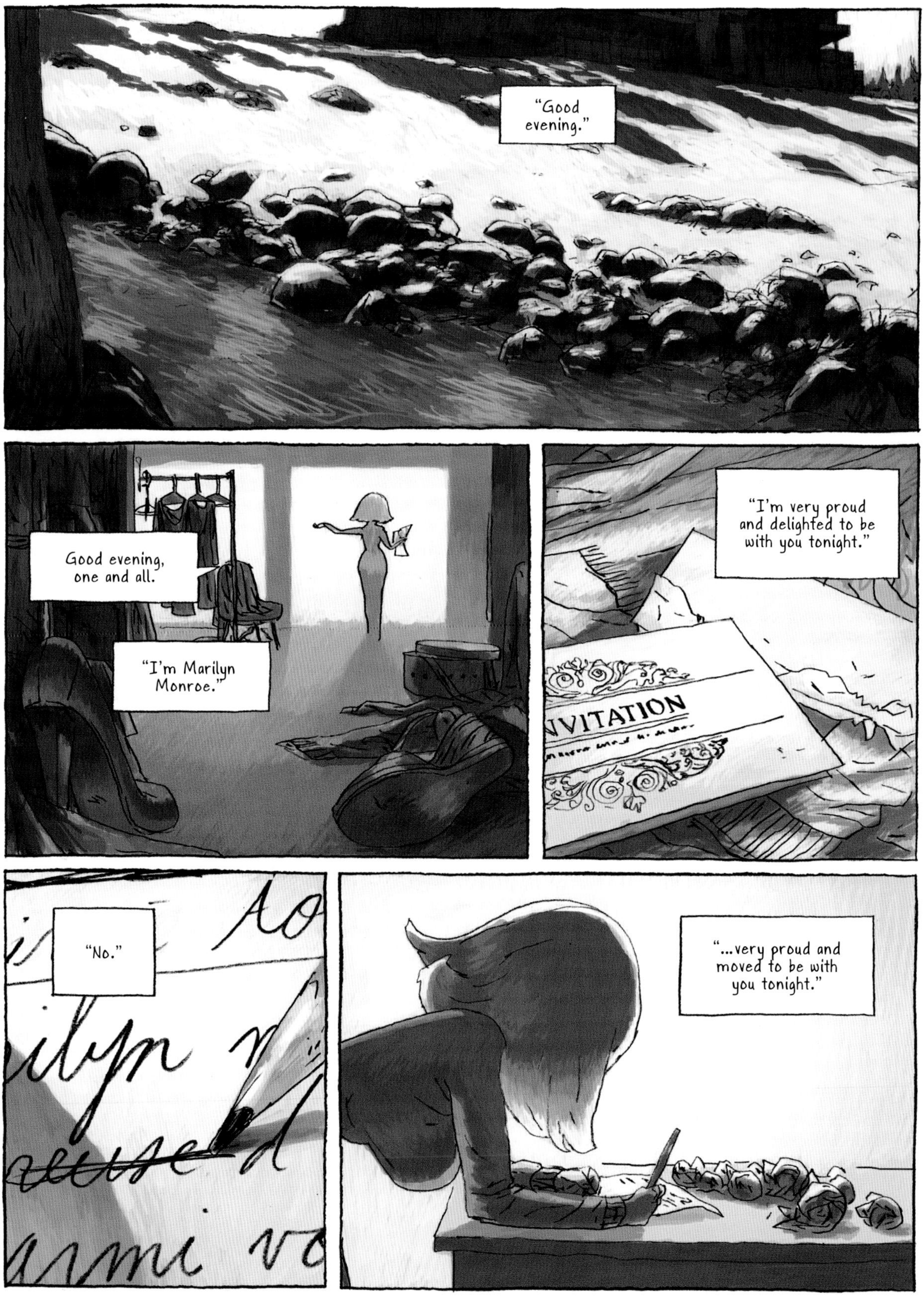
"Good evening."
Good evening, one and all.
"I'm Marilyn Monroe."
"I'm very proud and delighted to be with you tonight."
INVITATION
"No."
"...very proud and moved to be with you tonight."

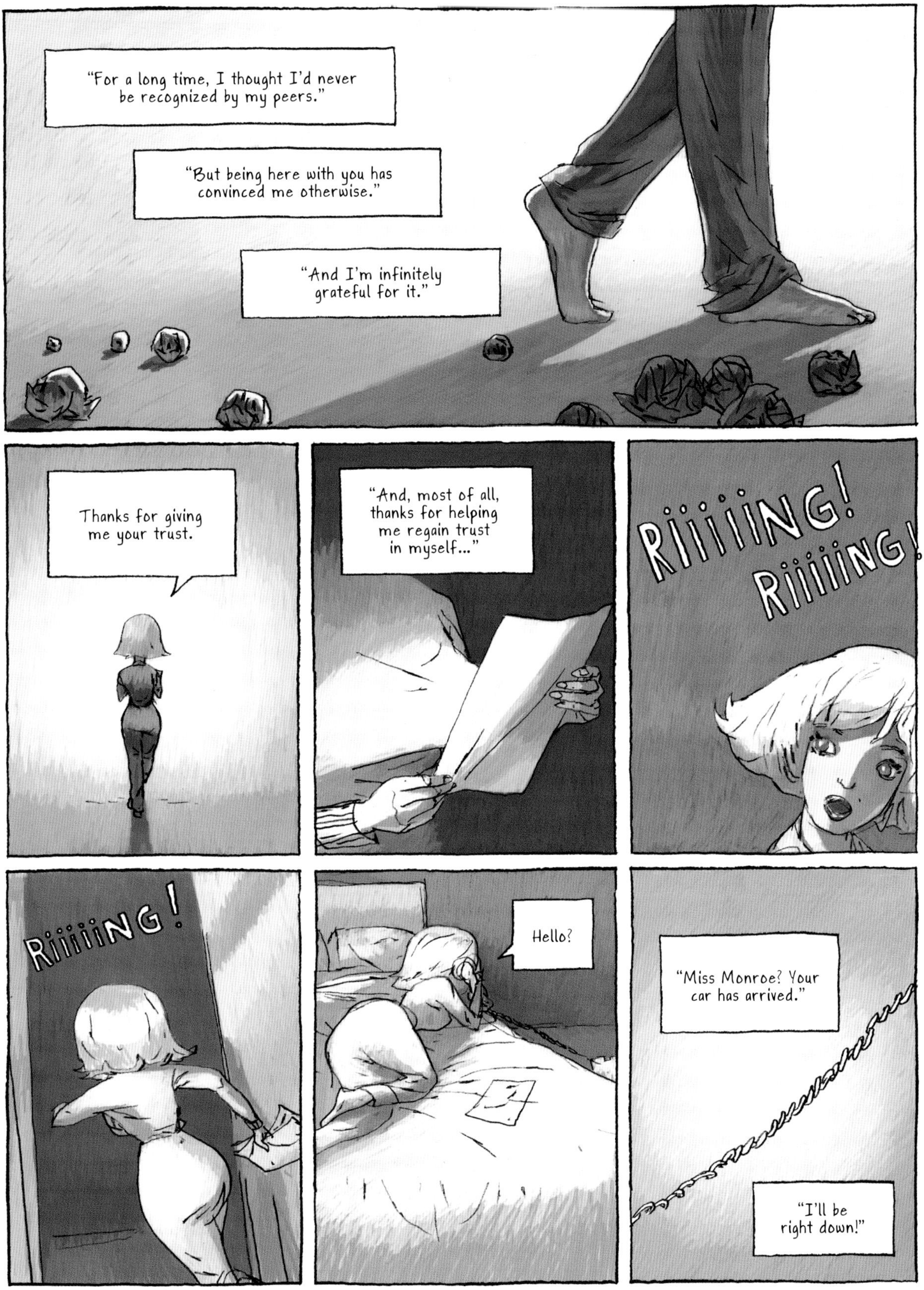
"For a long time, I thought I'd never be recognized by my peers."
"But being here with you has convinced me otherwise."
"And I'm infinitely grateful for it."
Thanks for giving me your trust.
"And, most of all, thanks for helping me regain trust in myself..."
Riiiiing!
Riiiiing!
Riiiiing!
Hello?
"Miss Monroe? Your car has arrived."
"I'll be right down!"

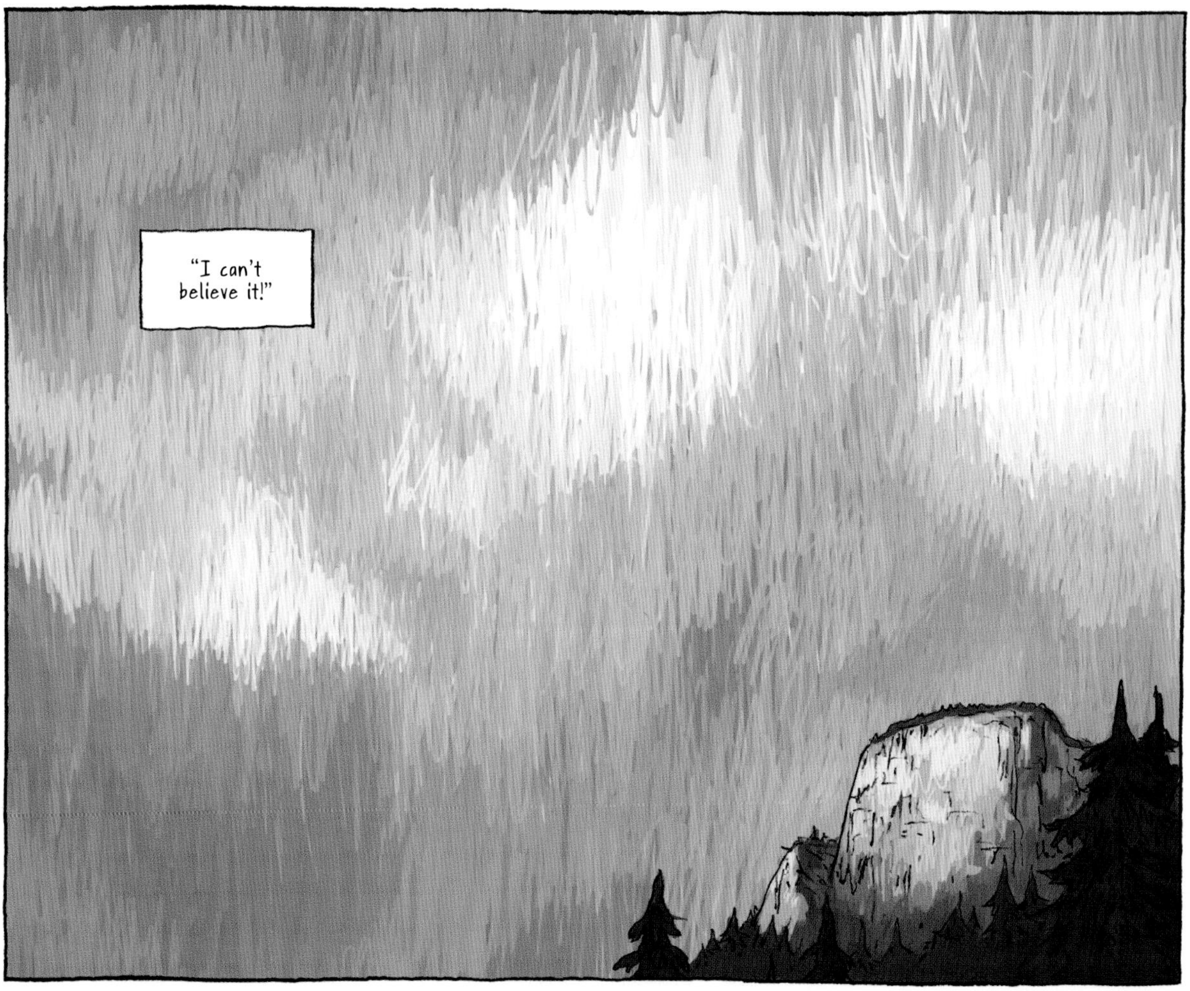
"I can't believe it!"

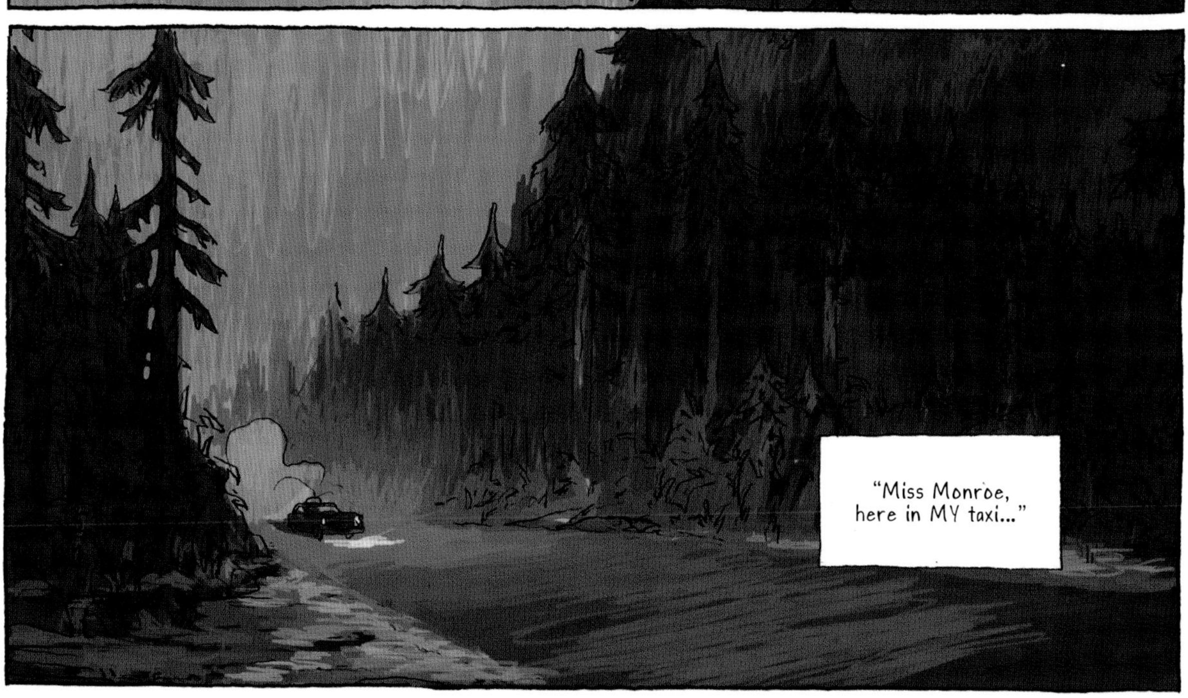
"Miss Monroe, here in MY taxi..."

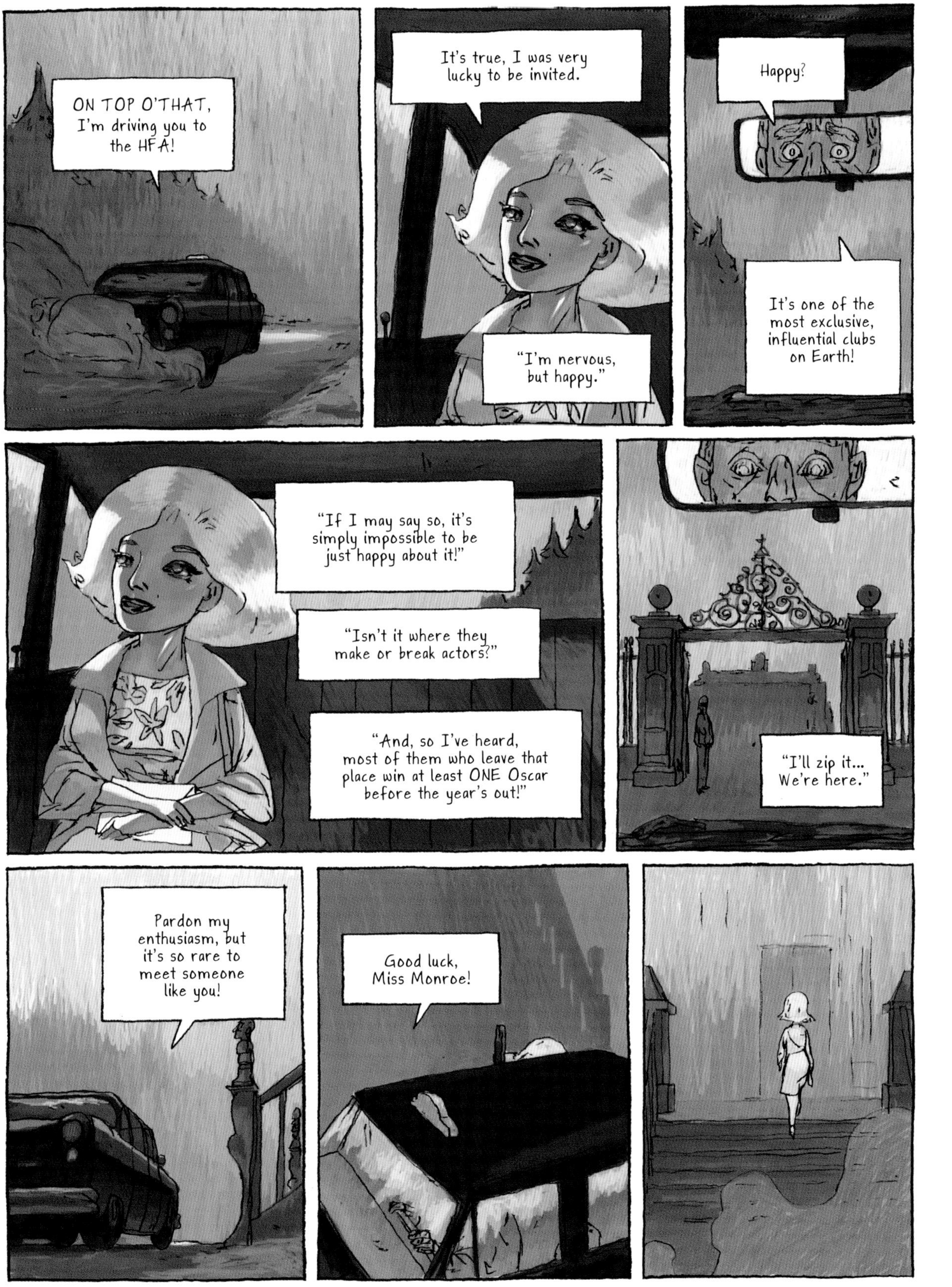
ON TOP O'THAT, I'm driving you to the HFA!
It's true, I was very lucky to be invited.
"I'm nervous, but happy."
Happy?
It's one of the most exclusive, influential clubs on Earth!
"If I may say so, it's simply impossible to be just happy about it!"
"Isn't it where they make or break actors?"
"And, so I've heard, most of them who leave that place win at least ONE Oscar before the year's out!"
"I'll zip it... We're here."
Pardon my enthusiasm, but it's so rare to meet someone like you!
Good luck, Miss Monroe!

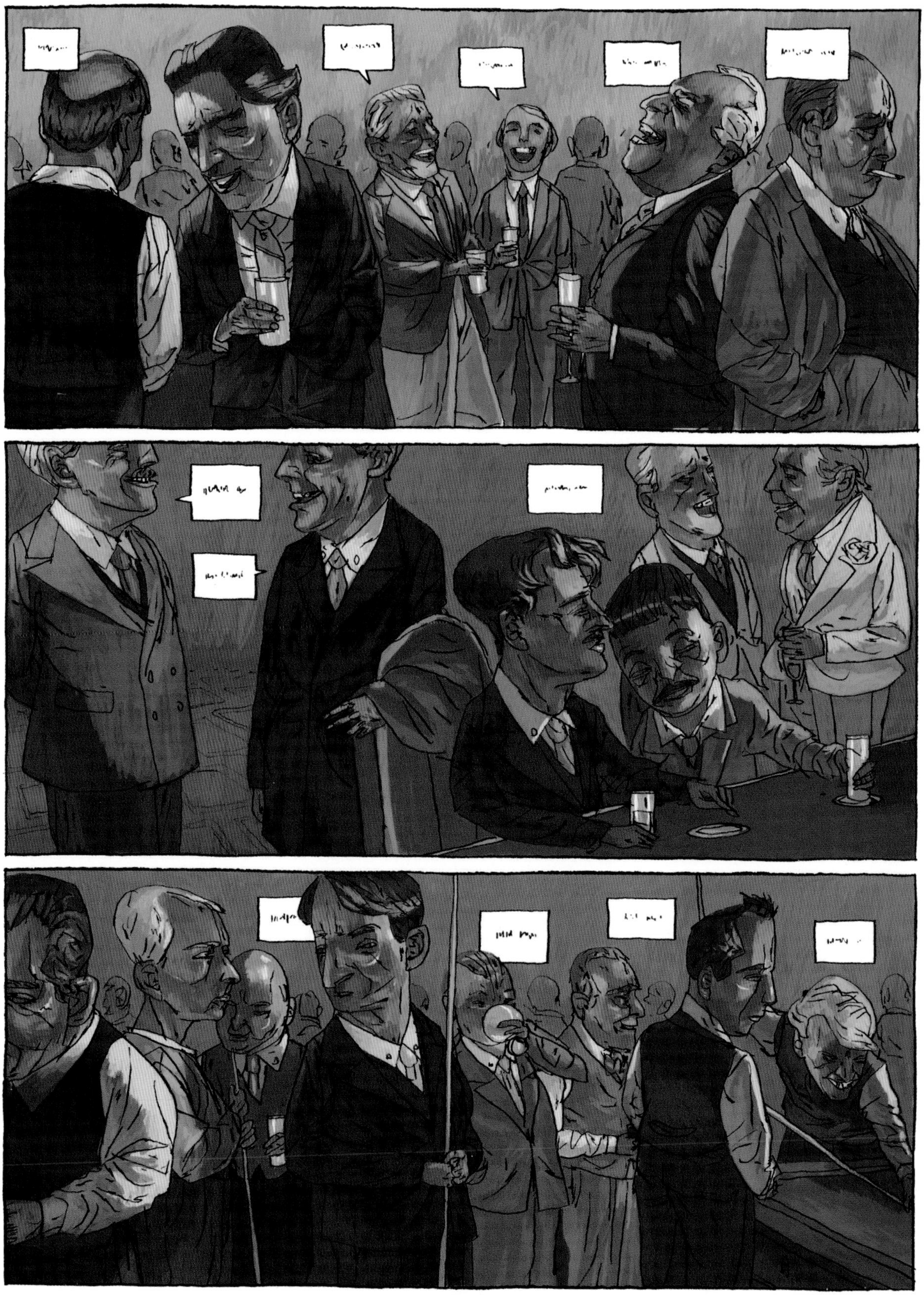

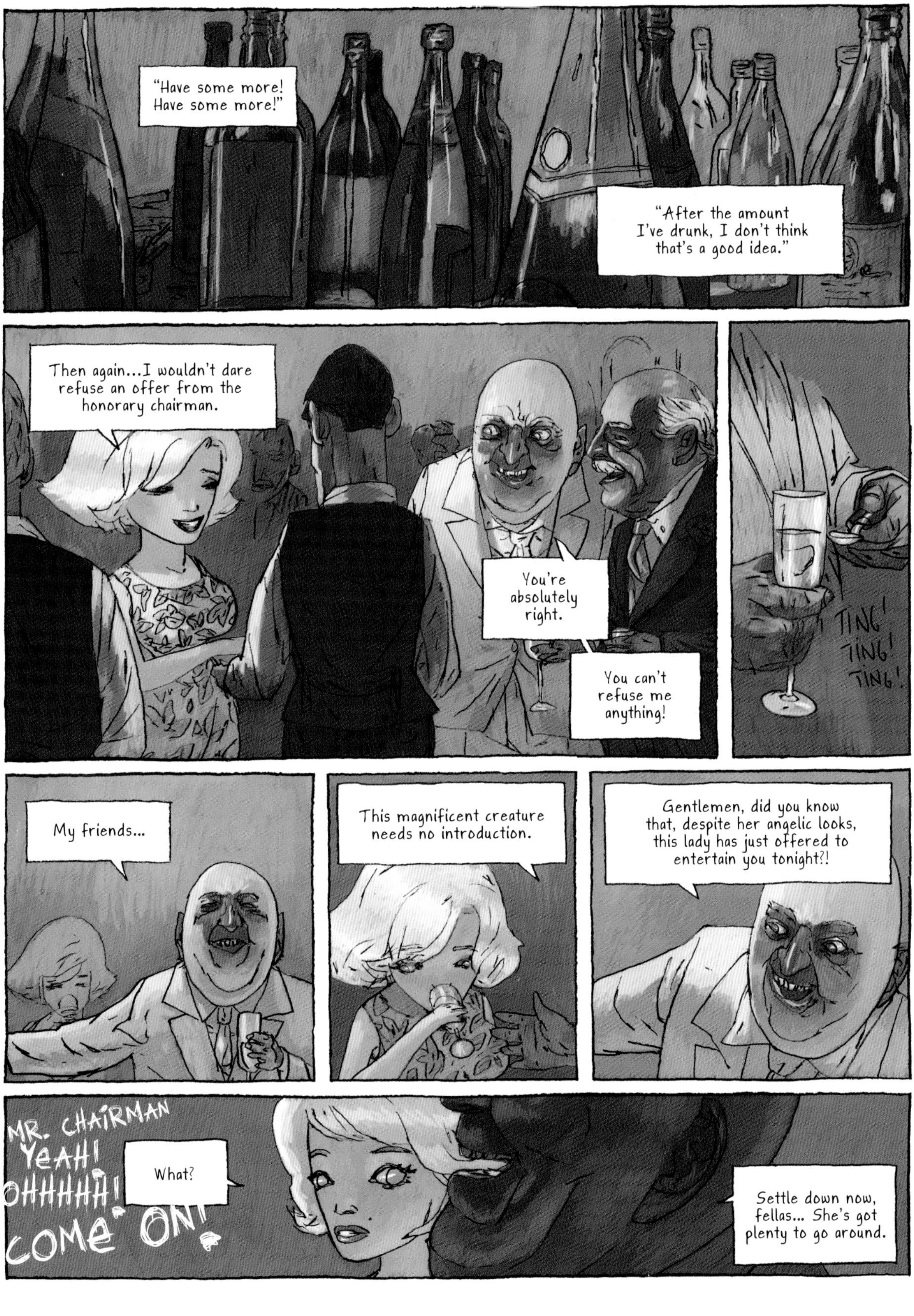
"Have some more! Have some more!"
"After the amount I've drunk, I don't think that's a good idea."
Then again...I wouldn't dare refuse an offer from the honorary chairman.
You're absolutely right.
You can't refuse me anything!
TING! TING! TING!
My friends...
This magnificent creature needs no introduction.
Gentlemen, did you know that, despite her angelic looks, this lady has just offered to entertain you tonight?!
MR. CHAIRMAN
YEAH!
OHHHHH!
COME ON!
What?
Settle down now, fellas... She's got plenty to go around.

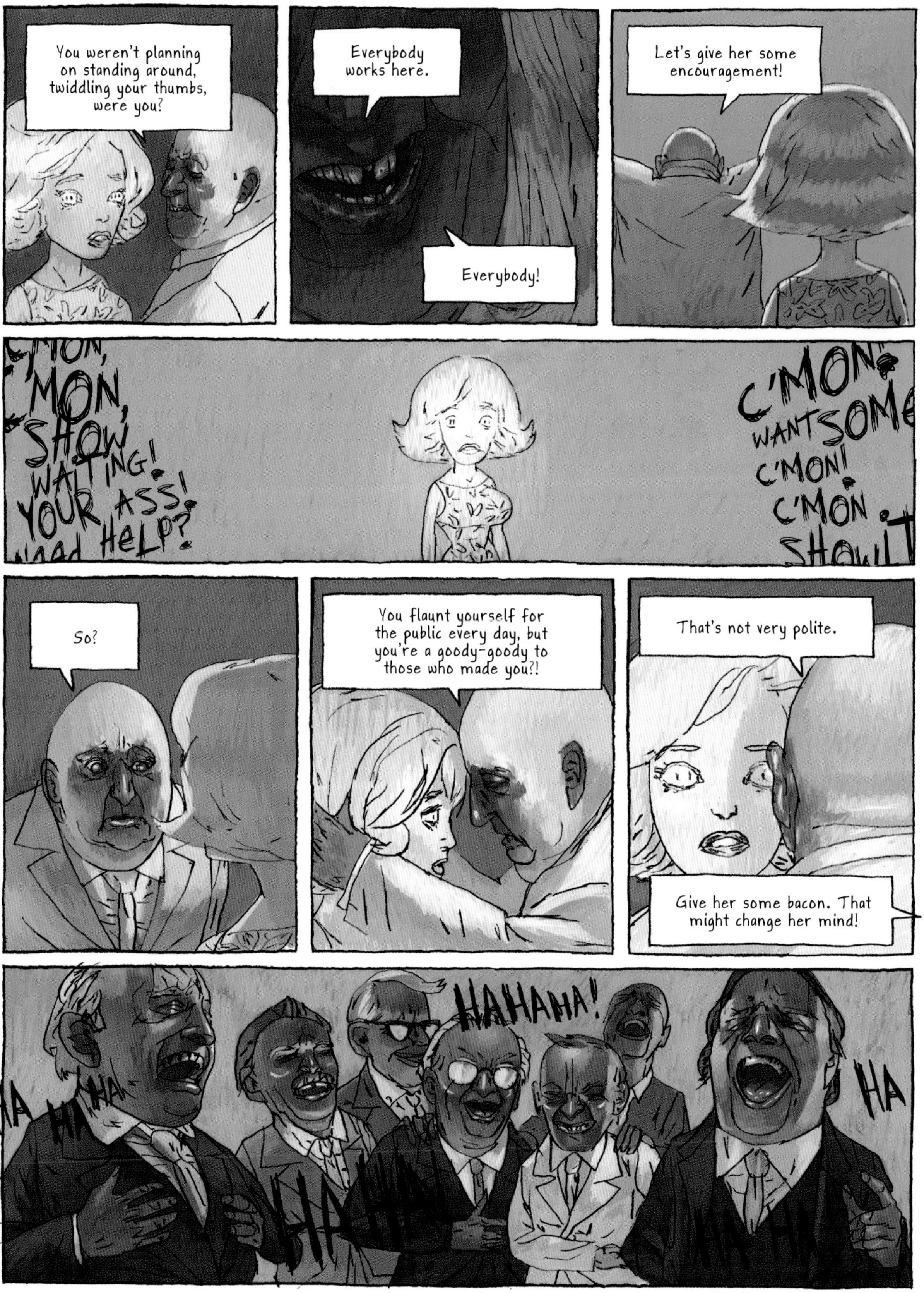

You weren't planning on standing around, twiddling your thumbs, were you?
Everybody works here.
Everybody!
Let's give her some encouragement!
MON,
SHOW
WAITING!
YOUR ASS!
HELP?
C'MON
WANT SOME
C'MON!
C'MON
So?
You flaunt yourself for the public every day, but you're a goody-goody to those who made you?!
That's not very polite.
Give her some bacon. That might change her mind!
HA HA HA
HAHAHA!
HA

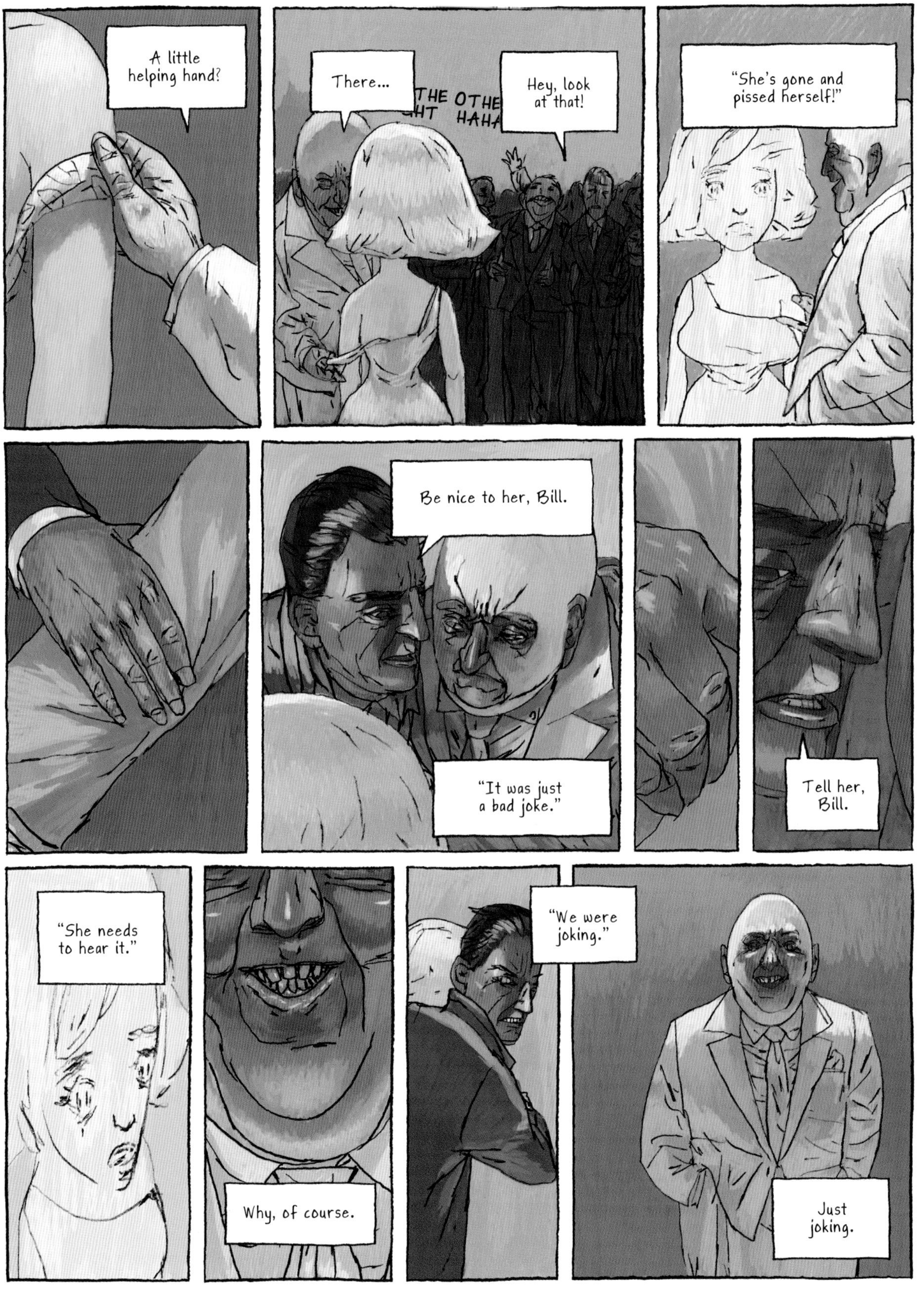
A little helping hand?
There...
THE OTHE
HT HAHA
Hey, look at that!
"She's gone and pissed herself!"
Be nice to her, Bill.
"It was just a bad joke."
Tell her, Bill.
"She needs to hear it."
Why, of course.
"We were joking."
Just joking.

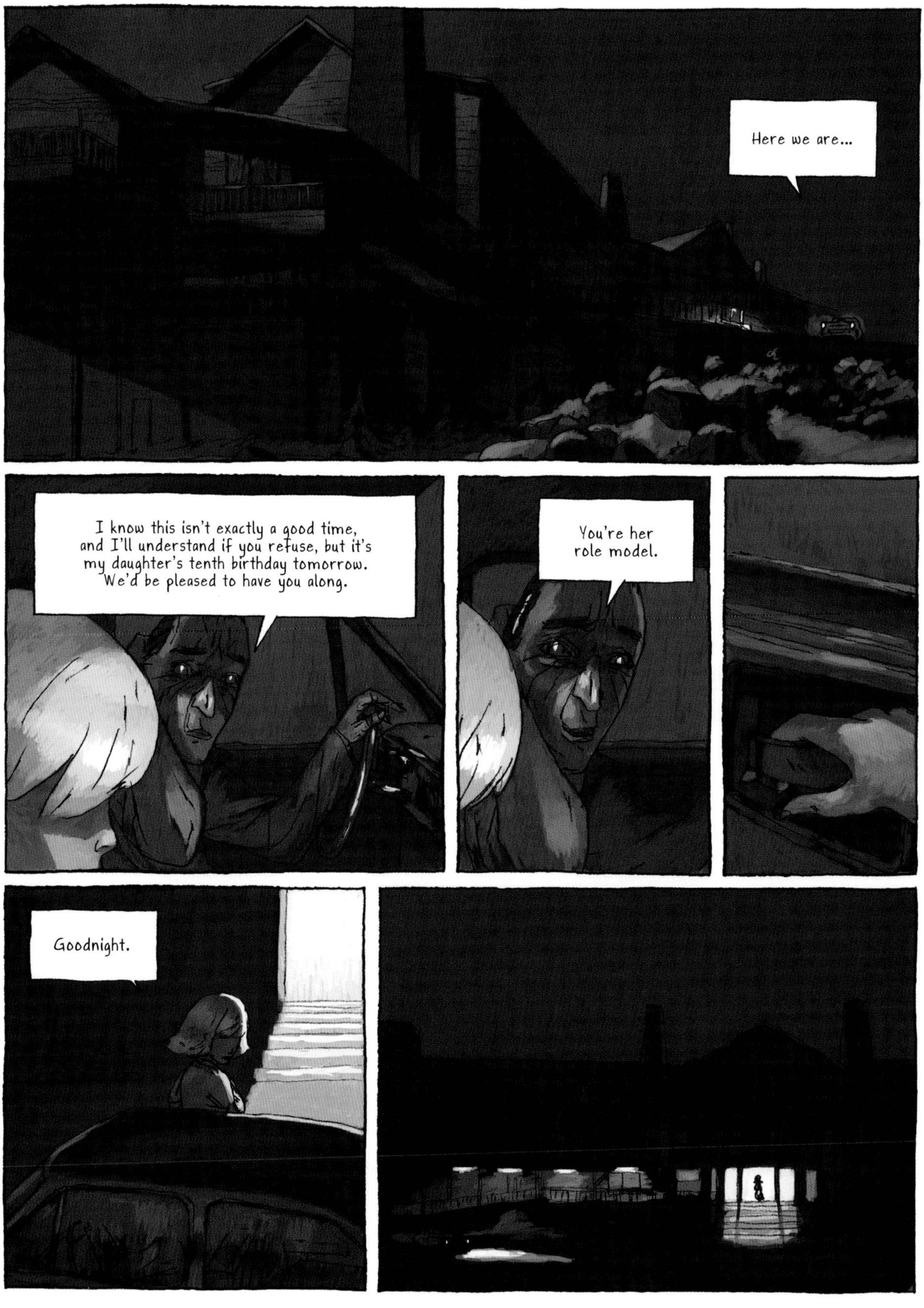
Here we are...
I know this isn't exactly a good time, and I'll understand if you refuse, but it's my daughter's tenth birthday tomorrow. We'd be pleased to have you along.
You're her role model.
Goodnight.

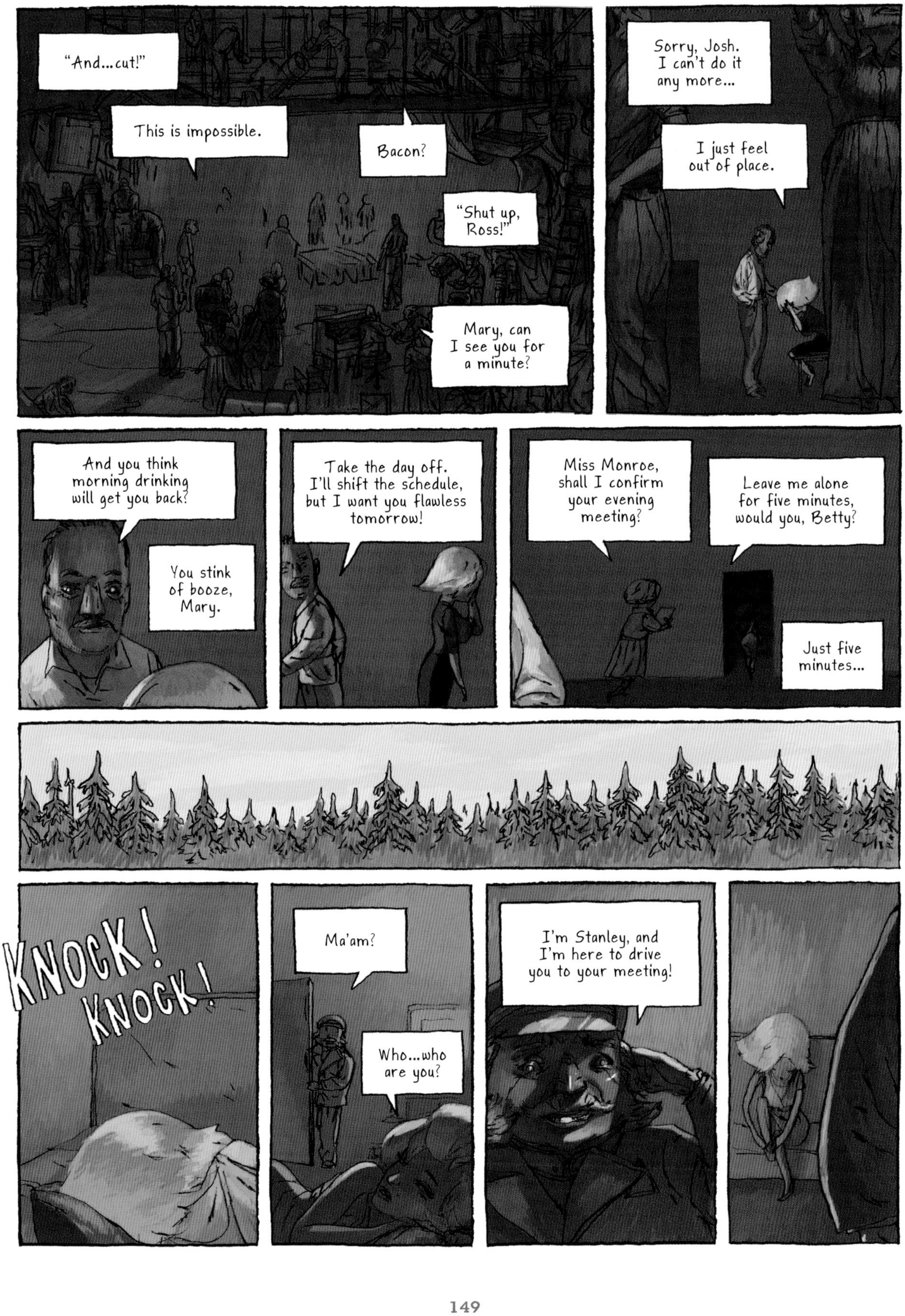
"And...cut!"
This is impossible.
Bacon?
"Shut up, Ross!"
Mary, can I see you for a minute?
Sorry, Josh. I can't do it any more...
I just feel out of place.
And you think morning drinking will get you back?
You stink of booze, Mary.
Take the day off. I'll shift the schedule, but I want you flawless tomorrow!
Miss Monroe, shall I confirm your evening meeting?
Leave me alone for five minutes, would you, Betty?
Just five minutes...
KNOCK! KNOCK!
Ma'am?
Who...who are you?
I'm Stanley, and I'm here to drive you to your meeting!

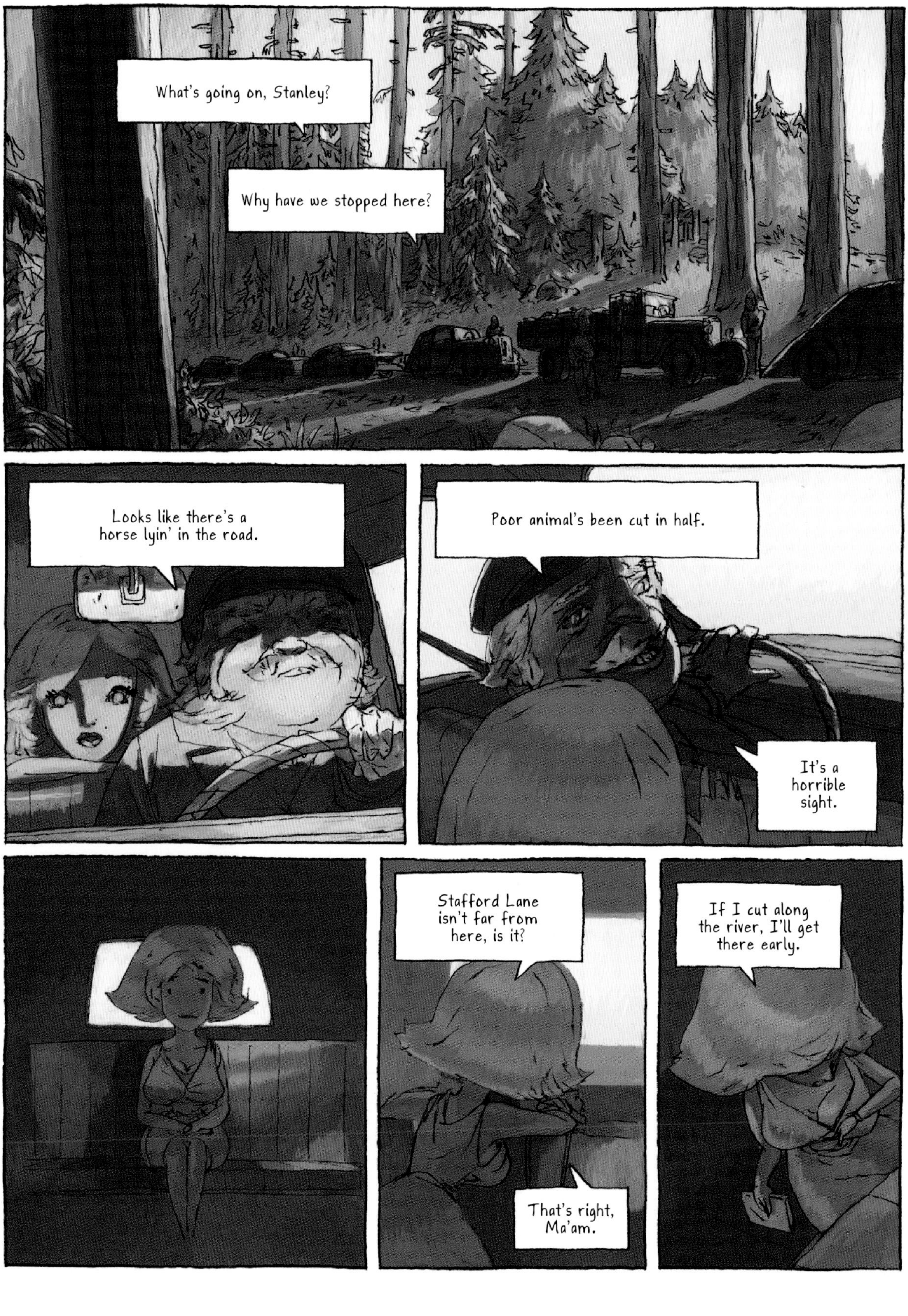
What's going on, Stanley?
Why have we stopped here?
Looks like there's a horse lyin' in the road.
Poor animal's been cut in half.
It's a horrible sight.
Stafford Lane isn't far from here, is it?
That's right, Ma'am.
If I cut along the river, I'll get there early.

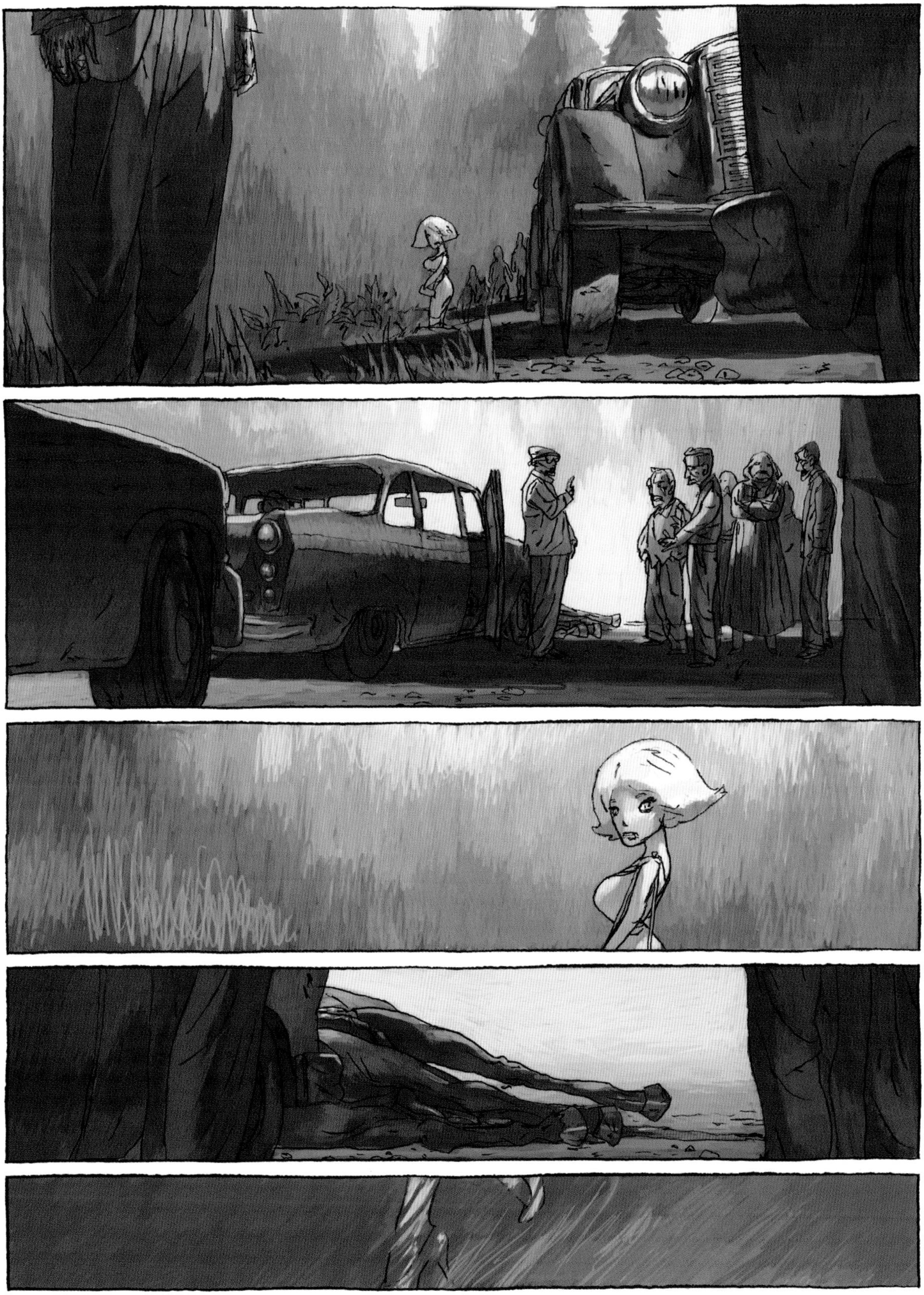

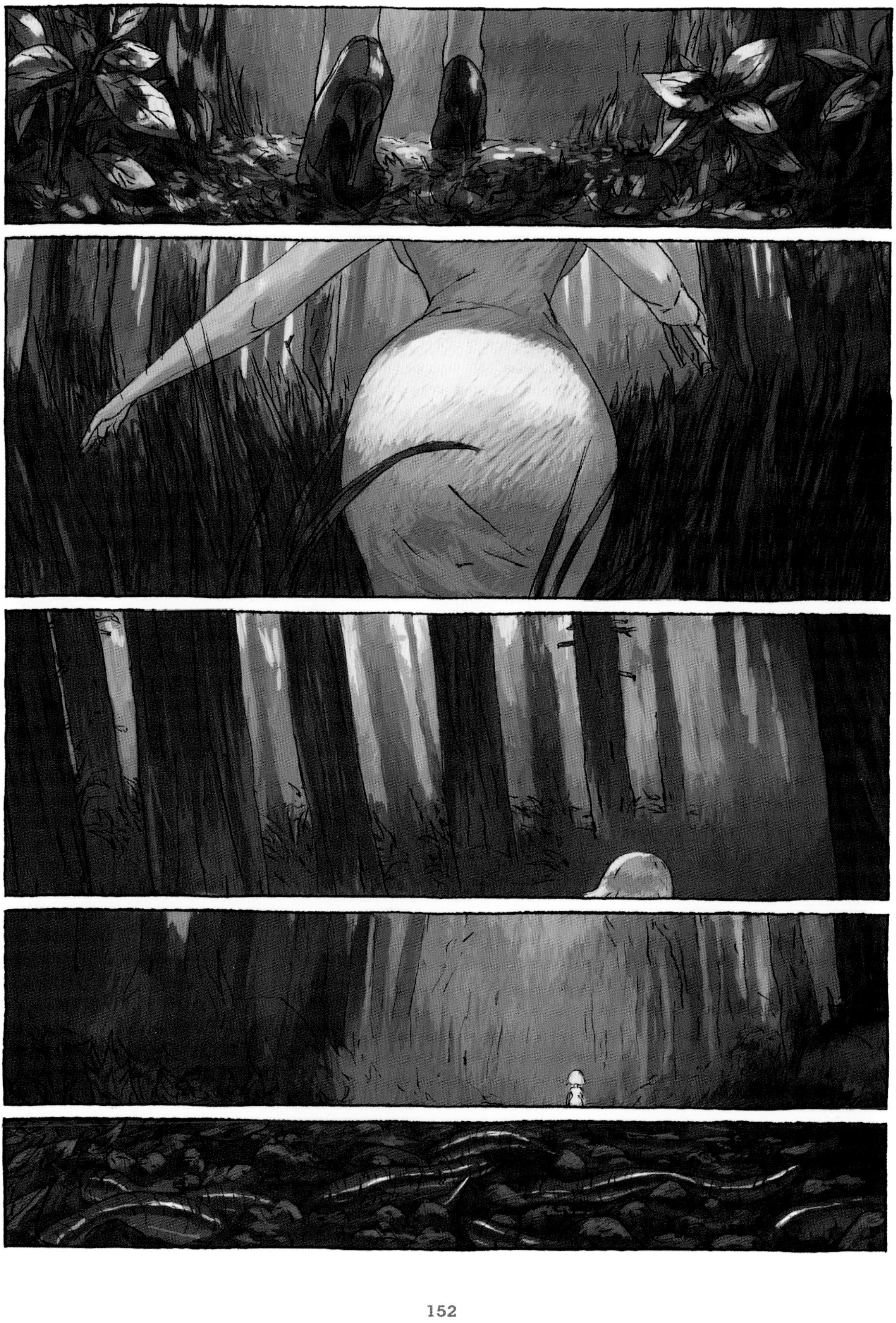

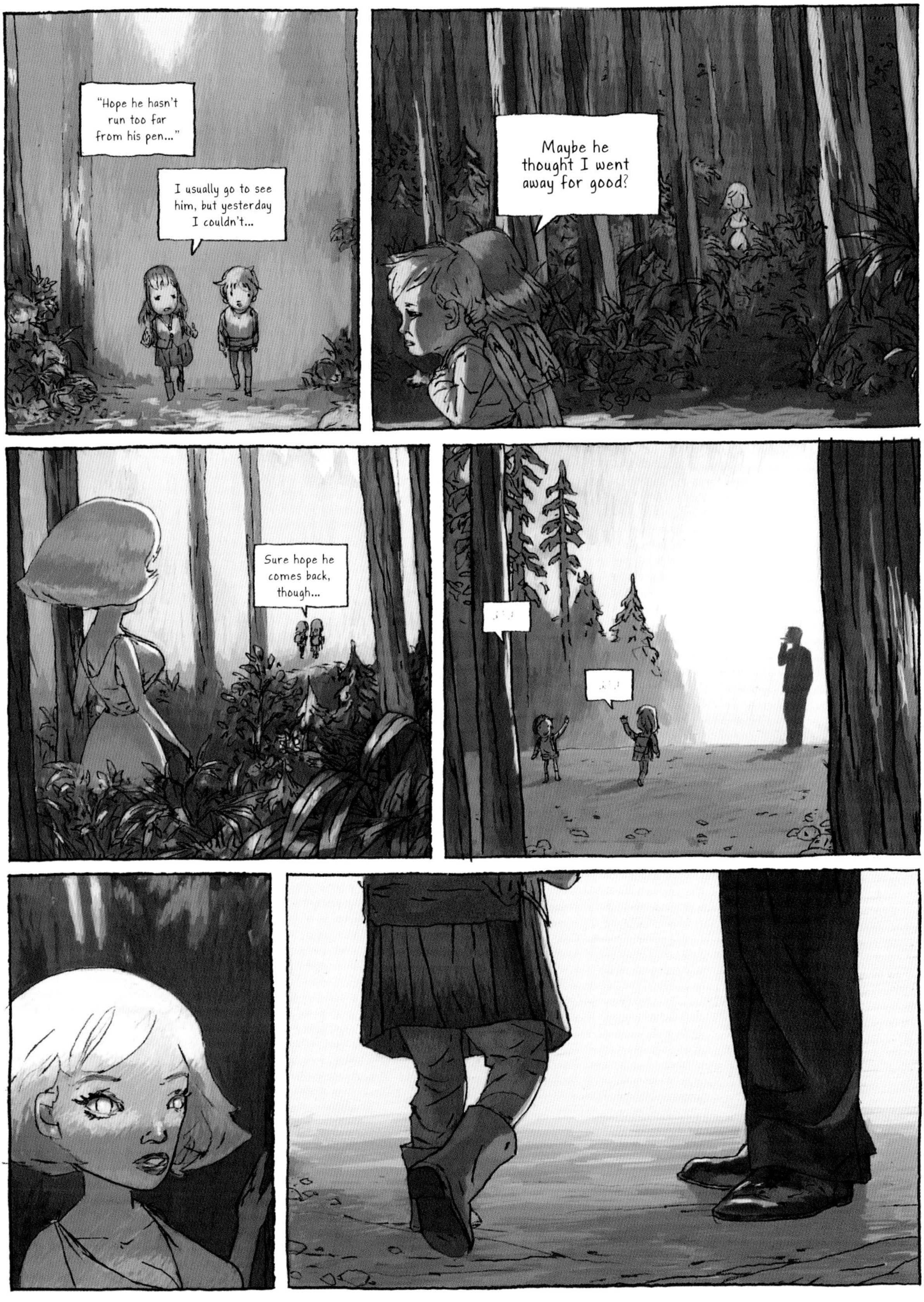
"Hope he hasn't run too far from his pen..."
I usually go to see him, but yesterday I couldn't...
Maybe he thought I went away for good?
Sure hope he comes back, though...

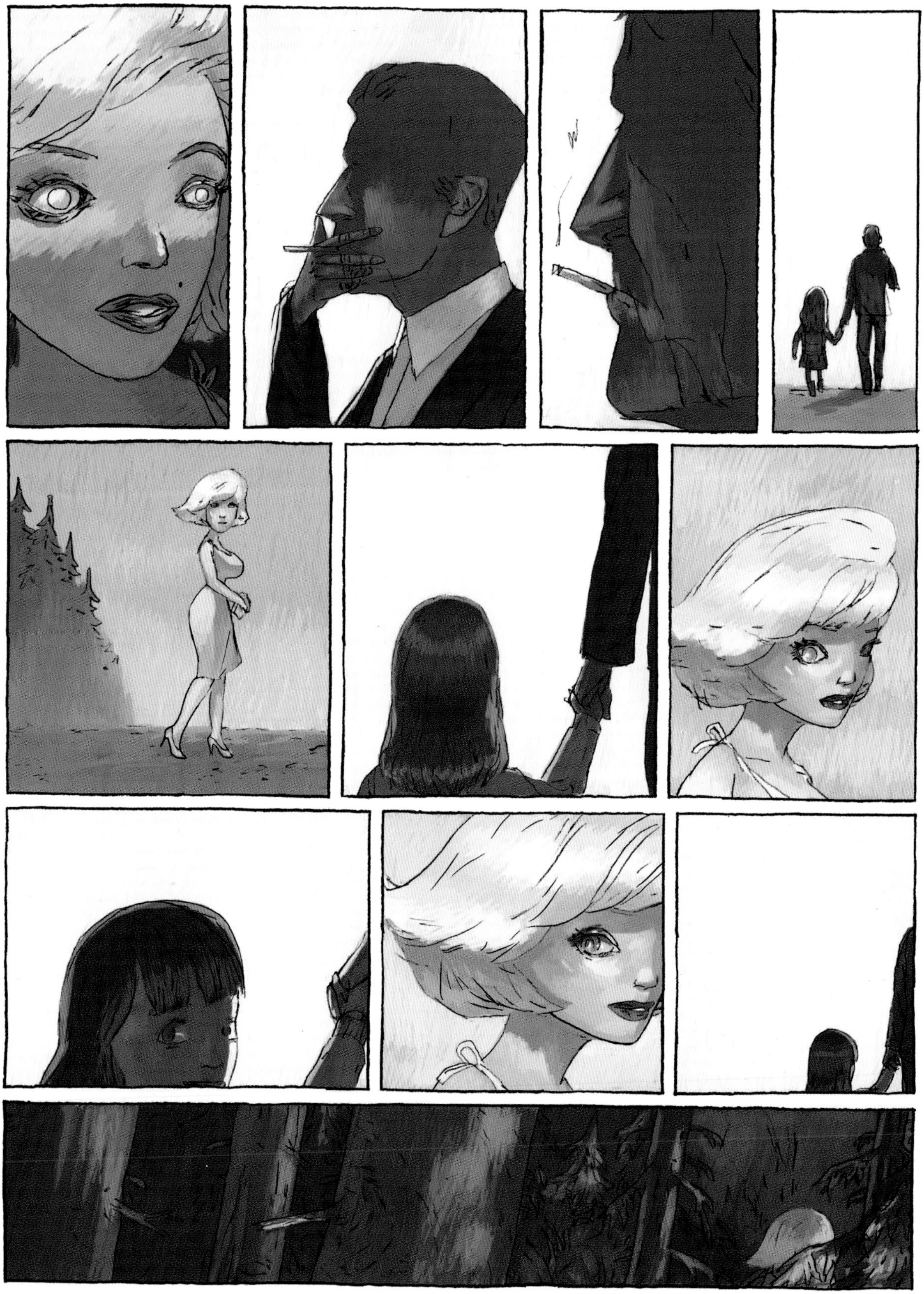

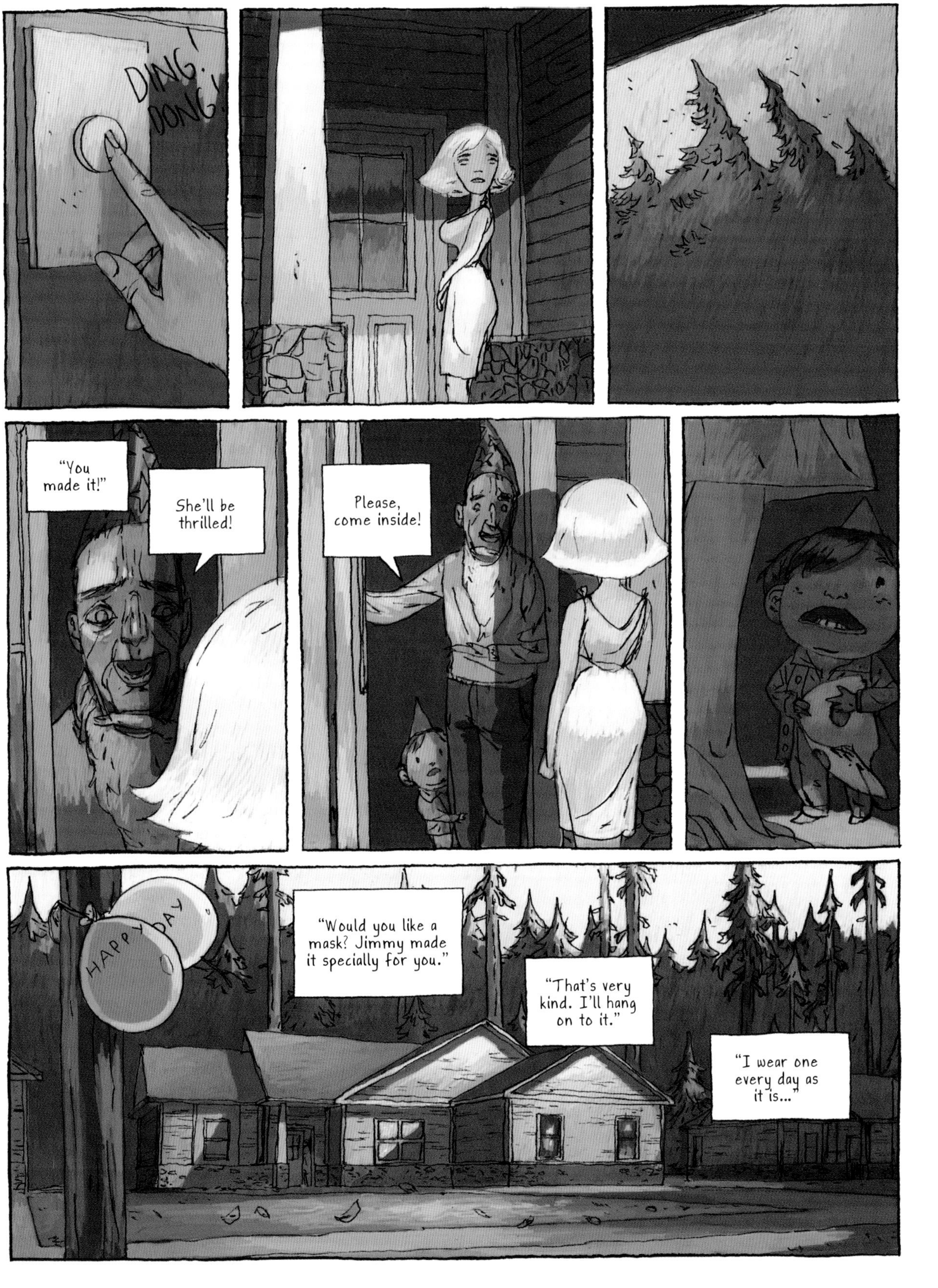
DING! DONG!
"You made it!"
She'll be thrilled!
Please, come inside!
HAPPY DAY
"Would you like a mask? Jimmy made it specially for you."
"That's very kind. I'll hang on to it."
"I wear one every day as it is..."

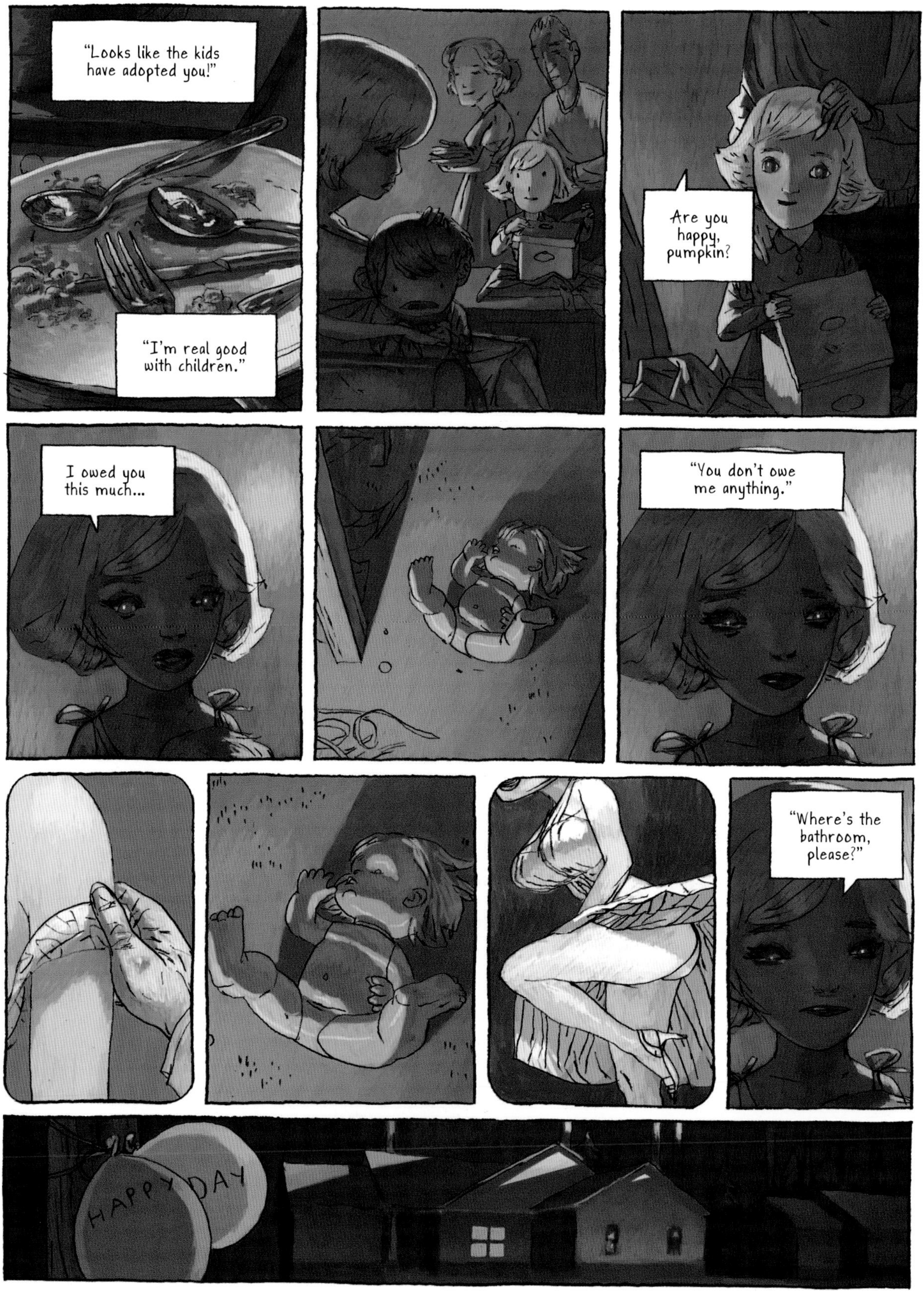
"Looks like the kids have adopted you!"
"I'm real good with children."
Are you happy, pumpkin?
I owed you this much...
"You don't owe me anything."
"Where's the bathroom, please?"
HAPPY DAY

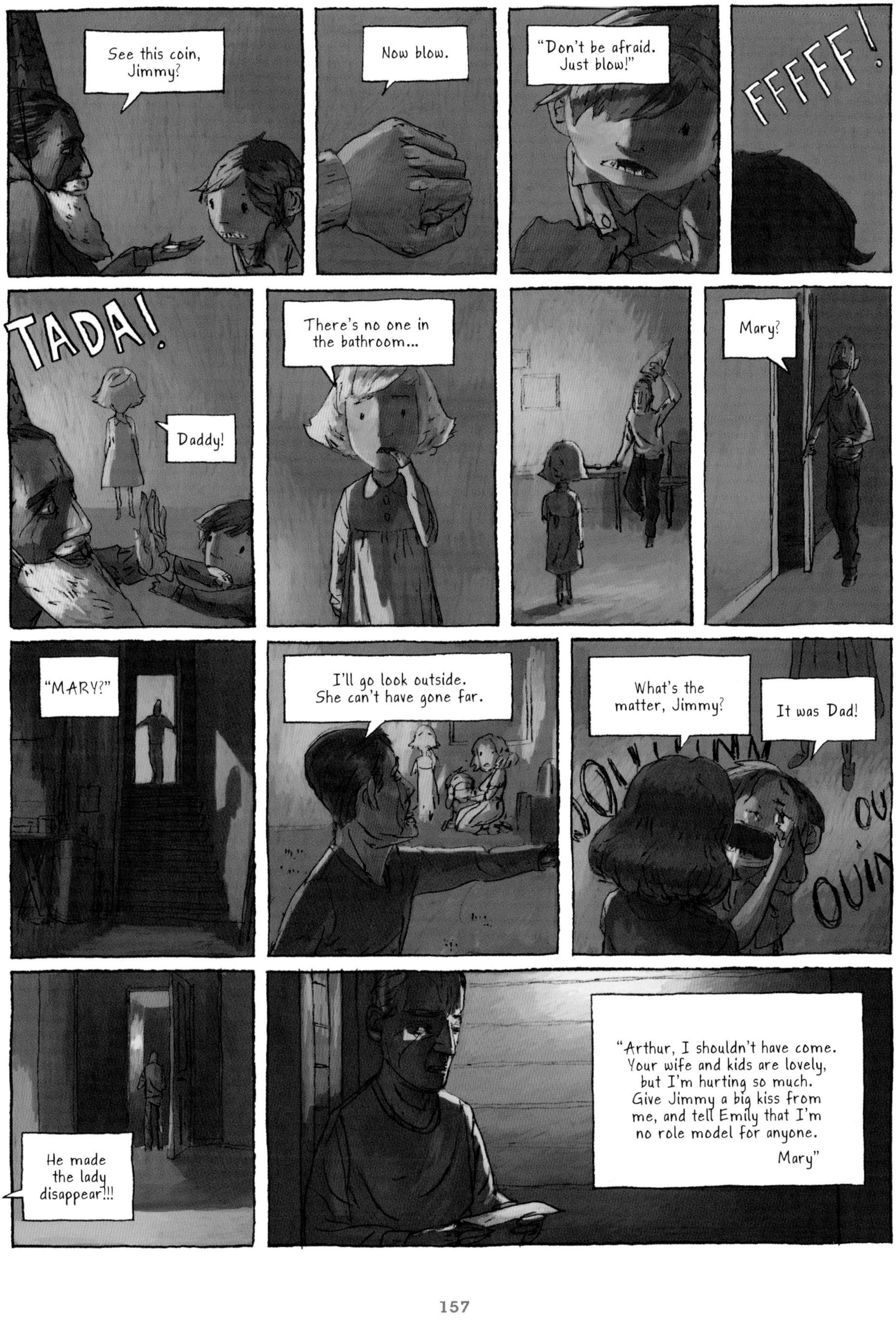

See this coin, Jimmy?
Now blow.
"Don't be afraid. Just blow!"
FFFFF!
TADA!
Daddy!
There's no one in the bathroom...
Mary?
"MARY?"
I'll go look outside. She can't have gone far.
What's the matter, Jimmy?
It was Dad!
OUIN
He made the lady disappear!!!
"Arthur, I shouldn't have come. Your wife and kids are lovely, but I'm hurting so much. Give Jimmy a big kiss from me, and tell Emily that I'm no role model for anyone.
Mary"

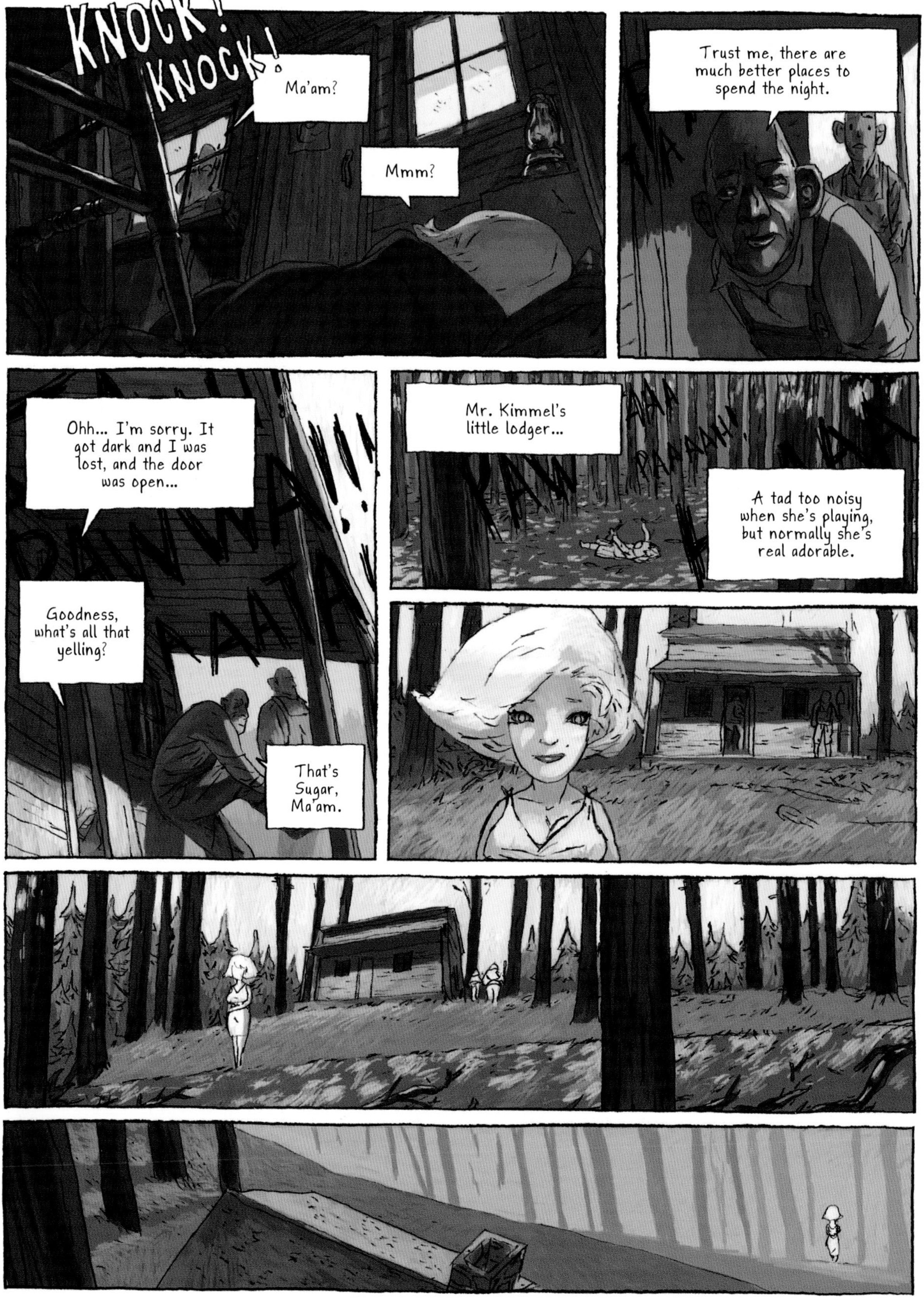
KNOCK! KNOCK!
Ma'am?
Mmm?
Trust me, there are much better places to spend the night.
Ohh... I'm sorry. It got dark and I was lost, and the door was open...
Goodness, what's all that yelling?
That's Sugar, Ma'am.
Mr. Kimmel's little lodger...
A tad too noisy when she's playing, but normally she's real adorable.

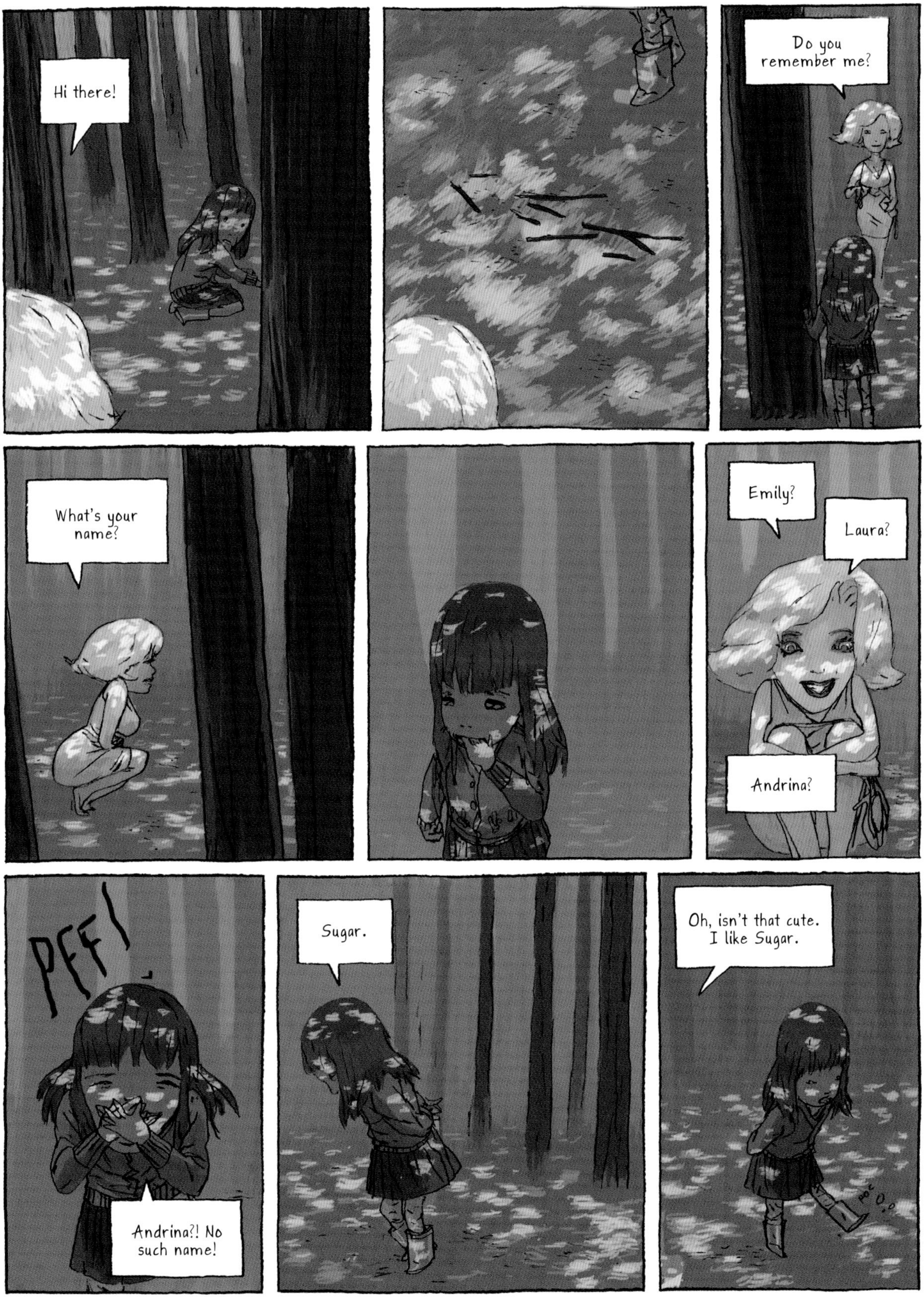
Hi there!
Do you remember me?
What's your name?
Emily?
Laura?
Andrina?
PFF!
Andrina?! No such name!
Sugar.
Oh, isn't that cute. I like Sugar.

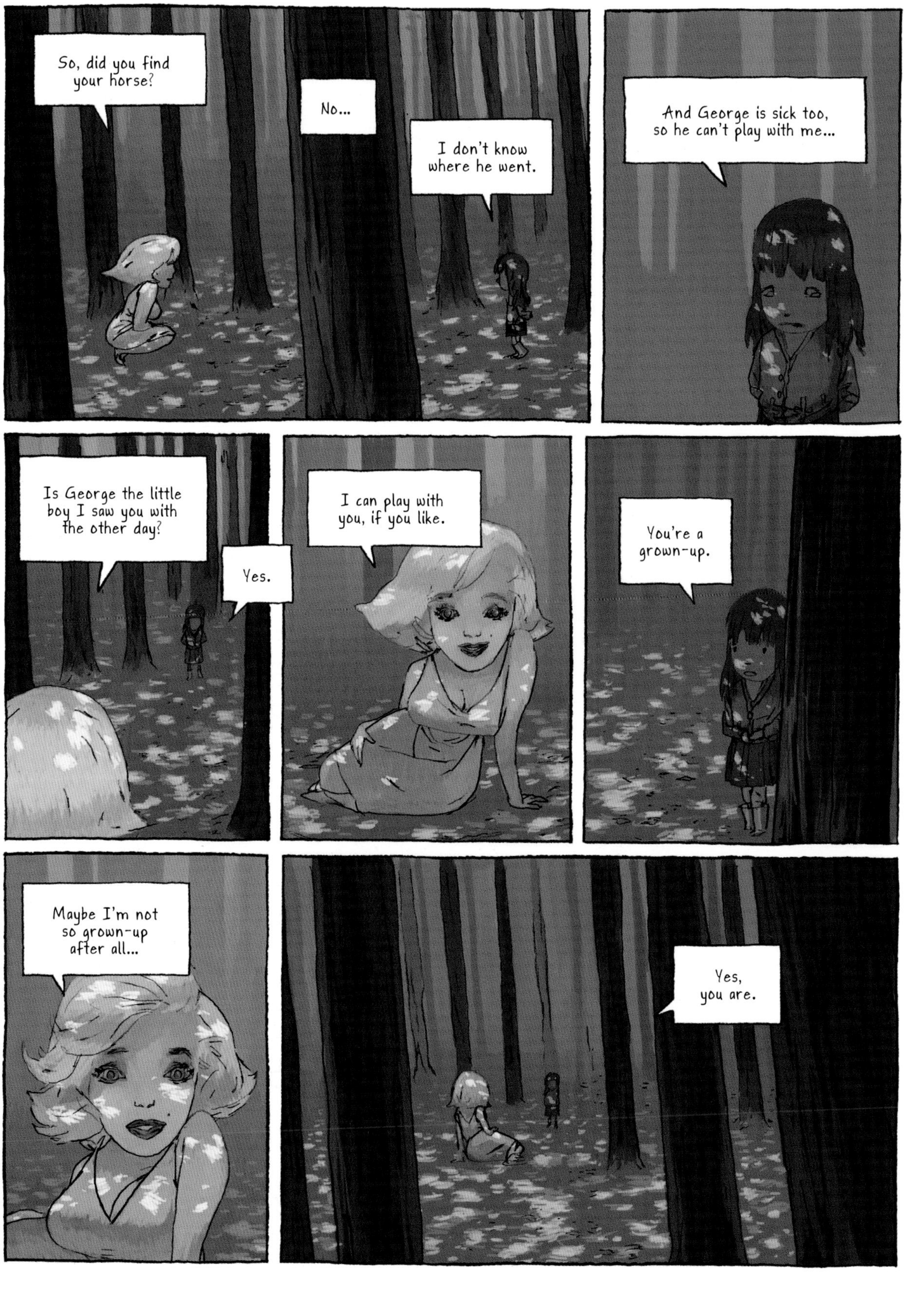
So, did you find your horse?
No...
I don't know where he went.
And George is sick too, so he can't play with me...
Is George the little boy I saw you with the other day?
Yes.
I can play with you, if you like.
You're a grown-up.
Maybe I'm not so grown-up after all...
Yes, you are.

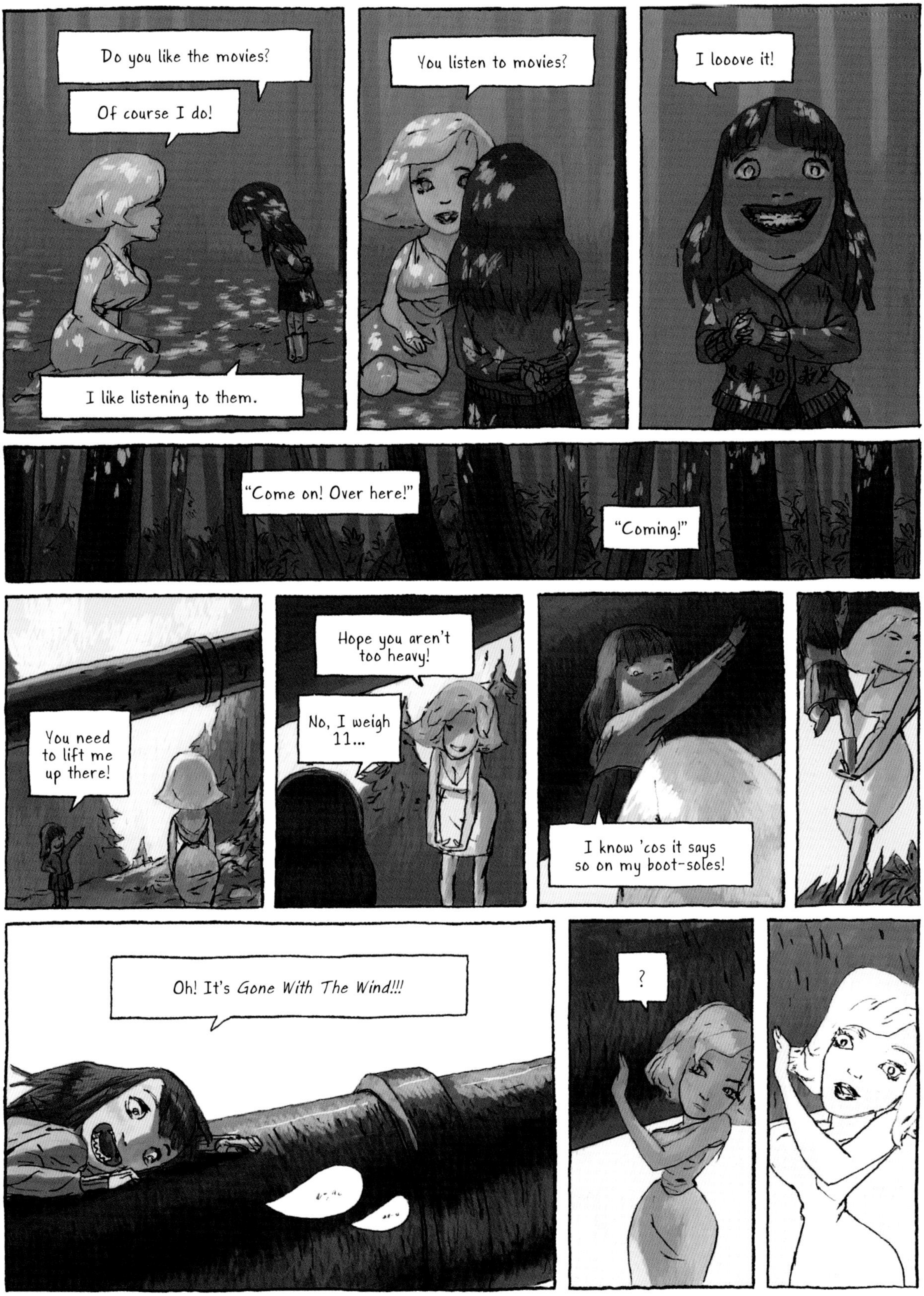
Do you like the movies?
Of course I do!
I like listening to them.
You listen to movies?
I looove it!
"Come on! Over here!"
"Coming!"
You need to lift me up there!
Hope you aren't too heavy!
No, I weigh 11...
I know 'cos it says so on my boot-soles!
Oh! It's *Gone With The Wind*!!!
?

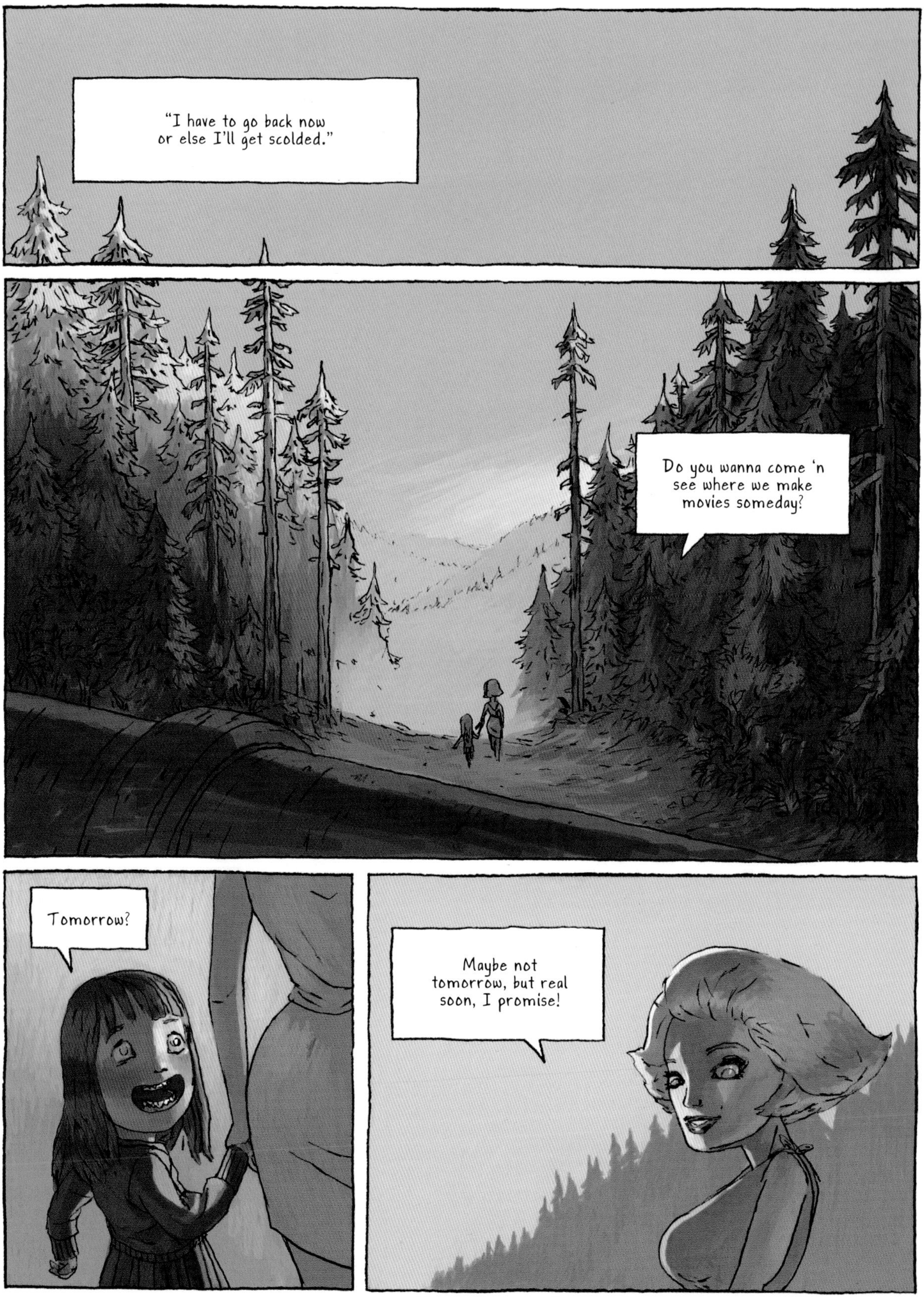
"I have to go back now or else I'll get scolded."
Do you wanna come 'n see where we make movies someday?
Tomorrow?
Maybe not tomorrow, but real soon, I promise!

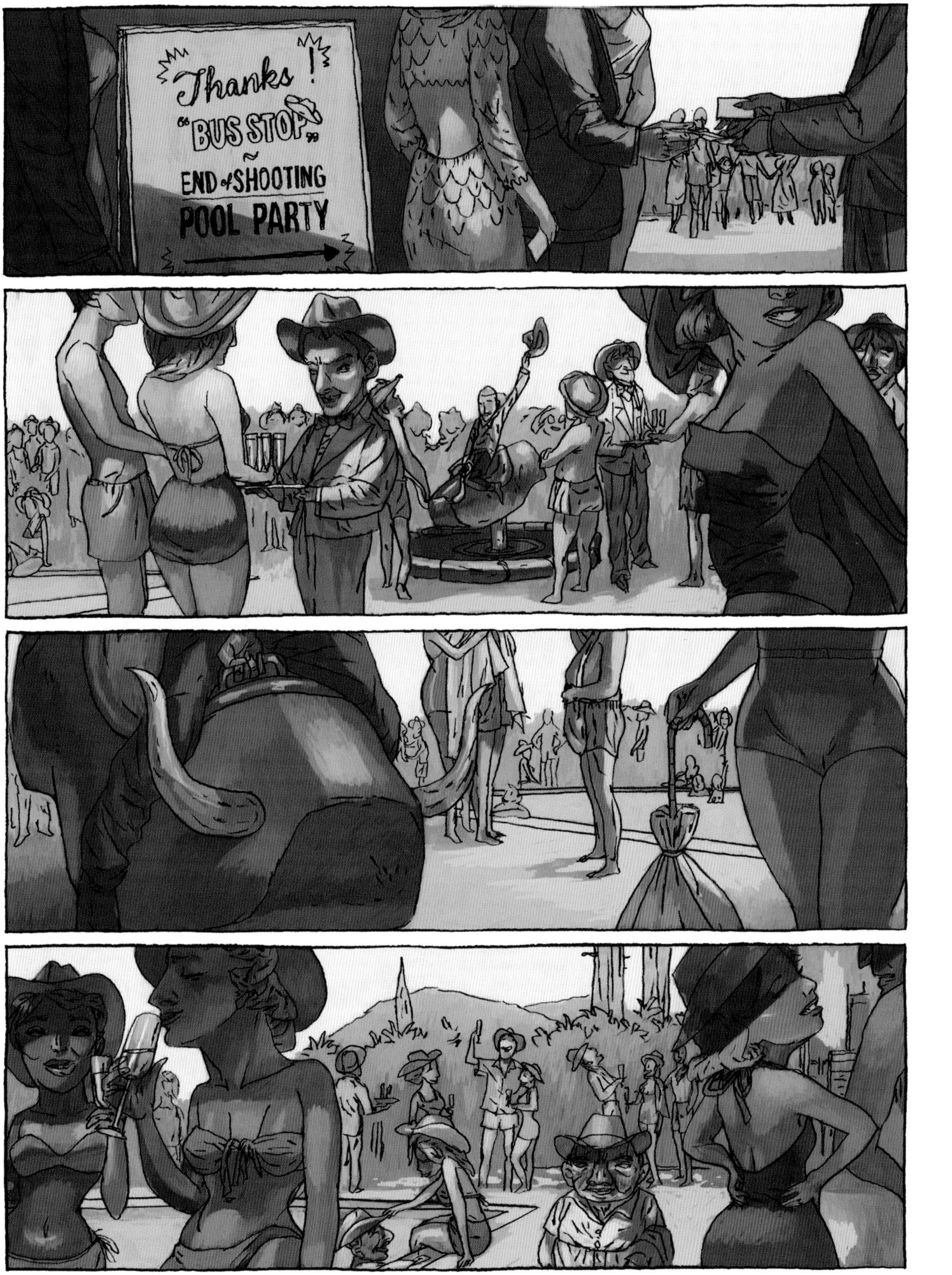
Thanks!
"BUS STOP"
~
END of SHOOTING
POOL PARTY

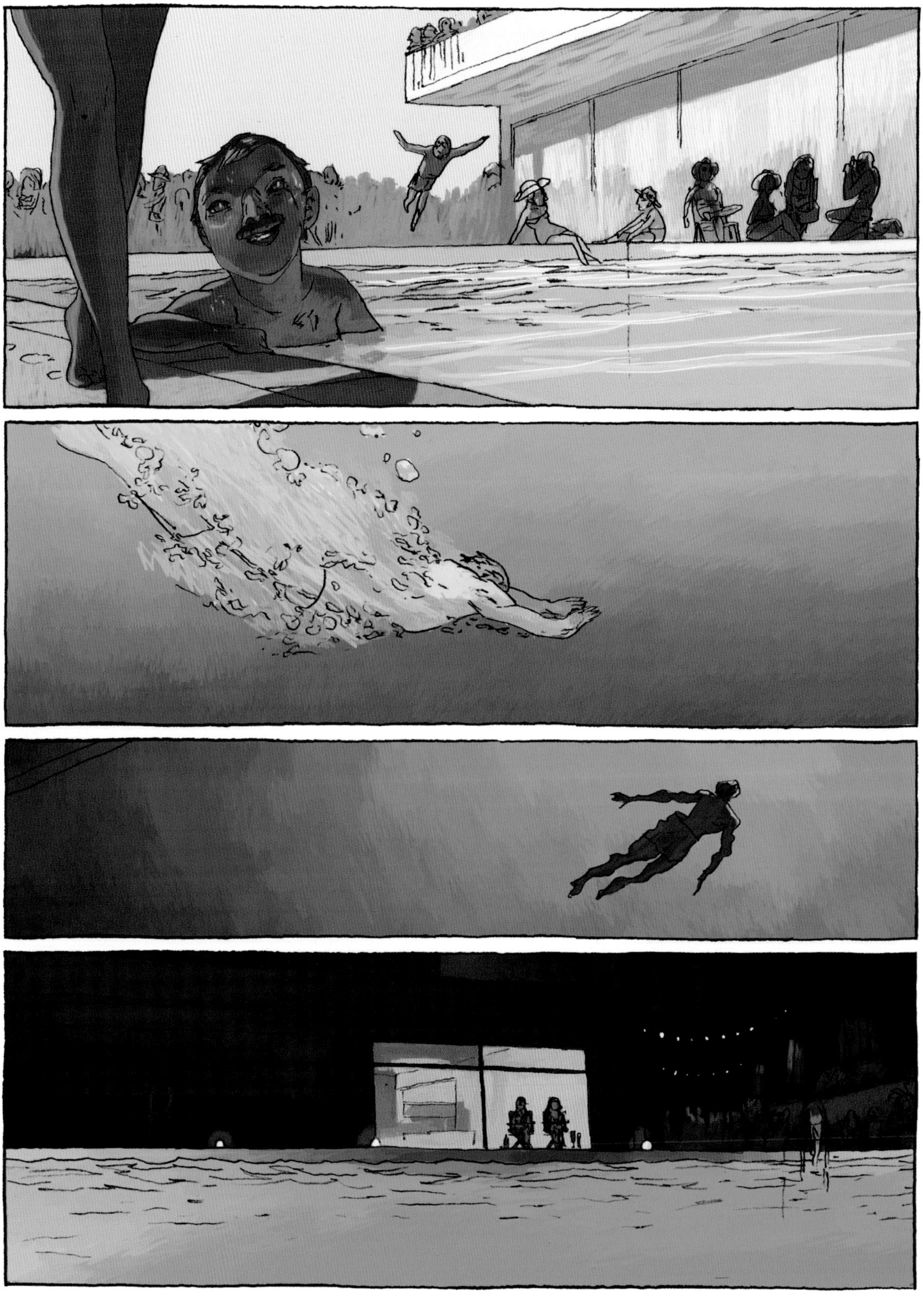

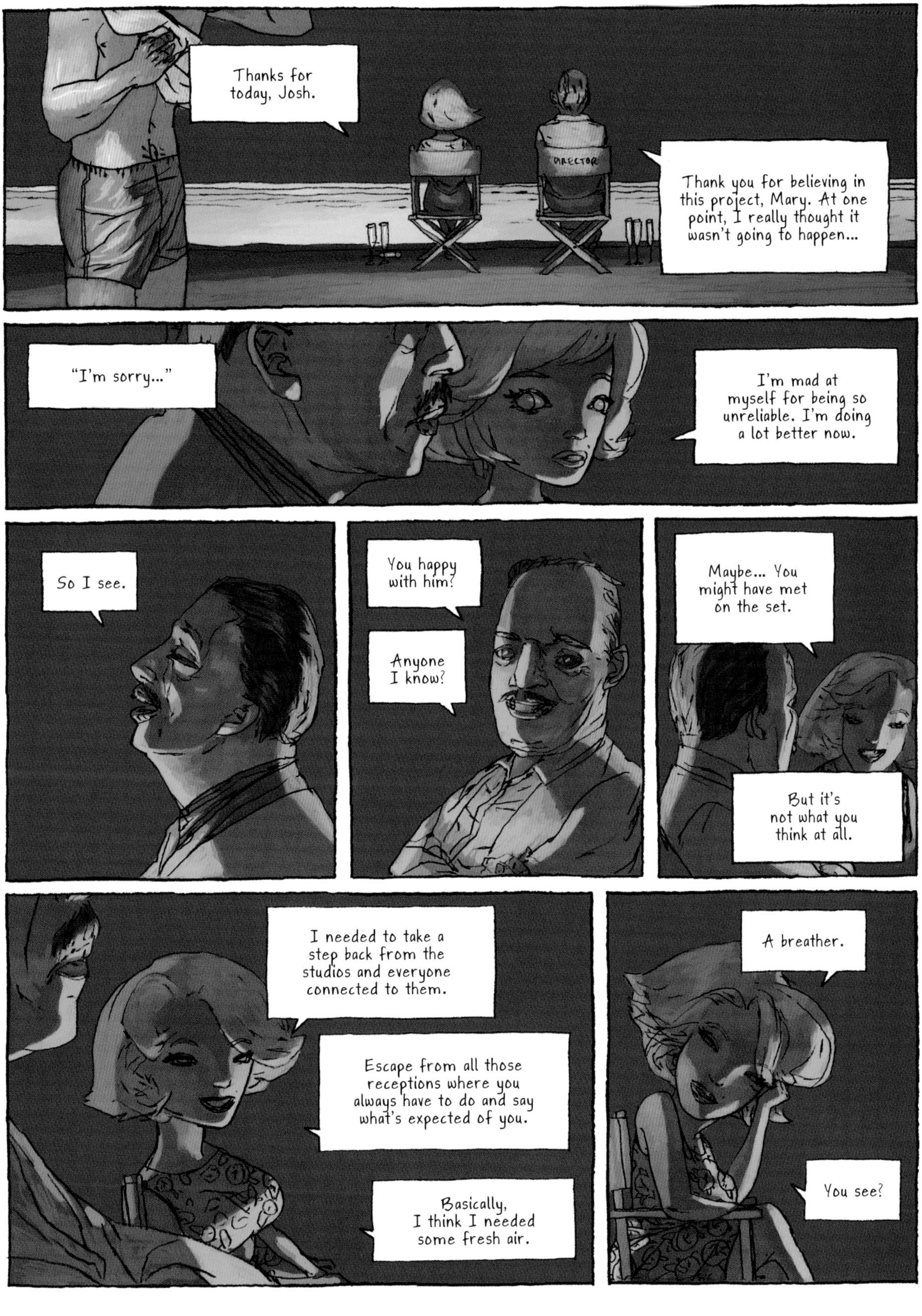
Thanks for today, Josh.
Thank you for believing in this project, Mary. At one point, I really thought it wasn't going to happen...
DIRECTOR
"I'm sorry..."
I'm mad at myself for being so unreliable. I'm doing a lot better now.
So I see.
You happy with him?
Anyone I know?
Maybe... You might have met on the set.
But it's not what you think at all.
I needed to take a step back from the studios and everyone connected to them.
Escape from all those receptions where you always have to do and say what's expected of you.
Basically, I think I needed some fresh air.
A breather.
You see?

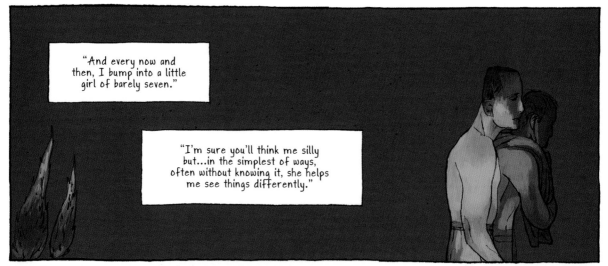

"And every now and then, I bump into a little girl of barely seven."

"I'm sure you'll think me silly but...in the simplest of ways, often without knowing it, she helps me see things differently."

You worry me, Mary. You'll be talking about wanting a baby next.

No, I think this goes beyond that.

She makes me feel alive.

"It's strange, but I've realized that simplicity tends to be a luxury here."

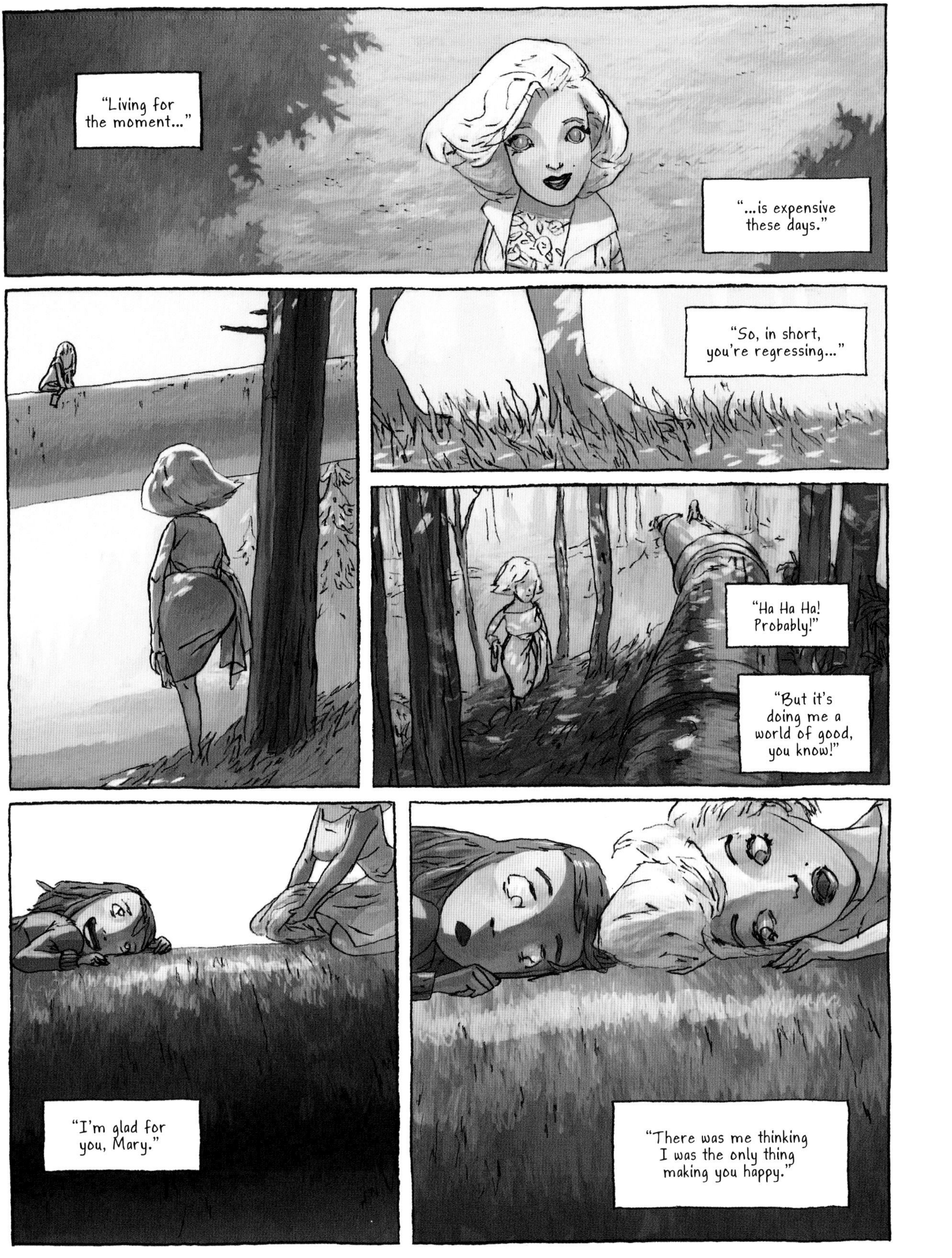
"Living for the moment..."
"...is expensive these days."
"So, in short, you're regressing..."
"Ha Ha Ha! Probably!"
"But it's doing me a world of good, you know!"
"I'm glad for you, Mary."
"There was me thinking I was the only thing making you happy."

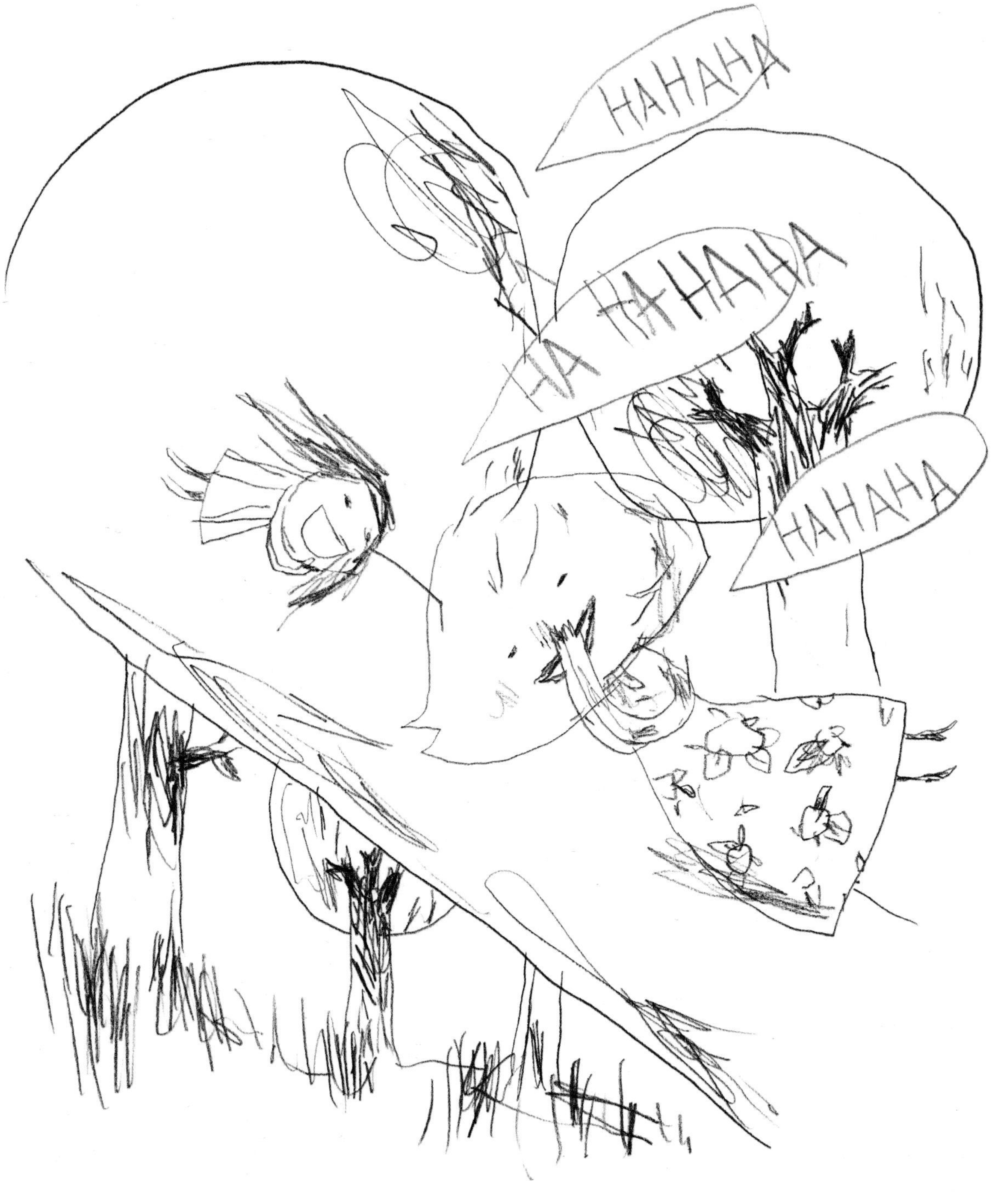
HAHAHA
HA HAHAHA
HAHAHA

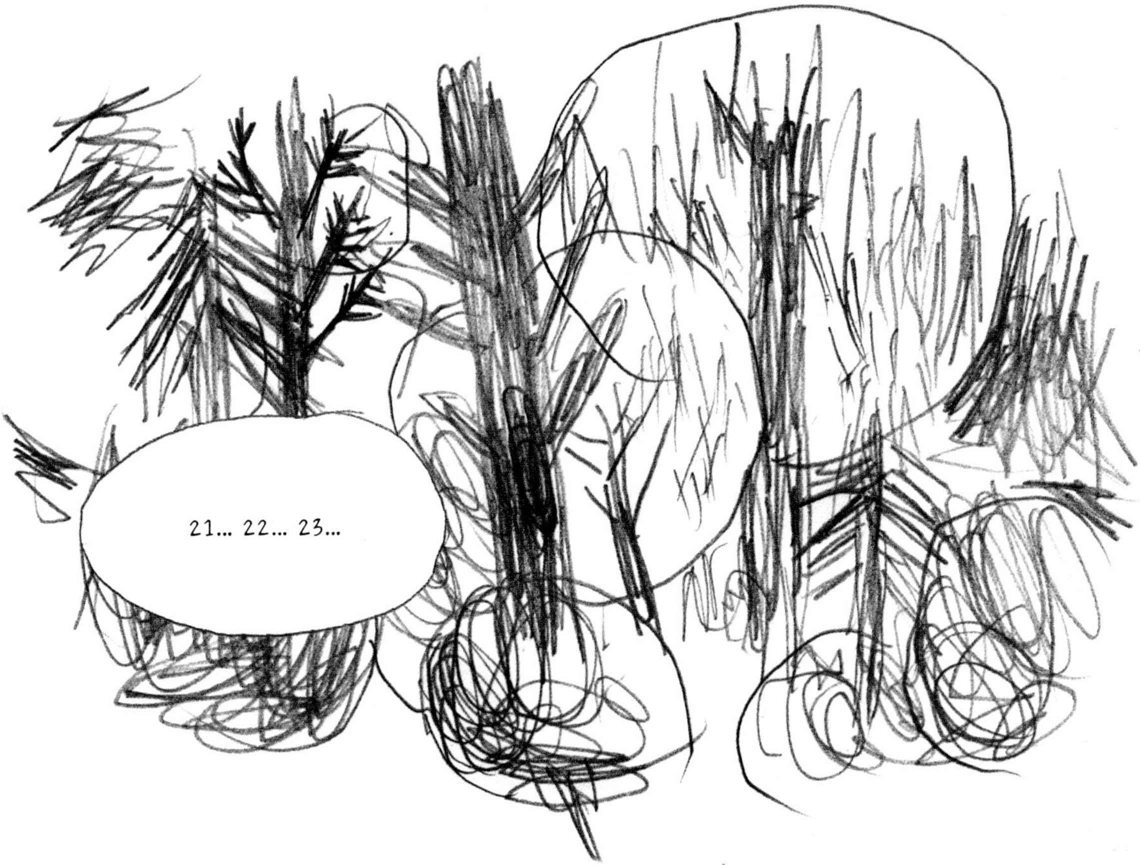
21... 22... 23...

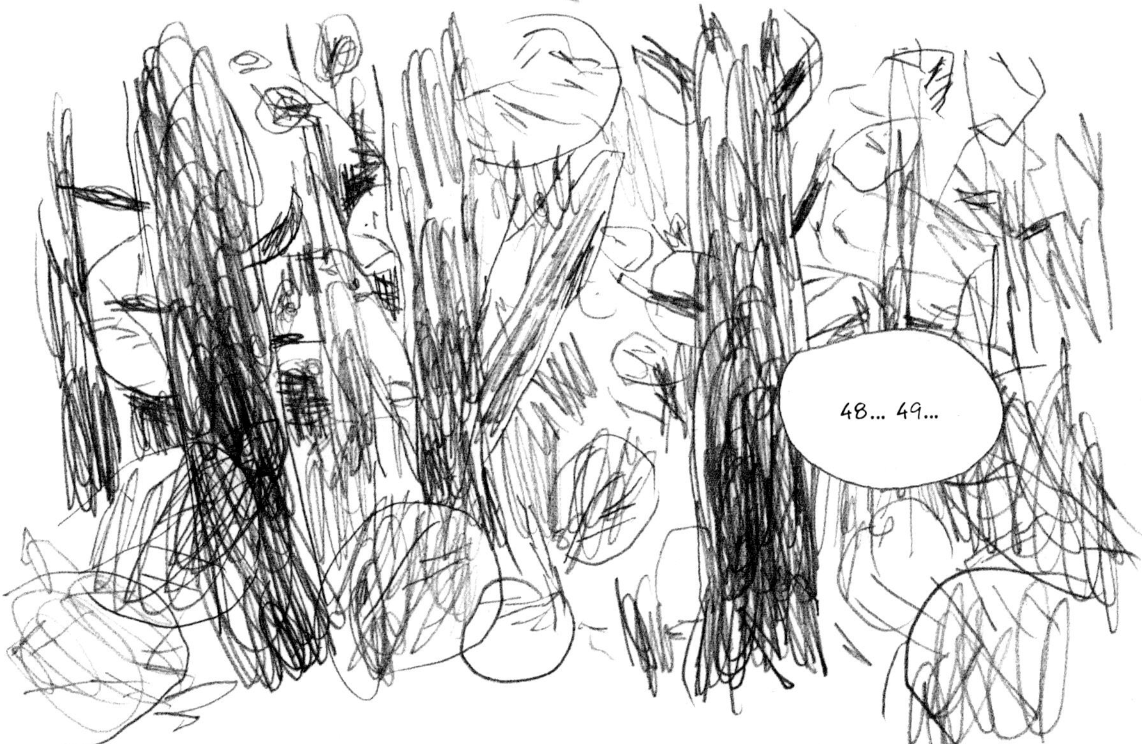
48... 49...

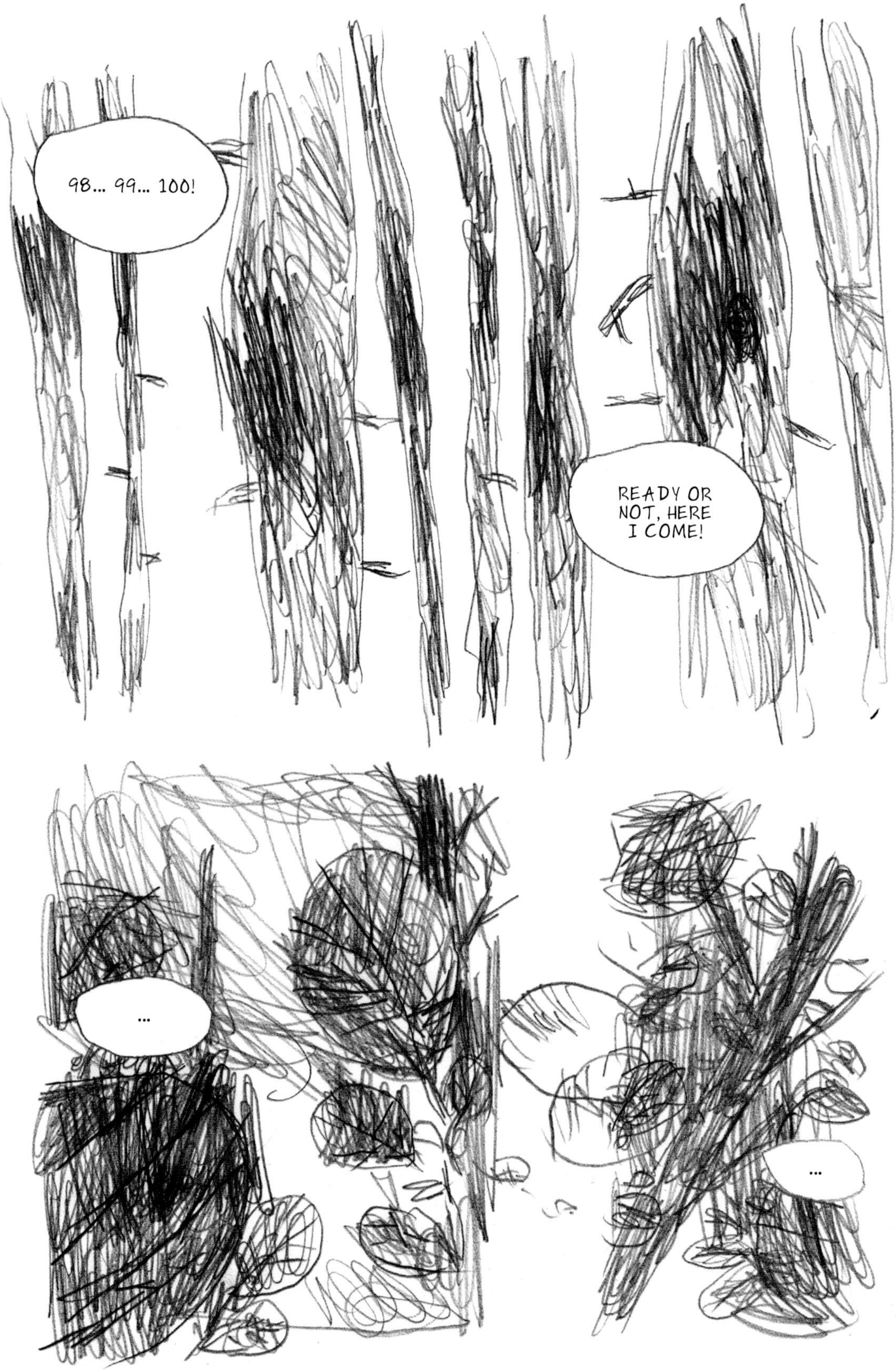
98... 99... 100!
READY OR NOT, HERE I COME!
...
...

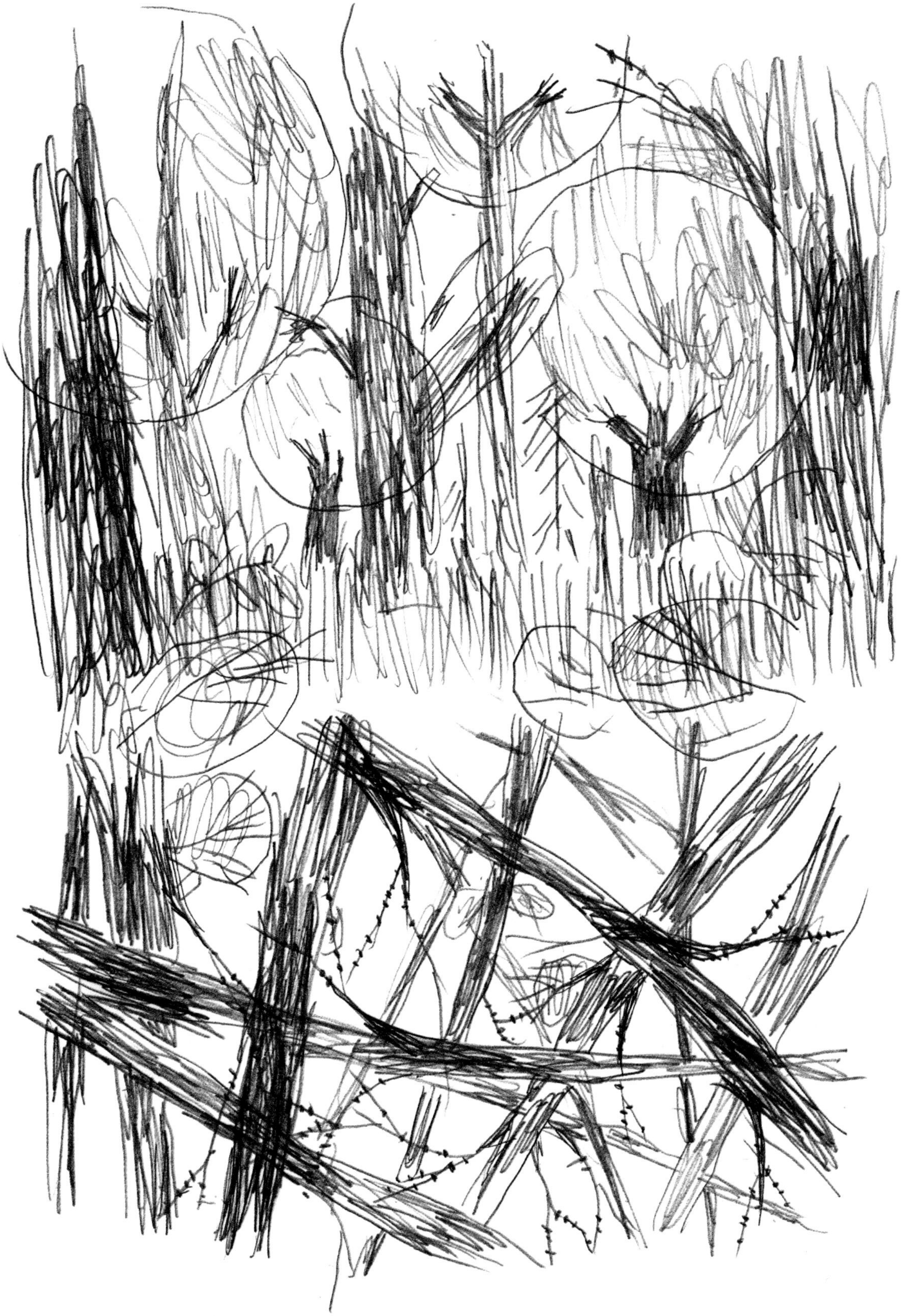

CHAPTER 3
HIDE
& SEEK

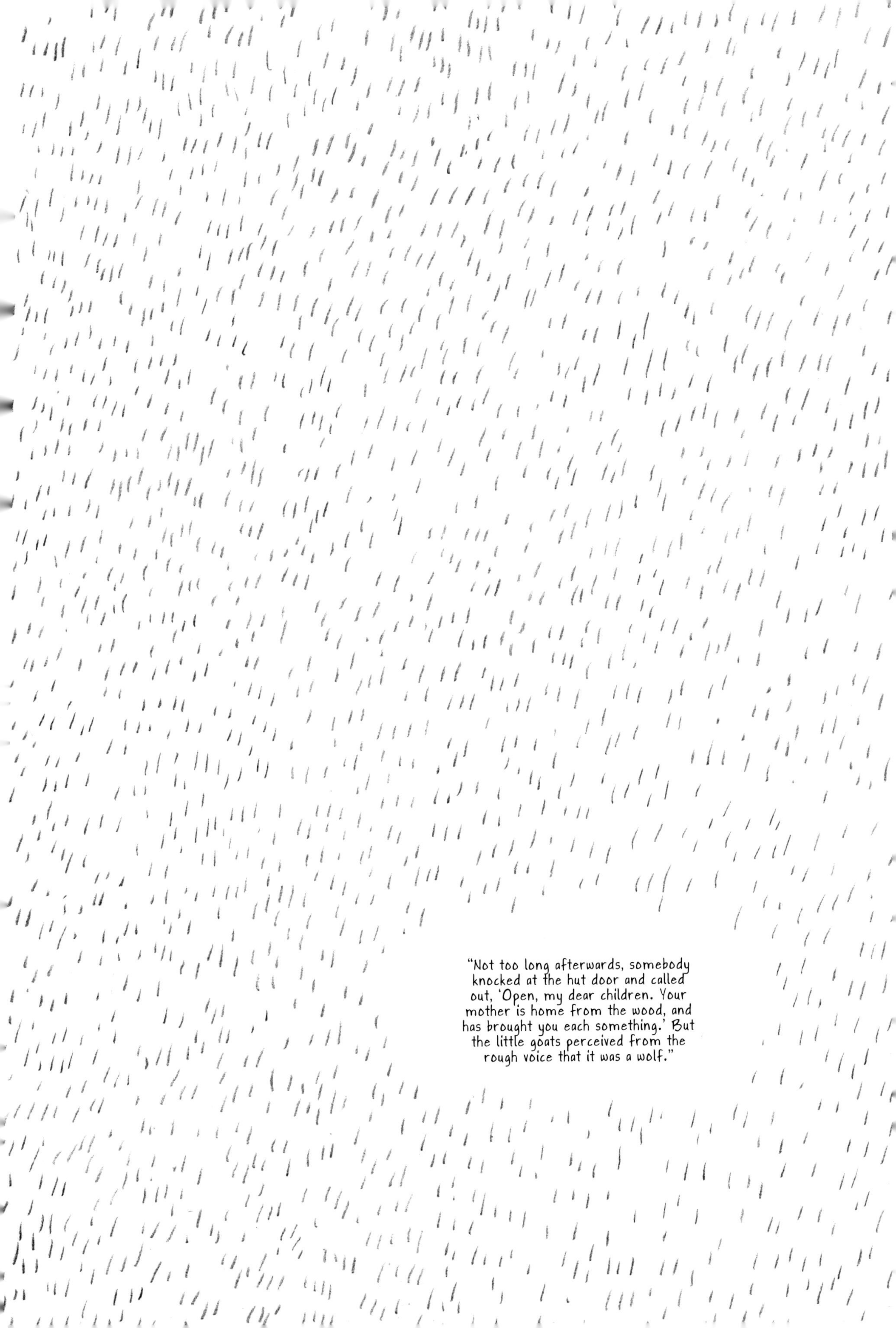

"Not too long afterwards, somebody knocked at the hut door and called out, 'Open, my dear children. Your mother is home from the wood, and has brought you each something.' But the little goats perceived from the rough voice that it was a wolf."

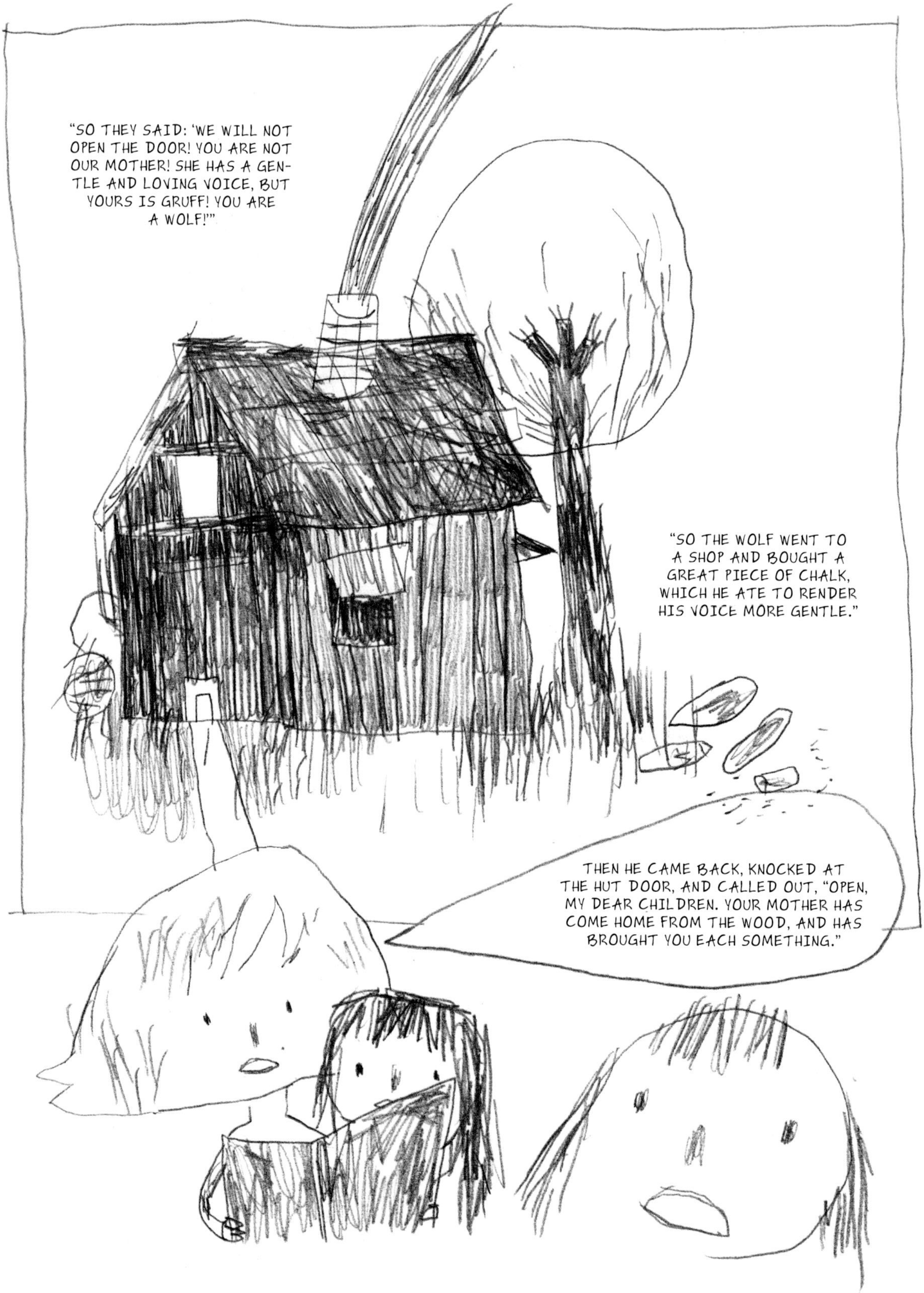
"SO THEY SAID: 'WE WILL NOT OPEN THE DOOR! YOU ARE NOT OUR MOTHER! SHE HAS A GENTLE AND LOVING VOICE, BUT YOURS IS GRUFF! YOU ARE A WOLF!'"
"SO THE WOLF WENT TO A SHOP AND BOUGHT A GREAT PIECE OF CHALK, WHICH HE ATE TO RENDER HIS VOICE MORE GENTLE."
THEN HE CAME BACK, KNOCKED AT THE HUT DOOR, AND CALLED OUT, "OPEN, MY DEAR CHILDREN. YOUR MOTHER HAS COME HOME FROM THE WOOD, AND HAS BROUGHT YOU EACH SOMETHING."

"BUT THE WOLF HAD PLACED HIS BLACK PAW UPON THE WINDOW-SILL, SO THE GOATS SAW IT AND REPLIED:"

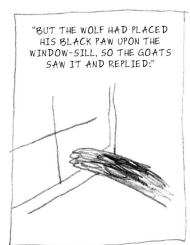

"'NO, WE WILL NOT OPEN THE DOOR! OUR MOTHER HAS NOT BLACK PAWS! YOU ARE A WOLF!'"

"SO THE WOLF WENT TO THE BAKER AND SAID:

I HAVE HURT MY PAW, PUT SOME DOUGH ON IT."

"THE BAKER WAS AFRAID, SO HE POWDERED THE WOLF'S PAW WITH FLOUR."

"NOW THE VILLAIN WENT FOR TO THE HUT FOR THE THIRD TIME, AND KNOCKING ON THE DOOR, HE CALLED OUT:"

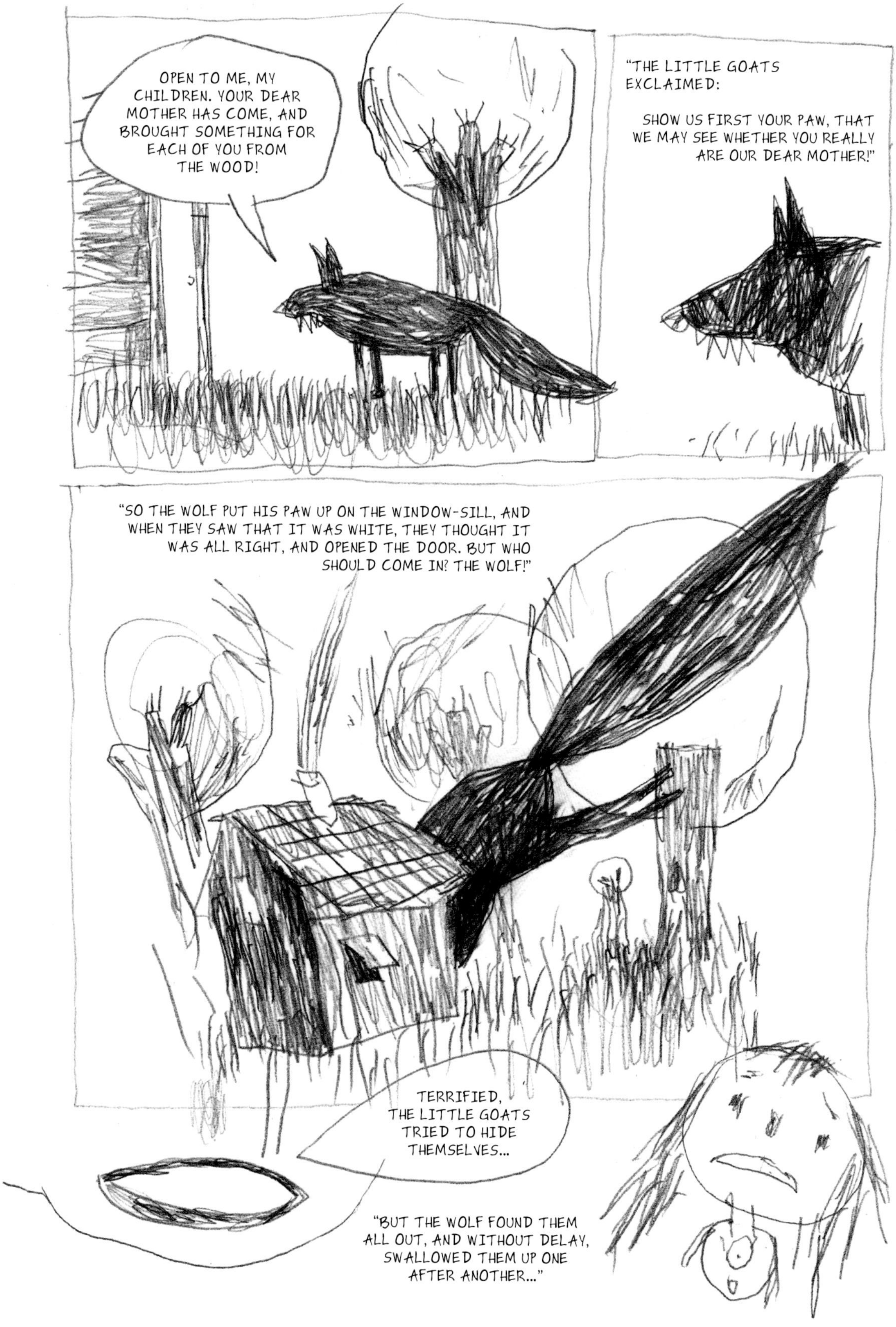

OPEN TO ME, MY CHILDREN. YOUR DEAR MOTHER HAS COME, AND BROUGHT SOMETHING FOR EACH OF YOU FROM THE WOOD!
"THE LITTLE GOATS EXCLAIMED:
SHOW US FIRST YOUR PAW, THAT WE MAY SEE WHETHER YOU REALLY ARE OUR DEAR MOTHER!"
"SO THE WOLF PUT HIS PAW UP ON THE WINDOW-SILL, AND WHEN THEY SAW THAT IT WAS WHITE, THEY THOUGHT IT WAS ALL RIGHT, AND OPENED THE DOOR. BUT WHO SHOULD COME IN? THE WOLF!"
TERRIFIED, THE LITTLE GOATS TRIED TO HIDE THEMSELVES...
"BUT THE WOLF FOUND THEM ALL OUT, AND WITHOUT DELAY, SWALLOWED THEM UP ONE AFTER ANOTHER..."

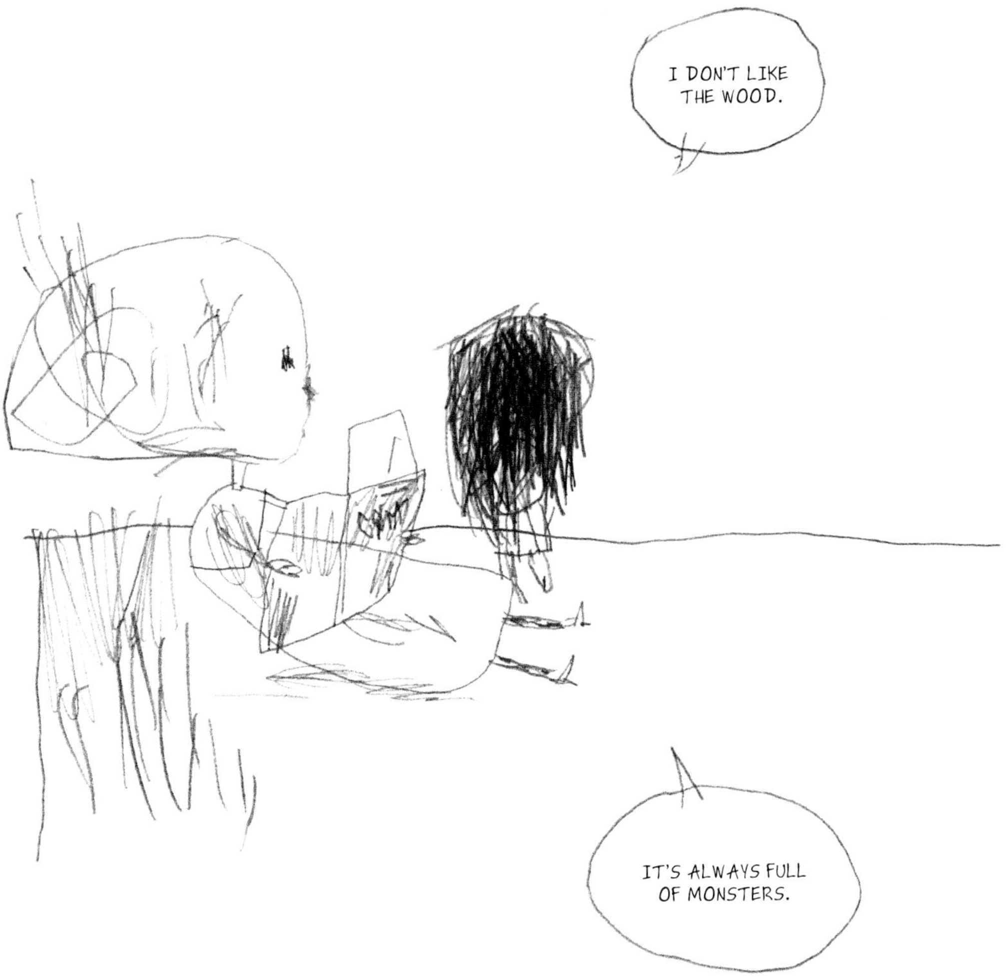
I DON'T LIKE THE WOOD.
IT'S ALWAYS FULL OF MONSTERS.

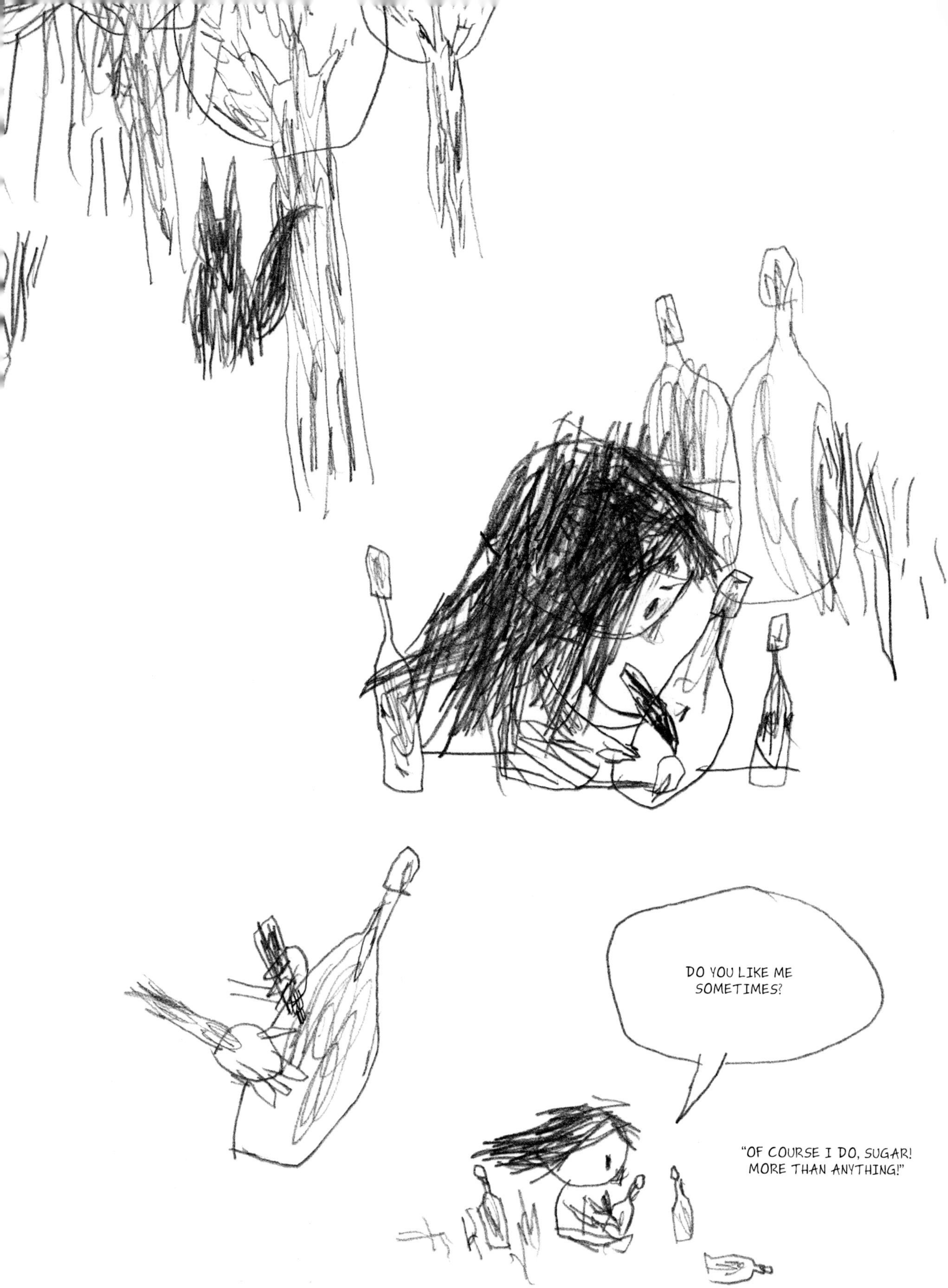
DO YOU LIKE ME SOMETIMES?
"OF COURSE I DO, SUGAR! MORE THAN ANYTHING!"

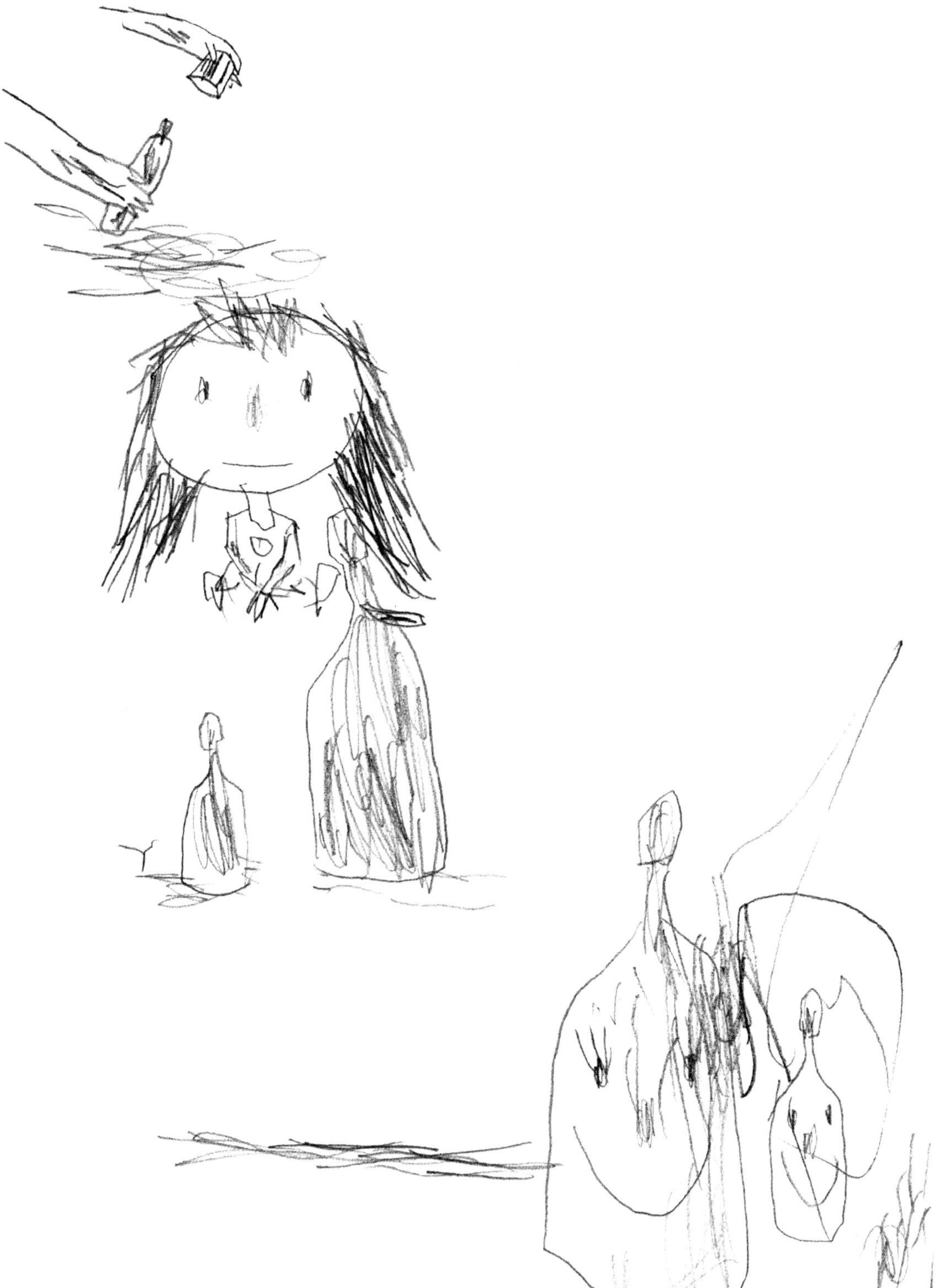

"I WISH I COULD BE WITH YOU ALL THE TIME..."

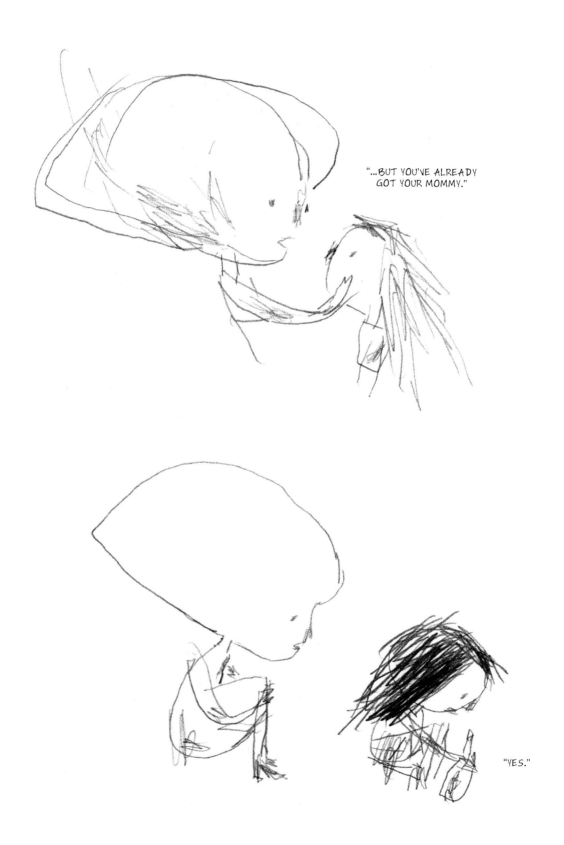

"...BUT YOU'VE ALREADY GOT YOUR MOMMY."

"YES."

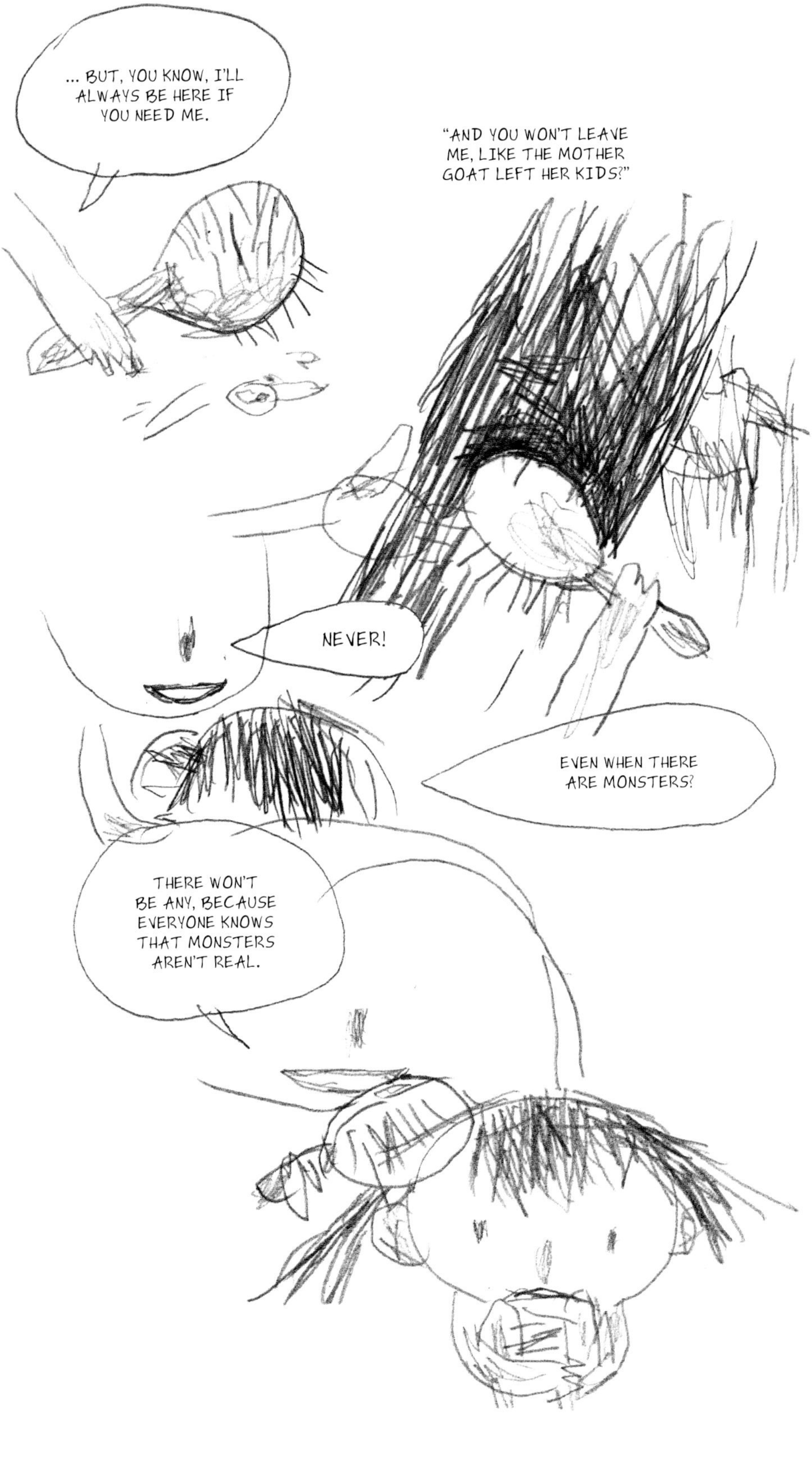
... BUT, YOU KNOW, I'LL ALWAYS BE HERE IF YOU NEED ME.
"AND YOU WON'T LEAVE ME, LIKE THE MOTHER GOAT LEFT HER KIDS?"
NEVER!
EVEN WHEN THERE ARE MONSTERS?
THERE WON'T BE ANY, BECAUSE EVERYONE KNOWS THAT MONSTERS AREN'T REAL.

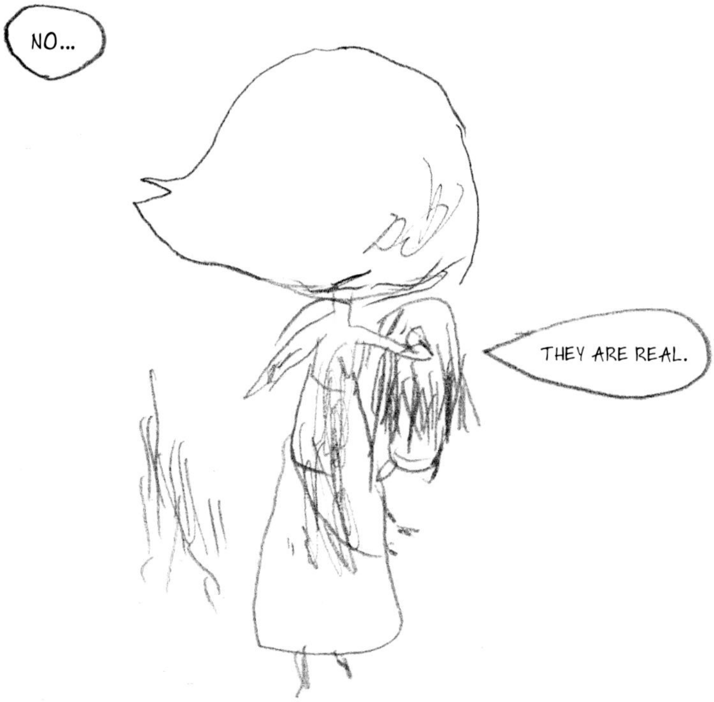
NO...
THEY ARE REAL.

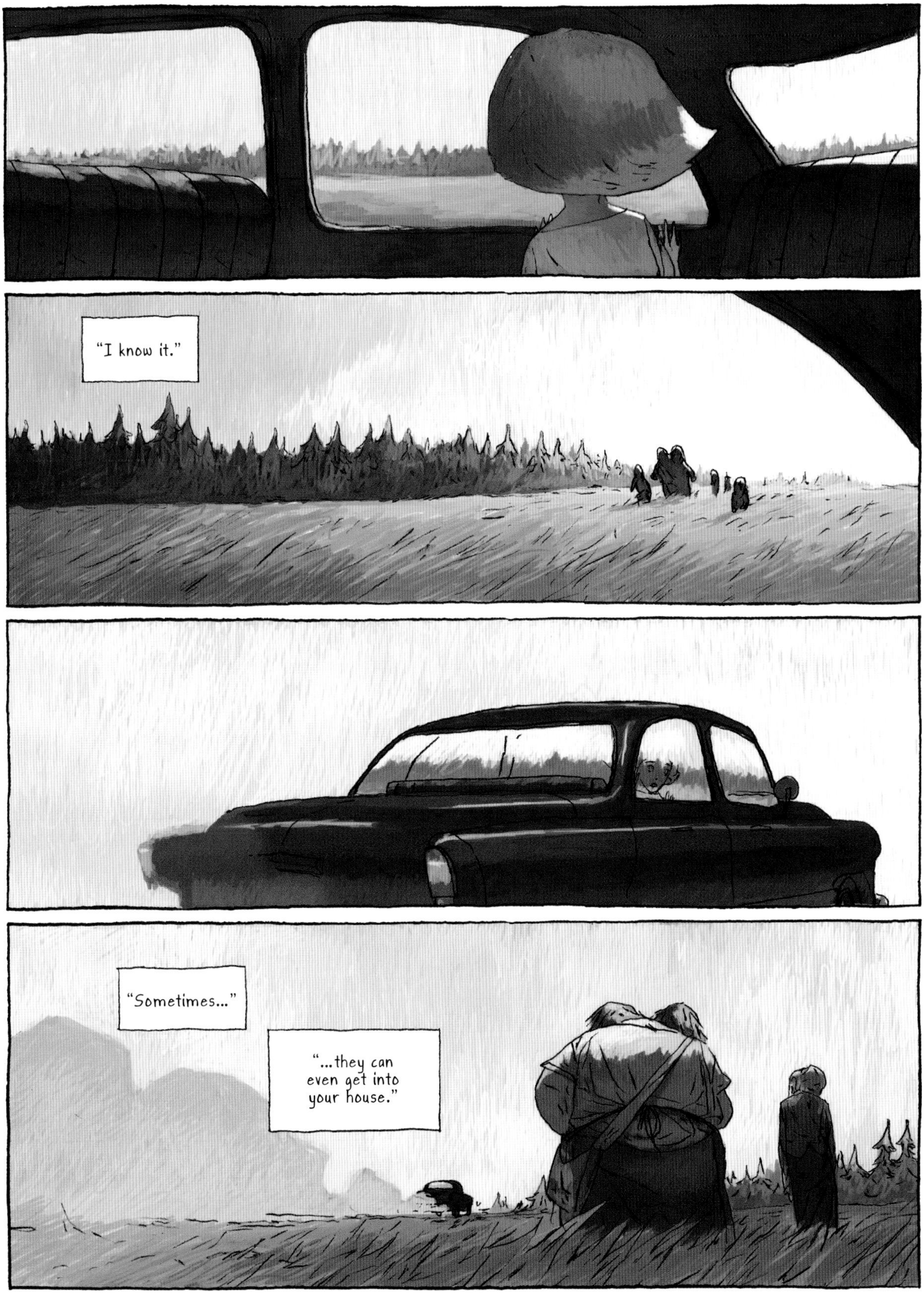
"I know it."
"Sometimes..."
"...they can even get into your house."

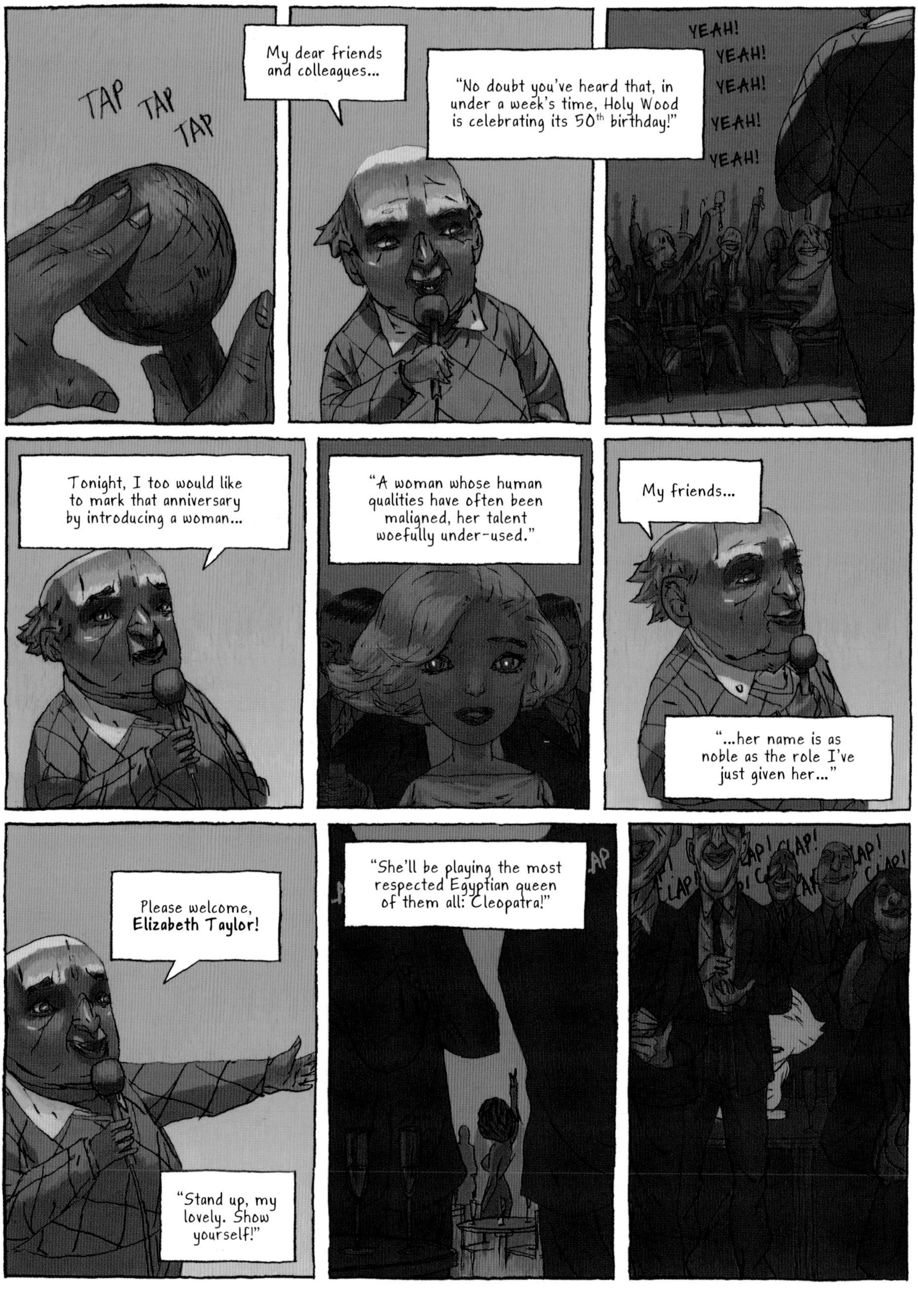
TAP TAP TAP
My dear friends and colleagues...
"No doubt you've heard that, in under a week's time, Holy Wood is celebrating its 50th birthday!"
YEAH! YEAH! YEAH! YEAH! YEAH!
Tonight, I too would like to mark that anniversary by introducing a woman...
"A woman whose human qualities have often been maligned, her talent woefully under-used."
My friends...
"...her name is as noble as the role I've just given her..."
Please welcome, **Elizabeth Taylor!**
"Stand up, my lovely. Show yourself!"
"She'll be playing the most respected Egyptian queen of them all: Cleopatra!"
CLAP! CLAP! CLAP! CLAP!

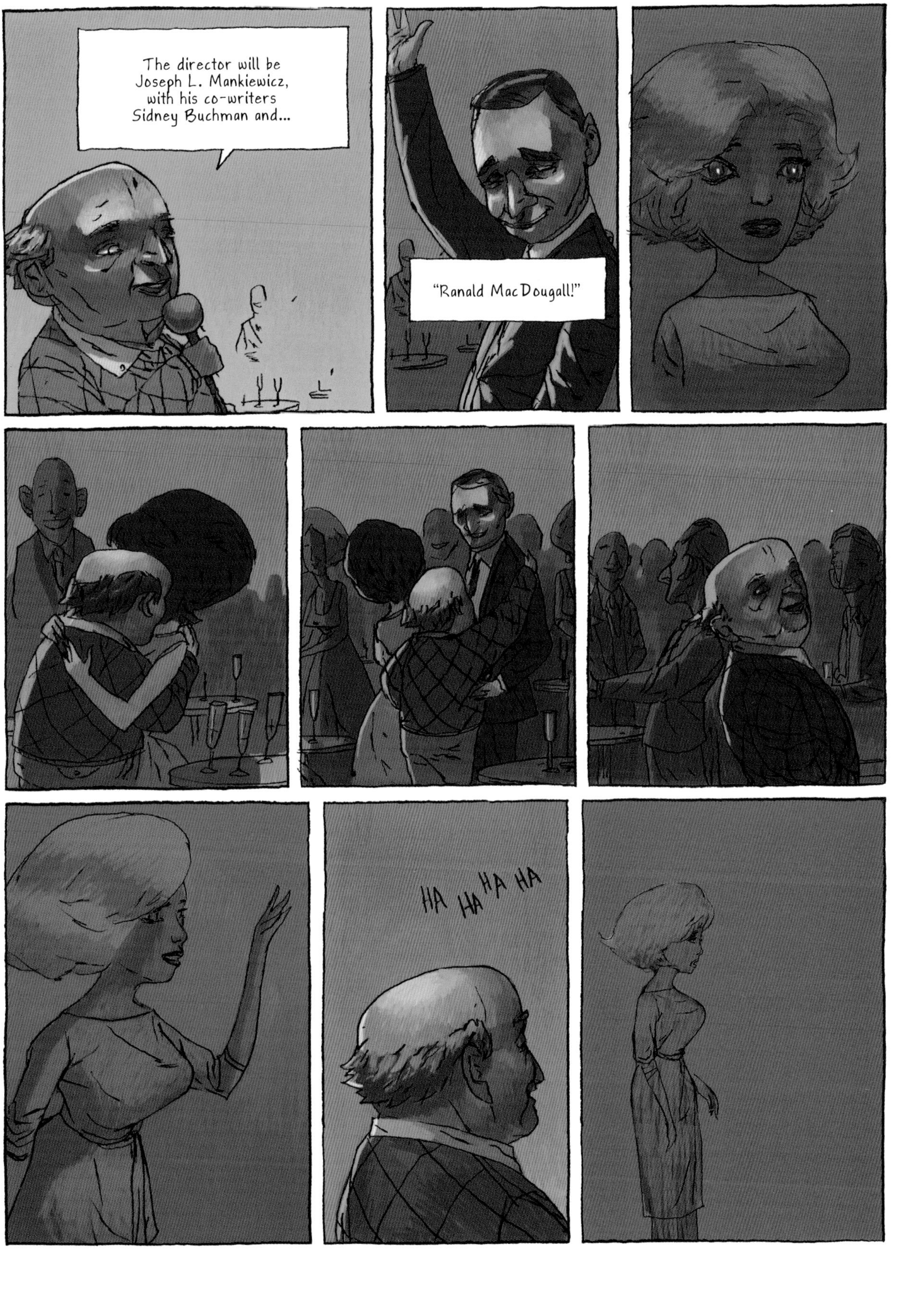

The director will be Joseph L. Mankiewicz, with his co-writers Sidney Buchman and...
"Ranald MacDougall!"
HA HA HA HA

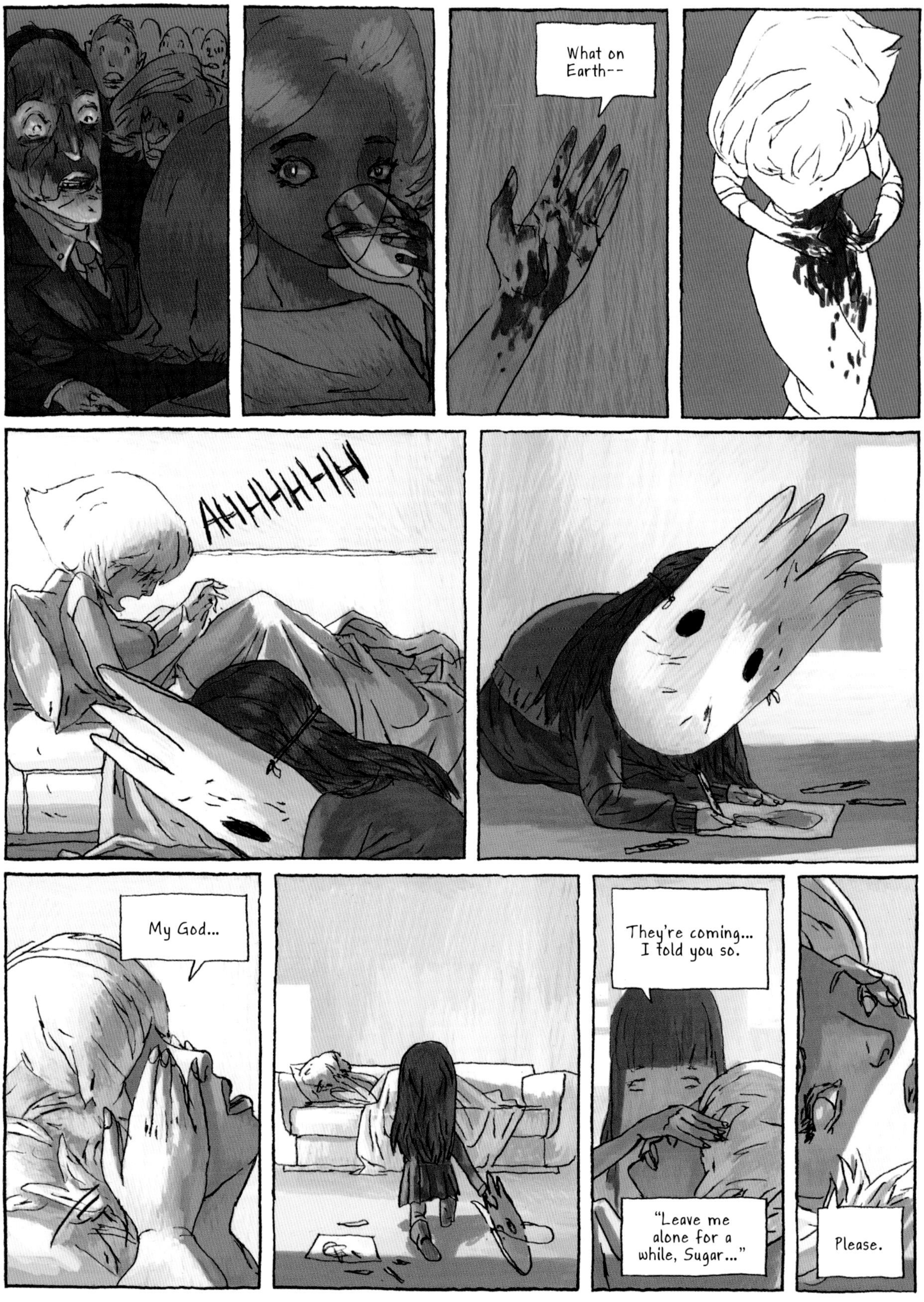
What on Earth--
AHHHHHHH
My God...
They're coming... I told you so.
"Leave me alone for a while, Sugar..."
Please.

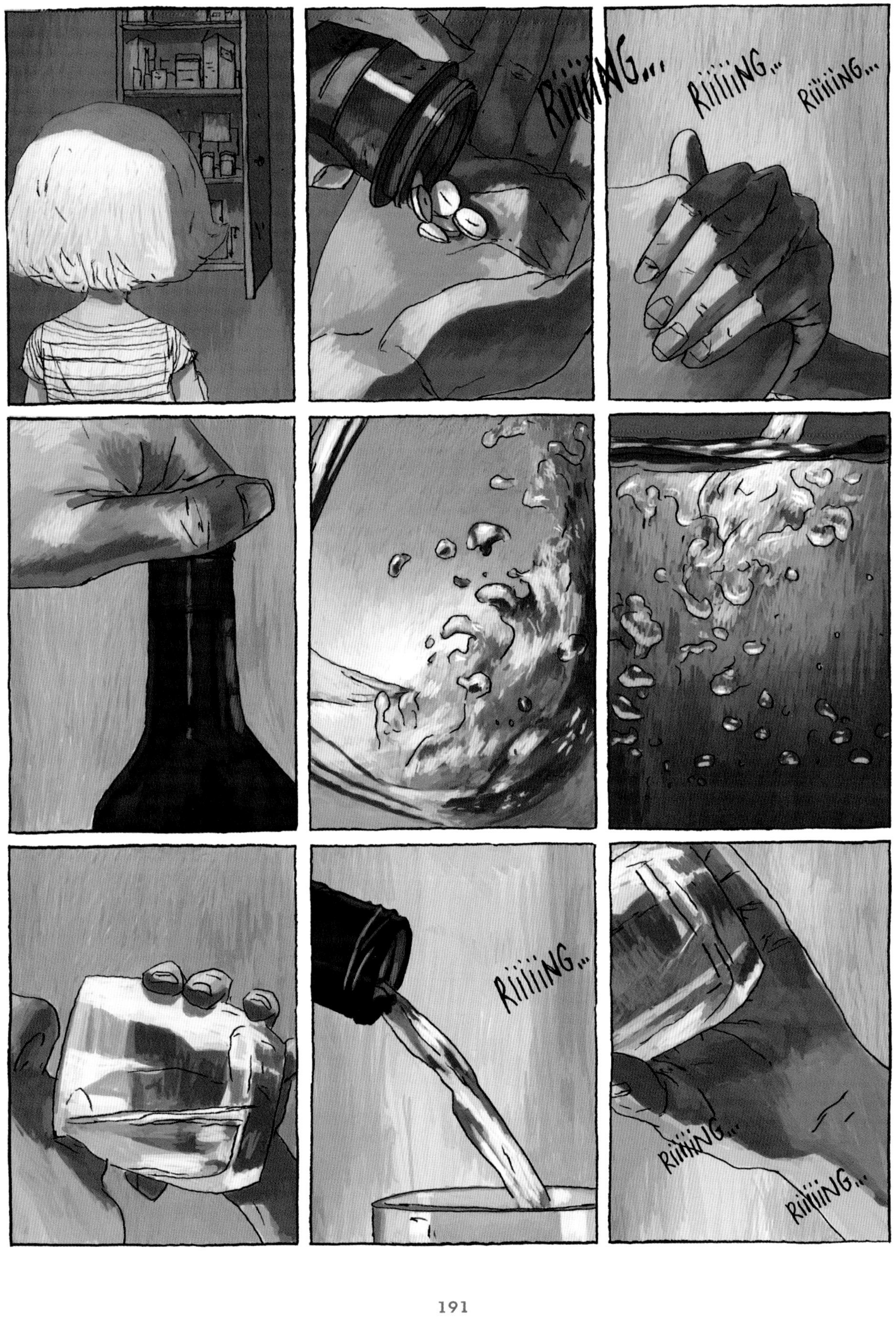
RiiiiNG...
RiiiiiiNG...
RiiiiiNG...
RiiiiiNG...
RiiiiNG...
RiiiiNG...

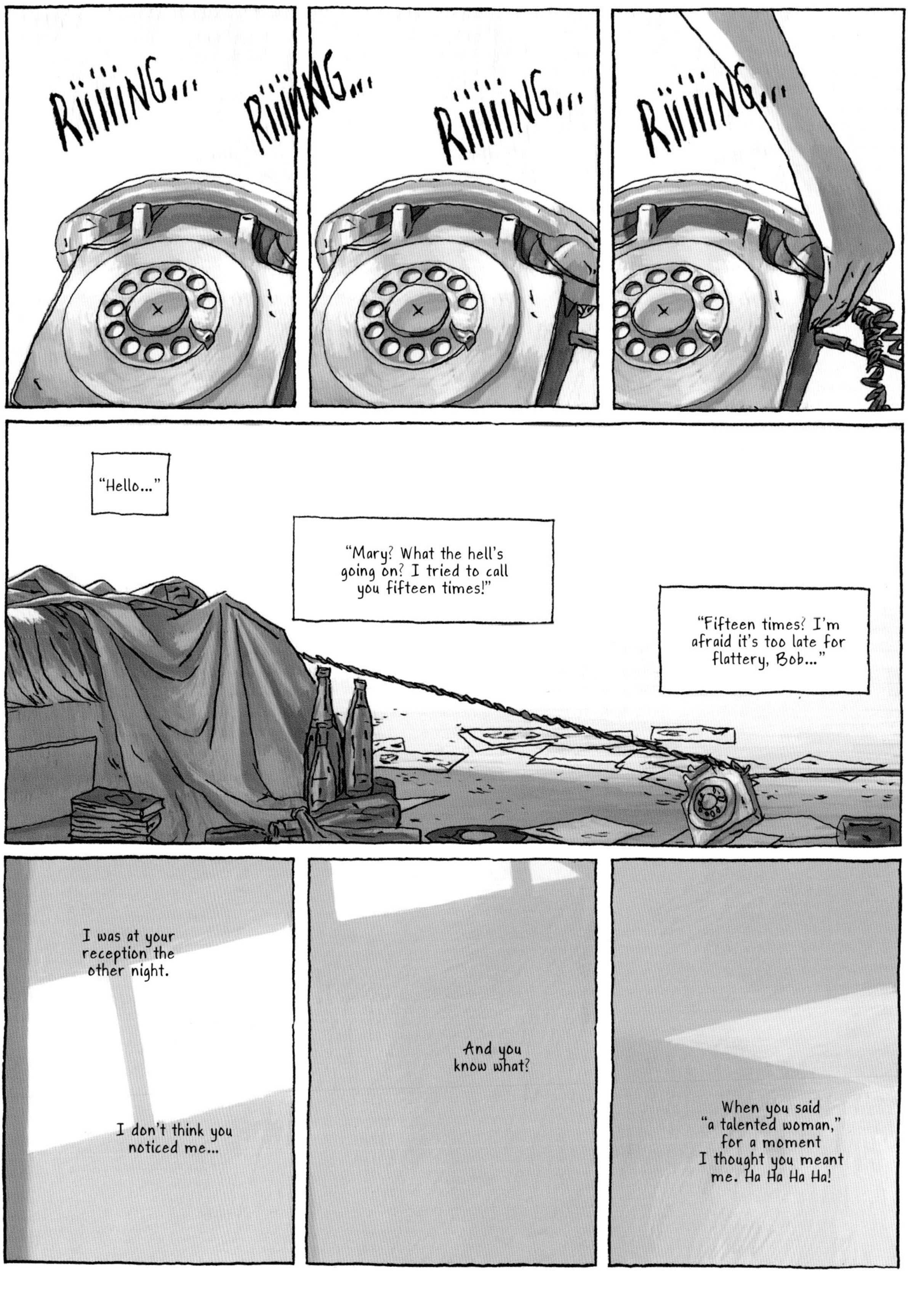
RIIIING...
RIIIING...
RIIIING...
RIIIING...
"Hello..."
"Mary? What the hell's going on? I tried to call you fifteen times!"
"Fifteen times? I'm afraid it's too late for flattery, Bob..."
I was at your reception the other night.
I don't think you noticed me...
And you know what?
When you said "a talented woman," for a moment I thought you meant me. Ha Ha Ha Ha!

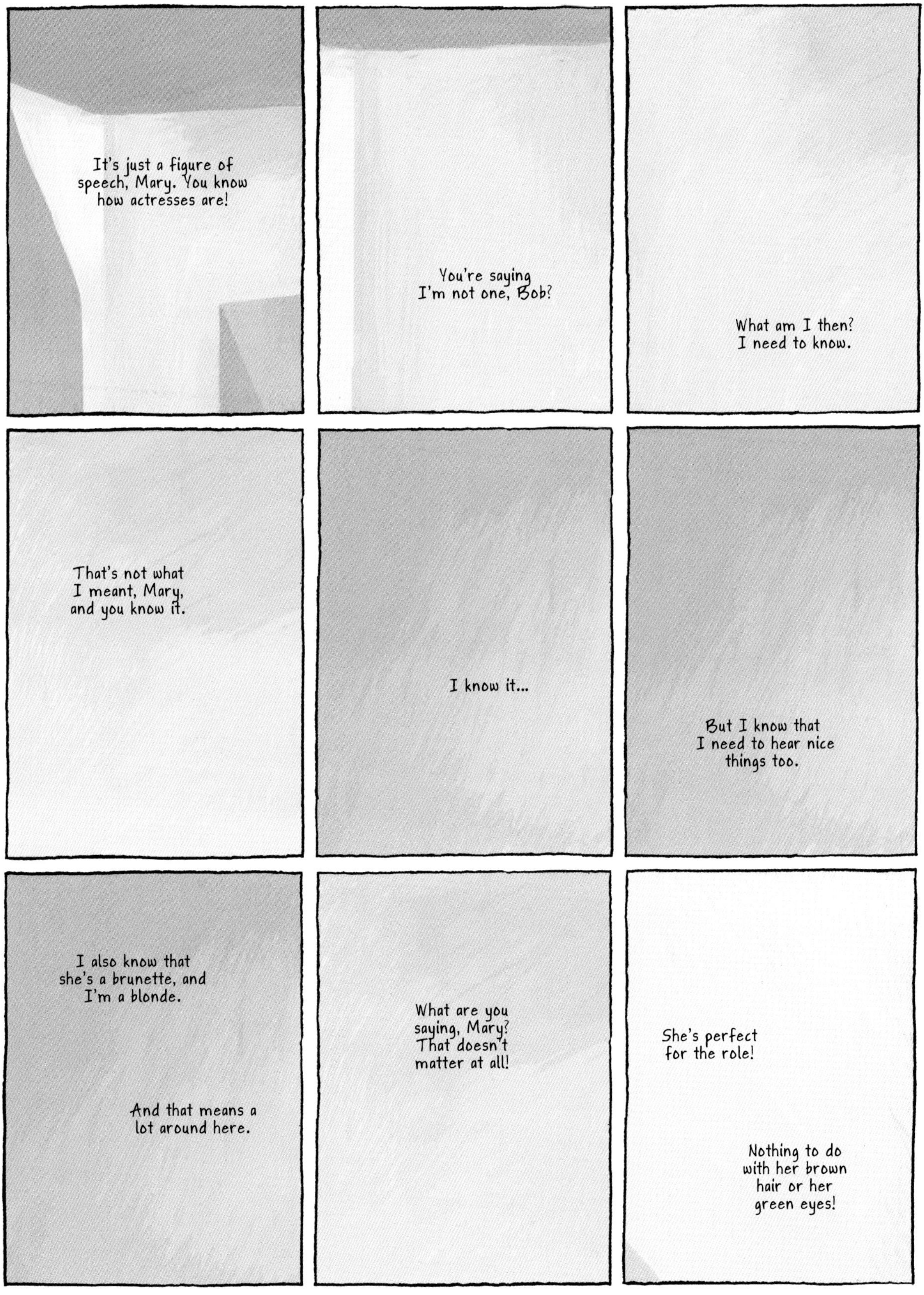
It's just a figure of speech, Mary. You know how actresses are!
You're saying I'm not one, Bob?
What am I then? I need to know.
That's not what I meant, Mary, and you know it.
I know it...
But I know that I need to hear nice things too.
I also know that she's a brunette, and I'm a blonde.
And that means a lot around here.
What are you saying, Mary? That doesn't matter at all!
She's perfect for the role!
Nothing to do with her brown hair or her green eyes!

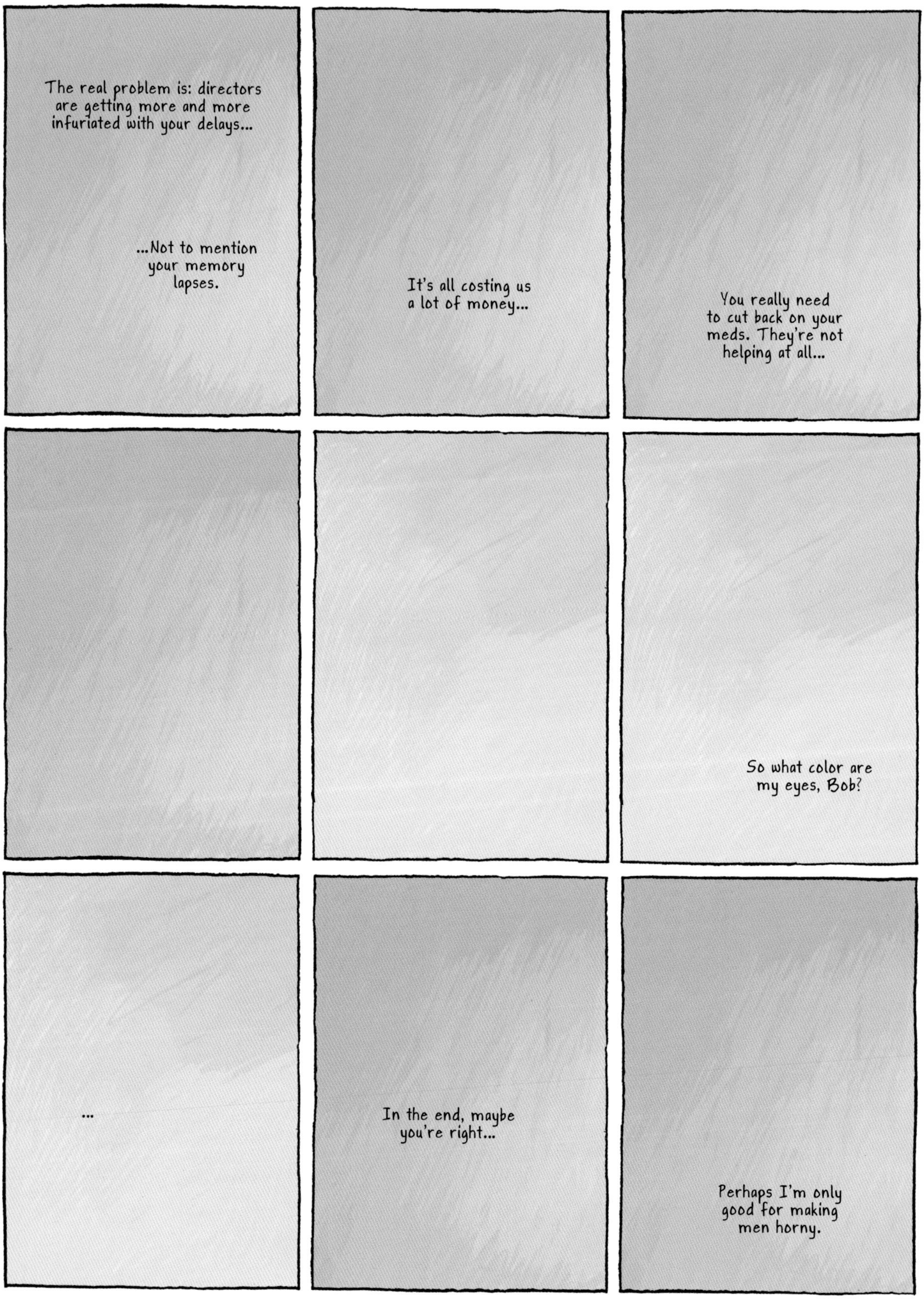
The real problem is: directors are getting more and more infuriated with your delays...
...Not to mention your memory lapses.
It's all costing us a lot of money...
You really need to cut back on your meds. They're not helping at all...
So what color are my eyes, Bob?
...
In the end, maybe you're right...
Perhaps I'm only good for making men horny.

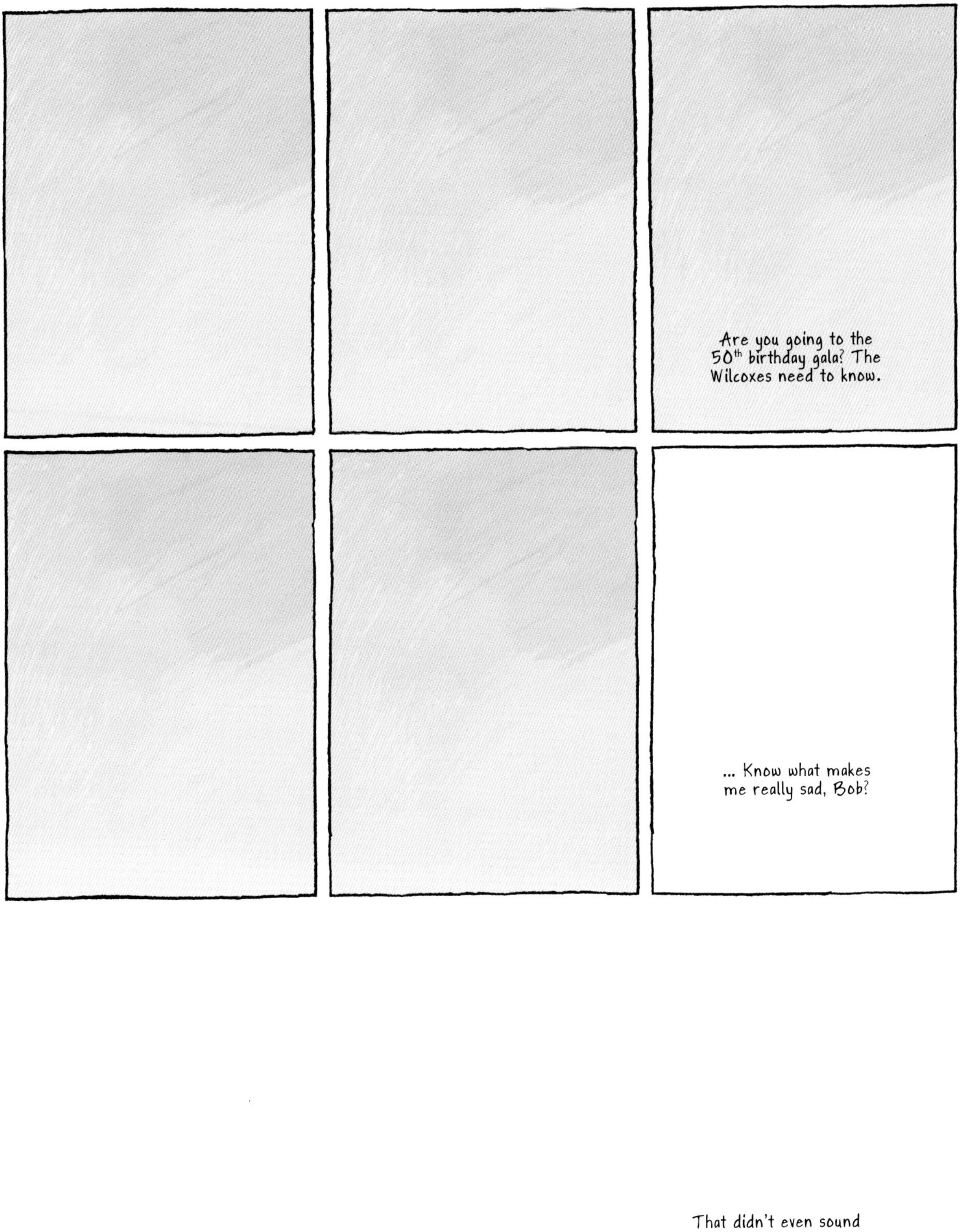
Are you going to the 50th birthday gala? The Wilcoxes need to know.
... Know what makes me really sad, Bob?
That didn't even sound like an invitation.

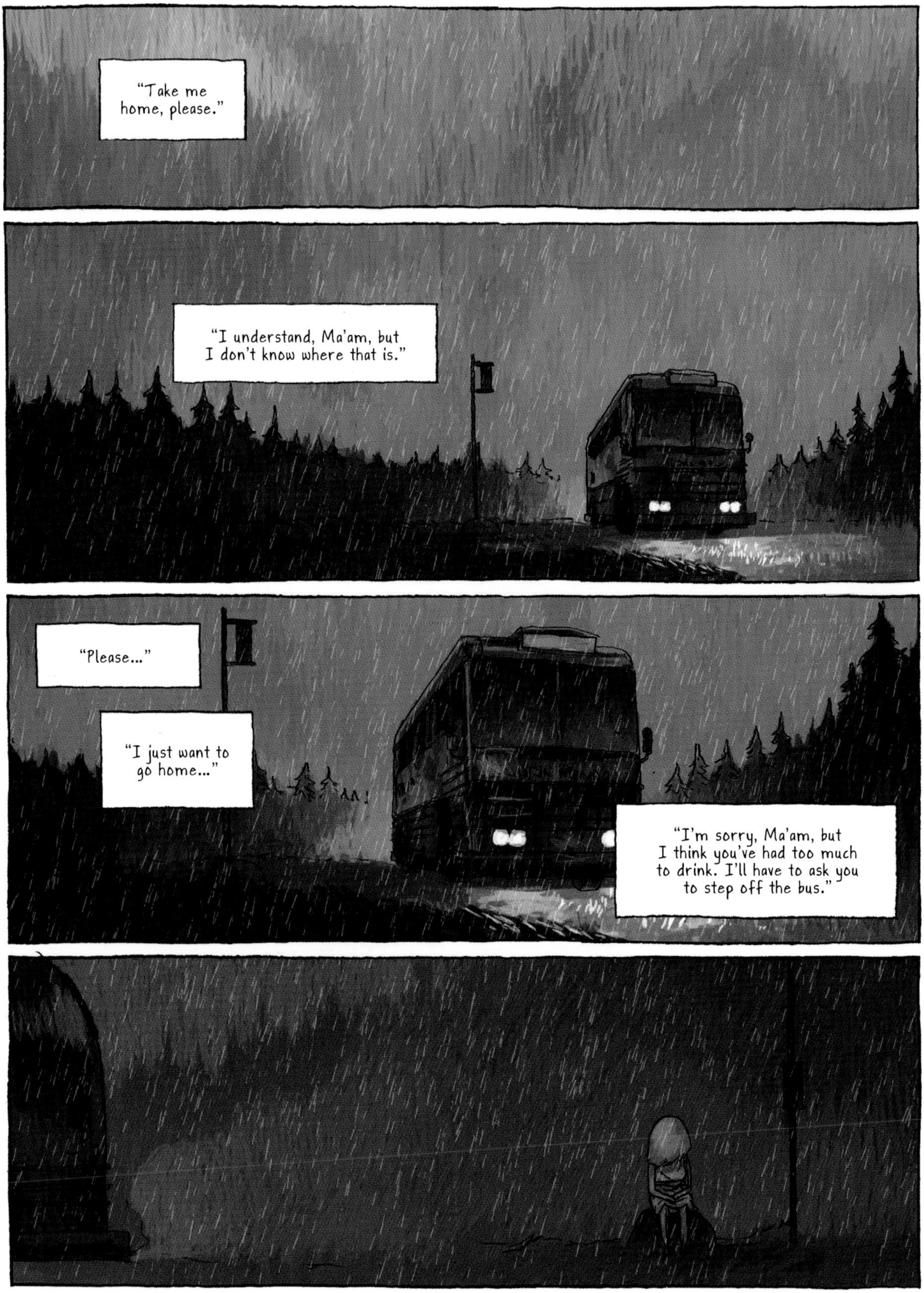
"Take me home, please."
"I understand, Ma'am, but I don't know where that is."
"Please..."
"I just want to go home..."
"I'm sorry, Ma'am, but I think you've had too much to drink. I'll have to ask you to step off the bus."

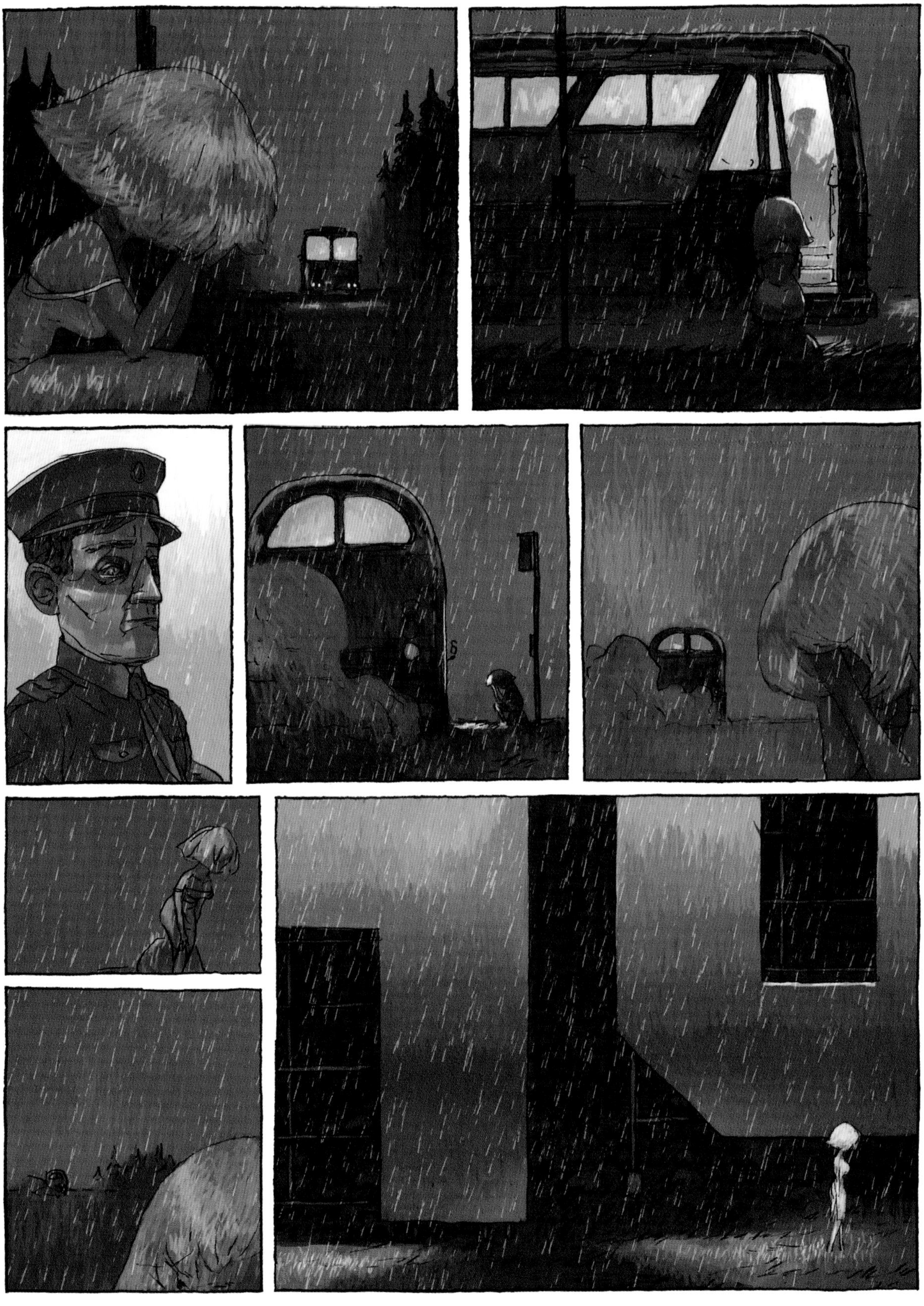

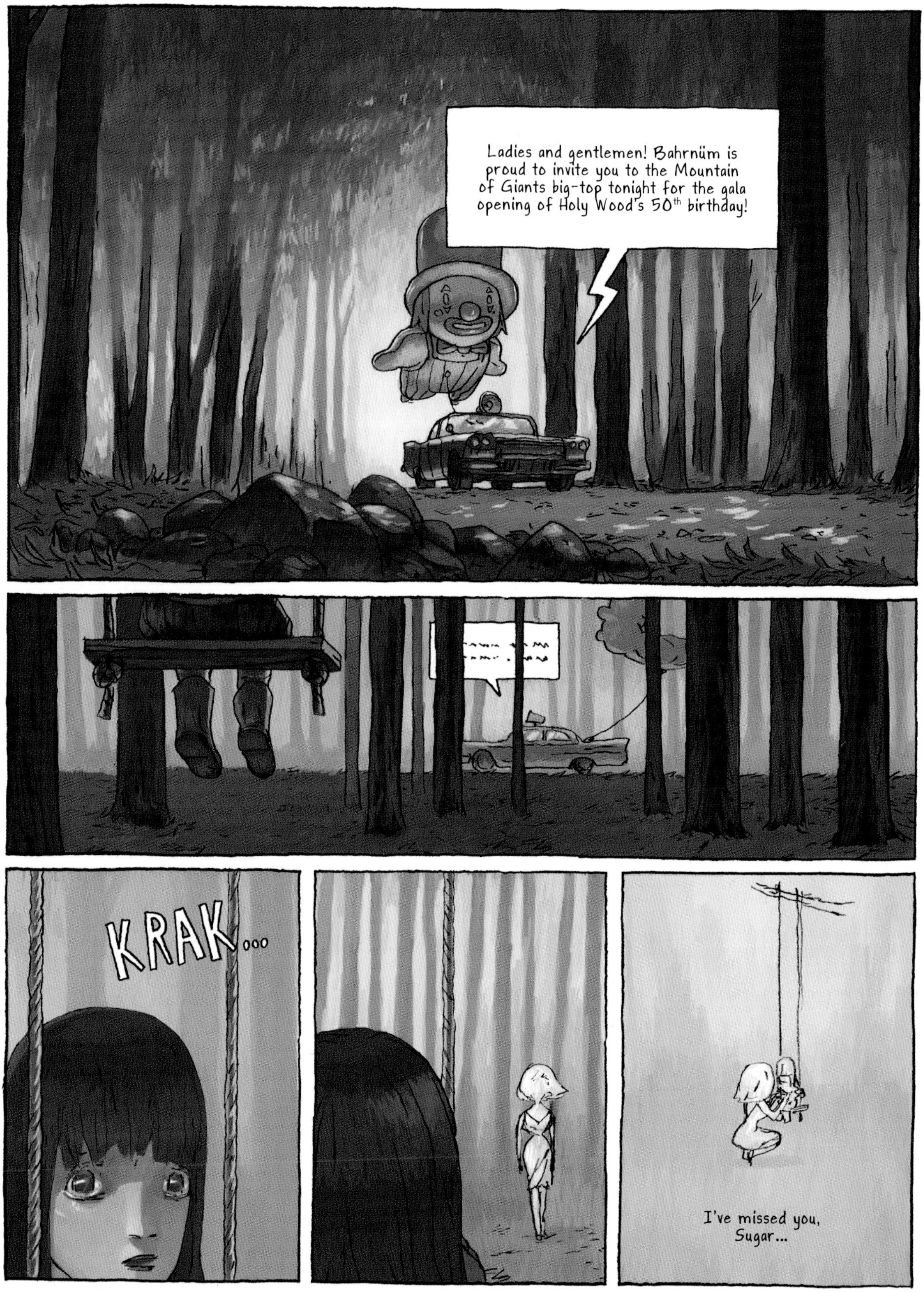

Ladies and gentlemen! Bahrnüm is proud to invite you to the Mountain of Giants big-top tonight for the gala opening of Holy Wood's 50th birthday!
KRAK...
I've missed you, Sugar...

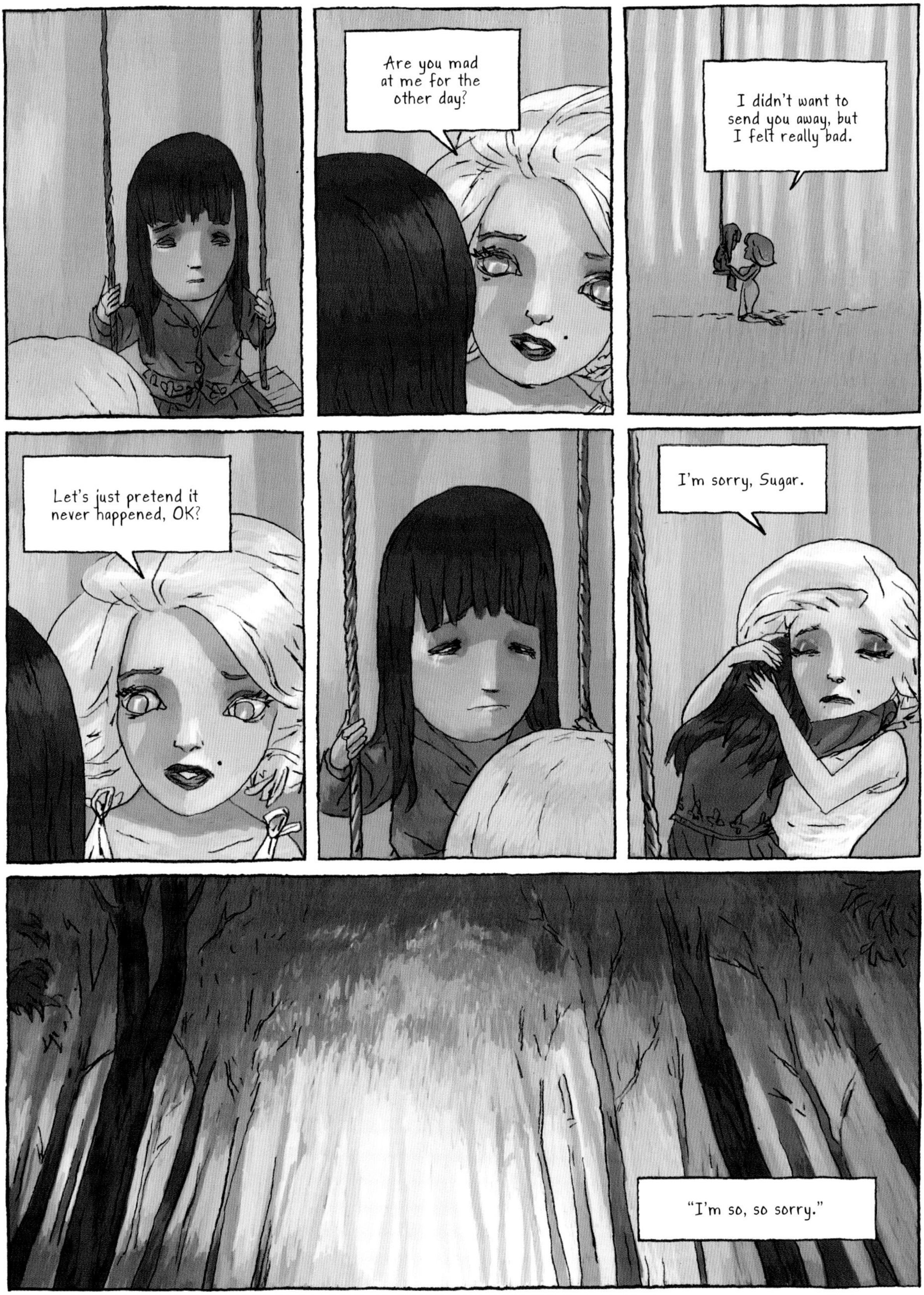

Are you mad at me for the other day?
I didn't want to send you away, but I felt really bad.
Let's just pretend it never happened, OK?
I'm sorry, Sugar.
"I'm so, so sorry."

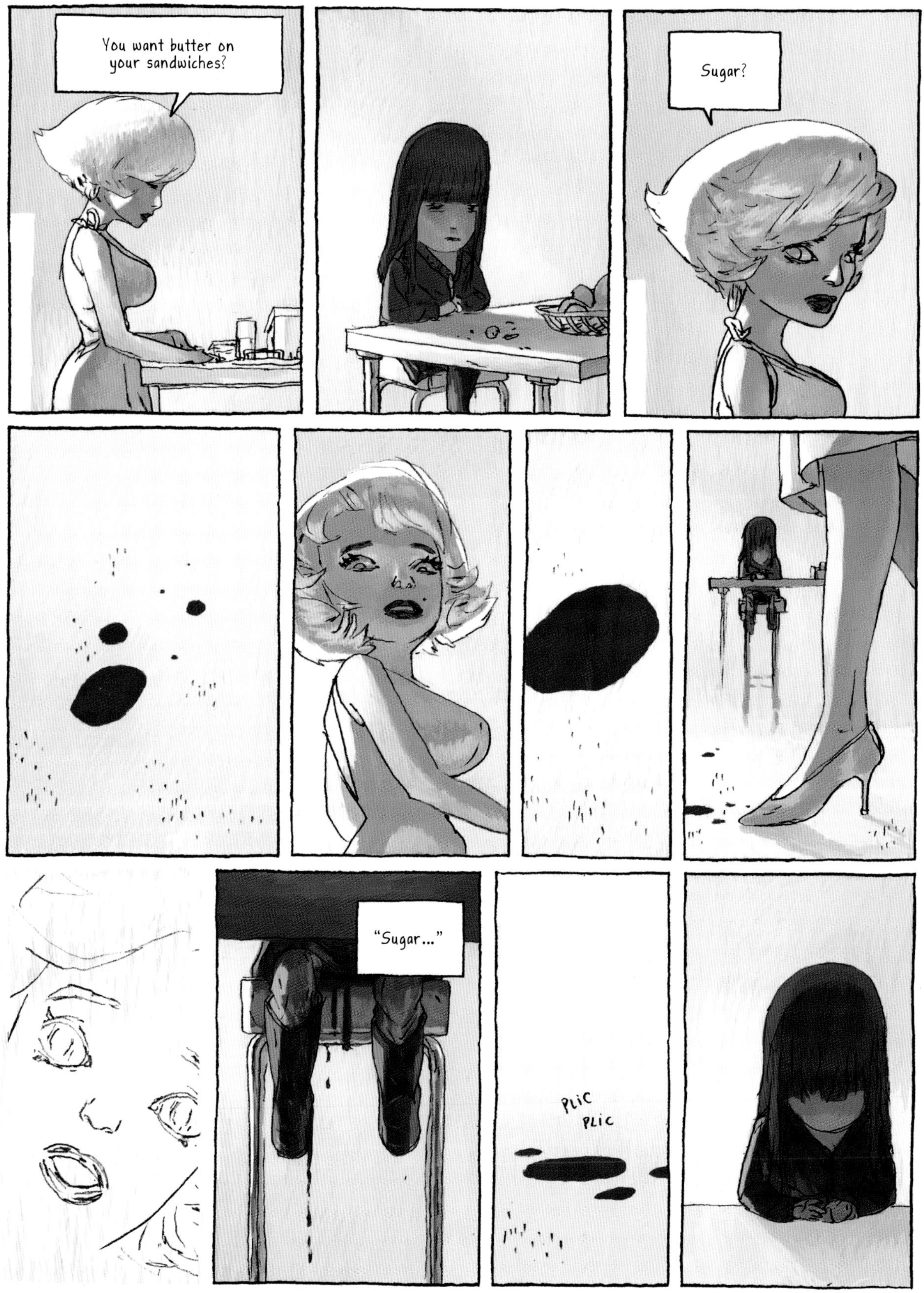
You want butter on your sandwiches?
Sugar?
"Sugar..."
PLIC
PLIC

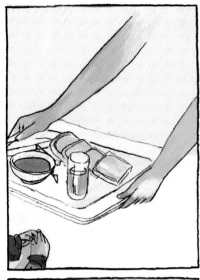

What's the matter, Sugar?

I-I-it's...

I-it's th-the monsters...

Th-Th...

Th-They...

f-foun'...

m-m-me...

An' n-now they're e-e-eatin' me up... Th-They e-eat m' words so I w-won' t-talk 'bout th-them...

Th-They d-don' l-like b-bein' t-talked 'bout.

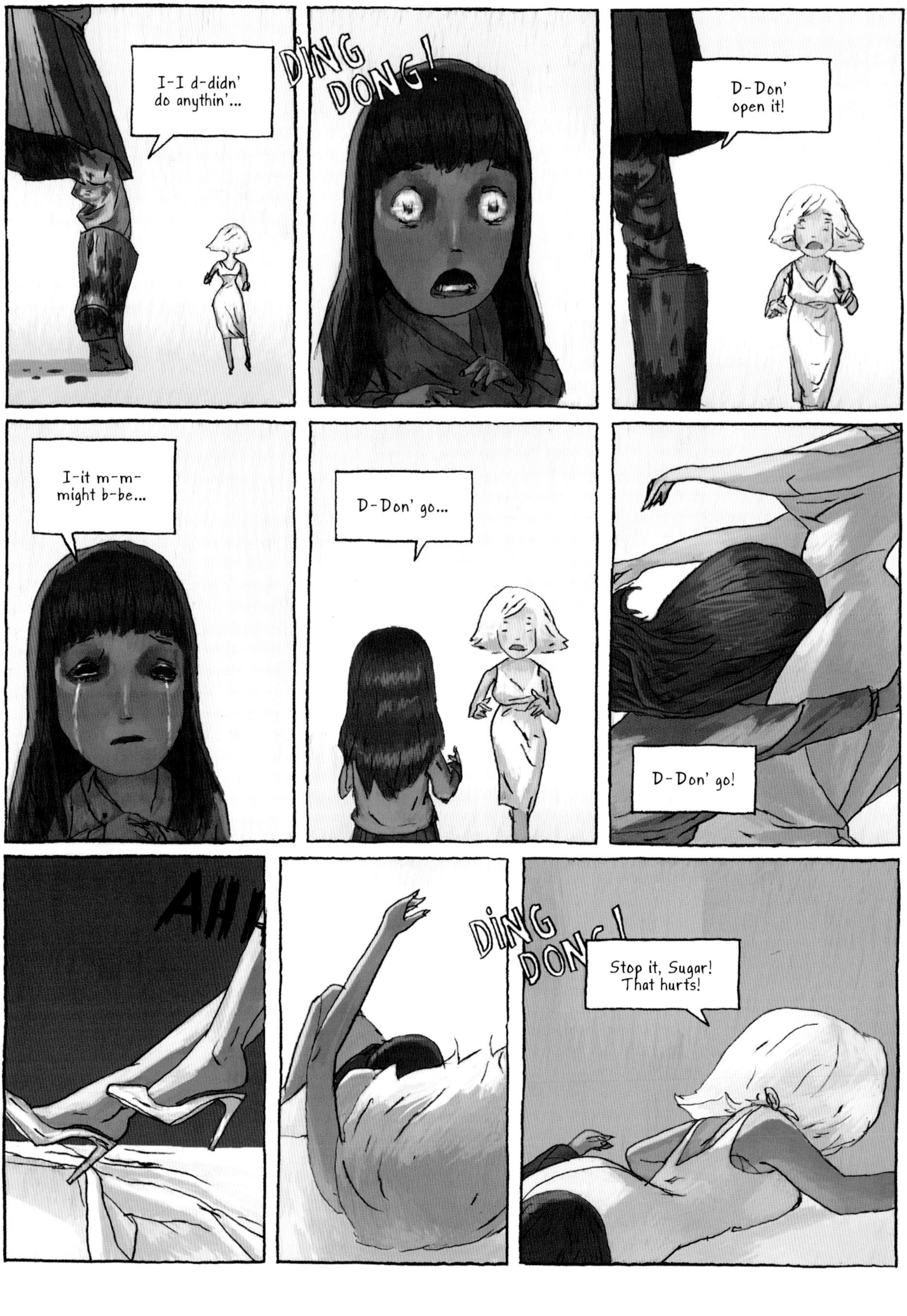
I-I d-didn' do anythin'...
DING DONG!
D-Don' open it!
I-it m-m-might b-be...
D-Don' go...
D-Don' go!
DING
Stop it, Sugar! That hurts!

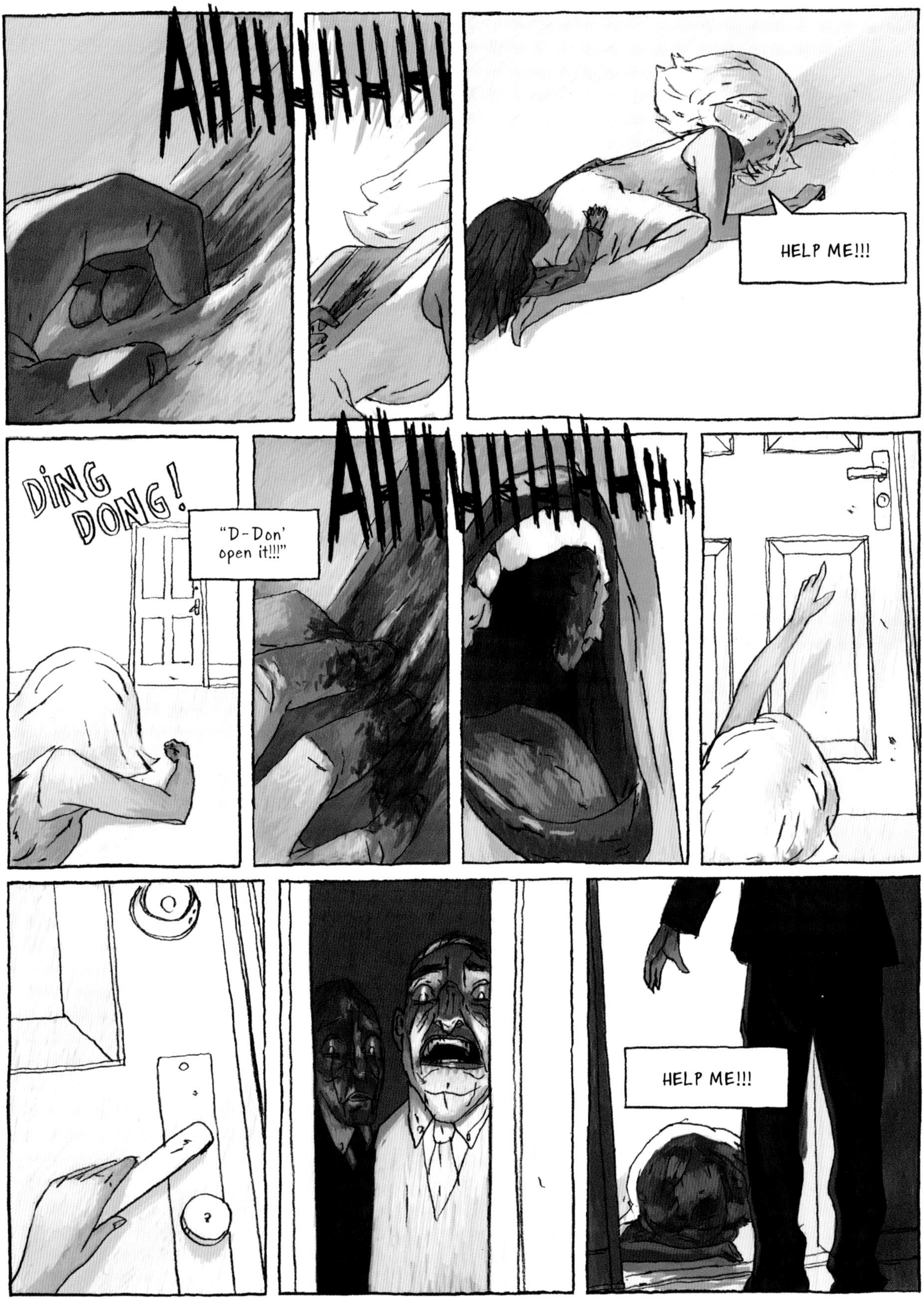
AHHHHHHHH
HELP ME!!!
DING DONG!
"D-Don' open it!!!"
AHHHHHHHHHhh
HELP ME!!!

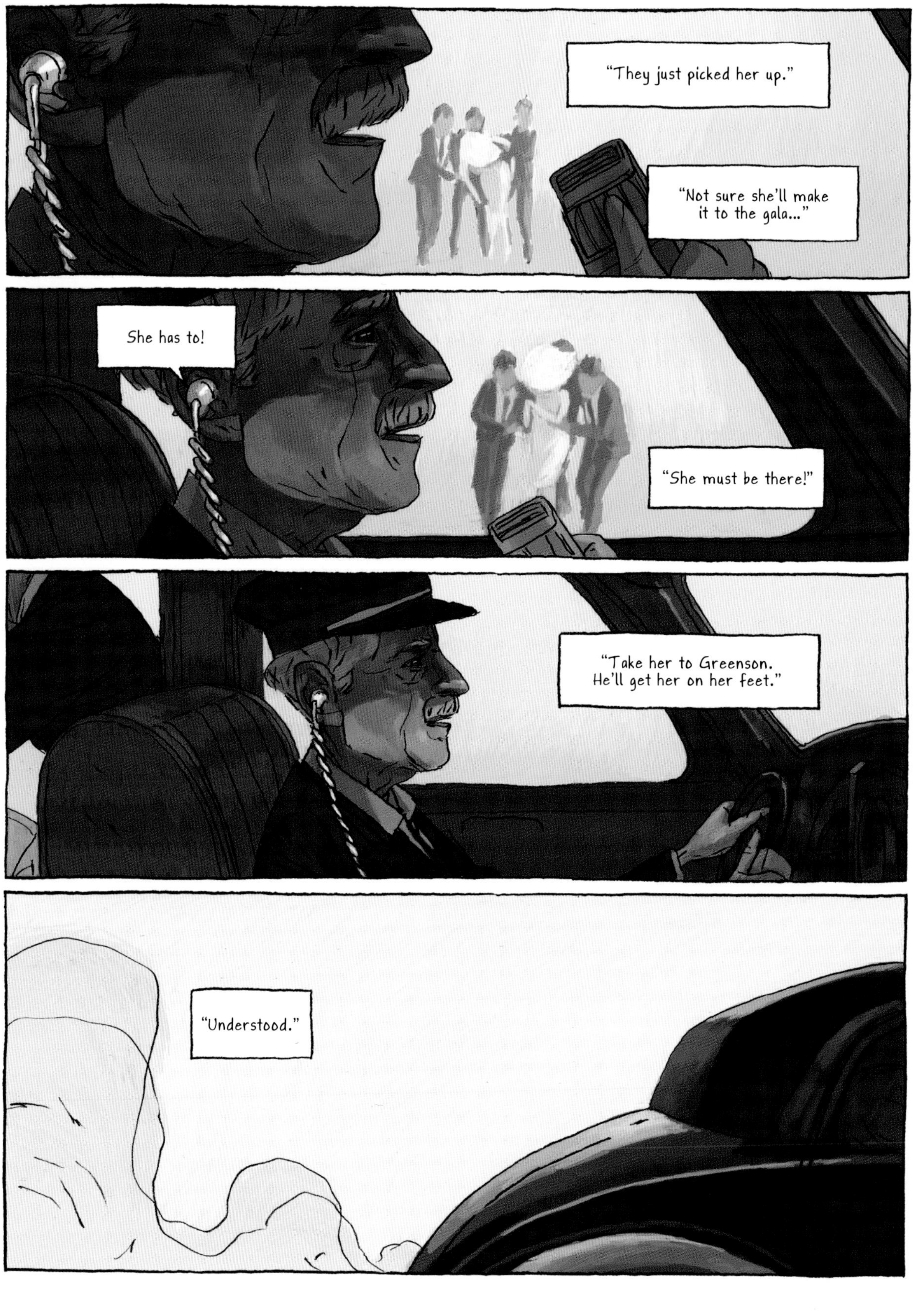
"They just picked her up."
"Not sure she'll make it to the gala..."
She has to!
"She must be there!"
"Take her to Greenson. He'll get her on her feet."
"Understood."

I don't want to talk to you, doctor. I've got nothing to say.

All this is none of your business.

When I really needed you, doctor, you were never there! You should have been there! it's your job to be there!

But we had our sessions...

...almost every day.

"We've accomplished a lot, and I must say, the trust you've placed in me has paid off."

"In fact, your anxiety attacks are much less frequent."

But The Founders know your weak spot.

NORMA JEANE BAKER

PHOTOS
TOP SE-

What's this?

Open it.

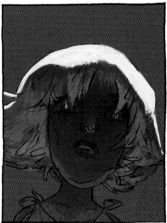

205

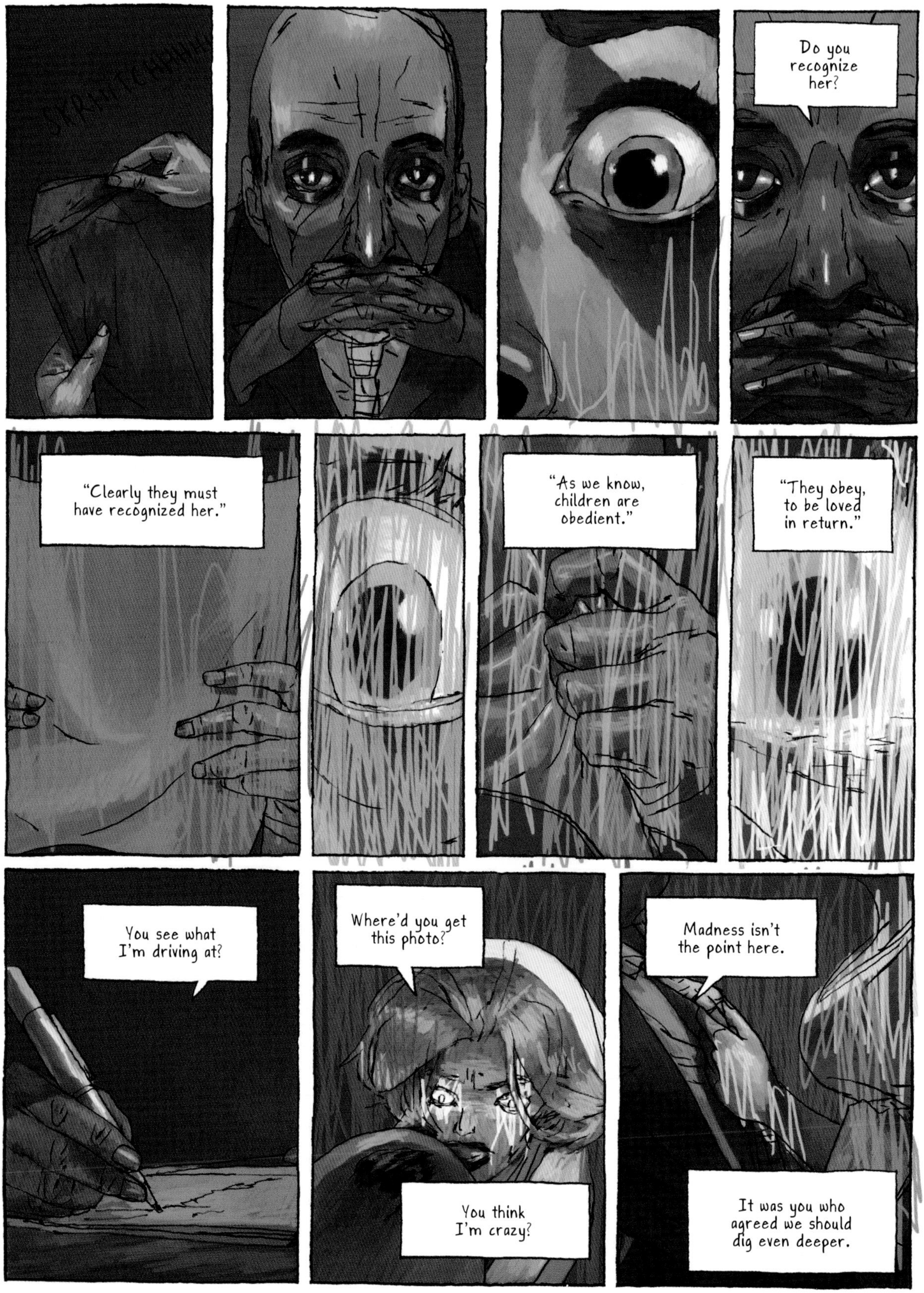
Do you recognize her?
"Clearly they must have recognized her."
"As we know, children are obedient."
"They obey, to be loved in return."
You see what I'm driving at?
Where'd you get this photo?
You think I'm crazy?
Madness isn't the point here.
It was you who agreed we should dig even deeper.

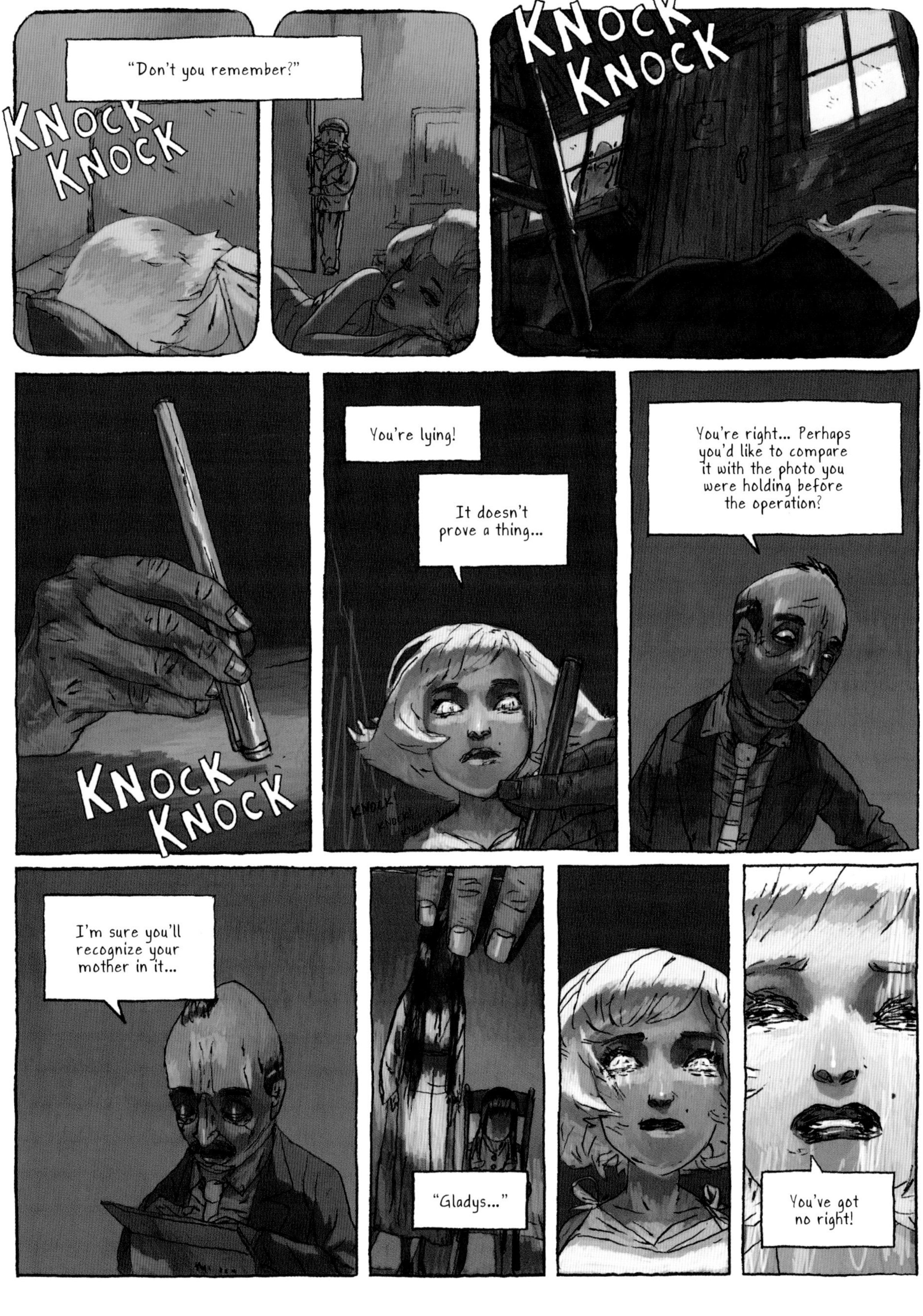
"Don't you remember?"
KNOCK KNOCK
KNOCK KNOCK
KNOCK KNOCK
You're lying!
It doesn't prove a thing...
You're right... Perhaps you'd like to compare it with the photo you were holding before the operation?
I'm sure you'll recognize your mother in it...
"Gladys..."
You've got no right!

I'm not the villain here.

I'm on your side.

"Sadly, your decision to break off our sessions has left us no opportunity to understand the origins of what's troubling you."

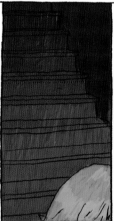

"And your drug cocktails combined with your alcohol intake only aggravate your mental state."

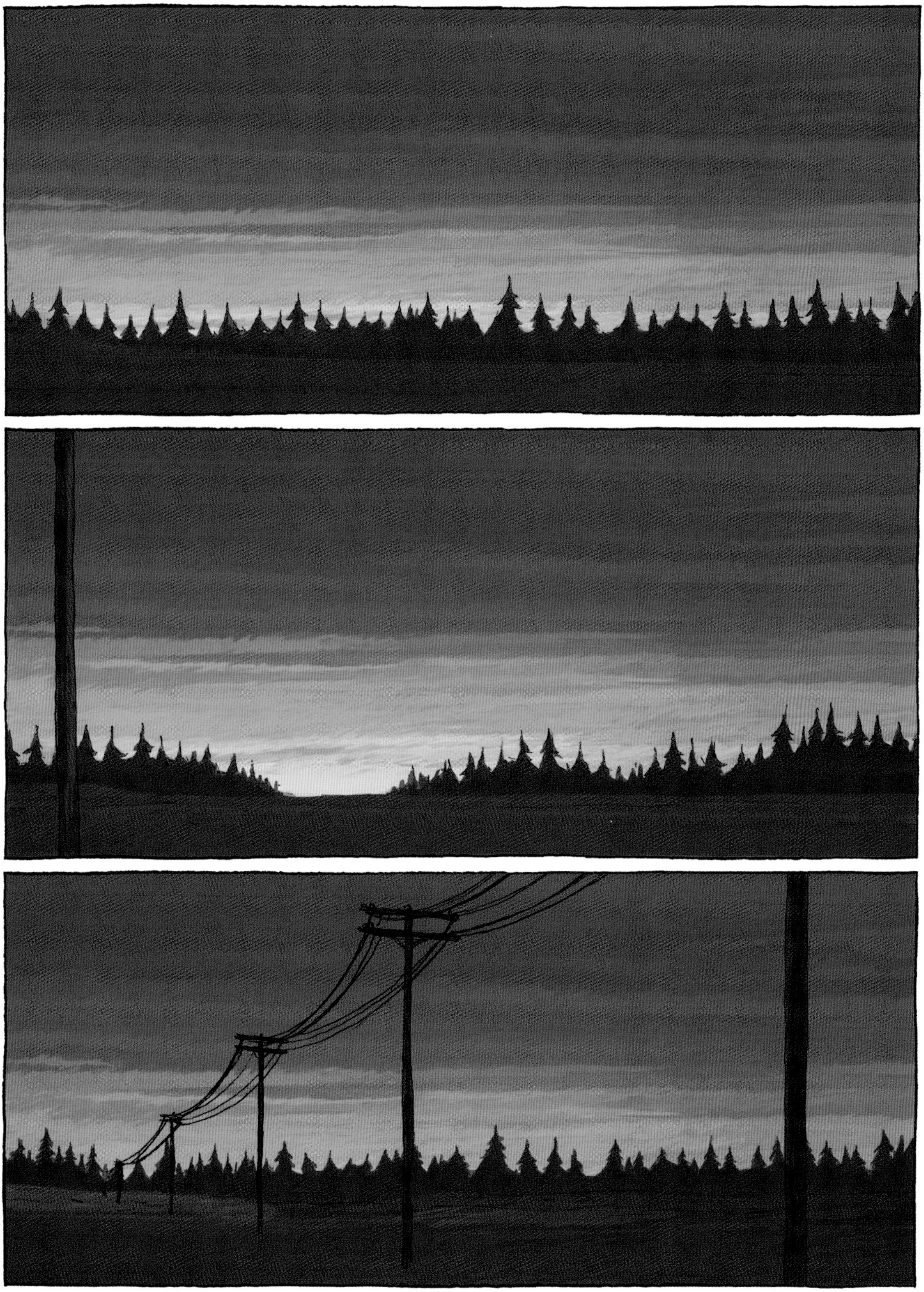

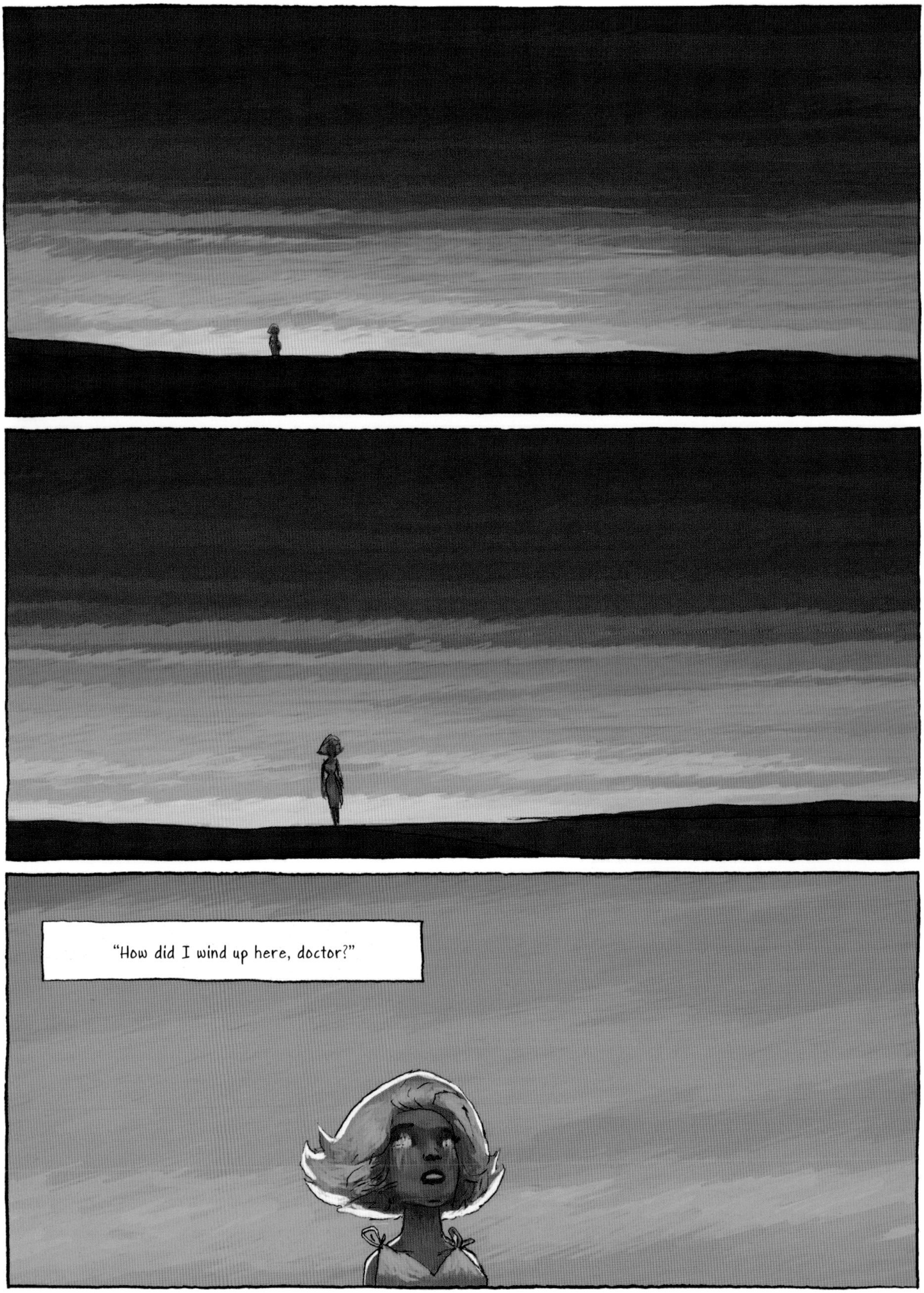
"How did I wind up here, doctor?"

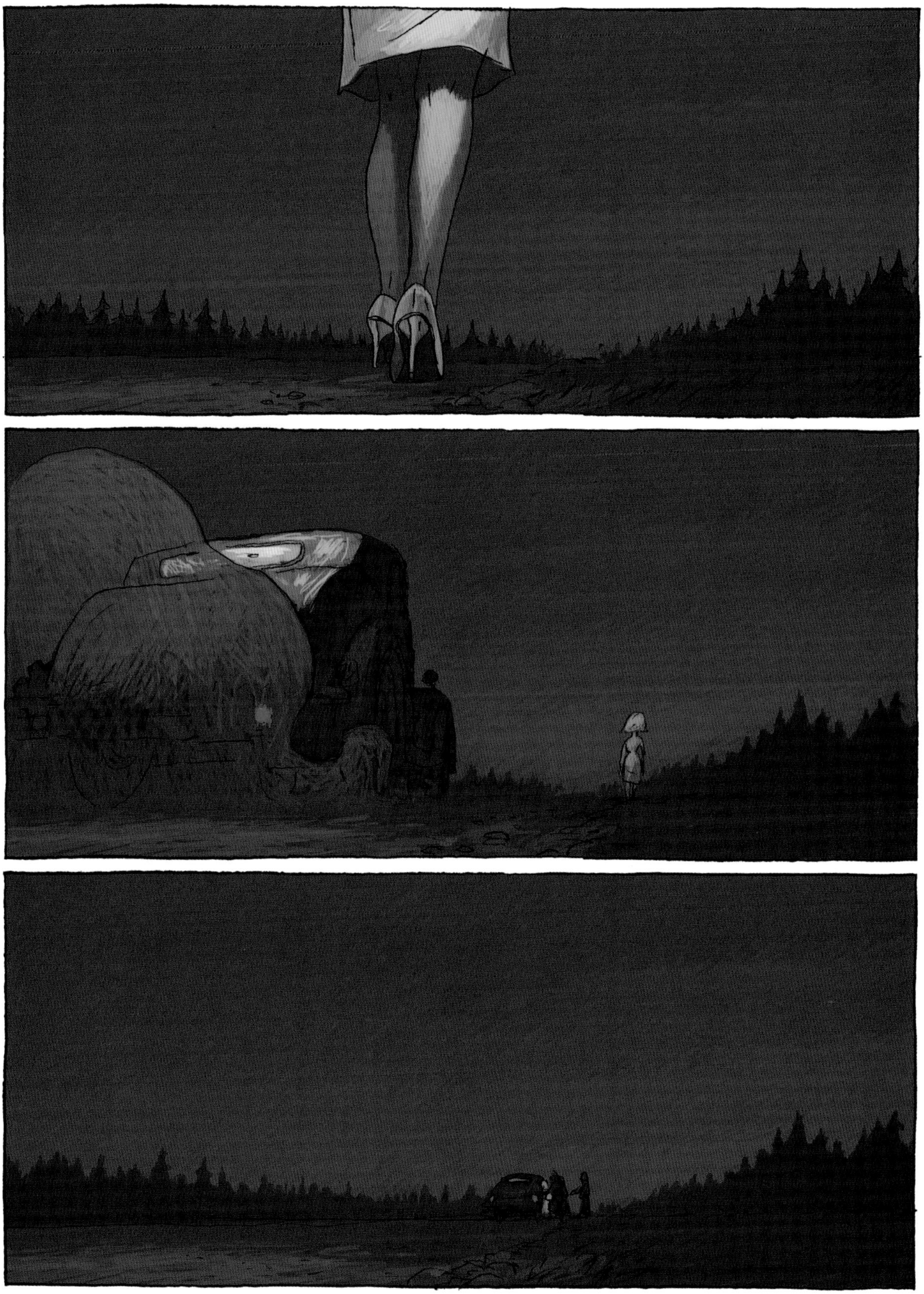

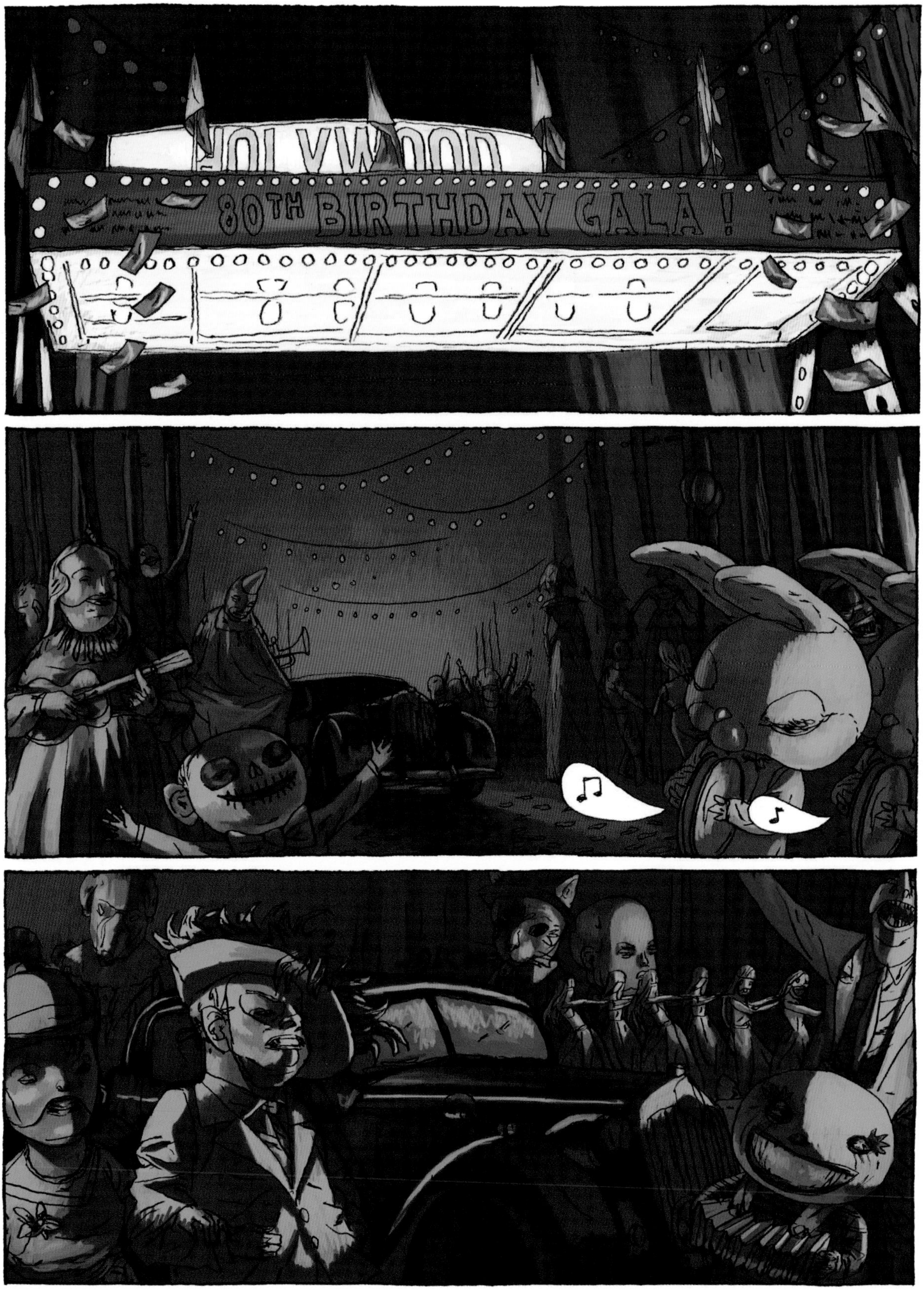
80TH BIRTHDAY GALA!

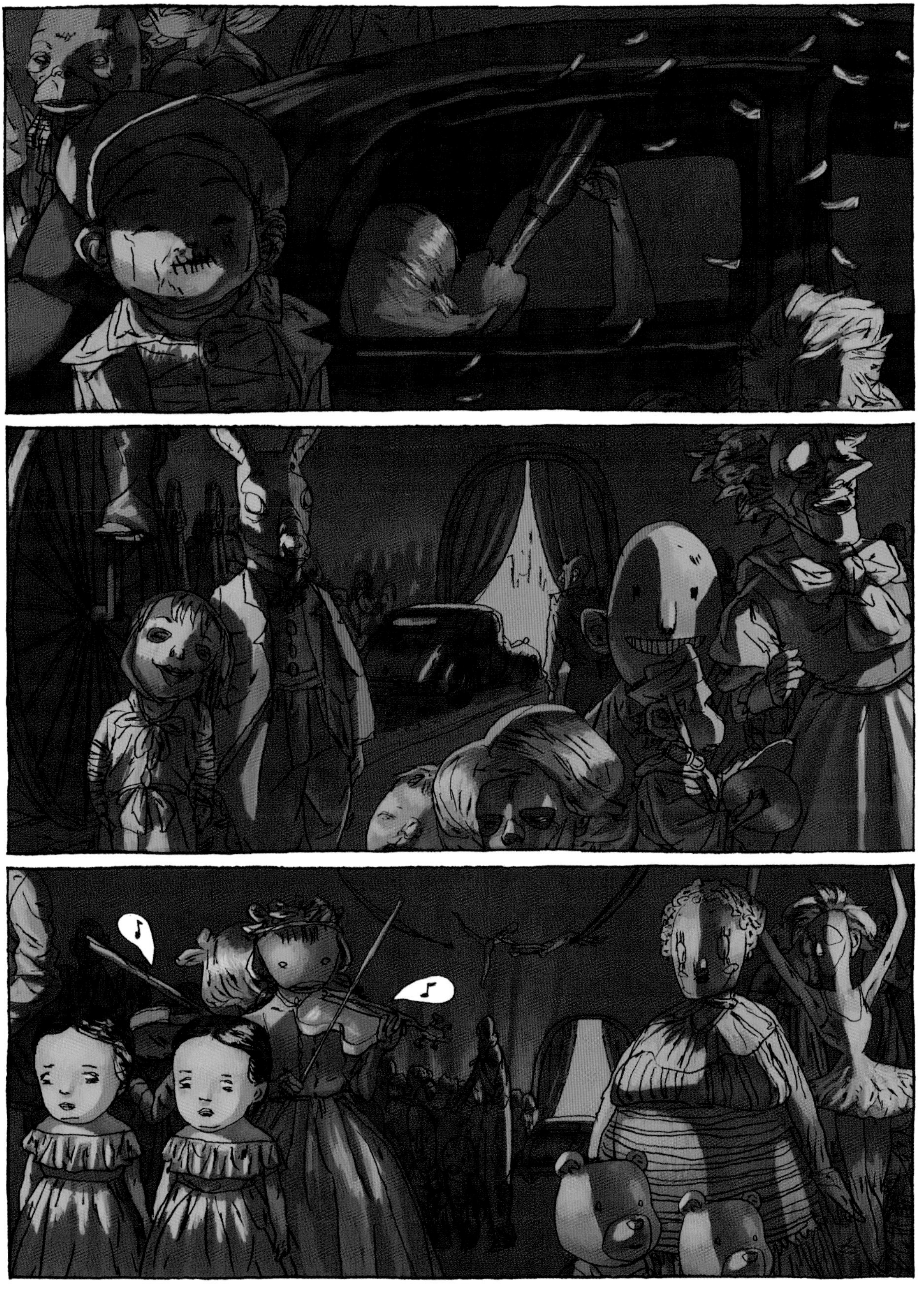

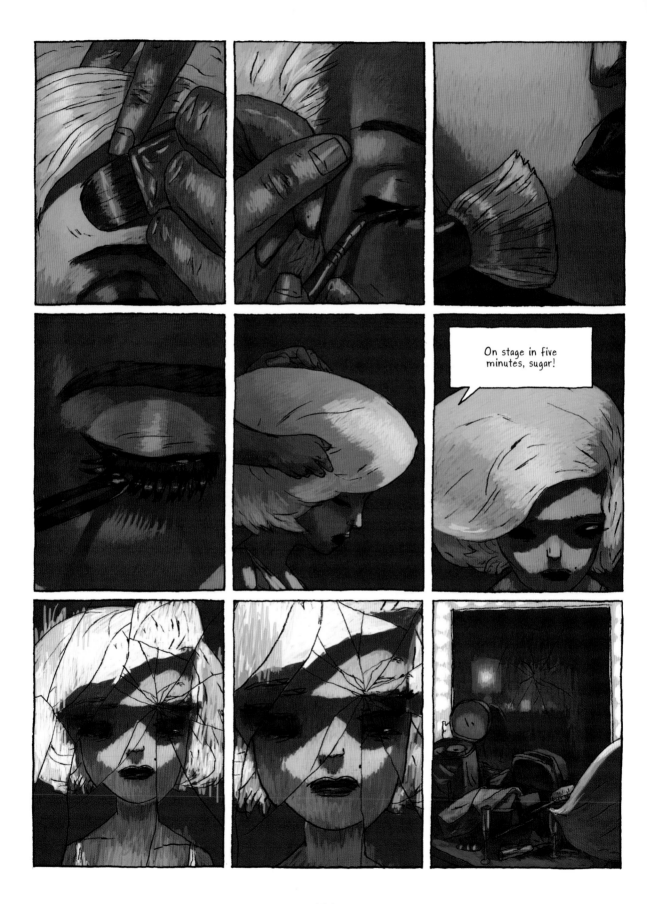

On stage in five minutes, sugar!

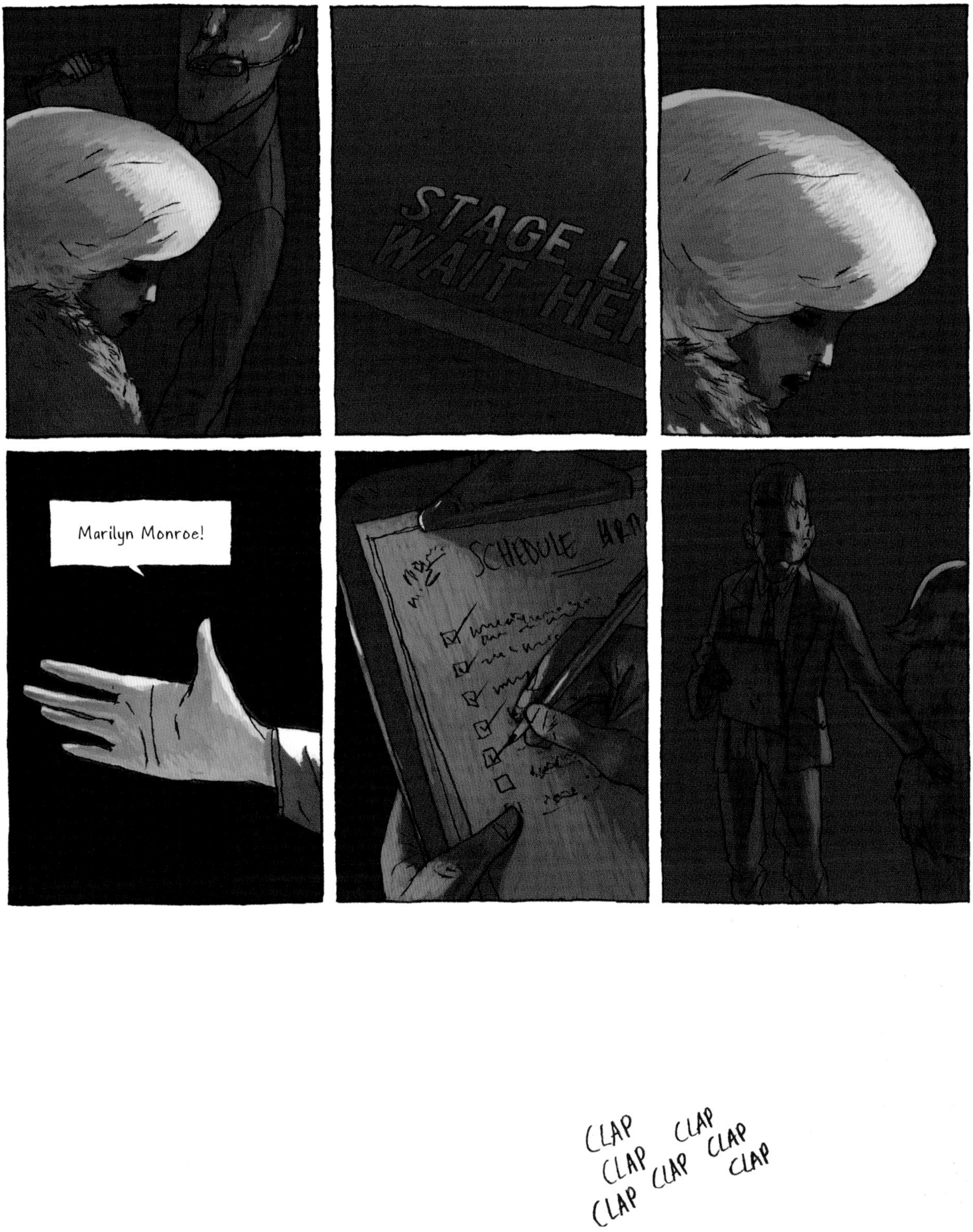
Marilyn Monroe!
SCHEDULE
CLAP CLAP
CLAP CLAP
CLAP CLAP CLAP
CLAP

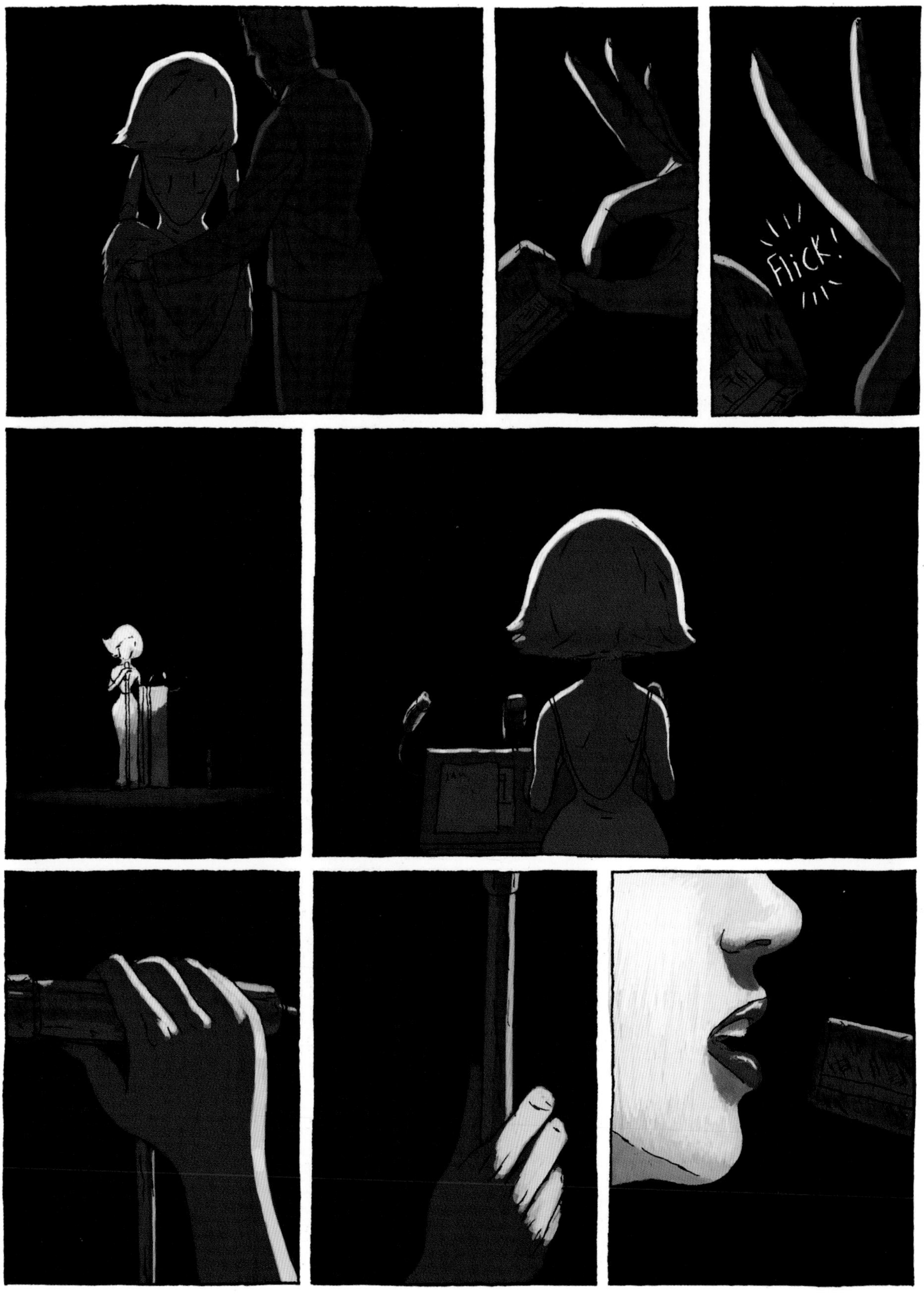
FLICK!

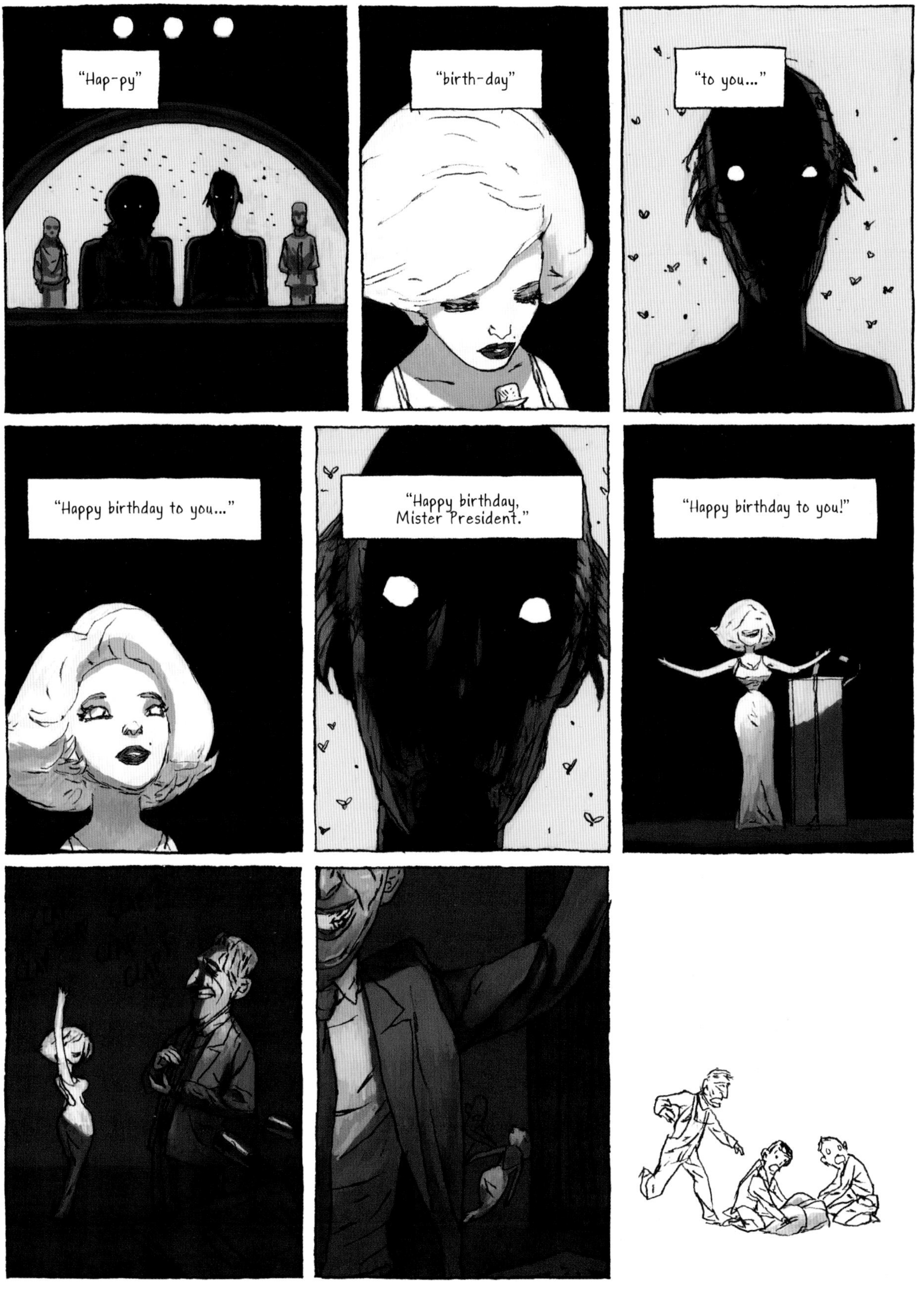
"Hap-py"
"birth-day"
"to you..."
"Happy birthday to you..."
"Happy birthday,
Mister President."
"Happy birthday to you!"

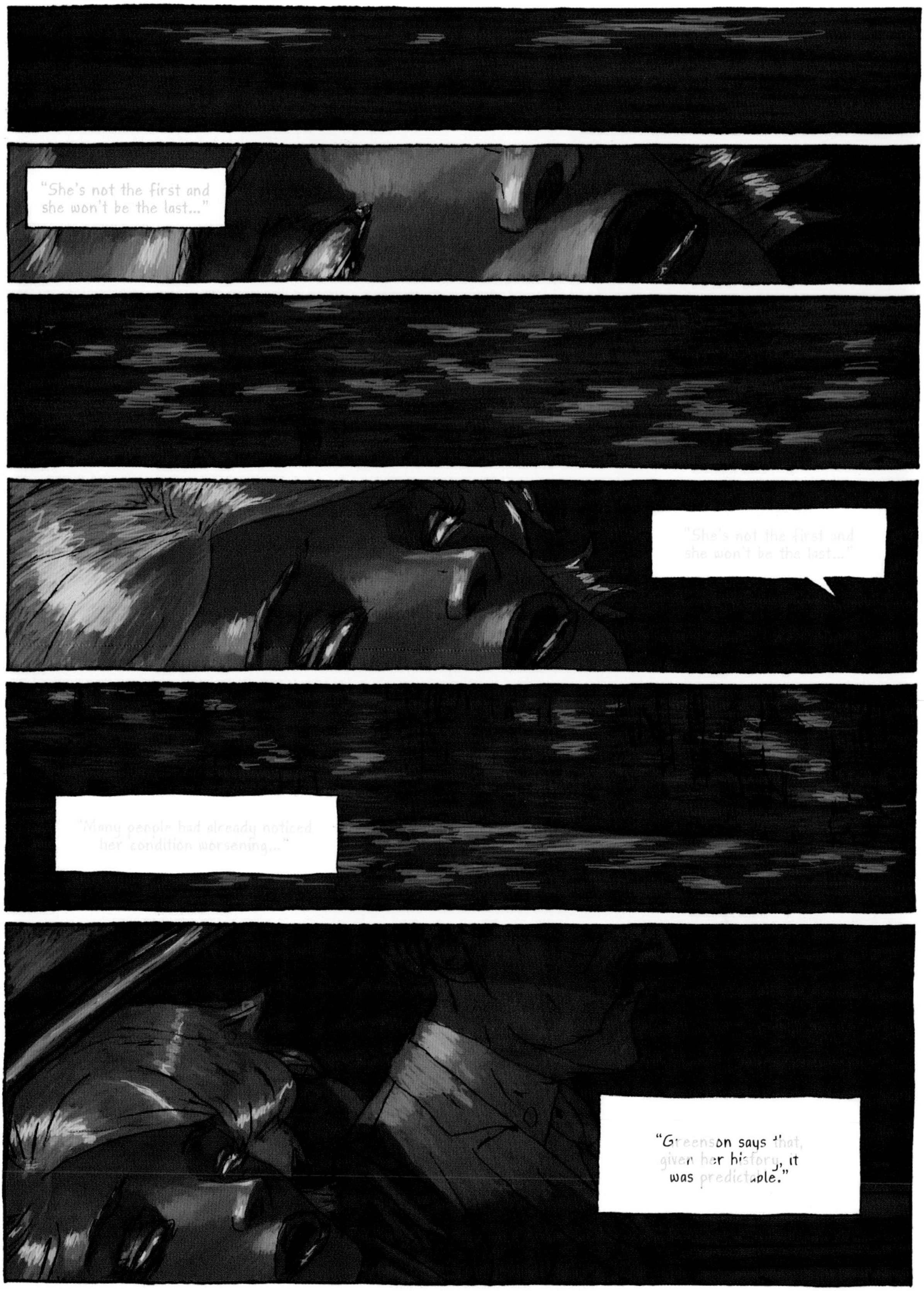
"She's not the first and she won't be the last..."
"She's not the first and she won't be the last..."
"Many people had already noticed her condition worsening..."
"Greenson says that, given her history, it was predictable."

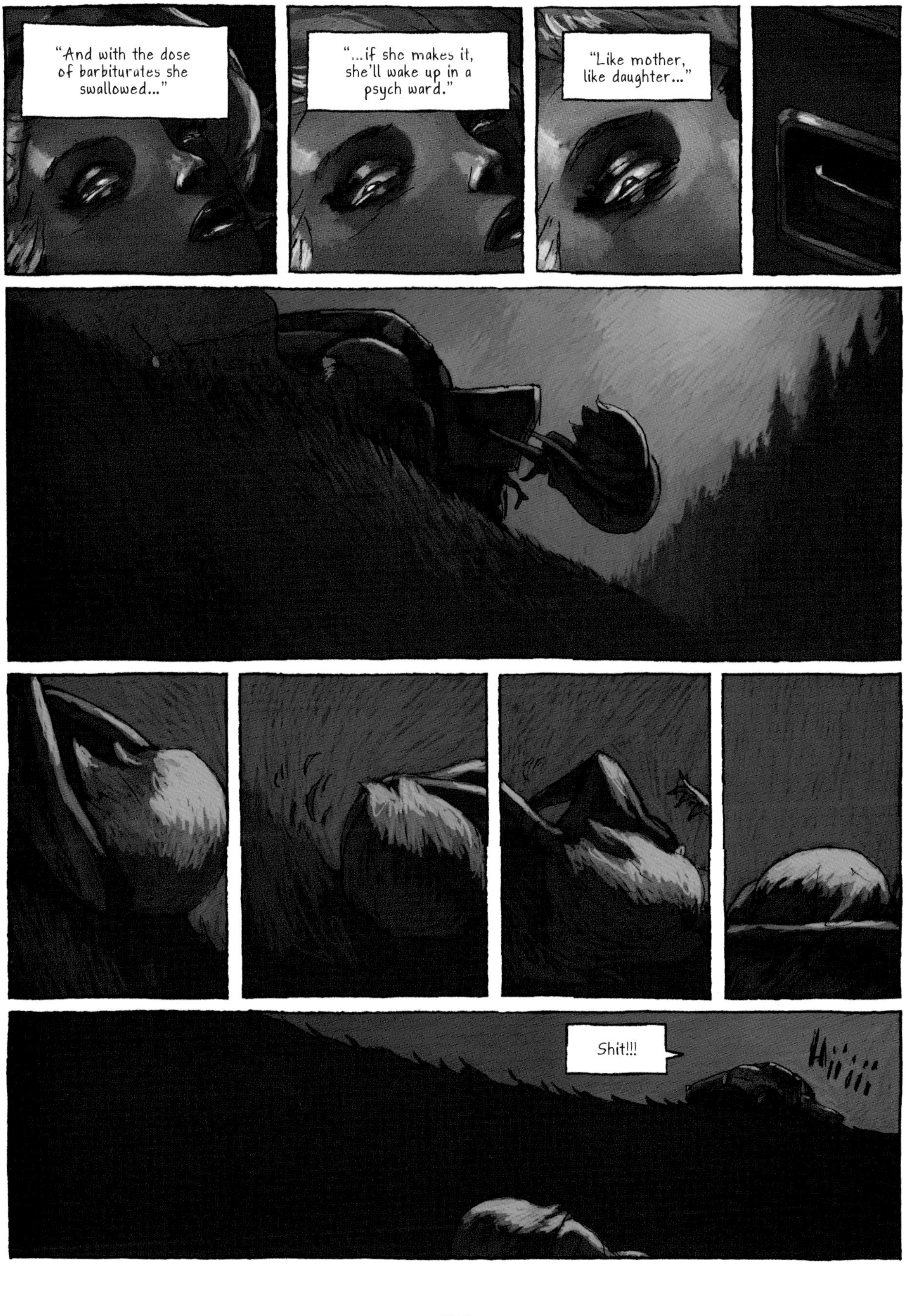

"And with the dose of barbiturates she swallowed..."
"...if she makes it, she'll wake up in a psych ward."
"Like mother, like daughter..."
Shit!!!

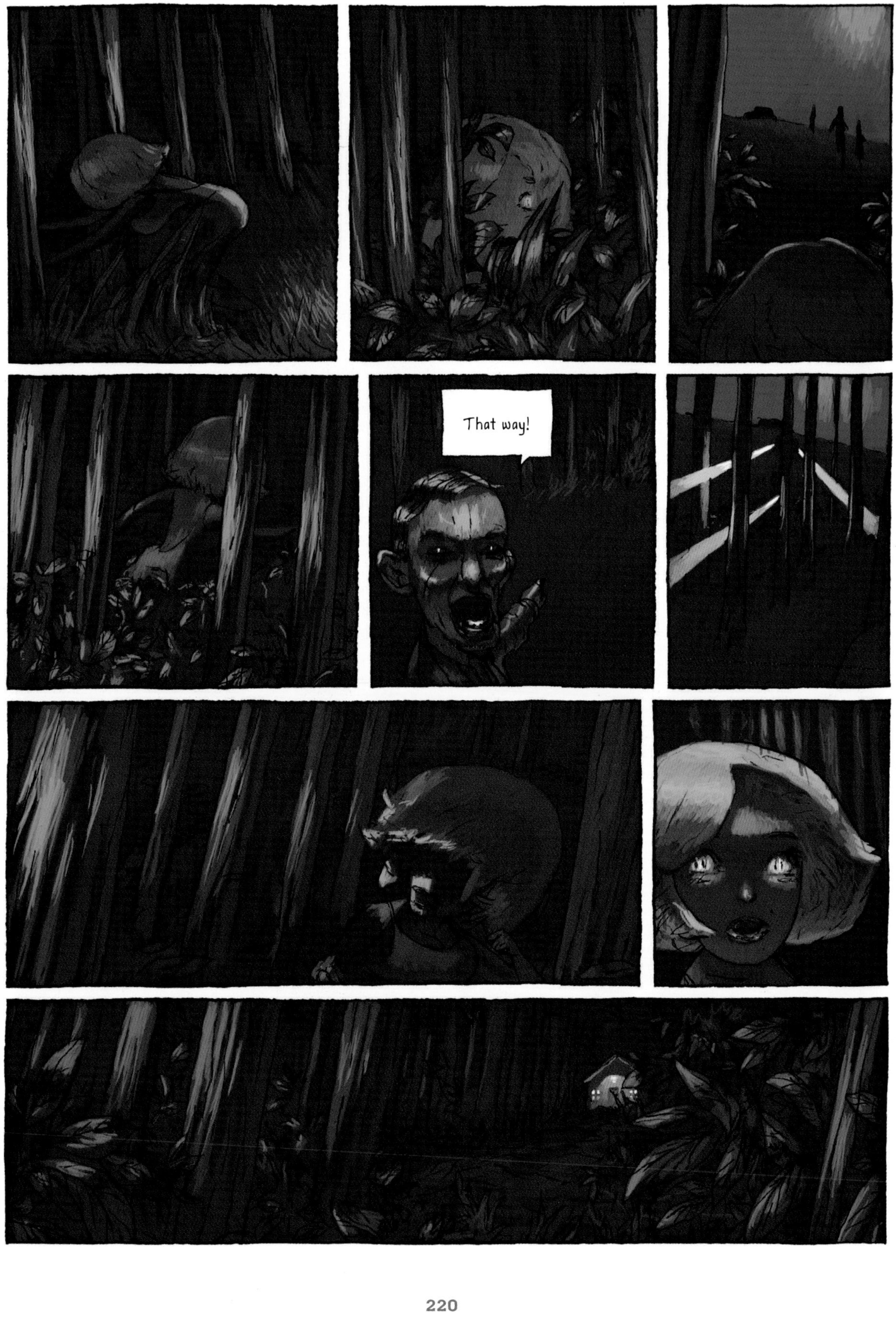
That way!

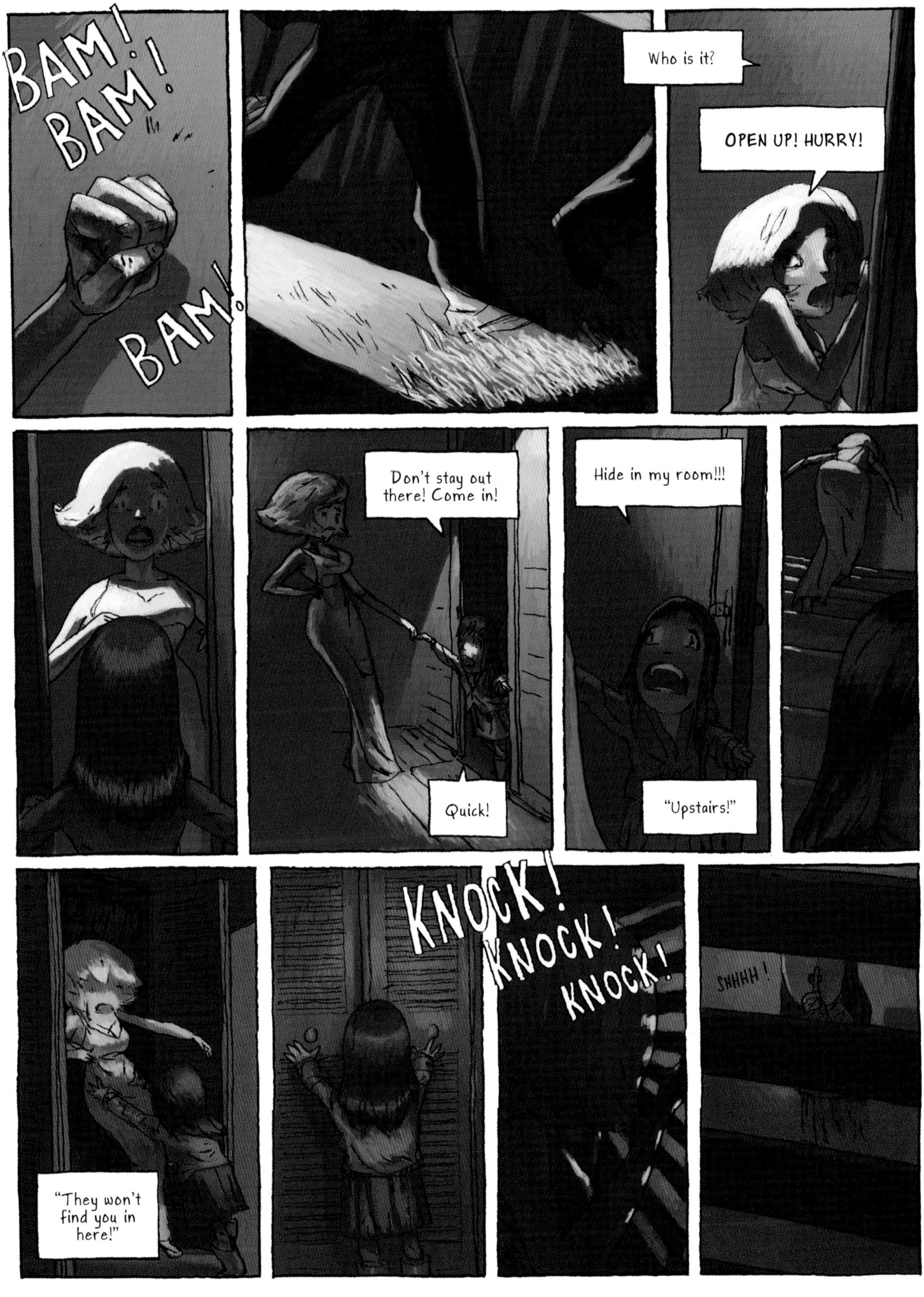
BAM! BAM!
BAM!
Who is it?
OPEN UP! HURRY!
Don't stay out there! Come in!
Quick!
Hide in my room!!!
"Upstairs!"
"They won't find you in here!"
KNOCK! KNOCK! KNOCK!
SHHHH!

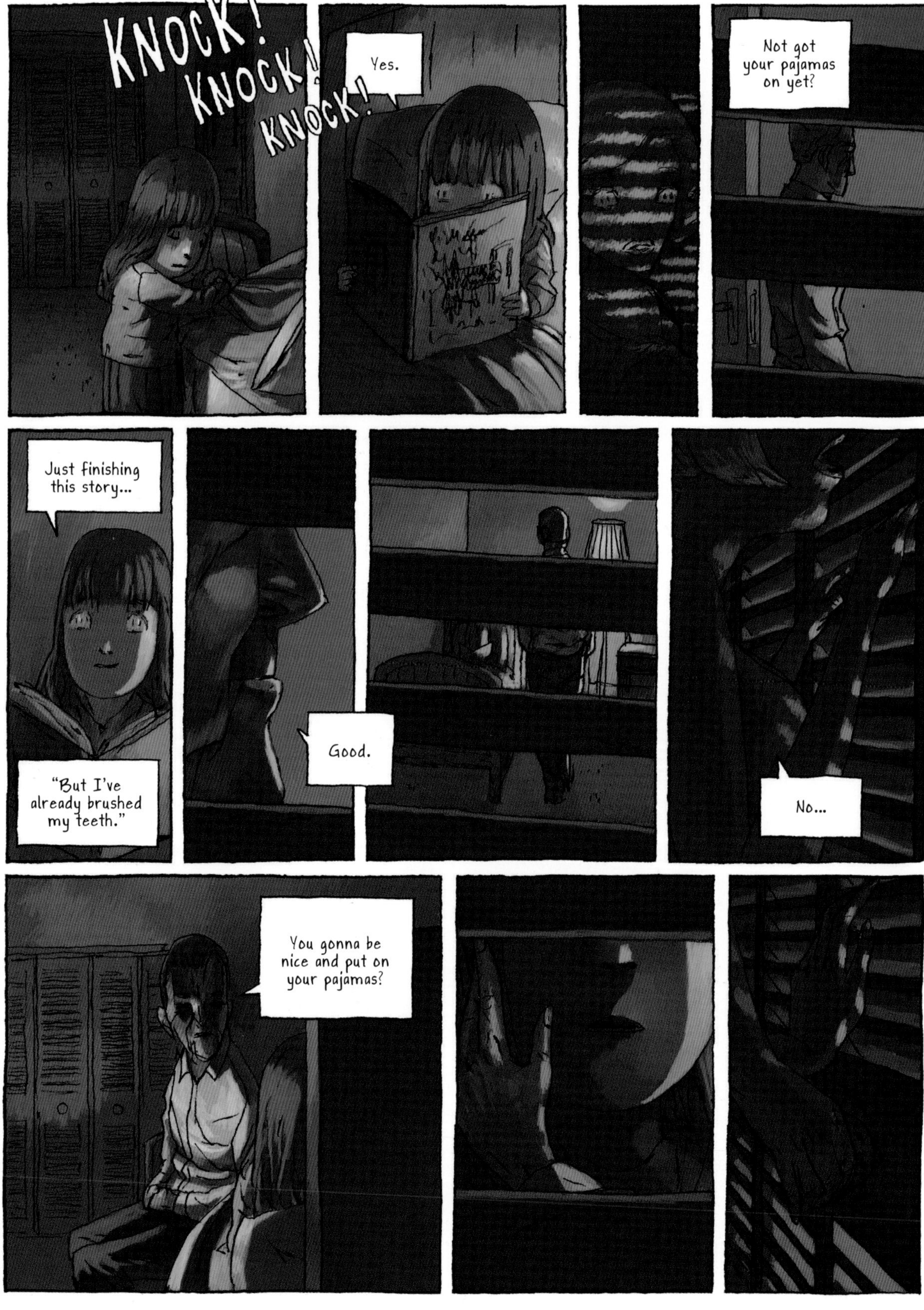
KNOCK! KNOCK! KNOCK!
Yes.
Not got your pajamas on yet?
Just finishing this story...
"But I've already brushed my teeth."
Good.
No...
You gonna be nice and put on your pajamas?

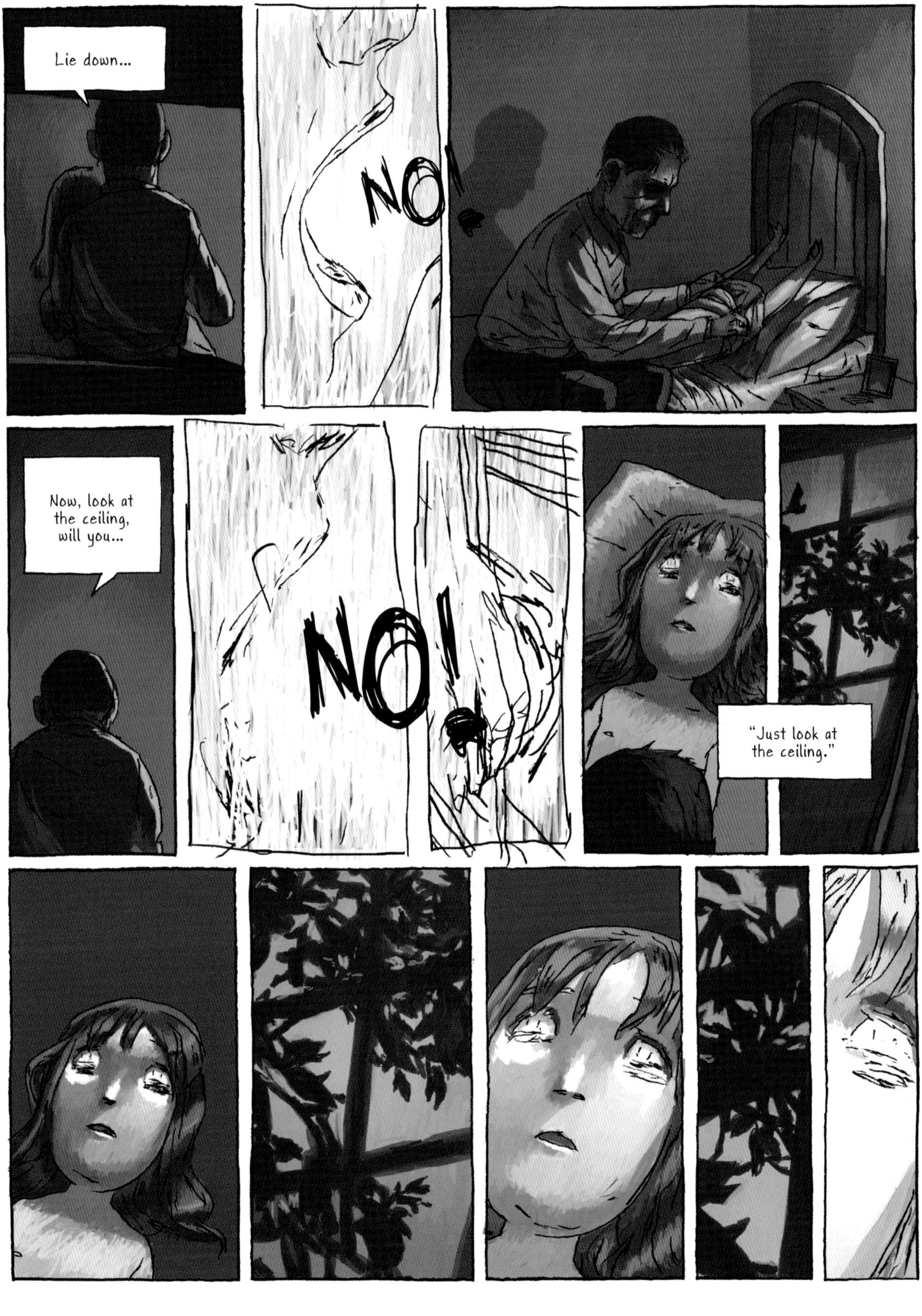
Lie down...
NO!
Now, look at the ceiling, will you...
NO!
"Just look at the ceiling."

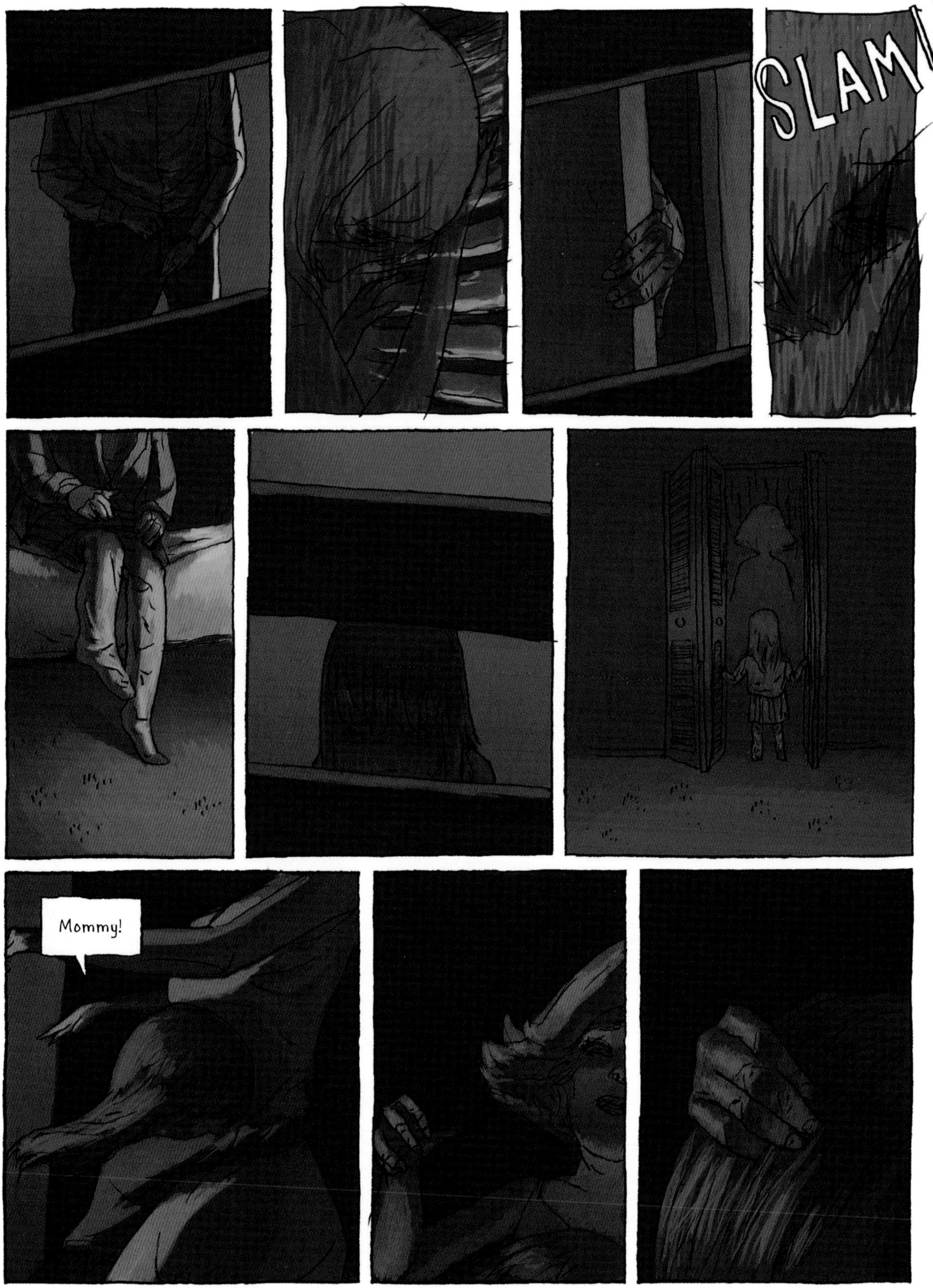
SLAM!
Mommy!

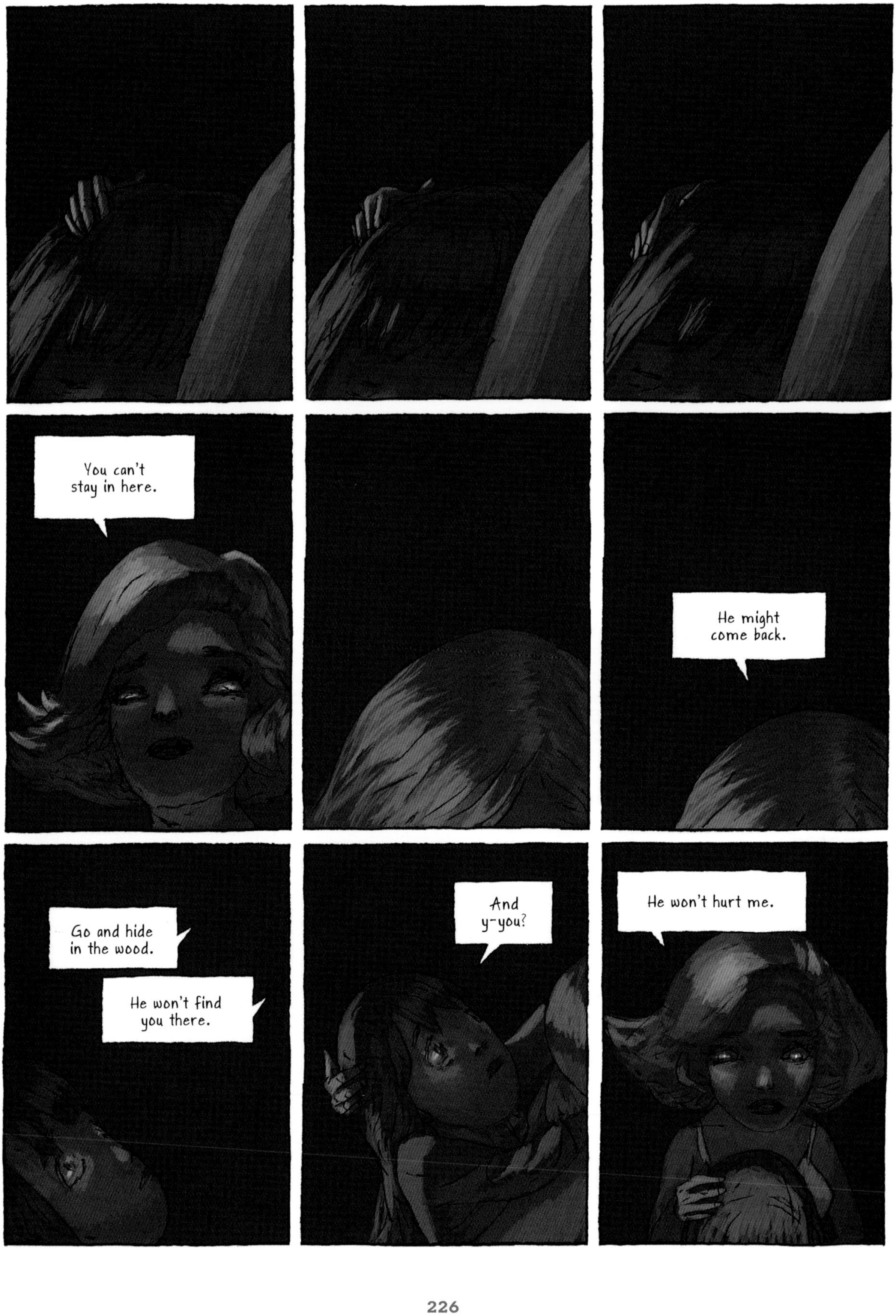

You can't stay in here.
He might come back.
Go and hide in the wood.
He won't find you there.
And y-you?
He won't hurt me.

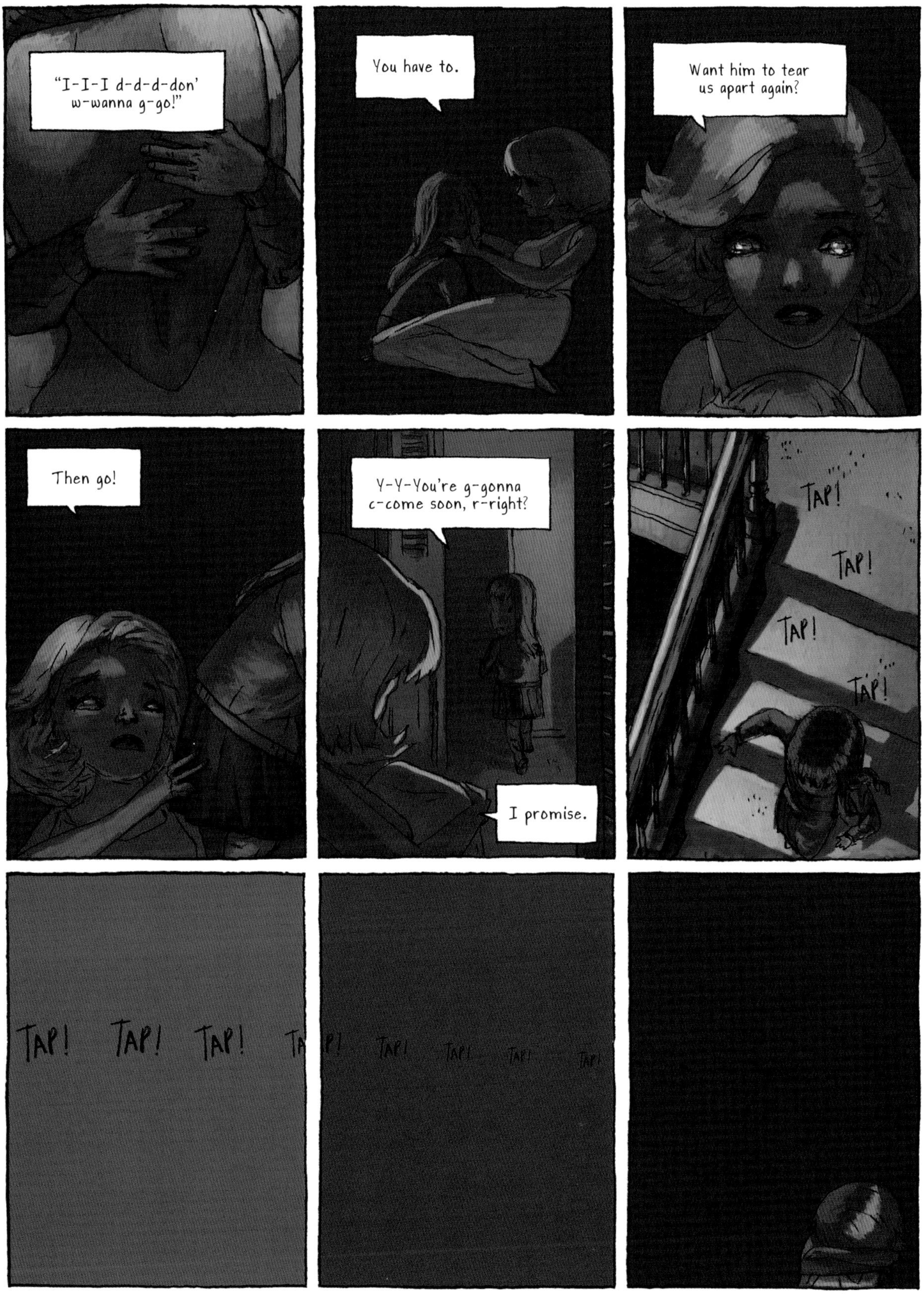
"I-I-I d-d-d-don' w-wanna g-go!"
You have to.
Want him to tear us apart again?
Then go!
Y-Y-You're g-gonna c-come soon, r-right?
I promise.
TAP!
TAP!
TAP!
TAP!
TAP! TAP! TAP! TAP! TAP! TAP! TAP! TAP! TAP!

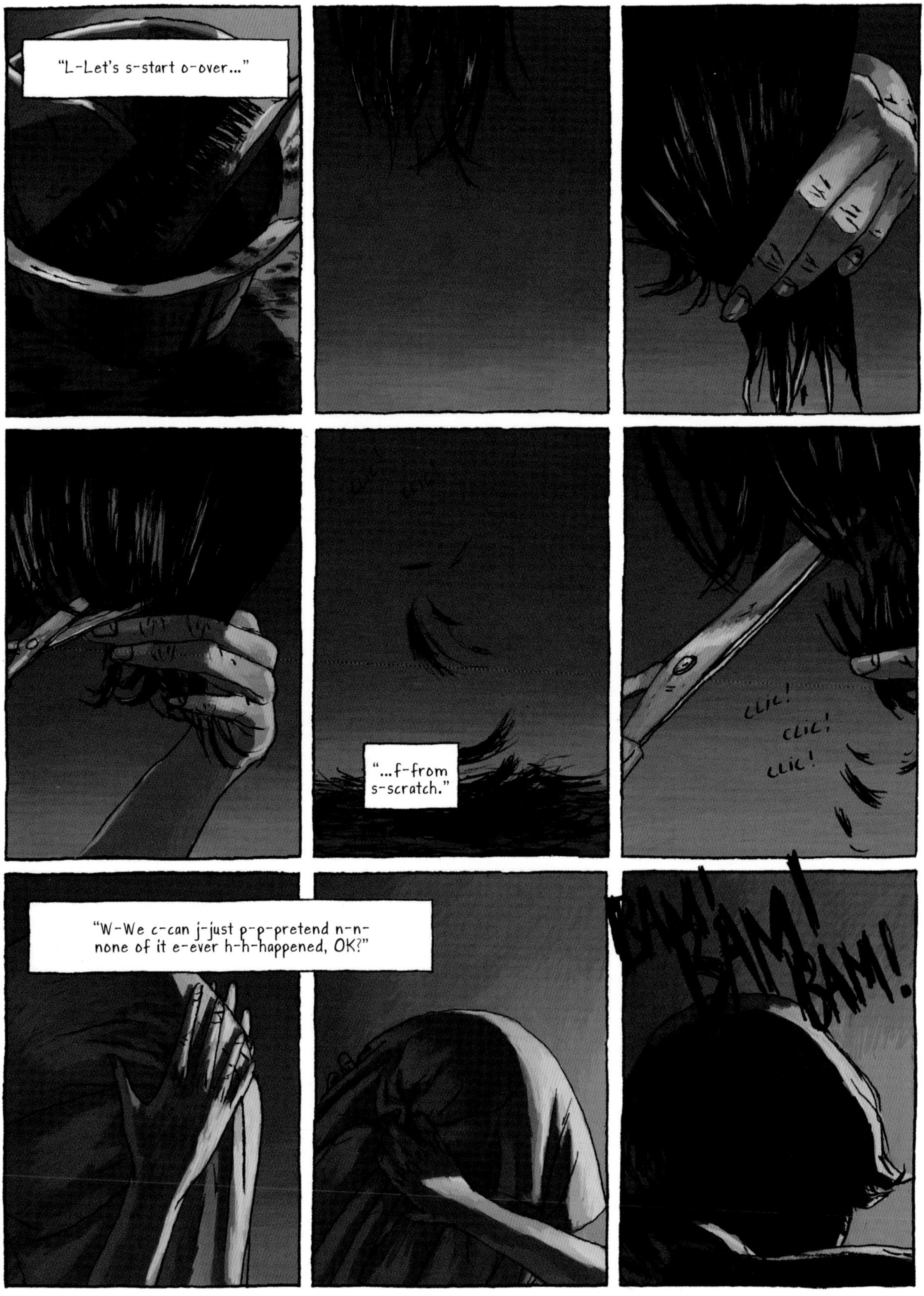
"L-Let's s-start o-over..."
"...f-from s-scratch."
CLIC!
CLIC!
CLIC!
"W-We c-can j-just p-p-pretend n-n-none of it e-ever h-h-happened, OK?"
BAM! BAM! BAM!

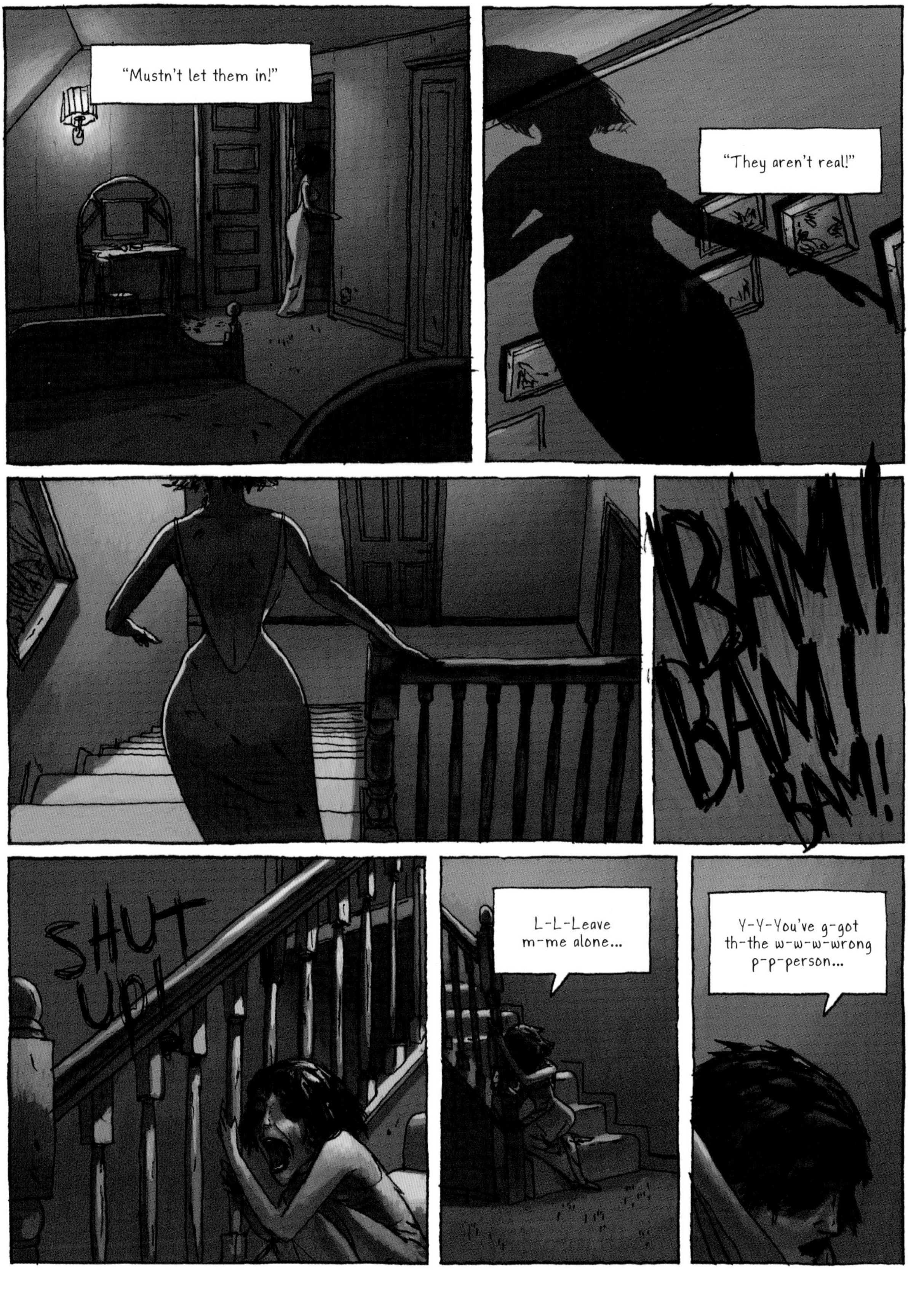
"Mustn't let them in!"
"They aren't real!"
BAM! BAM! BAM!
SHUT UP!
L-L-Leave m-me alone...
Y-Y-You've g-got th-the w-w-w-wrong p-p-person...

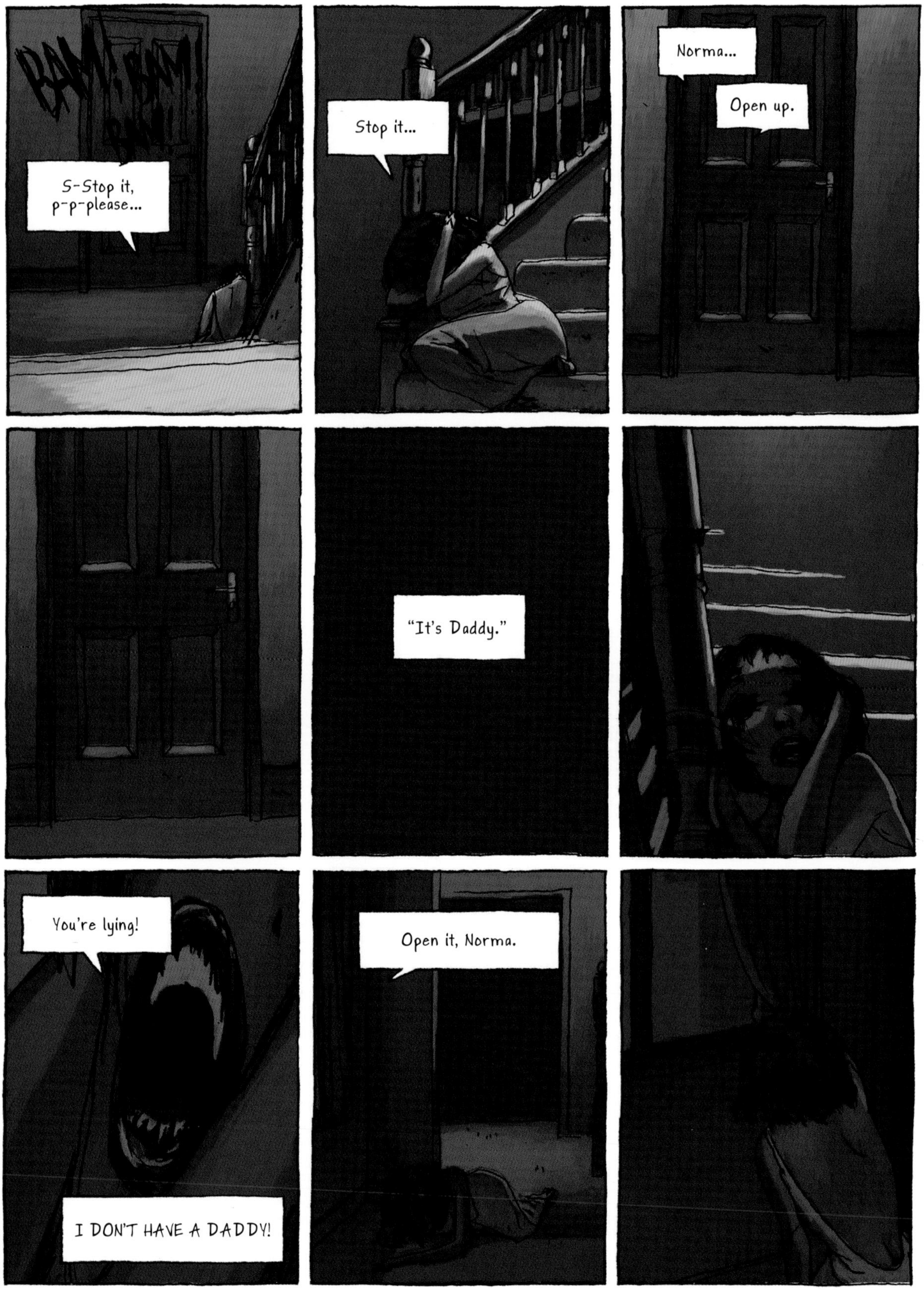
BAM! BAM! BAM!
S-Stop it, p-p-please...
Stop it...
Norma...
Open up.
"It's Daddy."
You're lying!
I DON'T HAVE A DADDY!
Open it, Norma.

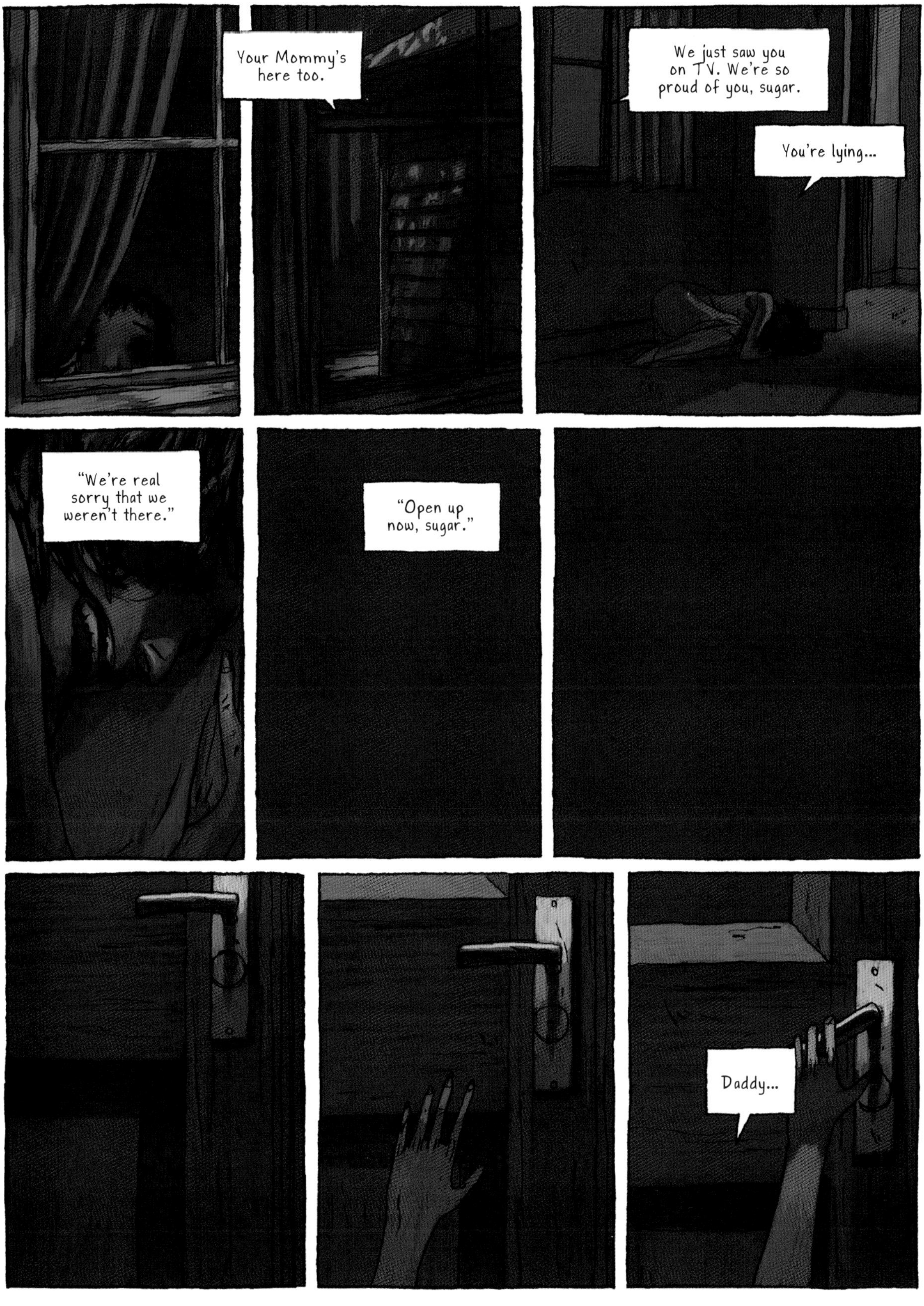
Your Mommy's here too.
We just saw you on TV. We're so proud of you, sugar.
You're lying...
"We're real sorry that we weren't there."
"Open up now, sugar."
Daddy...

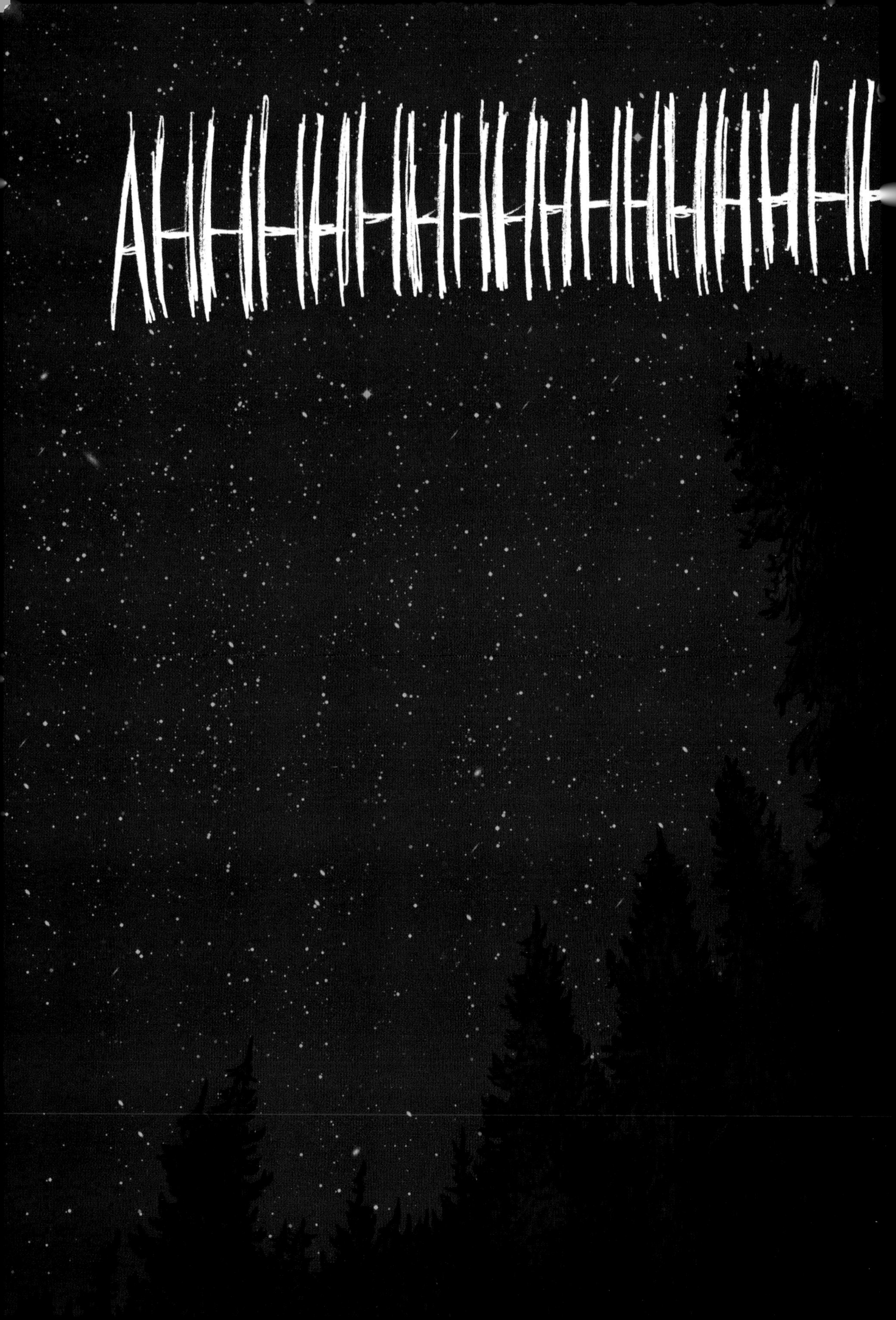
AHHHHHHHHHHHHHHHH

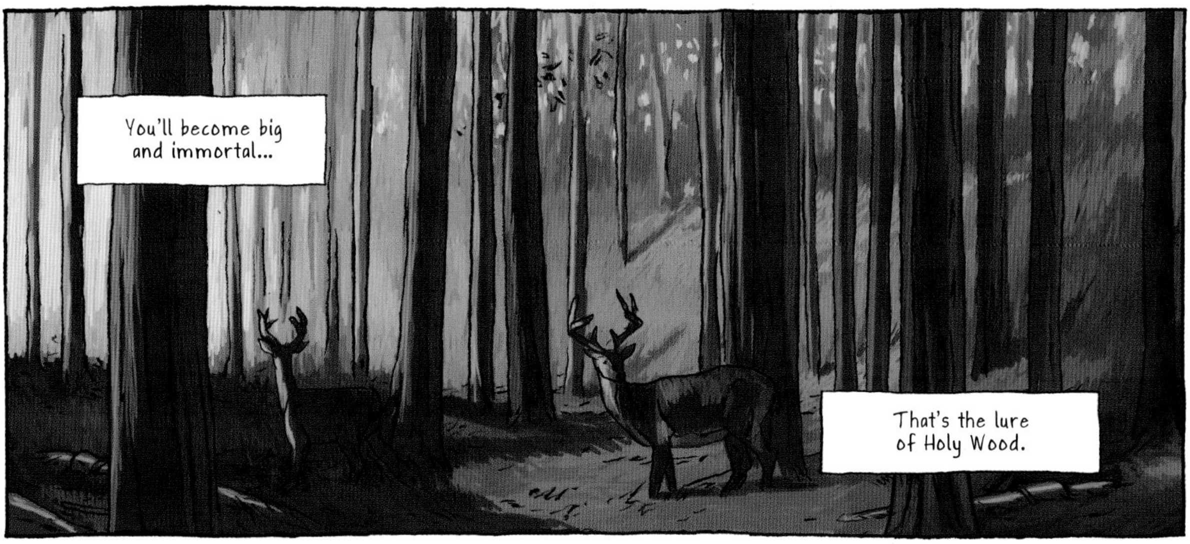
You'll become big and immortal...
That's the lure of Holy Wood.

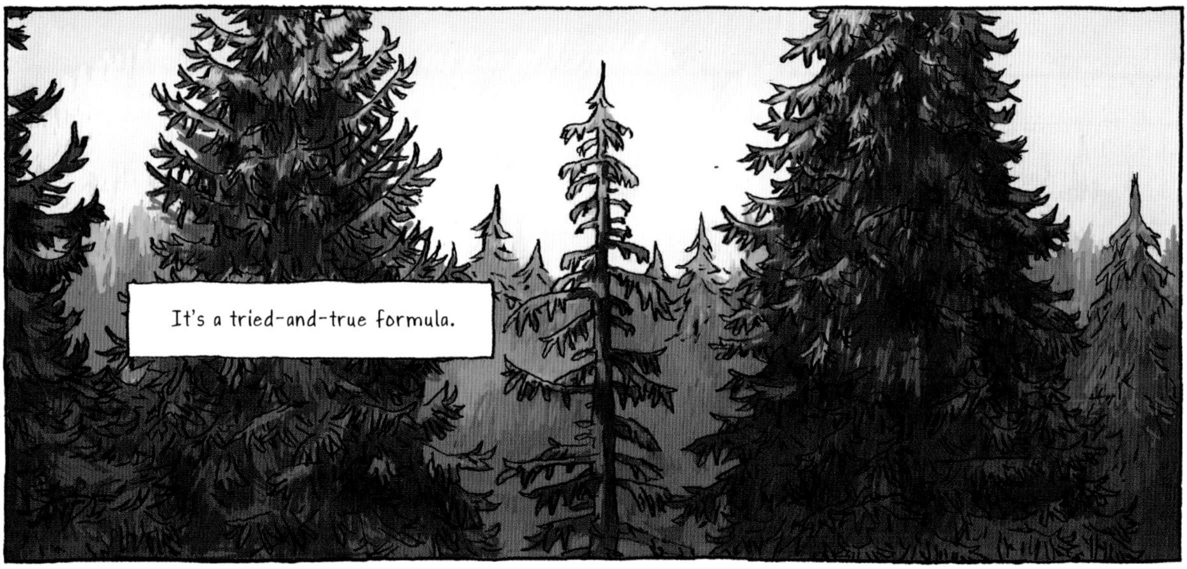
It's a tried-and-true formula.

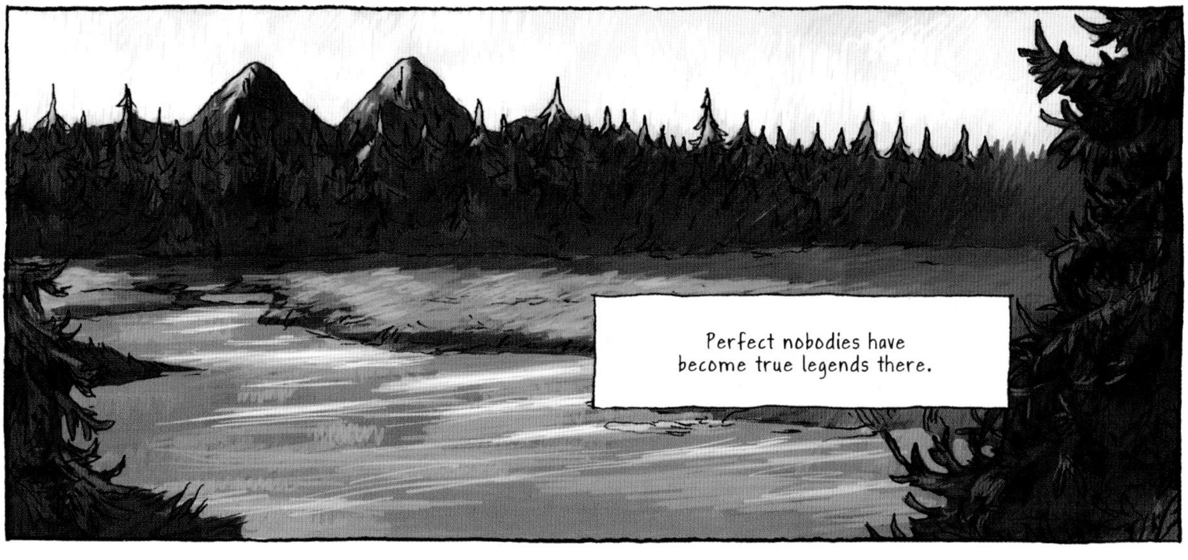
Perfect nobodies have become true legends there.

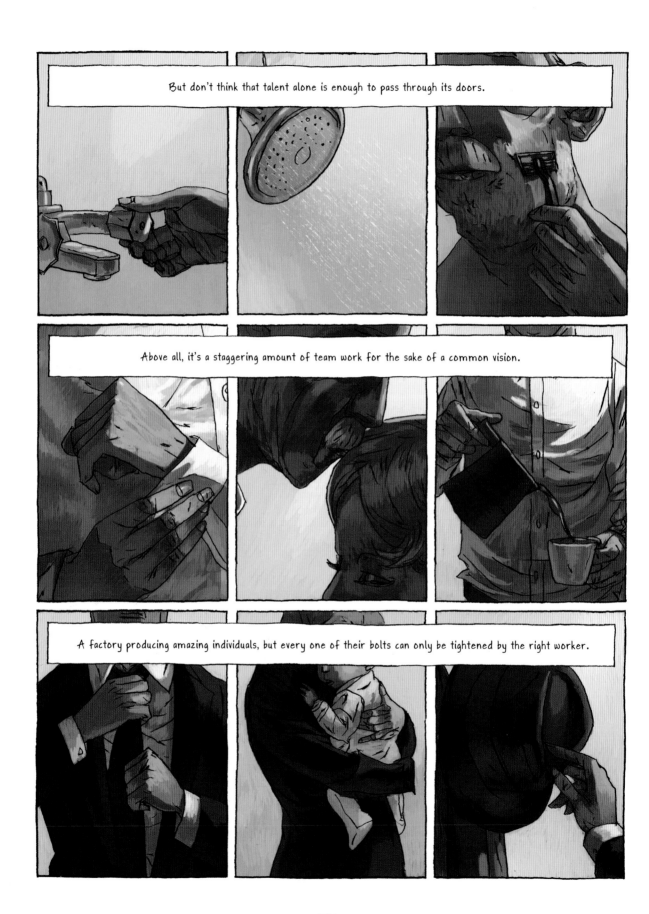

But don't think that talent alone is enough to pass through its doors.

Above all, it's a staggering amount of team work for the sake of a common vision.

A factory producing amazing individuals, but every one of their bolts can only be tightened by the right worker.

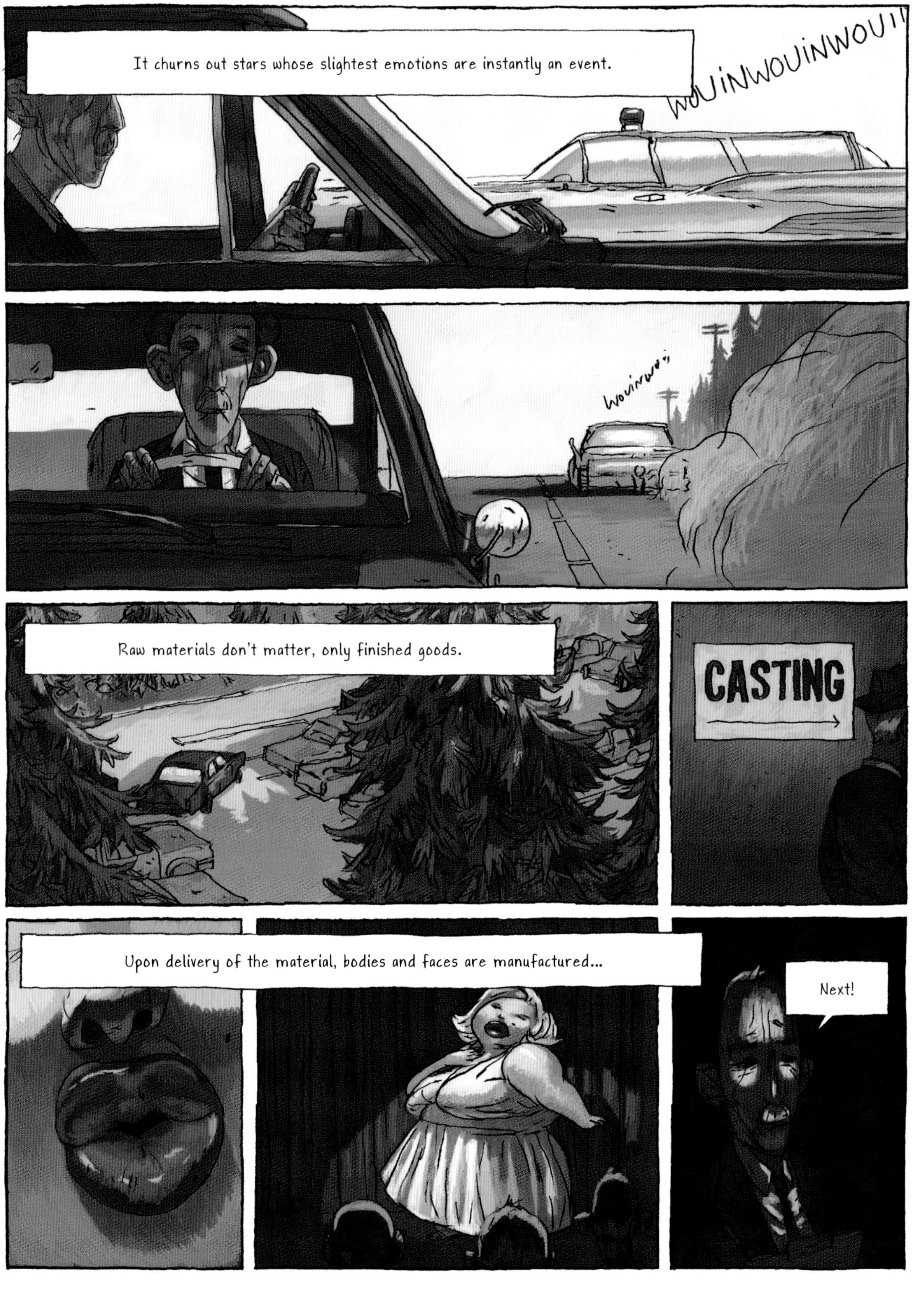
It churns out stars whose slightest emotions are instantly an event.
WOUINWOUINWOU!!
wouinwou
Raw materials don't matter, only finished goods.
CASTING
Upon delivery of the material, bodies and faces are manufactured...
Next!

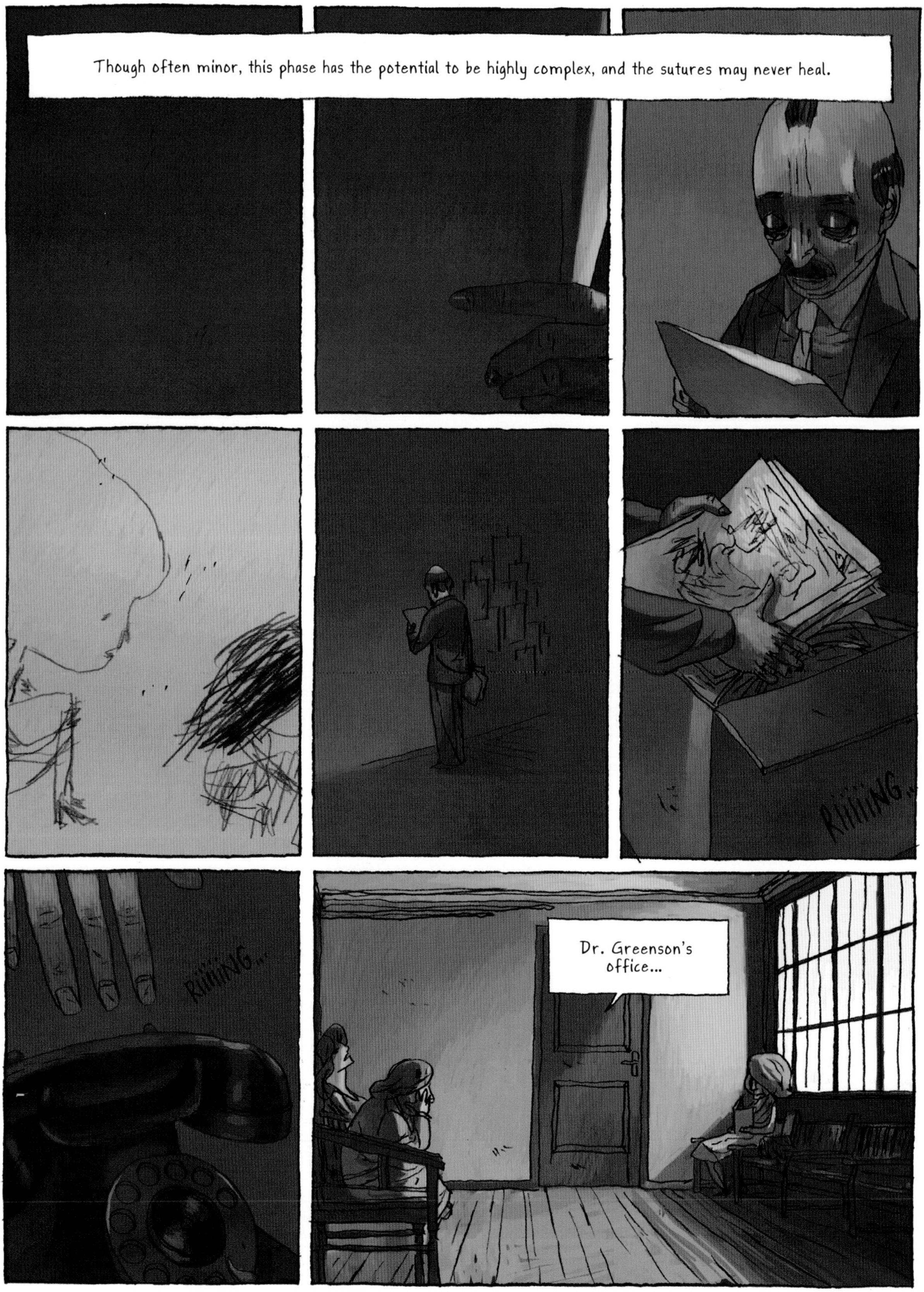
Though often minor, this phase has the potential to be highly complex, and the sutures may never heal.
RIIIING...
RIIIING...
Dr. Greenson's office...

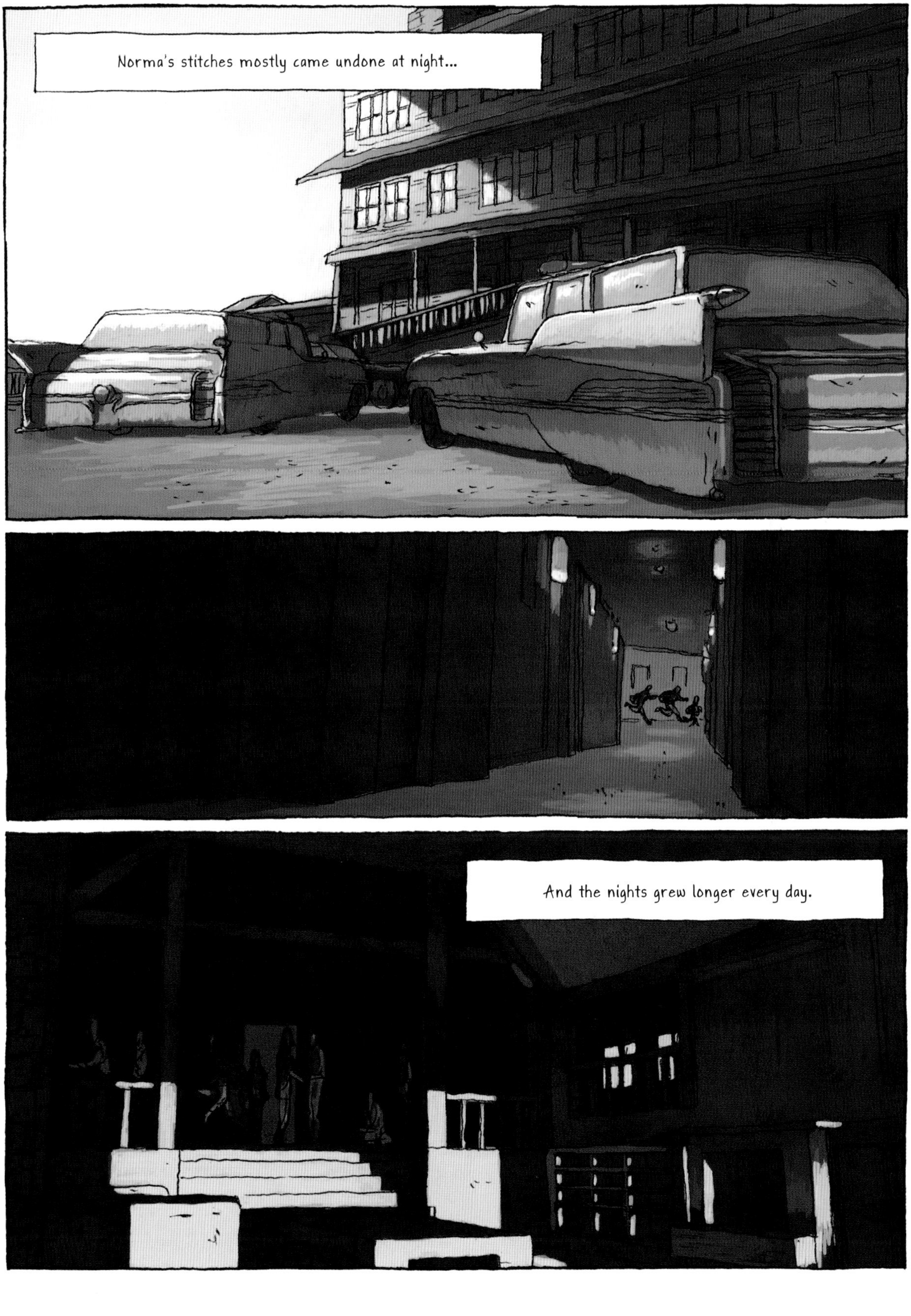
Norma's stitches mostly came undone at night...
And the nights grew longer every day.

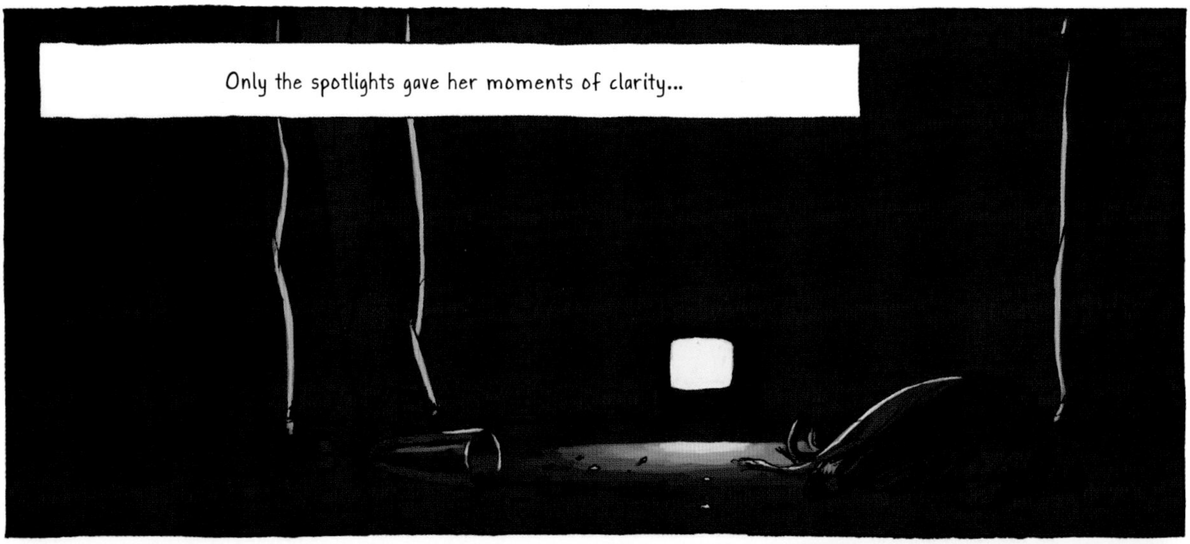
Only the spotlights gave her moments of clarity...

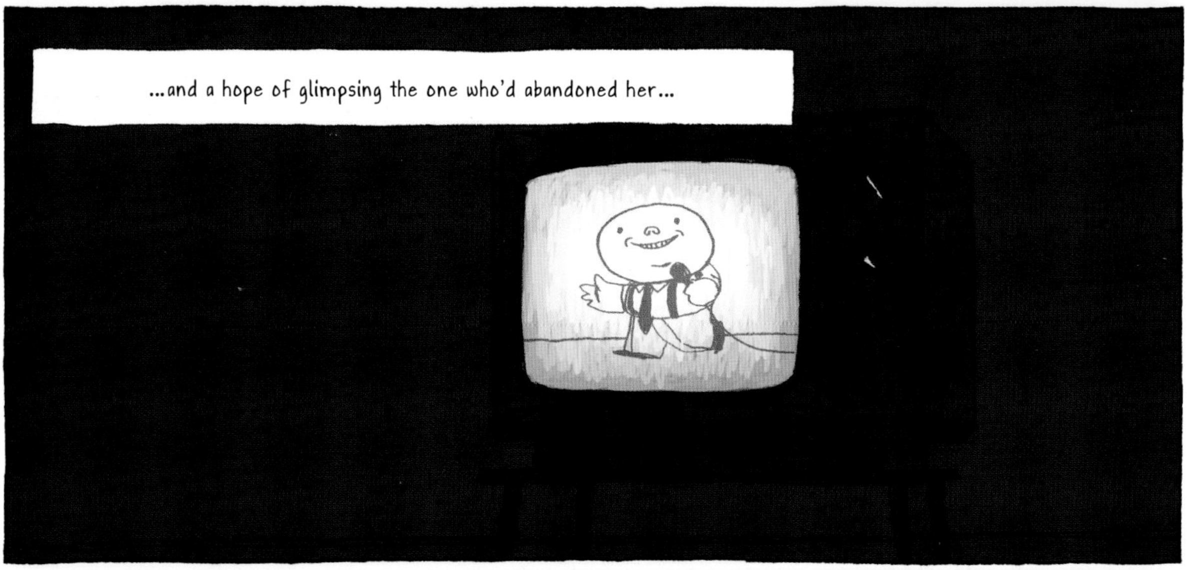
...and a hope of glimpsing the one who'd abandoned her...

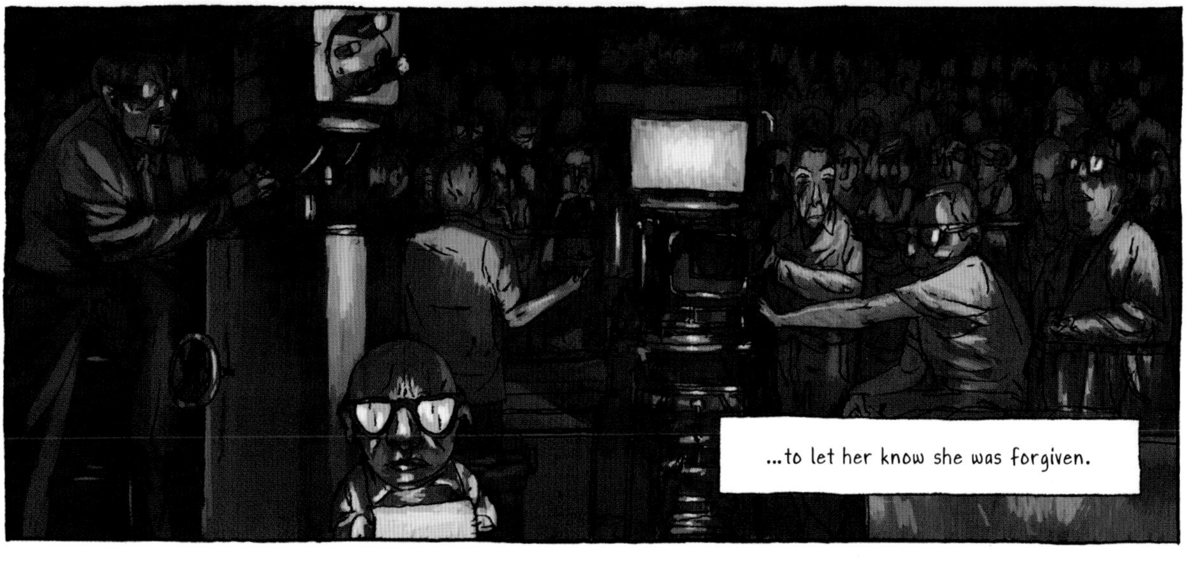
...to let her know she was forgiven.

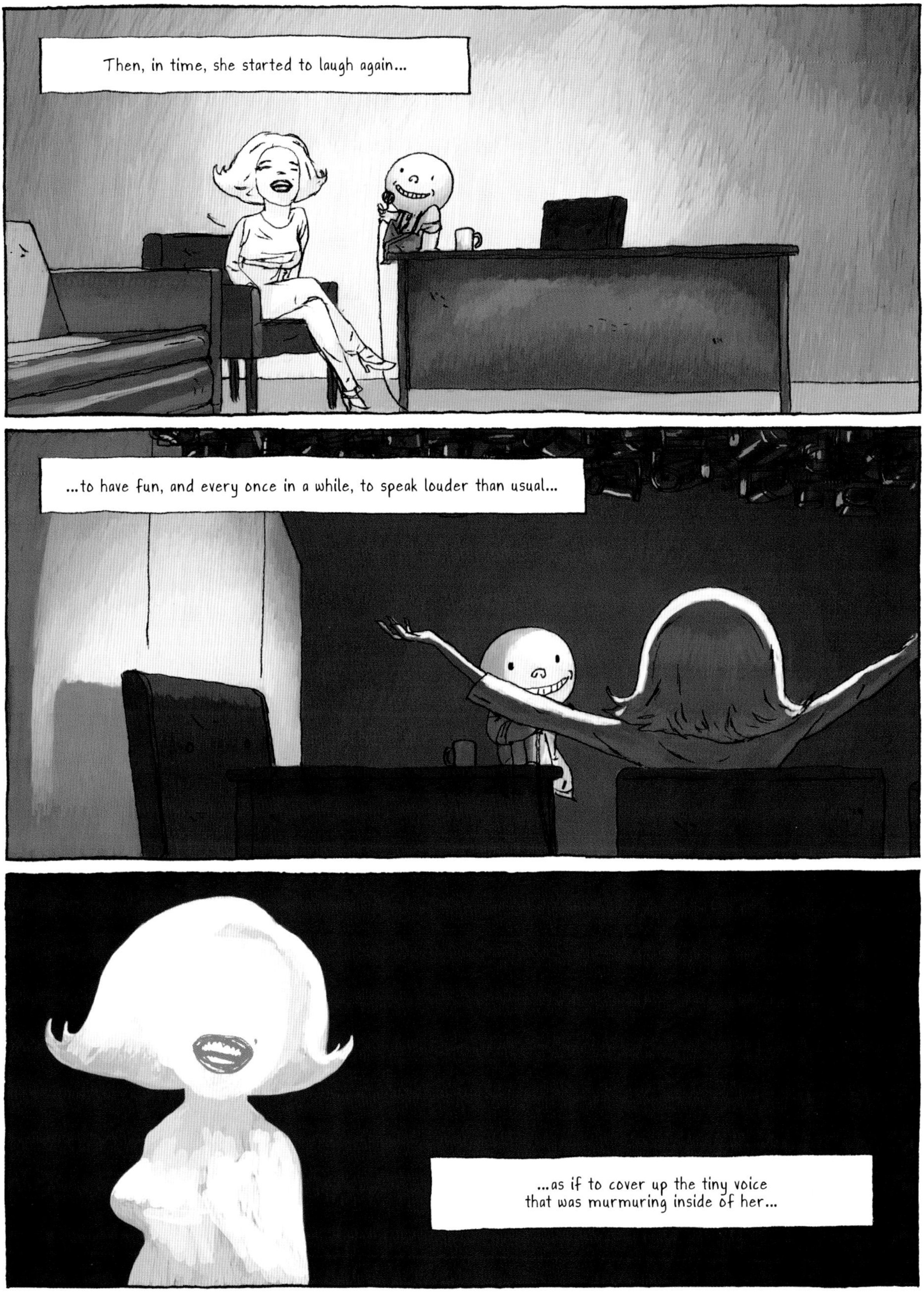

Then, in time, she started to laugh again...
...to have fun, and every once in a while, to speak louder than usual...
...as if to cover up the tiny voice that was murmuring inside of her...

The voice whispering that the worst thing about playing hide-and-seek
is knowing there's no one coming to find you.

BONUS
MATERIAL

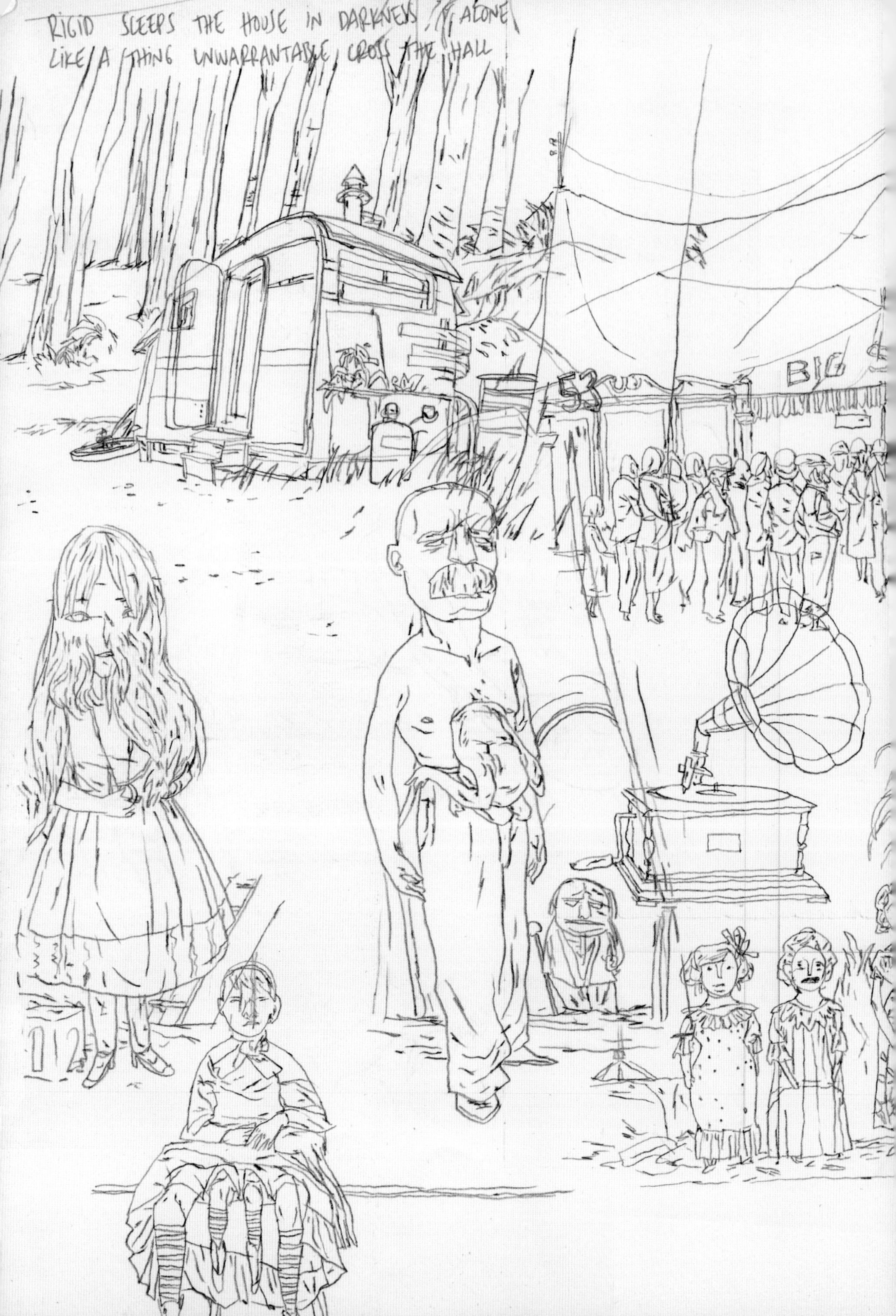
RIGID SLEEPS THE HOUSE IN DARKNESS, I ALONE
LIKE A THING UNWARRANTABLE CROSS THE HALL
53
BIG
112

AND CLIMB THE STAIRS TO FIND THE GROUP OF ....
STANDING ANGEL - STERN AND TALL....

I WANT MY OWN ROOM ...... WHAT IS THIS
THRONG OF STARTLED BEINGS SUDDENLY THROWN
IN CONFUSION AGAINST MY ENTRY ? IS IT ONLY THE TREES
LARGE SHADOWS FROM THE OUTSIDE STREET LAMP BLOWN

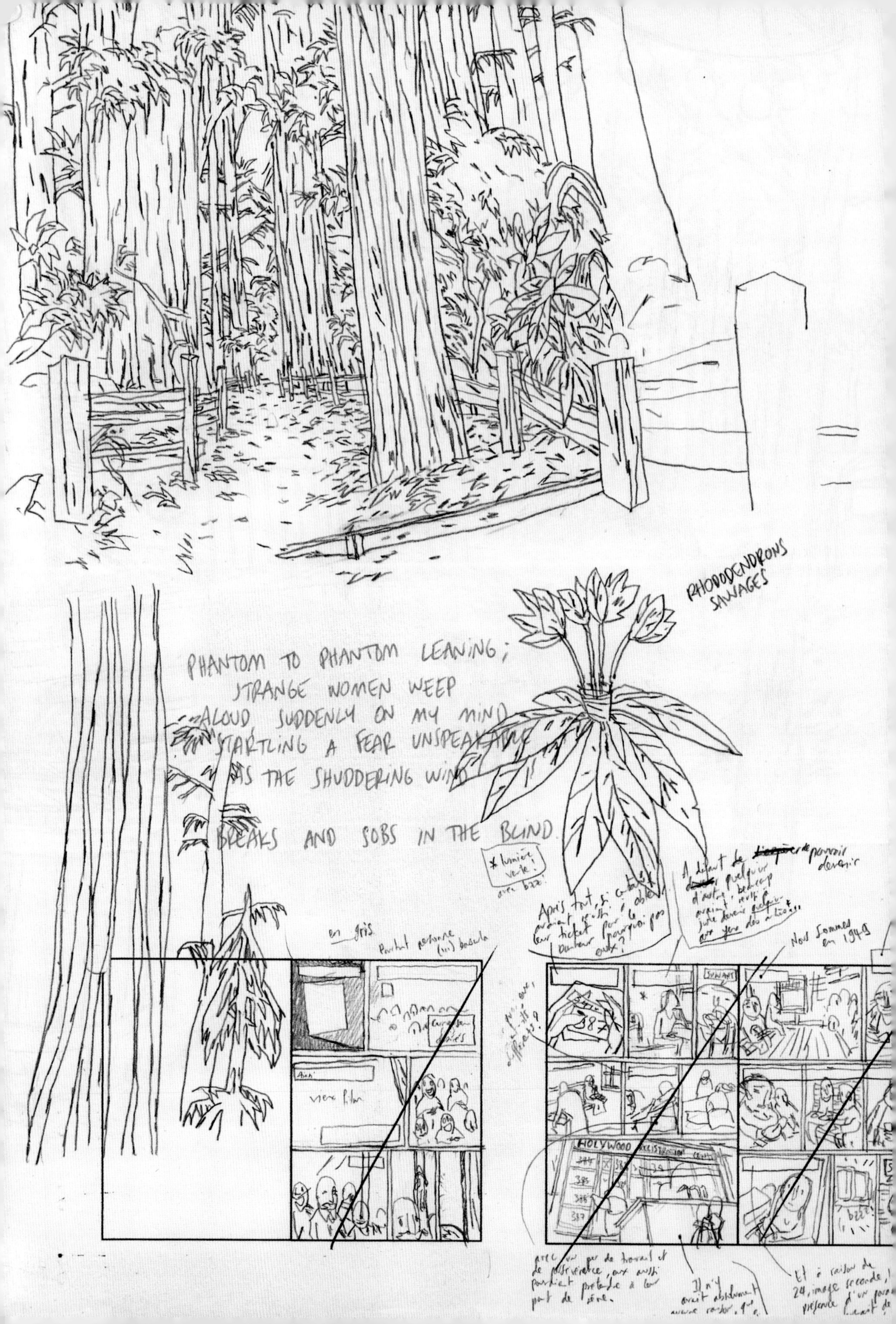
RHODODENDRONS SAUVAGES
PHANTOM TO PHANTOM LEANING;
STRANGE WOMEN WEEP
ALOUD SUDDENLY ON MY MIND
STARTLING A FEAR UNSPEAKABLE
AS THE SHUDDERING WIND
BREAKS AND SOBS IN THE BLIND
* lumière verte !
avec bzz !
Après tout, si certains avaient réussi à obtenir leur ticket pour le bonheur pourquoi pas eux ?
Nous sommes en 1949
en gris
SUIVANT
HOLYWOOD REGISTRATION
bzzz !
avec un peu de travail et de persévérance, eux aussi pourraient prétendre à leur part de rêve.
Il n'y avait absolument aucune raison
Et à raison de 24 images seconde,

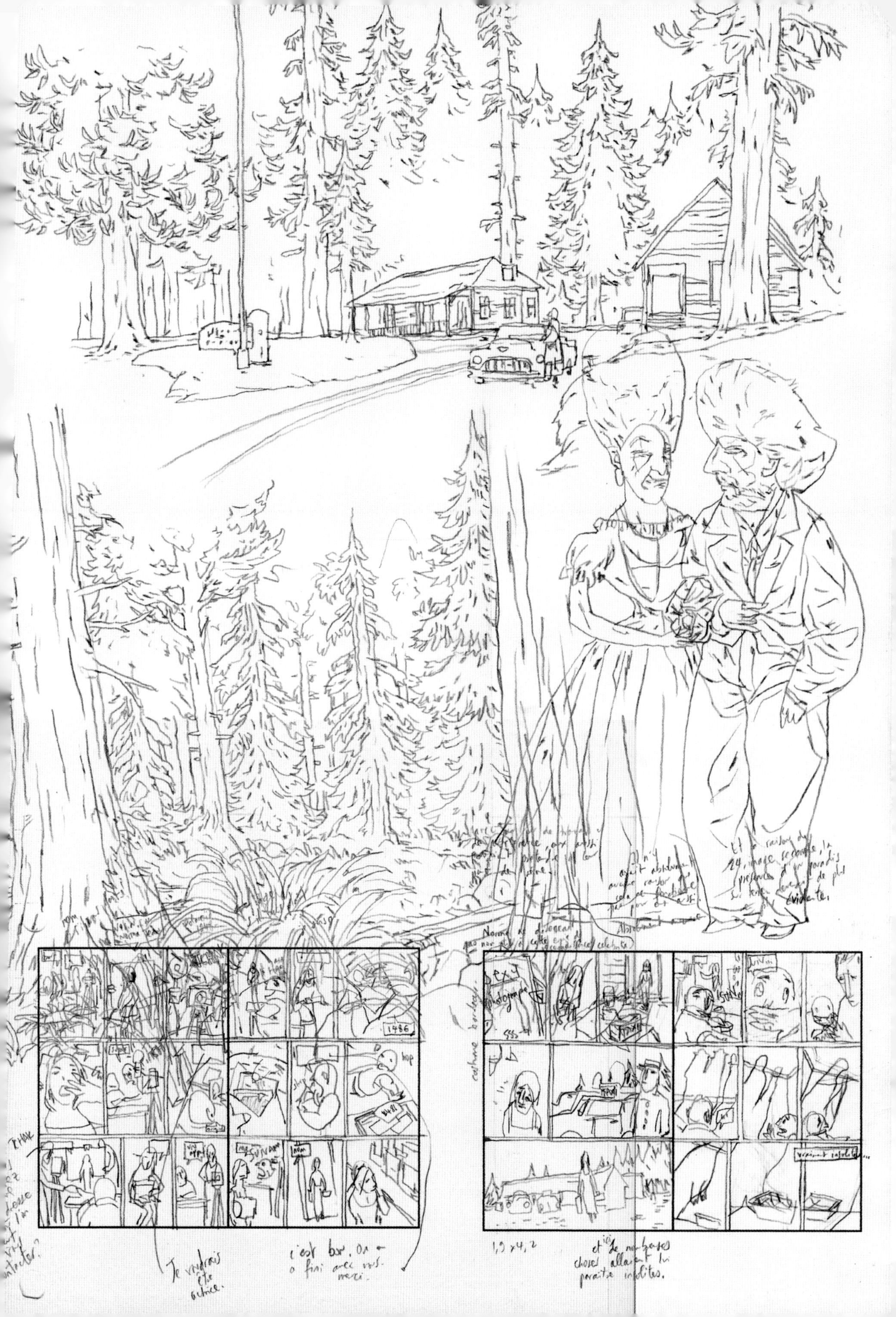

Je voudrais être actrice.
c'est bon. On a fini avec vous. merci.
1,9 x 4,2
et ici de nombreuses choses allaient lui paraître insolites.

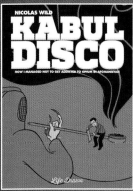

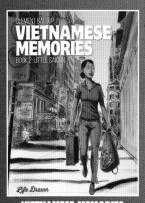
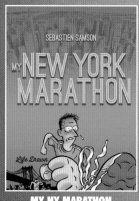